Robert Musil
and the Crisis of
European Culture
1880-1942

Photo courtesy Robert-Musil-Archiv, Klagenfurt.

Robert Musil and the Crisis of European Culture 1880-1942

DAVID S. LUFT

UNIVERSITY OF CALIFORNIA PRESS

BERKELEY / LOS ANGELES / LONDON

University of California Press
Berkeley and Los Angeles, California
University of California Press, Ltd.
London, England
© 1980 by The Regents of the University of California
Printed in the United States of America

1 2 3 4 5 6 7 8 9

Library of Congress Cataloging in Publication Data

Luft, David S
  Robert Musil and the crisis of European culture, 1880–1942.

  Bibliography: p.
  Includes index.
  1. Musil, Robert, 1880–1942—Criticism and interpretation.
2. Europe—Intellectual life. I. Title.
PT2625.U8Z795   833'.912   78-66008
ISBN 0-520-03852-5

Contents

LIST OF ABBREVIATIONS   i

PREFACE   iii

Introduction   1
   The Austrian Mandarin   5
   The Crisis of Liberal Culture   9
   The Generation of 1905   13
   Philosophical Essayism   18

1. The Young Musil: 1880-1905   23
   1. The Provincial Mandarin   24
   2. The Spiritual Revolution   35
   3. The Divided Self   52

2. Between Science and Art: 1905-1911   63
   1. The Berlin Years   64
   2. Philosophy and Science   78
   3. Metaphor and Soul   88

3. Ideology and Civilization: 1911-1924   99
   1. Ethics and Essayism: 1911–1914   100

2. The Revolt against Civilization: 1914–1919   121
3. German Culture as Symptom: 1919–1924   138

4. *Der Dichter*: 1918-1933   158
     1. The Creative Person and Bourgeois Culture   160
     2. Symbolism and "the Other Condition"   178
     3. Metaphysics and the Novel   198

5. *The Man without Qualities*   214
     1. Science and the Self   217
     2. The Search for Order   233
     3. The Condition of Love   249

6. *Geist und Politik*: 1933-1942   269
     The Exile   270
     National Socialism as Symptom   274
     Culture and Politics   279
     The Mystic in the Garden   286

Epilog   295

BIBLIOGRAPHY   299
     I. MUSIL'S WORKS   299   II. OTHER PRIMARY SOURCES 302
          A. Unpublished Sources
          B. Major Fiction   III. LITERATURE ON MUSIL   304
          C. Major Non-Fiction   A. Books and Dissertations
          D. Standard Editions   B. Articles
               1. German   C. Reviews by Contemporaries
               2. English
                                        IV. GENERAL WORKS   309

INDEX   313

List of Abbreviations

AHR	*American Historical Review*
DVJS	*Deutsche Vierteljahrschrift*
LWW	*Robert Musil: Leben, Werk, Wirkung*
MoE	*Der Mann ohne Eigenschaften:* vol. 1 of *Gesammelte Werke in Einzelausgaben*
Prosa	*Prosa, Dramen, späte Briefe:* vol. 3 of *Gesammelte Werke in Einzelausgaben*
Studien	*Robert Musil: Studien zu seinem Werk*
Tag. I and II	*Tagebücher* with *Anmerkung, Anhang, Register:* 2 vols.
TE	*Tagebücher, Aphorismen, Essays und Reden:* vol. 2 of *Gesammelte Werke in Einzelausgaben*
TLS	*Times Literary Supplement*

I am convinced that personal accomplishment means a hardly perceptible alteration of the spiritual riches which one receives from others, and . . . I believe this is true not only of what one attributes to the great traditions but also of what one takes in with every breath.

ROBERT MUSIL

Preface

I first read Robert Musil's *The Man without Qualities* in 1969, finding to my surprise that a writer of such intellectual and imaginative power was virtually unknown in the United States. At that time I wanted to write a broad study of the relationship between metaphysics and the novel in the early twentieth century. I was particularly interested in literary and cultural critics such as Benjamin, Lukács, and Bloch, and in novelists such as Thomas Mann, Kafka, Broch, Hesse, Döblin, and Musil. Except for Mann, the novelists had been left by historians to the province of literary criticism, and important figures such as Musil, Broch, Benjamin, Bloch, and even Lukács had hardly begun to receive the attention they deserved. I decided to begin with Musil, both because he merited an intellectual biography in his own right and because he represented so clearly the interconnections between philosophy and the novel in his generation. In 1972 I finished my dissertation on the early part of his life, and since then I have worked on the period after 1924, making use of the Musil *Nachlass* in Klagenfurt and exploring more fully Musil's relationship to the cultural crisis of his generation.

Musil did not believe that his perceptions could or should be reduced to a fixed conceptual order. Part of his genius was to capture the complexity and nuance of a pluralistic culture and to eschew the reassurance of a systematic image of the world. At the same time, his important thoughts are always partly feelings, and he makes the demanding claim that his reader experience this complexity, of feeling as well as thought. His alertness to complexity and his openness to feeling make Musil's writing unusually resistant to systematic academic presentation. But in both respects Musil was also the representative essayist of his generation, the master of the intermediate mode between metaphysics and the novel.

Musil's position on the borderline between modes of thought and feeling has made still more difficult the translation of words which have always been difficult to import from German culture. Thus, despite the highly intellectual quality of his writing, Musil thought of himself as a *Dichter* or poet, but in the German sense, which includes all forms of serious imaginative writing (novels as well as lyric poems). For Musil, it was important to distinguish *Dichter* from *Schriftsteller* (writer), much as other classical words such as *Geist*, *geistig*, *Bildung*, and *Kultur* have a "set-aside" quality in the German tradition. Particularly difficult problems of translation arise from the fact that the English word *spiritual* can refer to spirit or mind [*geistig*], to the soul [*seelisch*], or to the church [*geistlich*]. Ordinarily, *spiritual* appears in my translations for *geistig* as distinguished from *intellektuell*, while *seelisch* is often translated as *psychic* or *emotional*. In potentially ambiguous cases, I have tried to clarify with brackets: intellectual [*geistig*] and spiritual [*seelisch*]. The specifically religious term *geistlich* rarely appears in Musil's prose. In general I have tried to render my translations with as much consistency as possible in order to convey the structure and texture of the German. In my own prose I have interpreted and clarified, accommodating Musil's meanings to normal English usage.

I have translated *Geist* as *spirit* in order to convey a sense of *mind* which is not set in opposition to the feelings or isolated from them. *Mind* has much to recommend it as a translation, including its connotations of cosmopolitan, civilized, universal, and intellectual, and certainly the Anglo-Saxon philosopher will most often find clarification in the translations *mind/mental*. But *Geist* is by no means so clear and straightforward a word as *mind*, and that translation would leave incomprehensible Musil's need to defend the place of intellect (whether as *Intellekt*, *Verstand*, or *Vernunft*) in *Geist*. *Thinking* is closer to the sense of *Geist*, but imagination is also central to this word, and it depends on certain qualities of wit, will, and feeling. *Geist* is the creative, forming impulse in culture, and it refers to the shaping faculties of inwardness rather than the more receptive (and personal) faculties of *Seele* [*soul*]. *Geist* suggests not only logical thought but also those capacities for understanding which can be found in literature, religion, and other life-teachings. *Spirit* seemed the best way to convey this sense in English; it also conveys the quality of *Geist* as a word, its place in the structure of the German language, and its privileged status in the German tradition. Certainly *spirit* seems best for Musil's own understanding of *Geist* as "thinking in love."

Translation has been a major part of my task in writing on Musil. Most of his work is still not available in English; this includes his essays, plays, diaries, short fiction, and the *Nachlass* of *The Man without Qualities*, as well as his unpublished writings. In my discussions of these untranslated works (particularly the major essays and *Die Schwärmer*), I have been conscious of the need to provide the English-speaking world with a more complete picture of Musil's achievement as a writer. The major fiction has, of course, already been translated into English by Ernst Kaiser and Eithne Wilkins, and I have depended heavily on their work. I have not always followed their translations, however, and in the case of *Der Mann ohne Eigenschaften* I often began with my own. For the sake of simplicity and consistency I have always given my references to the German editions.

I am indebted to Dr. Karl Dinklage and the Vereinigung Robert-Musil-Archiv for so graciously making Musil's *Nachlass* available to me in 1973. Since then a complete edition of the diaries has appeared; wherever possible I have changed my *Nachlass* references to the 1976 Frisé edition, but I have otherwise kept all references to the earlier three-volume edition of Musil's works. Two other publications appeared too recently for me to use: Frisé's revised (1978) edition of Musil's prose, and Frederick G. Peters's study of Musil's major fiction.

During the ten years I have worked on this project, I have accumulated innumerable debts of knowledge and friendship. I would like to express my appreciation to the teachers, fellow students, librarians, and friends who have helped to make this book possible.

H. Stuart Hughes guided the dissertation on which this book was based and influenced my understanding of the field as a whole. The Danforth Foundation generously supported my graduate research with a Kent Fellowship between 1968 and 1972, and Erwin Hiebert and Dorrit Cohn kindly offered suggestions about my dissertation. In 1975 conversations with Carl Schorske encouraged me to confront more directly the specifically Austrian roots of Musil's experience.

Since 1972 the institutions and people of the University of California have aided my research in a variety of ways. I would particularly like to thank my senior colleagues in European history, Gabriel Jackson and Allan Mitchell, for their readings and criticism of my work. Two colleagues outside my field, James K. Lyon and Thomas A. Metzger, also provided valuable criticisms. Michael Parrish, Earl Pomeroy, Armin Rappaport, Barbara Shapiro, and Cynthia Walk all offered helpful suggestions: my thanks are due to them and to the many other colleagues of the University of California, San Diego, who have supported my work. Throughout the past seven years, I have benefited from the assistance of Paul Zarins and the staff of Central University Library, and more recently I have appreciated the people associated with the University of California Press who have encouraged and aided in the publication of this book.

In addition, I was fortunate to have several friends who were familiar with Musil and interested in my work. Susan Aborjaily, Rick Harmon, and John Toews all generously read and commented on my manuscript. I am particularly indebted to Carole Keim, who read the manuscript at several stages and perceptively heard my intent.

I am grateful to my family, friends, colleagues, and students for encouraging me throughout this project. I dedicate this book to all of them, but especially to Katie, who was conceived with the book, and to Sarah, who has supported my inquiry into Musil with her love and understanding.

University of California
San Diego
January 1979

Introduction

The Austrian novelist and essayist Robert Musil was one of the great critical and imaginative minds of the twentieth century. From his first responses to the psycho-sexual art of *fin de siècle* Vienna to his notes on Hitler in the 1930s, Musil's insights unveiled the structure of a culture in crisis. This crisis affected all of the traditional European ideologies from Christianity to Marxism, but at its center was the liberal culture of reason, individualism, and progress—and the educated bourgeois elite which had advocated these values since the eighteenth century. Not only was liberalism confronted by the political challenges of the mass parties, but something more diffuse with respect to the motivating power of culture seems to have been lost around the same time. The lack of a firm intellectual structure to inform the feelings and actions of the individual expressed itself during the early twentieth century in a period of cultural irrationalism and intense ideological conflict. For Musil, this twin crisis of culture and politics arose from the failure of the old ideologies to come to terms with modern science and mass, technological society. In *The Man without Qualities* (1930/1933) Musil summarized the spiritual problems of his generation and portrayed the ideological disorder of pre-war Vienna as a model of the crisis of European culture between 1890 and 1930. His vision of an unfirm self in an unfirm world was an attempt to overcome the rigidity and pathology of Europe's moral life.

Reared in the intellectual aristocracy of the Austrian *haute bour-geoisie*, Musil was both student and victim of the ideological upheaval of his generation in Central Europe. Trained as a soldier and an engineer, he turned to art in response to the cultural renaissance of the 1890s; and during his student years in Berlin between 1903 and 1910 he sought to balance his conflicting interests in science and literature. In the midst of thinking through the spiritual crisis of liberal culture, Musil was swept up in the war, revolution, and post-war reconstruction. For more than a decade he served the Austrian state as an administrator, soldier, and consultant, while establishing himself as a perceptive commentator on politics and culture in the literary periodicals of Germany. His burst of creativity in the dramas and novellas of the early 1920s crystallized his mature aesthetics, and he concentrated his energies after 1924 on *The Man without Qualities*. Living in Vienna and writing for a German audience, Musil felt equally rejected in Austria and in Germany; and he drifted steadily to the periphery to share in the oblivion of liberal intellectuals after 1933. Nazi rule and the exile of his audience silenced the cognoscenti's admiration for the first two volumes of his masterpiece, and the novel remained unfinished when Musil died in Switzerland in 1942. It was only after the Second World War that he became widely recognized in Europe as one of the great novelists of the twentieth century.

The central task of Musil's work was to mediate his culture's antagonisms between intellect and feeling, truth and subjectivity, science and art. Although best known as a master of the German novel, his training in engineering, experimental psychology, and philosophy set him apart from the conventional storyteller. His commitment to science, his mastery of the essayistic mode, and his dissolution of the story made his work exemplary for the crisis of the novel in his generation. Yet, he was above all a *Dichter*, an explorer of the imagination and borderline experiences of perception, sexuality, and emotion. From his satires of social life to his renderings of transformed states of consciousness, Musil's art sought to invent the inner person and to give expression to a complex and highly intellectual experience of reality. Uniting the objectivity of Mach with the lyrical inwardness of Rilke, Musil violated the boundaries between philosophy and literature in an effort to open both intellect and feeling to a more creative response to the world. In order to bring the ethical imagination into relation with modern science and society, he portrayed the objective functions which set limits for the expression of individuality, as well as the manifold motives of spiritual life.

Musil has been a difficult figure to define within the ideological conventions of the nineteenth century because his significance emerged at the point at which these conventions of ideology, form, and language began to break down. During his lifetime it was difficult for him to find an audience which could accept his peculiar blend of irony and mysticism. Since his death, Musil criticism has suffered from a polemical opposition between those who want to salvage Musil for a left-wing, Enlightenment tradition and those who are fundamentally apolitical and attracted primarily to his mysticism. The most basic level of this controversy concerns the philological problems of Musil's massive *Nachlass* and his intentions for the completion of *The Man without Qualities*.[1] The difficulty of resolving this debate lies not only in the open-endedness of Musil's work but also in his attempt to dissolve the polar style of thought which assumes the firm oppositions between romanticism and positivism, idealism and materialism. Insofar as the philological debate has been transcended, the literature has focused on reformulations of the various polarities of Musil's thought.[2]

1. Cf. Robert Musil, *Der Mann ohne Eigenschaften* (hereafter *MoE*), ed. Adolf Frisé (4th ed., Hamburg, 1968), vol. I of the *Gesammelte Werke*. This revised edition includes a large portion of Musil's unpublished drafts and some corrections in response to criticisms of the original edition. While I am responsible for all translations, I have also made use of the standard English version for those portions which have been translated: Robert Musil, *The Man without Qualities*, trans. Eithne Wilkins and Ernst Kaiser, 3 vols. (London, 1953/1954/1960).

Regarding the debate over how Musil meant to finish his novel, see Ernst Kaiser and Eithne Wilkins, *Robert Musil: Eine Einführung in das Werk* (Stuttgart, 1962); Helmut Arntzen, *Satirischer Stil. Zur Satire Robert Musils im "Mann ohne Eigenschaften"* (Bonn, 1960; second revised edition, 1970); and Wolfdietrich Rasch, *Über Robert Musils Roman "Der Mann ohne Eigenschaften"* (Göttingen, 1967). The late Wilhelm Bausinger's meticulous *Studien zu einer historisch-kritischen Ausgabe von Robert Musils Roman "Der Mann ohne Eigenschaften"* (Hamburg, 1964) makes clear that a great deal of work remains to be done before a genuinely scholarly edition will be possible, but he also establishes a secure basis for responsible criticism.

2. Hans-Peter Krüger, *Dichtung und Erkenntnis* (Tokyo, 1961); Gerolf Jässl, *Mathematik und Mystik* (Munich, 1964); Ulf Schramm, *Fiktion und Reflexion* (Frankfort, 1967); Elisabeth Albertsen, *Ratio und "Mystik"* (Munich, 1968); Ulrich Schelling, *Identität und Wirklichkeit* (Zurich, 1968); Stephan Reinhardt, *Studien zur Antinomie von Intellekt und Gefühl* (Bonn, 1969); Manfred Sera, *Utopie und Parodie* (Bonn, 1969); Christoph Hönig, "Die Dialektik von Ironie und Utopie" (Ph.D. diss., Berlin, 1970); Gerd Müller, *Dichtung und Wissenschaft* (Uppsala, 1971). This is only a sampling of the titles which fall into this pattern.

The vast bulk of the scholarship on Musil has been in the field of German literature, emphasizing individual works or literary themes.[3] Most of these studies concentrate on *The Man without Qualities,* although in the 1970s Musil's earlier work began to receive more serious attention. Even with the growing maturity and complexity of Musil scholarship, however, there has been little interest in the problems Musil shared with the liberal intellectuals of his generation in Austria and Germany, in the decade before the First World War and in the political upheavals after 1914. Musil's art and ideas are ordinarily treated abstractly, in isolation from his life and intellectual development. Yet Musil himself emphasized neither his individual literary works nor a fixed metaphysical position, but rather a process of valuing and a search for a method which could give form to the chaotic spiritual life of the early twentieth century.

Where Musil's work has not been treated in an abstractly literary manner, there has been a temptation to reduce him to the categories of Austrian ideology. The attempt to reserve Musil for a specifically Austrian tradition distorts his relationship to European science, the Enlightenment, German classical humanism, and the broadly shared concerns of his generation of intellectuals in Central Europe. Musil saw himself as a German poet and a European intellectual, not as an Austrian *Heimatdichter* or as the steward of the tradition of Grillparzer, Stifter, and Ferdinand von Saar. He did not intend *The Man without Qualities* as the long-awaited epic of the Habsburg Monarchy in decline, much less as an elegy for baroque or Biedermeier values. No less an authority than Hermann Broch has warned that "Nothing is falser than to count Musil among the indigenous *Österreichertum.*"[4] Musil

3. Musil scholarship has averaged about five monographs a year since 1962, and twice that many in 1969 and 1972. Cf. *Robert Musil: Leben, Werk, Bedeutung. Ausstellungskatalog,* ed. Karl Dinklage (Robert-Musil-Archiv: Klagenfurt, 1973), and Jürgen C. Thöming, *Robert-Musil-Bibliographie* (Berlin, 1968). For a valuable review of the formative stages of Musil scholarship, see Ulrich Karthaus, "Musil-Forschung und Musil-Deutung: Ein Literaturbericht," *Deutsche Vierteljahrschrift* 19, 3 (September 1965):441–83. A large number of articles and dissertations (many of them American) appear annually in German. Outside departments of literature, however, the English-speaking world has shown little interest; Musil's dramas, essays, diaries, and minor prose remain untranslated, and only two books have been devoted to Musil in English: Burton Pike's *Robert Musil: An Introduction to His Work* (Ithaca, N.Y., 1961), and Frederick G. Peters's *Robert Musil: Master of the Hovering Life* (New York, 1978).

4. Quoted in Robert Musil, *Tagebücher,* II (*Anmerkungen, Anhang, Register*), ed. Adolf Frisé (Hamburg, 1976), p. 1275. (This new edition of Musil's diaries will be referred to hereafter as *Tag.* I and II.) Broch characterized Musil's Austrianness as something sec-

was deeply influenced by the scientific and artistic values of *fin de siècle* Austria, but he was perhaps most Austrian in his cosmopolitanism, internationalism, and distaste for Austrian ideology. His real importance lies not in his relationship to Austrian tradition but in his search for a distinctively modern spirituality.

Socially, culturally, and intellectually, Musil was a transitional figure, on the threshold of the twentieth century. What is needed is a presentation which locates him socially and historically and portrays the evolution of his thought. This requires an examination not only of his major fiction, but also of his less well-known essays on politics and culture, his extensive diaries and *Nachlass*, and his dissertation on Ernst Mach. Musil's fiction appears here not primarily for the sake of its literary qualities, substantial as these are, but rather as an expression of the larger utopian thrust of his thought. This study's central task will be a clarification of the context, evolution, and characteristic form of Musil's thought. The first step toward understanding the form and meaning of Musil's development must be a presentation of the historical and cultural context in which he wrote.

THE AUSTRIAN MANDARIN

Musil's family belonged throughout the nineteenth century to the educated service-elite of the Habsburg Monarchy. This mandarin stratum of the Austrian *haute bourgeoisie* administered the conservative state and enjoyed an elevated social position just beneath the aristocracy. Its status derived from the dynastic state through its functions as a service class, through the system of state education and certification which it administered, and through the acceptance of its most successful members into the lower nobility. At the same time, it was the bearer of the values of the Enlightenment, European liberalism, and German classical humanism. It was to this professional stratum of intellectual workers that Musil was destined by birth and training to belong.

In his study of this professsional group in the German Empire, Fritz

---

ondary (*ein Nebenbei*) and called him "European, West-European" in his precision, one of the defining figures of "the spiritual-poetic physiognomy of Germany during the last decades." Broch added: "His real homeland is the spirit as such, in other words, that sphere which reaches beyond any sort of Austrianness, yes, even far beyond any sort of Europeanness. His Austrianness is the form of his irony" (ibid., p. 1276). But since neither Austria nor Musil is very familiar to Western historians, the advocates of Austrian tradition have been free to make rather extensive claims. See, for example, Friedrich Heer, "Humanitas Austriaca," pp. 17–105 in his *Land im Strom der Zeit* (Vienna, 1958).

Ringer defined the mandarins as "the social and cultural elite which owes its status primarily to educational qualifications, rather than to hereditary rights or wealth," composed of "doctors, lawyers, ministers, governmental officials, secondary teachers and university professors."[5] This stratum took shape during the eighteenth century in the German states of the Holy Roman Empire, and it was this group which gave German liberalism "its unambiguously academic-scholarly character."[6] Although it had social analogs in England and France, the mandarinate in Central Europe assumed its special importance in the context of delayed industrialization and the cultural dominance of a distinguished state-university system. Moreover, where liberalism developed under the shelter of the conservative German state, it was even more difficult than in Western Europe to identify its "traditional" and "progressive" features.

From its origins as a modern bureaucratic apparatus under Maria Theresa (1740–1780) and Joseph II (1780–1790), the mandarinate set the tone for the emergence of modernity in Austria. Created by the men around Maria Theresa, its initial task was the rationalization and centralization of the confusing maze of peoples and lands which the Habsburgs had acquired by mid-century. The mandarinate had its greatest impact in the Western half of the monarchy, in Austria and Bohemia-Moravia, which were administratively unified in 1749, just as the new system was being established. But even in Hungary (where the Magyars struggled to maintain their feudal independence from the Crown) this centralizing German bureaucracy left its mark. As late as 1914, long after the constitutional separation of Austria and Hungary in 1867, the central ministries of the empire were still overwhelmingly German. Given the indolence of the Austro-German aristocracy and the weakness of parliamentary institutions in Austria, it was the mandarins who effectively ran the state until 1918, though they took their lead socially from the aristocracy and served more as an administrative caste than as a ruling class.

In the second half of the eighteenth century, the mandarinate initiated the reorientation of baroque society to the secular goals of Enlightenment and *Bildung*. Directed in practice against the aristocracy and the church, this bourgeois service-stratum strengthened the central state

5. Fritz Ringer, *The Decline of the German Mandarins* (Cambridge, Mass., 1969), p. 5.
6. Georg Franz, *Liberalismus* (Munich, 1955), pp. 146–47.

and secularized the church's property and men as instruments of law and morality. This blend of enlightened absolutism and reform Catholicism came to be known in Austria as Josephinism, the dominant value-orientation of the educated elite from Maria Theresa to the liberal constitutions of the 1860s.[7] Inspired by the reformist impulse of Jansenism and the French Enlightenment, these sober, disciplined men sought to demonstrate the compatibility of reason and Christian morality in the legal order of the state. Their achievements—as lawyers, physicians, cameralists, clergy, professors, and schoolteachers—were primarily practical rather than ideological: they created a more secular, rational state within the context of Catholicism, absolutism, and German culture. It was also this stratum which set the tone for the emergence of bourgeois culture in German prose—and in the institutions of the university, theater, opera, salon, and newspapers. An important dimension of this new culture was the German classicism of the North, of Goethe and Lessing; and the values of *Geist* and *Bildung* shaped the mandarin's central commitment to education—both the cultivation of the personality and the moral education of mankind.

In reaction to the French Revolution the Josephinist bureaucracy assumed a more conservative form. During the Franciscan Era (1792–1835) the emphasis was on centralism, ideological control, and legal order, rather than reform. Political censorship repressed public debate, and Catholic restoration policed spiritual life in the direction of the more baroque religious ethos. As elsewhere in the German confederation, this apolitical atmosphere was compatible with the Biedermeier cultivation of private virtues, music, nature romanticism, and inner peace. Austria had its forms of romanticism, from Schlegel to Raimund to Beethoven, and the mandarin ethic of duty and mastery of passion existed in tension with the sentimental culture of the salons. The dominant ethos of the early nineteenth century, however, emphasized classical harmony and the reconciliation of the individual to a rational, objective order continuous with traditional values. It was during this period that Austria began to emphasize its peculiar identity and tradition, setting its aristocratic, Catholic, and realistic ethos in opposition to Protestant, idealist, subjectivist "Germany." Despite the conservative objectives of this imperial myth of order, it also stressed the ideological

7. Cf. Fritz Valjavec, *Der Josephinismus* (Munich, 1945); Eduard Winter, *Barock, Absolutismus und Aufklärung* (Vienna, 1971); Paul P. Bernard, *Jesuits and Jacobins* (Urbana, Ill., 1971).

continuity with the Enlightenment. Thus, in the early nineteenth century the educated stratum of the Austrian Empire accommodated itself to the conservative state in terms of Leibniz and Wolff rather than Kant and Hegel. This assimilation of Protestant rationalism to the Catholic context emphasized the reality of the social and natural orders against the subjectivist aspects of German idealism and romanticism. Austrian ideology offered sustenance to a hierarchical social order, but it also emphasized reason, empiricism, and a high moral tone of service.[8]

This mandarin blend of baroque and enlightened values set the terms for traditional liberal culture in Austria. The Josephinist stratum assumed the absolutist state, the religious basis of social and moral order, and its own elite role, but it was committed to social progress through education and reform, to free thought, science, art, and internalized professional values. The mandarin ethos found expresssion in Grillparzer's classical dramas, in Stifter's blend of Catholic piety and German *Bildung*, and in Bolzano's reconciliation of science, Catholicism, and progressive social thought. During the restoration, the liberal impulse in this tradition was submerged or insecure, but after 1835 Josephinism began to blur with early liberalism and with the challenges to a discredited absolutism. In 1848 the liberal mandarinate found itself trapped between the conservative state and radical German nationalism, establishing the predicament of German liberalism that would last until 1938. But the failure of the democratic, nationalist revolutions of 1848 and the collapse of neo-absolutism in 1859 paved the way for the constitutional monarchy of high liberalism.

The mandarinate defined the moral, intellectual, and political tone for the union of *Besitz und Bildung* (capital and culture) in the liberal era.[9] Its blend of dynastic loyalty, moral earnestness, positivism, and educational idealism established the norms for the *haute bourgeoisie* as a whole. There were tensions, to be sure, in the decline of the Josephinist tradition; and Stifter's suicide symbolized the conservative pessimism of

8. The historiography of this period suffers from a split between the language of Western and German scholarship and studies that stress the peculiarities of the Austrian experience. Two important studies by Roger Bauer that examine Austrian literature and philosophy in detail are *La Realité royaume de Dieu* (Paris, 1965), and *Der Idealismus und seine Gegner in Österreich* (Heidelberg, 1966). Cf. Eduard Winter, *Romantismus, Restauration und Früh-liberalismus im österreichischen Vormärz* (Vienna, 1968), and Robert A. Kann, *A Study in Austrian Intellectual History* (New York, 1960).

9. On Austrian liberalism see Franz, *Liberalismus;* Karl Eder, *Der Liberalismus in Alt-österreich* (Vienna, 1955), and Eduard Winter, *Revolution, Neoabsolutismus und Liberalismus in der Donaumonarchie* (Vienna, 1969).

Bildung in the face of an industrial capitalism which no longer gave art a social-moral function.[10] But in the 1860s tensions between culture and capital were submerged in the common moralistic-rational style and the common participation of professsors, lawyers, and businessmen in the new parliamentary institutions. The new arrangements of 1861 signaled the victory of achieved status and progress in capitalism and education, and the mandarin ethos of disciplined pragmatism was continuous with the values of high liberalism. The capitalist bourgeoisie emulated the cultural style of the mandarinate, and the great achievements of the liberal era were largely mandarin triumphs: the modernization and secularization of education, the rebuilding of Vienna in relation to the symbols of mandarin culture—the *Rathaus*, the university, the parliament, and the *Burgtheater*—and the extension and regularization of law through the bureaucracy. The mandarinate was the defining element within the liberal *haute bourgeoisie*, but it was also the stratum whose values of disciplined service were most threatened by the narcissism of its offspring in the 1890s.

THE CRISIS OF LIBERAL CULTURE

The Austro-Hungarian monarchy, or Kakania, as Musil called it, was a characteristically late-nineteenth-century blend of aristocracy and middle class, of authoritarianism and liberalism. Despite, or even because of, the peculiar roles of a Catholic aristocracy and a multinational population, the Dual Monarchy which held Central Europe together between 1867 and 1918 was an especially clear case of the problems of modernity.[11] Recently, historians have been attracted to this period of Habsburg history both as a key to anti-liberal mass movements of the twentieth century and as a center of cultural modernism.[12]

10. Carl E. Schorske, "The Transformation of the Garden: Ideal and Society in Austrian Literature," *AHR* 72, 4 (July 1967): 1303.

11. Musil and Broch both emphasized this point. On the other hand, both were concerned with the problems of the German elite, with German culture, and with universal features of the problem of value in modernity, not with the whole range of nationalities and classes in Kakania. The term *Kakania* takes on the qualities of an ideal type or fantasy in *The Man without Qualities*, but its literal meaning is simply *kaiserlich und königlich*, Imperial and Royal, Austrian and Hungarian, k-k-nia. Cf. *MoE* I, chap. 8.

12. See Carl Schorske's seminal articles in the *AHR*; William M. Johnston, *The Austrian Mind* (Berkeley, 1972); William J. McGrath, *Dionysian Art and Populist Politics in Austria* (New Haven, 1974); Allan Janik and Stephen Toulmin, *Wittgenstein's Vienna* (New York, 1973); and C. E. Williams, *The Broken Eagle* (London, 1974). General cultural portraits as well as studies of individual figures such as Karl Kraus, Sigmund Freud, and Ludwig Wittgenstein have recently emphasized Austria's peculiar sensitivity to the crisis of European culture.

Investigations of these issues have focused primarily on the Austrian half of the Dual Monarchy and the experience of its German liberal elite. The experience of this threatened elite provides the extreme instance of the crisis of liberal values throughout Europe in the late nineteenth century. The challenges to liberal reason from the unconscious and from mass politics (dramatically symbolized by Austrians as different as Freud and Hitler) became most apparent through the experience of Austrian liberalism. This highly self-conscious version of the crisis of European liberalism was Musil's personal inheritance and the perspective from which he experienced the breakdown of the old regime in Central Europe.

Austrian liberalism in the late nineteenth century shared the values, successes, and anxieties of the *haute bourgeoisie* throughout Europe, but the predicament of this liberal elite, caught in the transition from traditional-status to industrial-class society, was particularly apparent in Austria. There, liberalism's ascendancy was concentrated in a period which lasted at most for a generation, and neither democracy nor nationalism provided an ideological veil for its fragile eminence. As a group, the Austrian *haute bourgeoisie* was dependent on the Habsburg dynasty and the still dominant aristocracy, yet it embraced an ideology (of freedom, reason, and progress) and a practice (of capitalism and science) which disintegrated traditional society and invited a new one that challenged liberal leadership and values. Between 1860 and 1890 Austrian liberalism moved from confidence to doubt, from the secure, repressive style of a new elite to the gracious, pleasure-loving style of an impotent minority. The fate of the German-speaking *haute bourgeoisie* became so tied to the traditional order, in the face of nationalism and industrial mass society, that in the political debacles between 1890 and 1918 the failures of liberalism and of the Habsburg Monarchy were virtually indistinguishable.

The victories of *Besitz und Bildung* in the 1860s were part of a wave of successes for European capitalism and constitutionalism. Austrian liberalism was much like positivism elsewhere in Europe: its commitment to the free, rational individual was part of a framework of assumptions about legal order, capitalism, and evolutionary progress. But its constitutional parliamentarism was not joined with national triumph as in Bismarck's Reich; instead, these liberal forms were the residue of the monarchy's defeats at the hands of the Italians (1859), the Prussians (1866), and the Magyars (1867). The end of the German connection in

1866 left the liberals as a national minority in a multi-national state, and even in its finest hour Austrian liberalism made little contact with the masses who had scant grasp of the significance of the constitution.[13] Its German culture, its capitalism, and its ideological attacks on the church all tended to underscore the class character of Austrian liberalism; and its individualism and parliamentarism opened the door on a political and cultural pluralism which went beyond its own assumptions.

Liberalism's dependence on the traditional power structure became more apparent after the Crash of 1873, as anti-capitalist and anti-Semitic feeling mounted in the lower classes. The economic model of progress and upward mobility became less plausible in the Great Depression of 1873–1896. Moreover, German liberalism's brief period of dominance in the *Reichsrat* came to an end in 1879, and the prospects of liberalism dimmed still further with the emergence of the mass parties in the 1880s. The industrialization of Bohemia and Moravia did not create recruits for German liberalism, but offered the new challenge of the Young Czechs. Even among the mainly German parties of the 1880s and 1890s, the enemy was consistently the German liberal, whether for his dynastic loyalties, his opposition to Catholicism, his capitalism, or his assimilation of Jews into the German *haute bourgeoisie*. Envisioning itself as the harbinger of modernity and progress, liberalism found itself dependent on the conservative establishment; its opponents were often anti-intellectual and anti-Semitic, but they were almost always more democratic. The German liberal was trapped politically: from above by Franz Joseph, the conservative aristocracy, and the bureaucratic state; from below by the new nationalities, the lower-middle-class shopkeepers, and the working class. The primarily negative achievements of liberalism in breaking the bonds of tradition left a vacuum after 1880, an uncertainty about how to create new forms and meaningful connections with the rest of society.

This political predicament gave significance to the distinctive feature in the ideological inheritance of the Austrian liberal: the social and cultural emulation of an aristocracy which was neither militarist like the Prussian Junkers nor political like the British landed elites, but an aristocracy of display, cultivated pleasures, and social grace. The political

13. Valjavec, *Josephinismus*, p. 167. This class division intensified the split in the Josephinist state church between an urbane, secular, often deist elite and the baroque Catholicism of the rest of society.

impotence of the upper middle class was dramatized in the 1880s by its
devotion to pleasure and decorative art, to a leisure of conspicuous con-
sumption and gratification, detached from the practical problems of reality. Vienna became the *Kunststadt* par excellence, though its art was
one of ornament and status rather than moral education. Strauss waltz-
es, Makart's luxurious spectacles, the entertainments of the Prater, the
pretty songs and poems of the salon, intimations of dead glories in the
architecture of the *Ring*—all expressed the passivity and value-empti-
ness of the gay apocalypse (*die fröhliche Apokalypse*) around 1880.[14]
Elsewhere in Europe, even in Paris, the terms *aestheticism* and *decadence* referred to a handful of artists and intellectuals who affected
aristocratic styles and repudiated bourgeois values. By and large such
people were a shock to the earnest and repressive attitudes of the middle
class. In Austria the political impotence of the *haute bourgeoisie* and
the leading role of a Catholic aristocracy encouraged the distinctive
"evolution of the aesthetic culture of the educated bourgeoisie after the
mid-century. . . . [O]ut of it grew the peculiar receptivity of a whole
class to the life of art, and, concomitantly at the individual level, a sensitivity to psychic states."[15] Facing the challenges of modern industrial
society, Austrian liberals turned not to bourgeois idealism or nationalism but to an aristocratic culture which was more aesthetic than moral,
more psychological than political, more inclined to respond to the in-
roads of mass society with an ironic smile. The hero in this culture was
the artist rather than the politician, and his genius was for introspection
rather than domination. Schnitzler, Bahr, Hofmannsthal, and Altenberg
matured in the salon and café culture of *haut bourgeois* Vienna, and
they expressed the ultimate refinement of its world-weariness and impressionism.

The decadence of Young Vienna should be distinguished from the
class phenomenon of decadence apparent by 1880. It was in the work of
these writers of the 1890s (and their contemporary Sigmund Freud) that
the contradictions of Austrian liberal culture became explicit and fruit-

14. Hermann Broch, "Hofmannsthal und seine Zeit," in *Dichten und Erkennen: Essays I* (Zurich, 1955), p. 76. 1880 is often referred to as the nadir of European bourgeois
culture, especially in Germany. Cf. Henry Hatfield, *Modern German Literature* (Bloomington, Ind., 1966), pp. 1, 150n; H. Stuart Hughes, *Consciousness and Society* (New
York, 1958), pp. 40–41; and Egon Friedell, *A Cultural History of the Modern Age*, vol. 3,
trans. Charles Francis Atkinson (New York, 1933).

15. Carl E. Schorske, "Politics and the Psyche in *fin de siècle* Vienna: Schnitzler and
Hofmannsthal," *AHR* 66, 4 (July 1961):933.

ful. These figures consummated the decline of traditional liberalism and opened the door on the psychological man of modern art, social science, and mass politics, "preoccupied with the problem of the nature of the individual in a disintegrating society."[16] The searchlight of science turned inward to explore the vacuum of motivation. The application of intellect to the pretty emotions of kitsch, to the pain of the psyche and the unconscious, held the danger that the bases of culture might be undermined. The project of demystification, begun in the abstract conflict between science and religion and in the social conflict between industrialization and tradition, now threatened the last fortress of the unconscious self. For the artists of the Café Central this meant a complete enervation of the will, the conscious and articulate expression of bourgeois decadence. Yet in withdrawing to a psychological and sexual art, these Austrian intellectuals suffered the "persistent presence of conscience in the temple of Narcissus."[17] In their first uncertain attempts to overcome the world-weariness of the 1890s, the aesthetes of Young Vienna led the way for the younger writers of the generation of 1905—Kraus, Weininger, Broch, the later Hofmannsthal, and, of course, Musil.

THE GENERATION OF 1905

Toward the end of his study of European social thought in the generation of the 1890s, H. Stuart Hughes described a slightly younger generation of "essayists or imaginative writers" who "still thought of themselves as direct participants in the decisive experience of their elders." Roughly half a generation younger than such great innovators of modern social thought as Freud, Weber, and Bergson, these writers "were just reaching manhood in the first decade of the twentieth century." Hughes defined this generation of intellectuals in terms of an uneasy balance between respect for the intellectual giants of the 1890s and a desire to reach a popular rather than an academic audience. Confronted by the split in modern social thought between social science and imaginative writing, they tended toward the latter. Hughes called this "the generation of 1905," defining it in relation to the First Moroccan Crisis and the beginning of this generation's period of mature creativity in the decade before the war. Although Hughes emphasized the younger, more

16. Ibid., p. 931.
17. Ibid., p. 936.

irrationalist members of this group, his concept of "the generation of 1905" is an ideal characterization of Musil's generation.[18]

Musil defined his own generation as those who were between twenty-five and forty-five when World War I began, or, alternatively, as those born between 1870 and 1890. He thought of his generation in European terms, as a first attempt to move beyond traditional liberal culture to forge a genuinely modern culture, appropriate to life in modern, technological civilization. The *fin de siècle* looked decadent to the liberal generation of the 1870s, and certainly positivism had lost its optimistic appeal, but to be young and culturally aware at the turn of the century meant a sense of standing at the beginning of something new and exciting in every area of the arts. Here art took up the central position as the wellspring of the ethical and the source of transforming power and vision. Falling between the impressionists and the expressionist generation of the war years, these figures were old enough to share in the intellectual revolutions of the 1890s, but young enough to go to the front during their creative years. For most of them it was not until the 1920s, between the collapse of the old Europe and the victory of fascism, that their mature efforts came to fruition.

The generation of 1905 should not be too sharply distinguished from the intellectual revolutionaries of the older generation. It was, after all, the generation of the 1890s and the still older Nietzsche who had shown the way; and most intellectuals of the generation of 1905 looked up to the accomplishments of Mach, Dilthey, Weber, Freud, and the artists of the *fin de siècle*. Intellectually, their legacy was a more modest and specialized vision of science and reason, a less dogmatic understanding of history and human action, and a heightened awareness of the problems of motivation and the unconscious. What was new for

18. Hughes, *Consciousness and Society*, pp. 336–38. Hughes gives the birthdates 1856–1877 for this cluster of creative genius in the generation of the 1890s, but the figures he considers most important for modern social thought—Freud, Durkheim, Bergson, Weber, and Croce—were all born between 1856 and 1866, and two other major figures—Sorel and Pareto—were born in the 1840s. I find it more helpful to define this generation as those born in the 1850s and 1860s. Thus, the generation of the 1890s would mean those who were in their thirties during that decade. At the margin of this group would be those who were slightly older, but did not have much impact before the 1890s, such as Sorel and Pareto, or, arguably, even Nietzsche, Dilthey, and Mach. At the other limit, the figures Hughes mentions who were born between 1871 and 1877—Proust, Péguy, Jung, Thomas Mann, Michels, and Hesse—tend to be more imaginative types and (as Hughes himself points out, p. 377) blur into the generation of 1905. The writers Hughes mentions who were born in the late 1860s, particularly Gide and Pirandello, follow this same pattern.

those born after 1870 was the centrality of ethical questions, the intersection of the problems of philosophy and literature, and the actual historical experience of their mature years between 1905 and the 1930s.
These young readers of Nietzsche were aware of themselves as a generation and as a European phenomenon. Feeling themselves born into a
moral vacuum, they set out to answer the question of how to live in a
pluralistic, mass, industrial society.

   Within Austria the generation of 1905 had its peculiar characteristics.
The impressionism and decadence of the 1890s established norms of
aristocratic style, preoccupation with sexuality, and resistance to total
ideologies. Even in their moralistic attempts to overcome the decadence
of liberal culture, the writers of this generation were often stamped by
the atmosphere of Vienna 1900; this is apparent in the sexual theories
and suicide of Otto Weininger, as it is in Hofmannsthal's conservative
politics and Kraus's angry satires. But the achievements of modernism
in the work of Loos, Schoenberg, and the Secession were part of a
broader European transformation of culture apparent in Paris, Munich,
Dublin, London, and Berlin. Moreover, even those who emphasize the
peculiarities of the Austrian tradition have pointed out that this generation of Austrian intellectuals was self-consciously European and modern rather than Habsburg—and that this was particularly true of writers such as Musil, Broch, and Rilke.[19] Unlike their seniors, the
intellectuals of this generation often belonged only peripherally to the
mystique of Vienna itself, growing up in provincial cities or spending
their student years abroad. Moreover, their mature years were not
graced by the glamor of *fin de siècle* Vienna, but shattered by war, revolution, social dislocation, and exile.

   Not only was this generation cosmopolitan in the best Austrian tradition, but it emphasized the commonality of intellectual culture from
Vienna and Prague to Munich and Berlin. Austrians such as Musil,
Broch, Rilke, Kahler, Zweig, or Wittgenstein often thought of themselves as Germans or Europeans, and their practical dependence on the
cultural institutions of the German Empire was enormous even before
1914. For them, the Habsburg myth or the victory of Prussia in 1866
meant far less than the continuity of German culture and the shared
predicament of liberal intellectuals during the collapse of the old re-

   19. Cf. Joseph Strelka, *Brücke zu vielen Ufern* (Vienna, 1966), pp. 63–64, and Claudio Magris, *Der habsburgische Mythos* (Salzburg, 1966), pp. 21, 290–91.

gimes in Central Europe. This was particularly true of Musil, who refused to define culture in terms of states. He was concerned with the problems of philosophy and literature as mediated through the German language, and beginning in his early twenties he shaped his identity in terms of the wider sphere of German culture. He spent much of his adult life in Berlin, published his fiction and essays in Germany, and addressed himself to a German audience. Politically, he identified himself with the fate of the German nation; and he took the average German burgher—whether in Vienna or Berlin—as typifying the problems of the individual in modern civilization.

From the diplomatic revolution of 1905 to the triumphs of Hitler in the 1930s, the catastrophes of this generation were focused on Central Europe, and it was in Central Europe that the crisis of liberal culture came most strongly to consciousness in the generation of 1905. Within the German culture of Central Europe alone, Musil's definition of his generation encompasses an impressive array of creative writers, particularly in the fields of philosophy and literature. Among the older members of this generation, born in the 1870s, were Heinrich Mann (1871), Rudolf Kassner (1873), Karl Kraus, Max Scheler, and Hugo von Hofmannsthal (1874), Carl Jung, Emil Lask, Thomas Mann, and Rainer Maria Rilke (1875), Hermann Hesse (1877), and Martin Buber and Alfred Döblin (1878). Among those born in the 1880s were Musil himself, Osward Spengler, and Otto Weininger (1880), Stefan Zweig (1881), Karl Jaspers and Franz Kafka (1883), Ernst Bloch, Erich Kahler, and Georg Lukács (1885), Karl Barth, Gottfried Benn, Hermann Broch, and Paul Tillich (1886), Albert Paris Gütersloh, Georg Trakl, and Arnold Zweig (1887), and Martin Heidegger and Ludwig Wittgenstein (1889). At the extreme limit of this cluster, but identifying with the experience and problems of their older contemporaries, were Franz Werfel (1890), Walter Benjamin (1892), and Karl Mannheim (1893). These writers shared common problems, intellectual culture, and political experience. On the whole, those who were Austrian or slightly older tended to be more inhibited by their respect for reason, science, and liberalism, while those who were German or slightly younger were more likely to identify with vitalistic and anti-rational currents. Although the concept of the generation does not permit mathematical precision, it was central to Musil's experience and his sense of identity. And the task which he set himself was to think through the spiritual experience of his generation in Central Europe.

For the leading intellectuals of the generation of 1905, history seemed no longer to contain the cosmic secret, as the nineteenth century had believed. Setting out from the uncertainty of knowledge and the inadequacy of every form of dogmatism, the thinkers of this generation were conscious of the fragility and brevity of human civilization. Although they often moved to broader sociological and ideological analysis after World War I, their fundamental impulse was psychological, ethical, and aesthetic, focused on the inner crisis of their culture. Confronted with the decline of the old historical cosmologies of progress, they sought to reawaken the positive value of the unconscious, sexuality, and dream-life. This meant the new importance of symbolism, of language as a medium (or prison) unto itself, and of the unconscious as a source of creativity. Although they sought to overcome the pessimism of the 1890s, theirs was an optimism over the abyss, at the edge of suicide and despair, a vitalism in the face of a preoccupation with biological reductionism and death. It was in part their sense of the loss of a coherent ideology which eventually facilitated the rise of fascism. Although not the cause of fascism, it left an intellectual vacuum which fascism filled with charisma, heroism, and duty, investing the political order indiscriminately with an aura of ecstasy and purpose. In the absence of a firm intellectual order, the feelings sought to establish an order of their own.

For the intellectuals who faced the collapse of the authority of tradition and of the persuasiveness of liberal ideology, there were two basic options in their search to retrieve the ethical individual from the morass of bourgeois culture: either the pathos of absolute rebellion and irrationalism, or the attempt to maintain the ethical tension of the will, while honestly confronting the complexity and ambiguity of the actual world. Those who chose the latter option were more alert to the full meaning of this generation's experience; they were the essayistic novelists and literary philosophers who sought a creative resolution to the revolt against positivism and bourgeois culture, and who attempted in the 1920s to gain some retrospective understanding of the collapse of their world.

They represent a phenomenon of twentieth-century European thought which Merleau-Ponty identified in "Metaphysics and the Novel":

For a long time it looked as if philosophy and literature not only had different ways of saying things but had different objects as well. . . . Since the end of the nineteenth century, however, the ties between them have been getting closer and closer. The first sign of this reconciliation was the appearance of hybrid modes of expression having elements of the intimate diary, the philosophical treatise, and the dialogue.

In the generation of 1905 it was clearly the German-speaking intellectuals of Central Europe who were most preoccupied with a situation in which "philosophical expression assumes the same ambiguities as literary expression."[20]

PHILOSOPHICAL ESSAYISM

In the Central European realm of German culture, between Lübeck and Budapest, the intellectuals of the generation of 1905 moved outside the university and the intellectual conventions of the mandarinate and the liberal establishment in general. The leading figures of this generation were novelists and cultural critics, or philosophers on the margin of academic convention. This was the generation in which the novel reached its height in German culture, much later than in France or England, in the work of Broch, Döblin, Hesse, Kafka, Mann, and Musil. But these achievements occurred in the context of the breakdown of the typical literary form of bourgeois culture; the novel moved away from the story and immediate aesthetic totality in the direction of essayism, interpretation, and fragmented form. For these men, the novel became the vehicle for the continuation of metaphysics by other means: what was perceived elsewhere as the end of the novel was defined by these German writers as the characteristic fulfillment of the form. Walter Benjamin described his situation as one in which the story no longer spoke for itself,[21] and Georg Lukács defined the novelist as the philosopher par excellence, whose work "is like no other an expression of transcendental homelessness."[22] Taking the bleak landscape of literary naturalism as their point of departure, these novelists set out in quest of structures of meaning via the modes of indirection, irony, and self-conscious reflection.

The philosophers of the generation of 1905 shared this position between metaphysics and the novel. Systematic metaphysics seemed to have run its course, and the most eminent minds of the older generation—Simmel, Husserl, Mauthner, Weber, and Bergson—emphasized

20. Cf. Maurice Merleau-Ponty, "Metaphysics and the Novel," pp. 26–28 in his *Sense and Nonsense*, (Evanston, 1964).

21. Walter Benjamin, "The Storyteller" *Illuminations* (New York, 1969), pp. 83–110.

22. Georg Lukács, *Die Theorie des Romans* (Berlin, 1968; originally appeared 1915–1916), p. 2.

that the important issues lay in the realm of the philosophy of culture and language, expressed in an essayistic mode.[23] This invitation was welcomed by the finest minds of the younger generation, in the work of thinkers as different as Lukács, Wittgenstein, Bloch, Benjamin, and Musil. As early as 1911 Lukács identified the importance of the essay as an art form.[24] He pointed to what Matthew Arnold called "Criticism of Life," and noted that the criticized material was only the indirect occasion for the expression of something else. Though more removed from literary and cultural criticism, Ludwig Wittgenstein's devotion to the explication of language summarized his whole generation's conviction that an "expression has meaning only in the flow of life."[25]

The essayistic, indirect, and fragmentary style of this generation of philosophers was more than a formal similarity; it expressed the common predicament of the metaphysician in the midst of the breakdown of the assumptions of liberal culture. Whether in Benjamin's "interpolation in small" his concept of "the fragment as philosophical form," or in Lukács's notion of the Platonist choosing the essay as the appropriate form for a period of cultural transition, or in Wittgenstein's playful attempts to help the fly out of the bottle, or in Musil's elaboration of essayism as philosophy, the emphasis was always on the smallest step, the insight, the broken form.[26] In the essayists of this generation, the metaphysical impulse strayed beyond its traditional home in the university to literary criticism and the novel. Even Wittgenstein's ambivalent affair with academic philosophy confirms the appropriateness of Scholem's observation on Benjamin to this generation of philosophical essayists:

23. The leading figures of the generation of the 1890s founded a journal for the philosophy of culture in 1910, which Edmund Husserl introduced with a motto for the younger generation: "Our age does not stand under the rule of a single system": *Logos: Internationale Zeitschrift für Philosophie der Kultur* 1, 1 (1910):1. This remark is significant not only because of the date and the substance of the journal but because Husserl himself proved to be the most influential mentor for German philosophy after 1910.

24. Georg Lukács, "Über Form und Wesen des Essays," pp. 7–8 in his *Die Seele und die Formen* (Berlin, 1911). For Lukács, the essayist was the representative artist for an age without essence.

25. Ludwig Wittgenstein, quoted in Norman Malcom's *Ludwig Wittgenstein: A Memoir* (London, 1958), p. 93.

26. Cf. Theodor Adorno's introduction to Walter Benjamin, *Schriften*, vol. 1 (Frankfort, 1955), and Adorno, "Der Essay als Form," in his *Noten zur Literatur 1* (Frankfort, 1969). See also Ludwig Rohner, *Der deutsche Essay* (Berlin, 1966), and *Deutsche Essays*, vol. 1 (Berlin, 1968); Dieter Bachmann, *Essay und Essayismus* (Stuttgart, 1969); Erich Heller, *The Disinherited Mind* (New York, 1957), and *The Artist's Journey into the Interior* (New York, 1965).

He was a metaphysician; indeed, I would say, a metaphysician pure and simple. But it was borne in on him that in his generation the genius of the pure metaphysician would express itself more readily in other spheres, any other sphere than in those traditionally assigned to metaphysics, and this was precisely one of the experiences that helped him to mould his distinctive individuality and originality.[27]

The philosophical essayists were metaphysicians in disguise; the objectivity of the scientist and the irony of the artist were united with the discretion of the metaphysician behind the veil.

The leading writers of the generation of 1905 believed that the tasks of philosophy, literature, and cultural criticism had converged, and they shared the preference for hybrid forms, between metaphysics and the novel, which I call essayism. While the philosophers moved away from abstract system toward the concrete and the fragmented form, the novelists moved toward essayism, reflection, and the collapse of narrative coherence. This pattern emerged in the decade before 1914 in the work of the most gifted critics of the cultural crisis, and it became so widespread in the wake of the First World War that by 1924 Thomas Mann identified "the spiritual essay" or the "intellectual novel" as the dominant form of the day.[28] As with the young Lukács more than a decade earlier, Mann saw the origins of this form in the romantics and in Friedrich Schlegel's vision of the union of science and art, but the context of the project had been radically transformed in the course of the century by industrialization, by the example of Nietzsche, by the revolutions in science and art, and by the attempt to link up with a more worldly criticism in the Anglo-French tradition.

For the generation of 1905, the end of metaphysics and the crisis of the novel were parallel expressions of the crisis of traditional liberal culture which they expressed and explicated through the hybrid mode of essayism. Though the essayists may be seen as "theologians marooned in the realm of the profane,"[29] they were attuned to the wisdom of Nietzsche that the old language and concepts were dead. Though they brought about a brilliant renaissance of the novel, they did so with an emphasis on the broken form, the ironic distance, and the dying story. It was these philosophical essayists who revived the spirit of ethics and

27. Gershom Scholem, "Walter Benjamin," *Leo Baeck Memorial Lecture* 8 (New York, 1965), p. 9.
28. Thomas Mann, "Über die Lehre Spenglers," pp. 224–25 in his *Schriften und Reden zur Literatur, Kunst und Philosophie*, vol. 1 (Frankfort, 1968).
29. Scholem, "Walter Benjamin," p. 16.

criticism to bridge the inherited gap between positivist science and *l'art pour l'art*. For them, essayism seemed the most rigorous and effective form to employ in a search for a way beyond the collapse of progress and the isolation of the individual in pluralistic, mass society. Rudolf Kassner called essayism the high point of German prose, but Lukács argued that the essay had become too high a form, too formless and problematic, too free and intellectual.[30] It had lost its backdrop in life, and the obvious way to recover this was through the problematic form of the novel. Nowhere are these connections more apparent than in the work of Robert Musil.

Musil was the representative philosophical essayist of the generation of 1905 in Central Europe. From his fiction and essays of the pre-war years to *The Man without Qualities*, he explored the intermediate zones between philosophy and literature. But precisely in realizing the representative intellectual mode of his generation, Musil cut himself off from everything conventional and typical.[31] The irony and mysticism of his philosophical essayism established a distance from both the old bourgeois values and modern mass culture. His prose is often easy and graceful on the surface, having little of the typical German profundity about it, but there is a great deal of intellectual energy and complexity hidden in it. With an alertness rare in his own time, Musil saw that up and down, forward and backward, rational and irrational, good and evil, wise and stupid were confused in inconvenient ways; therefore his attempt to bring the individual into creative relation with the challenges of industrial society and modern culture offered no fixed image of the world and value. Living in a revolutionary era, Musil assumed an ironic distance from the collapse of the traditional liberal order and its ideologies in order to explore the relations between intellect and feeling,

30. Rudolf Kassner, "Der Dichter und der Platoniker," *Sämtliche Werke*, vol. 1 (Stuttgart, 1969), pp. 9–22. This essay on the critic helped Lukács formulate his own understanding of the essayist. Kassner called the critic "the philosopher without system, the poet without rhyme, the most solitary person in society," and he compared him with the Platonists of the ancient world, the mystics of the Middle Ages, the skeptics of the late Renaissance, the *moralistes* of eighteenth-century France, and the cultural critics of Victorian England. He described this type as negative, anonymous, relativistic, mistrustful, as a man without a fate who bears all possibilities within him. Lukács offered fundamentally the same description, and Musil lived out the typology.

31. Musil was also representative in the sense that he thought through the spiritual experience of his generation. Cf. Lucien Goldmann, *The Human Sciences and Philosophy* (London, 1969), p 59. It would not, however, be correct to think of him as typical of his generation as a whole. Cf. Kurt Tucholsky, "Die Assortieren," p. 765 in his *Gesammelte Werke* 3 (Hamburg, 1960).

worldliness and spirit. In *The Man without Qualities* he brought to its
most complex and critical fulfillment the hybrid mode for which the literary form of the essay seemed the most appropriate model:

An essay is not the provisional or incidental expression of a conviction that
might on a more favorable occasion be elevated to the status of truth or that
might just as easily be recognized as error . . . an essay is the unique and un-
alterable form that a man's inner life assumes in a decisive thought. . . . There
have been quite a number of such essayists and masters of the floating life
within, but there would be no point in naming them. Their domain lies between
religion and knowledge, between example and doctrine, between *amor intellectualis* and poetry; they are saints with and without religion, and sometimes too
they are simply men who have gone out on an adventure and lost their way.[32]

32. *MoE* I, chap. 62. The finest novelists of these years—Kafka, Broch, and Musil—
died without recognition. The greatest of the philosophical essayists left only fragments:
Wittgenstein his scattered notes, Benjamin his essays and his never-written mosaic of nineteenth-century Paris, and Musil his unfinished novel. These three, like most of the essayists, remained by choice or necessity outside the university, where a generation earlier they
would all no doubt have made their mark with proper attention to systematic form and
one-dimensional rationality.

CHAPTER ONE

The Young Musil: 1880-1905

There are all sorts of reasons why there is no past era one
knows so little about as the three to five decades between
one's own twentieth year and one's father's twentieth year.[1]

obert Musil was born in Klagenfurt, Carinthia, on November
6, 1880—in the symbolic year of the value vacuum of German culture and the gay apocalypse in Vienna. He spent his
childhood in the provincial cities and military academies
of Austria, and his family and education reflected the "ill-reconciled
moralistic and aesthetic components" of Austrian liberal culture.[2] He
grew up in a society which was strongly polarized not only according to
gender roles but also between forms of work and leisure, between the
moralistic-scientific values of the bourgeoisie and the gracious elegance
of the aristocracy. As a student of engineering in Brno, Moravia, between 1898 and 1901, Robert sought to come to terms with the cultivated leisure of the *haute bourgeoisie* and with the literary culture of
the *fin de siècle*. Emulating the decadence of Vienna and the symbolism
of Paris, the young scientist adopted the style of the aesthete while
seeking to transform his new perceptions in the direction of an ethical
art. After his year of military duty, Robert moved away from his family
in Brno, first to Stuttgart as an engineer and then, at the end of 1903, to
Berlin to study philosophy. His first novel, written between 1902 and
1905, portrays in the adolescent experiences of an Austrian mandarin
the tensions between the intellectual and emotional components of

1. *MoE* I, chap. 15.
2. Schorske, "Politics and the Psyche," p. 931.

Robert's own experience. In *Young Törless* Musil rendered a sensitive attempt to shape a self out of the cultural dis-ease of late nineteenth-century Austria.

1. THE PROVINCIAL MANDARIN

So his son was from boyhood well acquainted with the aris-

tocracy's talent for condescension, which unconsciously yet so

accurately weighed and measured out the exact quantity of

affability required; and he had always been irritated by this

subservience—of one who did, after all, belong to the intellec-

tual elite—toward the owners of horses, lands, and traditions.[3]

Robert's father, Alfred Musil (1846–1924), represented everything that was disciplined, rational, and dutiful in the mandarin tradition, and his virtues and achievements were continuous with the framework which his own father had defined. The grandfather, Dr. Matthias Musil, had left rural Moravia to make a career as a military physician, and around mid-century he settled in Graz, south of Vienna. Alfred Musil's interest in engineering nearly led him to follow his father and his brother into a military career, but he remained instead within the civilian and academic bureaucracy. Beginning in Klagenfurt, where he married Hermine Bergauer in 1874, he devoted himself to the study of machine construction and techniques of industrial engineering. Shortly after Robert's birth, the Musils moved from Klagenfurt, and for a decade Alfred Musil followed the spread of industrial growth via a number of research and administrative positions in Austria, Bohemia, and Moravia. His scholarly accomplishments as a mechanical engineer were distinguished, and his administrative work was honored by Franz Joseph; but his ambition and vitality ebbed when his hope for an invitation to Vienna or his home city of Graz was thwarted by an appointment to the faculty of the technical institute in Brno. Although his banishment to provincial Moravia was a disappointment, he continued to be a dedicated and respected member of his profession and received the ultimate reward of the mandarin, a patent of the lower nobility, just a year before the dynasty's demise.[4]

3. *MoE* I, chap. 3.
4. Unless otherwise indicated, the fundamental biographical material is available in Karl Dinklage, "Musils Herkunft und Lebensgeschichte," in *Robert Musil: Leben, Werk,*

Alfred Musil embodied an age of practical, technical achievement in a career marked by modest success within the given social order. His scholarly ambition and passionate devotion to mechanical engineering seem to have consumed most of his personality, but his ambition was leavened by a gentle temperament. Ideologically, he was typical of the liberal generation of the 1870s: irreligious, committed to positivism, rationalism, and pragmatism, though without political or combative overtones. Far from being an aggressive or dominant personality, he was, according to his son, not cowardly, but anxious and fearful. He "believed nothing and offered nothing as a surrogate" and later seemed to his son to typify the spiritual style of his generation: "This generation, which allowed itself to be governed and was not fanatical about progress, . . . thought stoically."[5]

Hermine Bergauer Musil (1853–1924) was seven years younger than her husband and an utterly different sort of person. She was the youngest and most favored child of a large, respected family whose connections with the mandarinate extended back to eighteenth-century Bohemia. The Bergauers, like the Musils, belonged to the pragmatic-utilitarian tradition of state service; Hermine's father had served the dynasty as an engineer and had played a major role in the construction of the first horse-drawn railway (Budweis-Linz) on the European continent. But while Alfred offered a model of disciplined practicality, Hermine was sensuous, high-strung, unpredictable, and artistic. In contrast to her husband's bourgeois approach to achievement and recognition, Hermine Musil displayed a more elegant, aristocratic culture and lifestyle. As a person and as a woman, she embodied the affective side of the Austrian liberal ethos—not only through her aesthetic and social interests, but in her unconventional personal life as well. This was most apparent in her relationship with a younger friend of the Musils, Heinrich Reiter (1856–1940), who fit the model of the dashing cavalier more nearly than her husband did. After meeting the Musils in 1881, Reiter regularly accompanied the family on summer vacations, became virtually a member of the family, and in 1900 took up residence in the Musil home. The exact nature of this intimacy, which lasted until Her-

Wirkung (hereafter *LWW*), ed. Karl Dinklage (Zurich, 1960), pp. 187–264 and in Adolf Frisé's scholarly edition of the diaries: *Tag.* I and II.

5. Robert Musil, *Tagebücher, Aphorismen, Essays und Reden* (hereafter *TE*), ed. Adolf Frisé (Hamburg, 1955), Vol. II of the *Gesammelte Werke*, p. 438. This original Frisé edition of the diaries has most of the fundamental material and is still the most generally available edition.

mine's death in 1924, was never made explicit to their son; but Reiter does seem to have become the center of Hermine's emotional life.[6] While Alfred Musil continued to love Hermine and adjust to her, he apparently remained in the shadow of his more mercurial wife.

It would be a mistake to suggest that Frau Musil was less ambitious for her husband than other wives or less obsessed than other mothers that her son be respectful and meticulous as a child and find a marriage and profession of importance as a man. All these conventional expectations remained in force, confirmed by the elevated social world of the Bergauers. The fact that her only other child, Elsa (born in 1876), died within a year of her birth made Robert even more the focus for such ambitions. But Hermine Musil did not fulfill the traditional ideal of the Victorian woman either as a wife or as a mother, and Musil's preoccupation with her was far greater than with his father, whose temperament and values were much easier for the young mandarin to accommodate.[7]

Robert's parents expressed the tensions in liberal culture between discipline and eros, state service and individualism, science and aestheticism, and the contradictory styles of his parents made a strong impression on Robert as a child. Musil later recalled that there had been something sexually polar in the way his parents had related to him. They fought for his love, but not for primacy of control over him. He recalled that his natural love for his father was greater than that for his mother, and it puzzled him that his mother had never tried to enfold him with tenderness. This duality between his parents was complicated further, not only by Reiter's frequent presence, but by the even more substantial presence of Robert's nurse. His oldest memories (from the age of sailor suits and high socks) were of Berta: "She was big, fat, and good-natured, and told me stories which I loved." Frau Musil's role seems to have been more elegant and remote, as Musil's memory of the odor of his mother's fur suggests: "I think that something sexual is mixed in this memory, although I do not at all recall anything of the sort." If it is fair to speak of Robert's two fathers, it is worth mentioning that the family life of the *haute bourgeoisie* in this period often provided two mothers.[8]

6. Cf. Karl Corino, "Ödipus oder Orest? Robert Musil und die Psychoanalyse," in *Vom "Törless" zum "Mann ohne Eigenschaften,"* ed. Uwe Baur (Munich, 1973), pp. 136–37. Despite some disclaimers from friends of the family, both Dinklage and Corino characterize this relationship as a *ménage à trois*.

7. The parallels with Rainer Maria Rilke's family and childhood are sometimes striking. Cf. Peter Demetz, *René Rilkes Prager Jahre* (Düsseldorf, 1953).

8. *TE*, pp. 462, 489, 176–77.

Robert's childhood was outwardly secure and unproblematic. Between 1884 and 1891 his family lived in Steyr, "the city without Jews," just south of Linz. There Robert enjoyed the "dreamily grandiose" world of the provincial mandarin, and frequent vacations and visits to his parents' families in Linz, Graz, and Salzburg extended his social universe to include grandparents, aunts, uncles, and cousins. As an only child, Robert became the recipient of two generations of attention and ambition, and he was impressed from an early age by the great expectations his parents had for him. He was often compared with his headstrong and successful paternal grandfather, and he came to believe that "by the time I was twenty I would have achieved great fame." But despite these visions of success, Robert felt isolated in an adult world. Moreover, although he was reared to have a sense of family and tradition, he felt no sense of a larger commonality beyond the family.[9]

His experience in Steyr, of being alone in a place where no one knew him, later seemed to him to have established the typical pattern of his life. He did well in school, but he had no close friends. Frequently ill and consistently younger and smaller than his classmates, Robert was eager to prove himself physically and he developed a passion for gymnastics and boxing which lasted throughout his life. If the route to school was interrupted by combat, the atmosphere of the home invited emotional withdrawal. Boring promenades with his parents did little to provide a world of play or enhancing intimacy. Although Robert seems to have felt loved by his parents, he never felt really at home in the lap of the family. He was lonely and unhappy much of the time—the recurring theme from his childhood memories was his "brooding in the melancholy of his room." He would sit, alone at his window or in the garden, in an island of private emotions, leading his well-meaning father to infer a scientific passion and to decide "to make a natural scientist out of him." Musil later saw his feelings of isolation from his family (the "submerged fantasy of the quiet child") as the beginning of the divergence of his line of development away from socially defined reality.[10]

Robert's loneliness as a child expressed itself mainly through fantasy and diffuse yearnings for companionship and adventure. He was conscious of replacing Elsa, and his capacity for something more than a stereotypical gender identity seems to have been established early in a desire to make up for the dead sister. Not only was Elsa the symbol for the companionship Robert missed, but he remembered wishing to be a

9. Ibid., pp. 480, 445, 28.
10. Ibid., pp. 469–72, 486.

girl himself before he had much idea of what this difference amounted to. Certainly, this childhood sense of himself set the tone for his curiosity about women and his exploration of the feminine side of his own personality. This curiosity about girls and a need for adventure apparently did find expression during his childhood in Steyr. His clandestine meetings with a neighbor named Albertine Barber provided him with his first opportunity to investigate female anatomy.[11] When Musil transposed this experience into his first attempt at a novel, he reflected on his motivation in asking to see the places where the girl had been beaten by her father: "Because an instinct tells him that it would be something new, not so boring. (That is the main thing!) The emptiness, sadness of being a child!"[12] Another antidote to his loneliness and boredom was apparently a more romantic attachment to Karla R., whom he still carried in his heart when his family moved to Brno in 1891.[13]

Robert's curiosity about sexuality was heightened by the repressive attitude toward the body in his home: "For at night he always had to sleep with his hands on top of the covers, and he had always been told that certain parts of his body were indecent." Whatever Robert's parents did say about sexuality seems to have been conventionally misleading, and Reiter's friendship with his parents cannot have made these mysteries easy to unravel. Robert apparently hoped that "seducing" the girl in the garden might provide some clarification, and he was never quite clear why unbuttoning his young friend's dress had actually been a disappointment. It was only after the move to Brno that he began to find answers to his frustrated curiosity. His new friend, Gustav Donath (1878–1965), was to play a major role in his life and in *The Man without Qualities*. Gustl was two years older, but weaker and in the same class, so they felt like equals. Once when Robert had stayed home from school for some time with an illness, it was Gustl who visited him to report the news about the mysteries of sexuality and procreation: "Only after Gustl left and night came did Robert comprehend this in its full force." Later, it was with Gustl that Robert shared his feelings about masturbation: "With Gustl it was more a pleasure, with Robert more a burden."[14]

Around the time of the move to Brno, Robert experienced a pre-

11. Corino, "Ödipus oder Orest?" p. 137.
12. *TE*, p. 47.
13. Reported by Gustav Donath in Dinklage, "Musils Herkunft," pp. 207, 260. Cf. *TE*, p. 530.
14. *TE*, pp. 48–52, 442.

cocious religious enthusiasm. This was a departure from convention, since both of his parents were atheists, and their free-thinking posture reached back another generation. In the best tradition of the Austrian mandarinate, Robert had been baptized as a Catholic but was not reared in the church. He grew up in an entirely secular atmosphere, virtually untouched by religion, much less by the stern Protestantism which shaped so many modern thinkers such as Emerson, Nietzsche, Weber, and Sartre. Robert's brief interest in religion may have been stimulated by the classes at the Realschule; in it there was almost certainly a dimension of rebellion or at least an attempt to extend his world.

Rebellion and conflict seem to have become the norm during the first year in Brno, and Musil recalled that he must have been a difficult child. Tensions between mother and son had been developing for some time, although the father had done his best to avoid these emotional conflicts except when they concerned education or career. Sometimes these confrontations were resolved by the dutiful husband, reluctantly beating his son under instructions from his wife. These punishments seem to have done little harm to Robert or to his relationship with his father, but the emotional life of the home was clearly hard on everyone. Eventually Frau Musil convinced her husband that Robert required the discipline of a military academy. Robert was delighted at the prospect of wearing long blue trousers and becoming a lieutenant at nineteen. From his parents' point of view, the choice of a military academy was consistent with the family tradition of service in the imperial army. Moreover, Hermine's most tangible impact on Robert as a child was her admiration for the heroic style of manhood suggested by her father and brothers and by Heinrich Reiter. Sending Robert away from home at the age of eleven corresponded to family expectations, to the child's Napoleonic romanticism, and to the needs of Frau Musil.[15]

Cut off early from the security of his family and friends, Robert was exposed for six years to an educational ideology of order, manliness, and aristocratic style. From 1892 to 1894 he attended a military Unter-realschule in Eisenstadt, south of Vienna. It was there that he experienced the first shocks of homesickness described in *Young Törless*; and he later saw this as a key turning-point in his development, one which forced him to fall back on his own emotional resources. He spent the

15. Ibid., pp. 488–89, 794.

next three years at the Oberrealschule in Mährisch-Weisskirchen (Hranice); this little Czech town ("the ass-hole of the devil") north of Brno provided the setting for his first novel. Many years later Musil looked back in amazement at these military academies, and he found it incomprehensible that his parents had never protested.

The cultural level of these schools was decidedly inferior to that of the gymnasia ordinarily attended by young mandarins, but this training allowed Robert to be educated with the social, political, and military elite of the Empire, and it encouraged a precocious emotional independence and maturity. Whatever defects these academies might have had, they were certainly not strongholds of bourgeois values and sexual restraint. Prostitution, homosexuality, and sadism did their part to educate the young officers, and for those who remained in the army only horses would surpass women as a diversion and topic of conversation. In the fall of 1897, Robert decided to explore an interest in science at the technical military academy in Vienna, but the conflict between the cultural excitement of Vienna and the intellectual banality of army life was too much: "The narrow comradeship and disciplined spirit had become offensive to him. . . . The fatalism of a hierarchical professional horrified him." At the end of 1897 he gave up on his first attempt to become a man of importance and returned to Brno to study engineering. At the age of seventeen he once again took up residence in his parents' home and began his studies at the technical institute where his father taught.[16]

Professionally, these years in Brno led Robert from the role of soldier to the role of engineer. Although he studied at the technical institute from 1898 to 1901, he also completed his year of voluntary service in Brno between 1901 and 1902, and it was not until January, 1903, that he became a reserve lieutenant. He left his military friends behind in 1897, but he had been socialized to the style of the smart young officer, and he was conscious of his maturity in relation to Gustl, "who was still very much the schoolboy." At this time Robert modeled himself on the cool political rationalism of Gentz. He later described the impact of the conservative army tradition: "Aristocracy is a priori the best principle of rule. So I thought when I was young. For the unpolitical, the political problem is easily resolved." At seventeen the refined barbarism of his military education had established the proud, trim, muscular look he kept all his life. He had already decided against a military career, but he

16. Ibid., pp. 480, 463, 53.

remained throughout his life in dress and bearing a product of the bourgeois accommodation to the style of the cavalier.[17]

Robert's technical education offered an alternative model of manhood and achievement; he later remarked that the decision to study engineering had meant "everything possible for his inner development." Technische Hochschulen in Austria were centers of liberal pragmatism and the upright moral style represented by his father. Here Robert cultivated the scientist's contempt for the anachronistic political and cultural attitudes of traditional students in the humanities. The shaping spiritual force was less political than technological, however, and the more fundamental reality was the cultivation of "that iron but indifferent application which was already characteristic of him as a boy." Most of the time Robert imprisoned himself in his room either with his technical studies or with some obscure philosophical treatise. He was often bored or frustrated with his work, but his thoroughness and determination carried him "like a destiny, like a dark, impenetrable drive." At times loneliness and overwork drove him from his room in search of some adventure, excitement, and sociability with harmless people.[18]

The night life of Brno seems to have offered some release from the almost pathological overwork of his years at the Technische Hochschule. Robert apparently had a period in Brno of openness to sensuality, although he remained ambivalent toward the world of the dance hall and its women. He experienced himself as sensuous, but his eroticism seemed to be stimulated more by the absence of women than by their presence. It was hard to say whether it was "chastity or awkwardness" that held him back from the whores and singers.[19] But it is clear that these years were marked by a preoccupation with sexuality and an ambivalence about such experiences. This attitude assumes a more than merely personal significance in the context of Austrian culture. For Austrian intellectuals at the turn of the century—Schnitzler, Kraus, Weininger, Schiele, and Freud—sexuality seemed to be the key to understanding this society. The *haut bourgeois* blend of hedonism and repression perceived sexuality as a feminine principle which fascinated and threatened the practical, rational male. The emphasis of the older writers, such as Schnitzler and Freud, was on the scientific portrayal of the social and psychological dynamics of sexuality, while the younger writers,

17. Ibid., pp. 53, 441, 401.
18. Ibid., pp. 795, 53–54.
19. Ibid., pp. 54–55.

such as Weininger and Kraus, developed a more moralistic critique of the conventions of sexuality, prostitution, and hypocrisy.

The external forms of sexuality were standardized for someone of Robert's social class. The bourgeois youth was expected to emulate aristocratic norms of easy decadence by gaining his sexual education from prostitutes, the *süsse Madel* (i.e., lower-middle-class or working-class shopgirls), or older married women. The ordinary period for these experiences was at the university or during the year of army service, when young men escaped from bourgeois convention and had the aristocratic model immediately available. These experiences offered a vision of woman as pure sexuality, as a necessary convenience maintained at the periphery of bourgeois life. Middle-class girls, however, were to be treated differently, in accordance with their cultivated ignorance and purity in matters of sexuality. For these young women, sex was a mystery, avoided by their elders as the unmentionable vulgarity. The salon within the bourgeois home became their proper preserve, where male hedonism was controlled and kept in tension with a more anaesthetic art: the world of *Lieder*, poetry, and evenings of music. The bourgeois salon in Austria was a matriarchy of purity, cut off from work and sexuality. And a young man like Robert was expected to divide his relations with women between the realms of feeling and sensation, culture and sexuality, to alternate between the kitsch of the salon and the syphilis of the dance hall. Nowhere were the contradictions of *haut bourgeois* culture more apparent or more stressful than in the realm of sexuality.

Robert seems to have experienced most of the stereotypical forms of sexuality in his culture, and his martial bearing made him the model of what his culture sought in these experiences. Certainly it was easier for an Austrian intellectual to give social expression to his erotic side than it was for a Max Weber, living with his family in Berlin. Presumably Robert's experiences were a disorderly combination of pleasure, boredom, and discomfort, sometimes clumsy, sometimes cavalier, but it is not always entirely clear in Musil's notes where autobiography ends and art begins, particularly in the realm of sexual fantasy. The norm of biography is to assume that the issue is simply a matter of establishing the names of the people with whom the hero lived out the two or three clichés of his culture: whether Robert "possessed" this or that woman. Musil believed that it was everything else that was important: the

thoughts, feelings, reactions, conversations, silences. These take form in
art and bear only the most tenuous relation to literal experiences.

The new importance of women in his life is clear, but it is difficult to
determine the exact nature of these relationships: with the whore, the
singer, the actress, the shopgirl, the matriarch of the salon, Gustl's
friend Alice, and his own mother. In 1901, probably during his year of
military service, Robert contracted syphilis; shortly thereafter he began
a relationship with a Czech working-class girl named Herma Dietz, who
later followed him to Berlin. During the years in Brno Robert lived the
sexual conventions of his culture and explored an accompanying world
of imagination. The former seems on the whole to have been stereotypical, while the latter was more essential to his significance as a writer.
The details of these experiences (and we will never strike the balance of
knowledge between a moment of sensuousness and a woman he never
touched) are less important than Robert's attempts to think through
their meaning and emotional content. How does an overcast day in
Brno compare with a sunny day in Vienna, or a clever conversation with
an awkward scene of sexual initiation? There is a great deal that can
never be known, enormous psychic spaces which will never be filled out
in a literal way. It is not very helpful, and potentially quite misleading,
to take too literally the few fragments of data we have, except as re-
minders of the culture which he lived.

The woman most dominant in Robert's life between 1898 and 1901
must certainly have been his mother, and her power as a person very
probably emphasized the difficulty of absorbing the irrational side of his
own personality. Karl Corino characterizes Robert's feelings toward his
mother at this time in terms of "incestuously fixated libido." He explains Robert's sympathetic attitude toward the women in the dance
halls in terms of the need "to save his mother in the whore"; and he
relates this to a tension in Robert between a grossly physical attraction
to sexual objects and a need to idealize.[20] This reduction of very limited
evidence to a peculiarly personal problem in the form of eternal, unconscious archetypes avoids the social reality that confronted a young man

20. Corino, "Ödipus oder Orest?" pp. 162–63. Cf. also TE, pp. 177, 426–27 for
Musil's recollections of seeing his mother partially naked during a family vacation at the
Wörthersee, and for his comments on the psychoanalytic view. For another Freudian
view, see Eithne Wilkins, "Musil's 'Affair of the Major's Wife' with an unpublished Text,"
The Modern Language Review 63, 1 (January 1968):74–93.

like Robert. The contradictory images of woman as object of gratification and as spiritual partner were givens of the culture. Robert's mother
could hardly avoid being implicated in these contradictions, particularly
since Reiter joined the household during this period. On the other
hand, it was presumably not only incestuously fixated libido which allowed Robert to notice that the women in the dance halls were persons
too.

There was clearly a long history of conflict between mother and son,
but the evidence does not permit a sweeping characterization of Robert's feelings toward his mother at this time. We know virtually nothing
about the substance of mother-son conflicts (or affinities) until 1902,
and still less about the daily flow of emotion. Even the social tensions of
Robert's integration into the local elite are mostly unstated. But Robert
was old enough now to talk with his mother as an equal, and living with
her made him conscious that mother-love was "the most powerful feeling of sympathy." This was the only period in his life when he was close
to his mother; he later reflected that only the bond of family relationship (pressed together in the same stall) permitted love to develop fully.[21] Whatever the nuances of this relationship at the time, it is apparent that Robert's feelings about women were much less effectively
worked through than the firm male norms of the army and engineering.
Robert's real challenge during these years was to absorb the impact of
the irrational in his own personality, and Austrian culture provided a
variety of forms for this project.

Robert's tour of duty in three military academies had done little to
meet the emotional needs of a sensitive young man, and he soon discovered that his childhood friend Gustav Donath had something he
lacked: a humanistic education. Despite his engineer's contempt for students of the humanities, Robert began attending lectures on literature.
He was eager to compensate for his meager cultural education and to
become an elegant, sophisticated man of the world rather than a military adventurer. In Brno he was exposed to educated society and introduced in a serious way to the *haut bourgeois* culture of feelings: to the
piano in the home, to theater and opera, the concert hall, the salon, and
the modes of sentimentality and decorum. This other side of liberal culture was softer, more feminine, more refined, but also highly formal-

21. *TE*, pp. 73–75. Twenty-five years later Musil attempted to portray something of
this relationship: "I did not succeed in the *Amsel* in expressing the power of my mother,
which apparently consisted in nothing" (*TE*, p. 441).

ized. Whatever Robert's uneven stages of cultural initiation, it seems
clear that he was more strongly attracted to literary than to musical
forms. He joined a literary club in Brno and developed a friendship with
Frau Tyrka, the wife of a government official, who encouraged the
efforts of young artists in her salon in Graz.

Robert's assimilation of the aesthetic side of bourgeois culture was
intimately entwined with his emotional and sexual maturation in relation to his family and the social style of the Austrian mandarin. On one
level, his exposure to high culture was a ritual of social adulthood and
status that invited him into the forms of class culture. He was growing
up, testing himself, and absorbing the values and ideas of cultivated
people. At the same time, he must have felt the excitement of experiencing any form of aesthetic or spiritual culture. This was an enormous
emotional compensation after the aridity of an adolescence spent with
horses and machines. Moreover, he discovered an alternative model of
humanity in the role of the artist and the mode of coffee-house aestheticism. All the various strands of Austrian culture were at work in
Robert's situation, but what stood out for him was the sense of intellectual and cultural change at the turn of the century. His dominant impression of these years was of a European-wide sense of participation in
a radical spiritual break with the past. In the midst of this exalted
awareness of cultural transformation, Robert began to write, to give
form to his own emotional confusions.

2. THE SPIRITUAL REVOLUTION

Out of the oil-smooth spirit of the last two decades of the

nineteenth century, suddenly throughout Europe there arose a

kindling fever. Nobody knew exactly what was on the way;

nobody was able to say whether it was to be a new art, a new

man, a new morality, or perhaps a reshuffling of society. So

everybody made of it what he liked. But people were standing

up on all sides to fight against the old way of life.[22]

The period of Robert's literary apprenticeship in Brno between 1898
and 1902 was a particularly exciting time for a young man to be alive.
In *The Man without Qualities* Musil portrayed the exhilaration with

22. *MoE* I, chap. 15, "Geistiger Umsturz."

which Robert and Gustl and Alice had responded to the revolution of
ideas and attitudes which swept across Europe, at least among "that
thin fluctuating layer of humanity, the intelligentsia." They "had been
just in time to catch a glimmer of it," and "entering into the world in
those days, even in coming around the very first corner, one felt the
breath of the spirit on one's cheeks."[23] They were conscious less of the
peculiarly Austrian aspects of this experience than of the accumulated
challenge of European artists and intellectuals to the values of the nineteenth century. Tolstoy and Dostoevsky, Wagner and Nietzsche, Ibsen
and Strindberg, Baudelaire and Mallarmé, Emerson and Wilde, Altenberg and Hofmannsthal—all of these writers helped to define a critical
distance from traditional liberal culture. Yet Robert and his friends saw
themselves, not as a decadent postscript to a dying world, but as an
intellectual avant-garde, setting out toward a new social and cultural
order: "It was a time of great ethical and aesthetic activity. One believed
in the future, in a social future, and in a new art."[24]

For Robert, the generational issue was prominent from the start. He
felt a distance from "the writers of the 1870s" and "their flat ideas,"
preferring "the illogical products from the early years of the *Wiener
Rundschau*, etc."[25] But if he was aware of his rebellion against his
father's generation, he was also identifying with those slightly older, the
generation of the 1890s and the writers and ideas that they brought to
the attention of young intellectuals at the turn of the century. For Musil,
the richness of the 1890s contained everything within it—the hero-cult
of Nietzsche and Carlyle as well as decadence, socialism, and nature
worship, the late romanticism of Emerson and the machine-worship of
the young. Musil later saw this as the classical period, the watershed for
the intellectual movements of the first third of the twentieth century, all
of which were "weaker in intensity and extent than the original movement and contained nothing which was not—even if less emphasized—
already present in it."[26] The earnest mandarins of the older generation
were inclined to describe this feverish cultural activity in terms of "mor-
bidity and decadence," and the dandies of Young Vienna were only too
happy to oblige such anxieties. But for Musil "these two negative defini-

23. Ibid.
24. Robert Musil, *Der deutsche Mensch als Symptom*, from the *Nachlass*, ed. Karl
Corino and Elisabeth Albertsen (Hamburg, 1967), p. 24.
25. *TE*, pp. 33–34.
26. Musil, *Der deutsche Mensch*, p. 26.

tions were only accidental expressions for the will to be different and to do things differently from people in the past."[27]

This sense of a radical break with the past had only slight political implications in the conventional sense. It was during this period that Robert moved away from "the class dictators" in the direction of socialism. As an *haut bourgeois* German in a predominantly Czech town, his class position was conspicuous, and Robert found himself sympathizing with socialism out of both personal need and rational considerations. In fact, he nearly made his literary debut as a theater critic for a working-class newspaper, the *Volksfreund*. This venture was stopped when the theater authorities abruptly decided to refuse to give the paper a seat. Even in this brief association with the working class, however, Robert was conscious of the huge aesthetic distance between his world and the atmosphere of working-class homes and meetings.[28] At any rate, his interest in socialism was short-lived, and his diaries make no mention of the convention of Austrian socialists held in Brno in 1899. For Robert, the spiritual revolution of the cultural elite held the center of the stage. Twenty years later, he lamented the ideological duality of the turn of the century: "Unkind fate: to bestow Nietzsche and socialism on a single age. Race ideology, elitism, and anti-democratic thought were tolerated because of Nietzsche."[29] Although Robert moved away from conservative politics, he, like most German intellectuals of his generation, looked for his heroes in the world of art rather than politics. The news from Vienna was not Badeni and Lueger, but Schnitzler, Hofmannsthal, and Altenberg.

It is hardly surprising that the European art movements of the late nineteenth century struck such deep roots in Austria. The ideology of *l'art pour l'art* was the *reductio ad absurdum* of the bourgeois goddess of kitsch, and it offered release from bourgeois society, often through immoralism, religion, or deviance. The aristocratic model in Austria helped to nurture a sense of style, and the contradictory cultural patterns helped to dissolve the sense of normalcy and to relieve that pressure to be righteous which Protestant and purely bourgeois traditions were more likely to emphasize. But these actual models of Austrian society were perceived mainly as additional forms of dead convention. Moreover, Musil was convinced that young men of genius do not study

27. Ibid., p. 24.
28. *TE*, pp. 441–42.
29. Ibid., p. 240.

literature according to national traditions, but instead let themselves be led by their instincts and talents. He was never really at home in any language except German (though he studied both French and Czech), but his response to modernism was decidedly European, rather than German in scope.[30]

In Brno, Robert was attracted to symbolism and Nietzsche, to the decadents, to Kant and Schopenhauer, rather than to more historical or realistic philosophies. The direct influence of German romanticism seems to have been relatively slight in this early period, descending for the most part via the French symbolists and the American transcendentalists. Musil was drawn to the leading writers of *fin de siècle* irrationalism, to Maeterlinck's understanding of the limits of language in capturing inwardness and to the sensuousness of D'Annunzio, which the romantics would have found "common." He liked materialism insofar as it was immoral and expressed a break with inherited orientations, but he rejected the various systems of late-nineteenth-century positivism. His disaffection from reason at this time was substantial, and he tended to exaggerate the distance "between the joy in logical speculation and that more 'lyrical' way of my recent times."[31]

Robert's enthusiasm for symbolism and irrationalism blended with the joy of discovering the literary education he had missed. From the French romantics and symbolists he learned that the virtues of the poet were the sense for the musical, the melodic, and mystical harmony, and "the gift for encompassing reality in an atmosphere of suggestion."[32] He was drawn to Mallarmé's view that art is not the rendering of some exterior reality but the portrayal of "a specific state of feeling of the poet."[33] Musil's diary quotations from the French symbolists make clear their powerful influence and their value in helping him come to terms with his own emotions and feelings of alienation. Emerson's expressive view of art made the same point: "For all people long in their spiritual anguish [*Seelennot*] for expression. In love, in art, in greed, in politics, in work and in play we seek to express our painful secret."[34]

30. Ibid., p. 440.
31. Ibid., pp. 83, 38.
32. From the *Nachlass*, H. 4, pp. 36–38 (cf. *Tag.* I, p. 12). Under the tutelage of Baudelaire and Mallarmé, Robert expressed the ambition to have "one beautiful thought daily" (*TE*, p. 32).
33. A. G. Lehmann, *The Symbolist Aesthetic in France, 1885–1895* (Oxford, 1968), p. 151.
34. *TE*, pp. 99–100.

But Musil's rejection of naturalism and realism in favor of the symbolist aesthetic was more than an adolescent enthusiasm or a passing fashion. In fact, it was not until later that he was able to make his break with realistic art fully explicit: "In recalling my first impressions about modern literature, this word [naturalism] always seemed to me an unredeemed promise." In his view, the concept of naturalism (and literary impressionism, which seemed to him the same mistake under a different name) was misguided, since it valued the artist as a literal reflector of external reality. But Musil was convinced that "the truth of a work of art is something different from its naturalism." While he later grew more aware that art is "a complicated social product," he never departed from his initial sympathy with the symbolist position that art is first of all "the expression of an individuality." This seemed to him so patent that he later saw the term "expressionism" as an obvious redundancy and doubted that any great writer had ever been an impressionist.[35]

This view of art had descended to Musil as a variation on Kant's *Critique of Judgment*, the classical rationale of modern art. Kant's emphasis on the incommensurability of the rational concept and the representation of the imagination (which corresponds roughly to Musil's later distinction between the realms of the *ratioïd* and the non-*ratioïd*) allowed art to be something more than an inferior form of science. For Kant, the aesthetic idea mediated between science and morality, between the phenomenal and the noumenal. After Schiller this connection began to disappear into pure subjectivity and contemplation for its own sake. In Schopenhauer the contemplative function of art corresponded to pessimism and the negation of the world of practical activity. With the decline of revolutionary liberalism after 1848, Schopenhauer defined the resigned terms of the split in European consciousness between positivism and aestheticism, between senseless activity and pure will-lessness. As Musil's generation (from Hermann Broch to Thomas Mann) received the Kantian doctrine and romantic aesthetics via Schopenhauer and Mallarmé, the emphasis was on subjective states and beauty for its own sake. To the symbolists, art was "the vehicle for realizing a state of mind which has no interest for science or ethics in the ordinary sense."[36] This interpretation of the Kantian aesthetic released art to a

35. *TE*, pp. 119, 199.
36. Lehmann, *Symbolist Aesthetic*, p. 32.

higher realm, completely separated from science and ordinary life. This view, particularly in its emphasis on psychic release and poetic states, appealed strongly to Musil. As he summarized it at the time: "The beauty of an idea is defined by the energy it radiates, through its power to create life in our soul."[37] Yet even in this formulation of aestheticism, the more decadent and passive style of the *fin de siècle* began to flow in the direction of ethics.

Here the decisive figure was Nietzsche, the ideolog of aestheticism, who transformed it from a life-denying to a life-affirming vision: "Fate: that I encountered Nietzsche for the first time precisely at the age of eighteen. Just after leaving the army. Just in such and such year of development." This grand formulation was in order, since Nietzsche proved to be the seminal intellectual influence in Musil's development. Nietzsche represented the intellectual toughness and asceticism of the fearless inquirer, in the context of the end of traditional objective values and bourgeois progress. Nietzsche led the way for Musil by identifying science as dead art, psychology as the queen of philosophy, grammar as the key to modern riddles. Nietzsche, rather than Freud, served as Musil's mentor in the realm of the unconscious, examining the relationships between drives and values. Still more importantly, Nietzsche offered a view of art, not as an escape, but as *the* fundamental human activity. Nietzsche had a tremendous impact on Musil's whole generation, and Musil kept returning to this fount of intellectual stimulation all his life. Much as Nietzsche influenced him in his youth, Musil thought even more highly of Nietzsche as he grew older, and he doubted whether he had even begun to take him seriously as a young man. He later concluded that the intensity of his affinities with Nietzsche and Emerson simply corresponded to the fundamental quality of the poet, but these affinities also pointed to similar attitudes toward philosophy and ethics.[38]

Nietzsche seemed to have defined the terms of any future philosophy or ethics, not as the dark prophet but as the critic and psychologist of *Beyond Good and Evil*, who "shows us all the ways in which our brains can work, but . . . follows none of them." Musil had already been attracted to Kant as the proper antidote to the historicist abdication of

37. *TE*, p. 33.
38. Ibid., pp. 37, 43. On Musil's strong sense of affinity with both Emerson and Nietzsche, see *Prosa, Dramen, späte Briefe* (hereafter *Prosa*), ed. Adolf Frisé (Hamburg, 1957), vol. III of the *Gesammelte Werke*, p. 706.

reason and will in the late nineteenth century. He rejected the tendency to discount Kant historically, preferring instead to use Kant to criticize the culture of the late nineteenth century, but he found Kant's systematic vision of truth unconvincing, and he felt ironic toward the attempt at a total vision of the world. Nietzsche pointed the way beyond systematic philosophy and firm social norms without falling into pessimism. His rejection of the principles of non-contradiction and systematic coherence opened the way for an essayistic form of truth which Musil found more congenial:

There are truths, but no Truth. I can perfectly well assert two completely contradictory things, and be right in both cases. One ought not to weigh one's insights against one another—each is a life for itself. See Nietzsche. What a fiasco, as soon as one wants to find a system in him, aside from the spiritual willfulness of the sage.

In these first responses Musil had already identified Nietzsche's central value for him: the sense of possibility, the subjunctive, combinations, what Musil called "the + + + brain of Nietzsche." In this apt description of his own mature art Musil prefigured the intimate connection between the essayistic form of truth and ethical possibility.[39]

Musil's enthusiasm for irrationalist art involved not so much a rejection of intellect as an attempt to overcome the division in bourgeois culture—between science and art, reason and feeling—from the side of art. He saw symptoms of decadence in the tendencies since romanticism toward a "one-sided overvaluing of reason" and a "lack of trust in the instincts."[40] Moreover, despite the tremendous progress of scientific knowledge since the seventeenth century, "the type of the man of intellect (the scholar, the researcher) has remained the same the whole time."[41] Nietzsche and the symbolists had not merely announced a new art and a new philosophy; they had condemned the psychic structure of the European burgher as an historical anachronism, cut off from its roots in Christian culture. This way of thinking appealed to Musil because of the failure of the empirical age to establish a connection be-

---

39. Ibid., pp. 31–40. The demanding task of reading Kant on his own led Robert to remark: "[I go on living] and do not fear that I must die from shame because another has already comprehended the world without remainder." When Kant set him to wondering whether Kant or anyone else had found the "eternal formula of this world and beyond," Robert satirized his own romantic lapse: "Oh, Robert, why do you use such pathetic words for things which are so indifferent to you!"

40. From the *Nachlass*, H. 4, p. 74. At the same time, he felt "the *monstrum in animo* as the general danger."

41. *TE*, p. 37.

tween science and personal values, but this was not simply an abstract conflict between positivism and aestheticism; it posed a quite personal conflict between the mandarin scholar and the cultural revolutionary. Musil found this conflict not only in the opposition between the technical institute and his circle of literary friends, but also in the dramatic tension between his repressed, scientific father and his volatile, musical mother. His life situation epitomized the confrontation of "the liberal culture of reason and law" with the "older aristocratic culture of sensuous feeling and grace" in *fin de siècle* Austria.[42]

The earliest literary attempts in Musil's diaries in Brno display the interconnections among decadence, psychological genius, and the creation of new ethical possibilities.[43] From the outset he kept his distance from the *Schwärmerei* of his friends, Gustl and Alice, who were more inclined to the prophetic, Wagnerian pose. Robert's pose when he began his diary as a literary workshop was the more sober image of *"monsieur le vivisecteur."* His characterization of this figure as "the prototype of the cerebral man to come" established the first of many prototypes of Ulrich.[44] He represented the ideal of the solitary explorer of consciousness and emotional relations, both a negating and an affirming principle: in the family, in friendships, and in love. Here and in his other early attempts Robert demonstrated a gift for the objective, impersonal, presuppositionless investigation of physiology, sexuality, emotions, gestures. His "adventures and wanderings of a surgeon of the soul at the beginning of the twentieth century" are not without the immaturity and incoherence one would expect from a young man, but the seriousness of his passion "to see and to learn to see" is as unmistakable as his skilled eye for emotional analysis as he transforms Gustl, Alice, his family, and his own emotional and sexual experience into art.[45] Musil transposed many portions of his early attempts into his later stories and novellas, and they initiated some of his characteristic patterns of expression and symbolism.

42. Schorske, "Politics and the Psyche," p. 934.

43. Regarding the dating of these early diaries from 1898 to 1900, see *Tag.* II, pp. 4–6, 9–11.

44. *TE*, p. 23. Robert was conscious of the complexity and multi-centeredness of the nervous system, a series of centers in a sophisticated organism. In a somewhat later note he suggested the ideal of no one center dominating, but with all centers integrated into the republic of the mind. Balancing these various aspects of the personality would also imply the creation of new forms of sexual life (*Tag.* I, pp. 71–72).

45. *TE*, p. 23. Robert called the 1890s an age of diaries (a time for analysis rather than art), though his diary is less like a conventional nineteenth-century diary than it is like the notebook Freud was keeping at the same time. Ibid., p. 31.

Writing was a creative response to solitude and feelings of alienation. He began his diaries as a night book, written by a meditative poet contemplating the "icy, polar regions" of the soul in the solitude of his room. This territory was forbidding, but he was conscious that it provided "perspective others never have." The night book offered a retreat from social life and the emotional drain of the day. He found himself refreshed by the night, in his element, alert to the economy of the psyche and his need for balance "between the altruism of the day and the egoism of the night." Night was not simply a time to sleep; it met a positive need to be alone and indifferent to responsibilities toward others.[46]

The perspective of night found its daytime analog in the role of the *flâneur* (which Robert learned from the French symbolists and Young Vienna): the poet as dandy, walking the streets and watching people, "tasting with impunity the colossal feelings of superiority over all other people. You sense the religion of the irreligious, the sadness of those who have long ago brushed aside all sadness, the art of those who smile today when they hear the name of art." He represented the solitary individual, living out the end of the bonds of family, traditional society, and firm moral order. The image of the *flâneur*'s isolation in the mass became more enhancing in Musil's mature art, but at the turn of the century this image belonged to a mood of "limitless hopelessness" (*Aussichtlosigkeit*), of world-weariness and emotional ground-zero. For all his excitement about the newness of his project, the brooding mood of spiritual exhaustion and sluggishness pointed to the underlying issue of motivation.[47]

Robert was intensely conscious of the precariousness of the project of being human and of the dark mysteries that lie beneath action. Reflecting on the Swedish fortifications he discovered during military maneuvers, Robert wondered what brutal, animal-like quality had brought these men so far to kill and conquer, but he questioned his right to judge, since his own life "conjures up such desperate emptiness." He felt the emptiness of leisure for the lost individual of the liberal era: "Each hour is the same gaping hole and child of death, which we must fill

46. Ibid., pp. 24–26. This attitude parallels Musil's early notes on Eduard von Hartmann's phenomenological description of "the essence of religion as an activity of consciousness which remains purely inward." Hartmann described it as "a sinking into oneself" in "moments of reverence" which are "times for the gathering of all energies" (*Tag.* I, p. 36).
47. *TE*, p. 30.

out." Given the bourgeois paradigm of self, time, and identity, he saw celebrations and anniversaries as ways of hurrying along a line to disappear into a hole. He found the weakness in his culture's way of living in the difficulty of getting through the dead hours. He sensed that religion had lost track of its basis in life, that the Sunday hour devoted to God had nothing to do with the rest of life. It puzzled him that people in his society had so much trouble enjoying themselves, and he wondered why his culture created no games for adults.[48]

Robert wanted a new objectivity which could investigate contemporary conditions and move beyond the beautiful as it was understood in bourgeois culture. He wanted to think and write beyond the assumptions of his own period, but he was conscious of language as an obstacle to new experience: "Two thousand years write with us. But most of all, our parents and grandparents." He later grew more classical, more conscious that one is less likely to say new things than to give new form; in this early period, however, Robert was determined to write only if it meant an increase of the spiritual treasure. Under the tutelage of the romantic and symbolist traditions, he committed himself to a severe conception of originality. He set his literary ambitions high in a search to break through the constraints of convention, syntax, and linear prose:

So long as one thinks in sentences with end-points, certain things cannot be said—at most, vague feelings. On the other hand, it would be possible to learn to write so that certain infinite perspectives, which today still lie on the threshold of the unconscious, then would become clear and comprehensible.

His writing problems were related to his attempts to see differently; he wanted new categories and a new image of the world.[49]

He was conscious of a tension between the one-dimensional logic of prose and the many-sided reality of experience. This difficulty was most apparent in dreams, which seemed to break down normal categories. But the same problem confronted the *flâneur* in the way the others reduced the street to a straight line, when it was a great deal else as well. This coding to stereotypical perceptions missed everything else and left nothing inwardly motivated. The gap between language and the puzzling individuality of emotions and experience made him uneasy about the literalness of "the two-times-two-is-four logic." He resisted the

48. *Tag.* I, pp. 13–15, 59; *TE*, pp. 32–33, 73.
49. *TE*, pp. 44–45.

temptation to accept the habituated assurance of formal logic in a way that discounted "that mysterious, discontinuous part of your inner self, which you call the emotional life, or nerves, or whatever." He wanted to see not only the measurable but also the intangible, to be alert to people and the flow of life. This vision included the unconscious, the "incalculable" within him, which sometimes began to move and to frighten him "as though [he were] confronted by an untamed animal." But he was not interested in artificially generating the mysterious. He wanted to resist the temptation of the age for brutal pathos, for the "dark, demonic, mystically gruesome," but rather to write as "we are . . . bright, airy, roomy."[50] He preferred the clarity and light in Nietzsche to the faked darkness and mystery of Wagner.

Musil kept his distance from the specifically musical logic of *fin de siècle* Austria: of Schopenhauer, Wagner, Strauss, and Mahler. Gustl often played the piano in the Musil home, but Robert apparently played no instrument, and he generally stood back from the musical enthusiasms of his peers. All this was more an accompanying awareness than his central concern. Yet his reservations about music have often been oversimplified because of his portrayal of Walter's relation to Wagner in *The Man without Qualities.* Although Musil was not very musical by the standards of his culture, music apparently did have considerable appeal for him. His early lyrical attempt, the "Paderewski-Phantasie" (ca. 1897–1900), suggests how powerfully music could affect him.[51] Yet Musil does seem to have felt an instinctive mistrust of the role of music in liberal culture, whether as the conventional leisure of the elite or in the more ideological new wave of Wagner. Music offered an escape from a world without value, whether as a meditative inwardness or as the annihilation of the ego in narcotic intoxication. As the extreme mode of the art ideologies of decadence, music made most conspicuous the limits of aestheticism, and Musil's attitudes toward music must be understood within the larger context of his inquiry into the relations among art, feelings, and life. As he put it forty years later in a critical reflection on music: "The question of whether a great goddess is ticklish under her arm is not one for the curious but for lovers."[52]

Robert was conscious of the parallel between music and erotic dream, and his own impulse was to give aesthetic consciousness personal form

50. Ibid., pp. 28–29, 33.
51. Cf. *Tag.* II, pp. 16–17.
52. *TE*, p. 560.

in his relations with women. As he learned to experience the concrete flow of life in more detail, he yearned for women who could transform life into beauty and happiness. He sensed a contradiction in his culture between the heightened spiritual significance which men ascribed to women and the continuation of narrowly intellectual forms. He wondered if it would not be possible to develop new models of male-female relations that balanced the intellectual and the physical, replacing the pederasty of the Greeks with the love of women. He dreamed of "someone who could spin out the soul again and again" for him and of the possibility that he might do this for himself. But this image of "another life" also meant a turning away from reality: "I felt that I would turn away from life and give myself entirely to this—since life is not in a position to offer me something of equal value."[53]

Aestheticism (whether in music or poetry) did not only underscore the inadequacy of life; it also lacked the factor of volume which might have filled life and made it enhancing. He saw what was fine, "the spiritual acts," as "abstractions of life, a kind of Holy Spirit, mysterium, a touching of the power," but the purely aesthetic lacked "psychic dimension" and thus did "not fill out the hours." Robert wanted to convert these moments of aesthetic arousal into life: "The decisive factor is the ethical condition into which they transform us and how long they affect us afterward." He wanted to unite the aesthetic with reality: "Since my youth I have looked upon the aesthetic as the ethical."[54]

Robert's feelings about women during the Brno years crystallized around an experience he associated with an actress named Valerie. Precisely what happened in reality, the extent to which Valerie was simply an objective correlative for Robert's inward explorations, makes very little difference. The "Valerie-experience," which provided the basis for the affair of the major's wife in *The Man without Qualities*, seems to have occurred in the fall of 1901, when Robert was almost twenty-one and about to enter his year of military duty:

It came as an overwhelming storm. For the first time his sensuousness wore the red, gold-embroidered mantle of love. His whole being was transformed. Something good, giving came over him. Wide stretches of thought, artfully entwined thoughts became clear. In a few weeks he matured beyond himself. His thoughts and feelings ordered themselves; the philosophy of maturity and stillness grew out of this. Then came the sobering. Simple, short, necessary. They finished with

53. Ibid., pp. 34, 55; *Tag.* I, p. 59.
54. *Tag.* I, p. 14; *TE*, pp. 39, 429.

each other. "It is immoral to stay together, if each hour does not bring growth to the soul," he said; "farewell."

To the sensuousness of his earlier sexual explorations was added an emotional experience which was startling to him in its intensity. Far from emphasizing the sentimental or romantic aspects of this experience (much less Valerie's person or their experiences together), Musil was fascinated by its autonomous impact on him and his personal growth. This sudden passion—and the equally sudden break—brought home to him the reality of the symbolist notion of the inaccessibility and irreducibility of peak experiences: "We cannot hold onto a great moment of recognition; it withers away, dries up, and leaves us nothing but the impoverished logical skeleton of the idea." The intensity and inexpressibility of such experiences, the connection between thought and feeling, and the factor of growth were all fundamental to the novel he began to write a year later.[55]

In the wake of the "Valerie-experience," Musil concluded that it was possible to give duration to such experiences only ethically. It was impossible to capture the insight except in the attempt to transform it into "Acts (either in Maeterlinck's or Emerson's terminology). Then we possess it." The "Valerie-experience" brought Nietzsche's anti-systematic theory of truth into relation with Robert's initial understanding of the ethical person:

Another species is made up of the great lovers—Christ, Buddha, Goethe— and myself in those autumn days when I loved Valerie.
They seek no truth at all, but they feel that something inside them comes together to a whole.
That is something purely human—a natural process.[56]

Robert's love-affair with Valerie seems to have marked the culmination of his irrationalist period and the beginning, in late 1901 or 1902, of a more positive attitude toward reason. The extent of his earlier disaffection from reason is suggested by his astonishment on reading Ernst Mach for the first time. The discovery in Mach's lectures on popular science of "a first-rate analytic mind of nonetheless great significance" reminded him to "be more cautious in the future." The quality of Mach's thought suggested that the polarity in his culture between sterile logic and Dionysian feeling was not necessary. The subjective,

55. *TE*, pp. 56, 34; cf. *Tag.* II, pp. 12–14.
56. Ibid., pp. 32–34.

impressionistic literary criticism of the 1890s began to look like an overreaction to the bureaucratic criticism of the positivist era. Musil grew more skeptical of the merely beautiful, more reserved toward *fin de siècle* decadence, more critical of the tendency he and Gustl had of overvaluing certain fine feelings: "With the subjective feelings one never finishes. The subjective feelings cannot decide." He criticized his earlier sloppiness of thought, recalling that when he first read Nietzsche at eighteen, he "was too easy-going toward every type of sensuousness, in that I took in and enjoyed everything that came in from the senses without further control." In retrospect, his initial response to aestheticism seemed excessive and self-indulgent:

With the 'sensuous' the fiasco is hard to avoid. It is laden with a certain unfruitfulness. . . . Characteristic of this unfruitfulness is that the "great work" seemed possible to me only with the stimulants of solitude, suggestion, and literally hallucinatory seclusion.[57]

Robert felt a need to move away from decadence, sensationalism, egoism, in the direction of reason and self-restraint, using the psychological with more finesse and caution. It seemed to him that he had been too preoccupied with moods, dreams, reveries, feelings which seemed to be fruitful but led to nothing. He wondered if his inability to transform a mood into some sense of purpose did not constitute a kind of "masculine hysteria." He sensed that art had become simply a substitute for life, "a form of illness" that disguised his resistance to the ethical, to giving his whole person to something instead of just thinking about it.[58]

The sobering seems also to have led to Herma Dietz and away from the expectations of his class. Robert apparently met Herma during his year of military service; twenty years later he portrayed her in the novella *Tonka*. In 1902 Herma seems to have become the center of Robert's emotional and sexual life—and the focus of conflicts with his mother, who could not accept her son's stubborn commitment to a mésalliance, particularly one which proved to be both inconvenient and traumatic. (The painful story of her pregnancy, venereal disease, and death in the hospital apparently did not take place until after she had followed Robert to Berlin.) Even in Musil's later portrayal of this relationship between the bright young mandarin and the shy, unimpressive working-girl, Tonka's appeal is never quite clear to the young scientist himself.

57. Ibid., pp. 35–38.
58. Ibid., p. 83.

Corino argues that Musil chose his sex object neurotically, below his own social level, as a means of dealing with his guilt about sexuality and his incestuous fixation on his mother.[59] In fact, Musil left very little record of his own motivation. Socially, such a relationship was one conventional solution, at least temporarily, for a young man of Musil's class. At the same time, it saved him from the normal socialization to the life of his class, from marriage and the automatic expectations which accompanied it. The literary evidence suggests the emotional and sexual uncertainty of both young people, as well as the tremendous anxiety which this relationship began to generate in the young man's parents and friends. Robert was conscious of his intellectual and cultural superiority to Tonka, but he seems to have valued her simplicity, unpretentious humor, and lack of affectation. To some extent, this relationship was simply a practical solution and an expression of Robert's de-romanticization of sexuality, although Herma did inspire feelings of loyalty and jealousy in Robert.[60]

Although Robert rejected his mother's advice about women, he was reluctant to disappoint his father's expectations of his pursuing a scientific career. Musil's talent for science and engineering was unmistakable, and in 1899 and 1901 he passed the state examinations in mathematics, physics, mechanics, and statistics. His development was so promising (and his connections certainly did him no harm) that he was offered a very flattering position as an assistant to Julius Carl von Bach at the technical institute in Stuttgart, then the most modern laboratory for mechanical engineering in Europe. After completing his army service in October, 1902, he followed his father's wishes and pursued the opportunity in Germany. But the social isolation of Stuttgart and the tedium of his laboratory work made clear that his second attempt to become a man of importance was as inconsequential as the first. The boredom and loneliness of a winter in Stuttgart drove him to begin his first novel, more as a way of passing time than out of literary ambition (or so he later claimed). Certainly, engineering no longer had any appeal for him, and in the spring of 1903 he seized upon the "madly attractive" decision to study philosophy.[61]

Between the spring of 1903 and the spring of 1905 Musil experienced

59. Corino, "Ödipus oder Orest?" p. 167.
60. See Robert Musil, *Tonka*, in *Prosa*, pp. 264–99; also *Tag*. I, p. 11, and much of H. 3, as well as *Tag*. II, pp. 11–12.
61. *TE*, p. 89.

a hiatus in his intellectual development, a transition between his career as an engineer and his studies in philosophy and psychology under Carl Stumpf in Berlin. In April he returned to Brno to live with his parents while he completed his reserve duty and finished the Gymnasium studies that would allow him to matriculate in philosophy. Though he left for Berlin in November, 1903, it was not until June, 1904, that he returned to Brno to take the *Maturitätsprüfung*. He continued his technical work, writing and publishing two engineering papers. He also devoted the better part of a year to the invention of a device for use in psychological experiments with light. This *Variationskreisel*, or color-wheel, a modification of an instrument already in use for optical experiments, constitutes the most tangible link between Musil's gifts as a mechanical engineer and his later interest in Gestalt psychology. At the time, he hoped that the *Variationskreisel* would be successful enough to make him financially independent, so that he could study philosophy on his own. Failing this, he considered dropping out of his social role altogether and giving up his class position: "Become a writer, boot-black, house servant, something American, and work your way up as a writer." There was no radical break, but Robert was moving steadily away from the expectations of his family. Although he remained financially dependent on his parents until 1911, his move to Berlin in 1903 established the distance he needed. It was to be more than seven years before Musil returned to live in Austria not as a student in his parents' home, but in Vienna as a married man, an established artist, and an independent mandarin.[62]

By the time he left for Berlin, Musil had achieved a partial reconciliation of the contradictory models provided by his parents, and in an undramatic, but substantial way had established his independence. In many respects Musil resembled his father: he was a contained and often cold person, distant and not particularly good at making friends. His life was marked by a few close relationships, but even here his lack of sentimentality was often breathtaking. His father would never have thought to employ his mandarin intellect on his own emotions, and Alfred Musil certainly never rejected his social order; but the elder Musil's patient, gentle, undogmatic style left its mark. Robert emulated the aristocratic-military style more closely than his father had, and he moved

62. Ibid., pp. 57, 46, 794–96 ("Der Variationskreisel nach Musil"). The two engineering papers were "Kraftmaschinen des Kleingewerbes" and "Die Beheizung der Wohnräume."

away from engineering and eventually from the university, but the transitions toward becoming an artist were always gradual and never involved rejection of his father's respect for science and intellect. He valued his father's rationality, discipline, and human tolerance, his renunciation of the spiritual comfort of Catholicism, and his devotion to science. The weak but decent image of authority provided by his father and the Austrian mandarinate was poor material for rebellion of the sort that Max Weber, the Freudian paradigm, or the German Youth Movement and expressionism represented; Musil's acceptance of his father mellowed in adulthood into a gentle irony toward authority and the past.[63]

Musil's relationship with his mother was far more difficult, and the contradiction between the contained style of her husband and Frau Musil's explosiveness must often have been hard for Robert to reconcile as he was growing up. Despite her long-standing affair with Reiter, her son's emotional and social life consistently met with Frau Musil's disapproval, most notably in the case of Herma. Musil's comments on these years of conflict emphasize his hostility toward Reiter and his inability to please or trust his mother. But while he challenged his mother's social expectations and her need to dominate emotionally, Robert admired her spirit of excitement and adventure, and the move to Berlin provided the distance he needed to begin to learn to accept her. Moreover, the contrasting temperaments of his parents obviously helped to shape his own style: "I am hardly to be thought of as an unclear mind, but not as a clear one either. . . . My father was very clear; my mother was characteristically confused. Like messy hair on a pretty face." The perceived disjunction suggests the difficulty of reconciling these moral and aesthetic traits in the liberal culture of Austria, and the polarity of intellectual styles in his parents seemed to him the source of his own distinctive mode of "'forming' thinking in place of the rational." Both his family and his culture attuned him to the androgynous values of his mature work.[64]

In Musil these opposites complemented each other as much as they conflicted, and this legacy seems to have provided some, if not all, of the tools he needed to cope with his development. Even his intense experi-

---

63. Cf. Max Weber's more dramatic relationship to his father in Arthur Mitzman, *The Iron Cage* (New York, 1971).

64. *TE*, p. 441. Cf. ibid., p. 70: "Mother too was once a girl, who would have suited Robert still better than Herma."

ences of loneliness—in Steyr, Eisenstadt, Mährisch-Weisskirchen, Stuttgart, and again in Berlin—equipped him for his mature exploration of
the isolation of the individual in modern urban society. In his studies,
his friendships, his diaries, and, above all, in his art, Robert gradually
found his way toward forms of expression that led him beyond his parents' world. The marks of conflict were clearest with his mother, but
even there Musil displayed a remarkable talent for growth, for moving
gradually but steadily beyond his past and learning to understand it. By
the time he finished his first novel, he had to an extraordinary degree
climbed out and beyond the emotional conflicts of his youth and gained
a certain distance from his childhood. The legacy remained in subli-
mated form, but he was now ready to give it expression and to test himself in the world.

3. THE DIVIDED SELF

The ego of Descartes is the last firm point in the critical-

epistemological train of thought; it is the certain, momentary

unity. The ego of which the mystics speak is the complex

ego. The former is the most certain, the latter the least

certain.[65]

The project that gave shape to the diffuse and anxious period between 1902 and 1905 was the writing of *Young Törless*, which Musil
began during the winter of 1902–1903 in Stuttgart. When he arrived in
Berlin, he gave little time at first to his studies and "rarely attended lectures." Though he was attracted to the new cultural ambiance of the
German capital, it was not until the spring of 1905 that he felt ready to
resume the "line of intellectual [*geistiger*] development" which had been
interrupted since 1901 by the army, Stuttgart, his conflicts with his family, and his Gymnasium examinations. The real turning-point was
finishing *Young Törless*. In a letter to Frau Tyrka dated March 22, 1905,
Musil reported that the novel had been finished "for weeks." His letter
expresses the relief of someone who at last has a difficult project behind
him. At this point his diaries resume with a vigor and detail which mark
a new stage in his own growth and his response to German culture.[66]

65. Ibid., p. 82 (1905).
66. Musil, "Briefe," in *LWW*, pp. 273–76; *TE*, pp. 439, 81.

Musil still suffered from the self-doubt of an unproven artist. He feared that the novel would be a disappointment even to the sophisticated public whose interest he hoped to attract. Rejections from three publishers confirmed these doubts, and he decided "to request a judgment from authority." His "choice fell to Alfred Kerr," then the leading critic and mentor of the literary revival in Berlin. As Kerr correctly judged, Musil's first novel was an extraordinary literary accomplishment, especially for such a young writer. Musil later recalled the support of Kerr and the success of *Young Törless* as one of the most beautiful moments in his literary career: Kerr championed *Young Törless* as "a book that will last," one "that had to be written." "Even though only a half dozen people have read it," Kerr was sure of its success and convinced that "sections of it" were "masterful."[67]

Kerr's review in *Der Tag* set the tone for the enthusiastic response the novel received when it appeared in 1906. He emphasized the stark realism of Musil's story and its affinities with naturalism and impressionism. Musil's tale of adolescent sadism and homosexuality "is without sentimentality. It does not, as it were, impose any lyricism. He is a person who sees into facts—only out of their factual relations does there arise for him that measure of 'lyricism' which is already in things." At the same time, Kerr saw that many readers would be offended not only by the portrayal of homosexuality, but also by the psychological reflections of the narrator, and he recalled the prejudices of the romantics against indecent explorations of the psyche: "A hundred years have passed. . . . Meanwhile Dostoevsky was there," but there would be an outcry, nonetheless. Yet even a critic who found Musil's subtle treatment of adolescent sexuality "too much honor for an episode" conceded that the novel demonstrated that the German language had refined itself in the previous twenty years to rival the French symbolists in "the portrayal of discreet and delicate human situations." Musil's contemporaries, on the other hand, praised the neo-romantic and generational aspects of the novel, and Oskar Maurus Fontana looked back on it in the wake of expressionism as "the work of a generation." But it was Kerr who came closest to taking the measure of Musil's intentions—neither sensationalism nor psychology, neither romanticism nor rebellion. According to Kerr, it was written "by an autonomous, search-

67. *TE*, p. 439; Alfred Kerr, "Robert Musil" (*Der Tag*, December 1, 1906) in *Robert Musil: Studien zu seinem Werk* (hereafter *Studien*) (Hamburg, 1970), pp. 240–45.

ing, and bold spirit, to whom everything base and untoward is foreign, because he is concerned on the whole with what is most important."[68]

Young Törless stands comparison with the best novels of the decade in its genius for language, its sensitive treatment of human motivation, and its force and reality as an act of the imagination—quite simply, as a good story. As in the work of Rilke and Thomas Mann during this period, the move toward Schopenhauer's novel of inner events is apparent in the use of inner monolog and psychological analysis, but the conventions of nineteenth-century narrative realism are still largely intact. Despite the novel's symbolism, Musil succeeded in controlling his analysis with a "lapidary" style that suppressed detail and went beyond the subjective to the creation of an objective world. The essayistic impulse was already apparent, but, as Musil later put it, "with *Törless* I still knew that one must be able to leave things out."[69]

The Confusions of Young Törless presents the development of a sensitive adolescent, finding his way through a series of emotional, sexual, social, and intellectual crises at a remote Austrian boarding-school.[70] In his homesickness and boredom, Törless comes to depend on the friendship of two unsavory characters named Beineberg and Reiting, the leading political manipulators in his class. When they catch their classmate Basini stealing money from their lockers, Reiting and Beineberg sadistically exploit his fear of betrayal and expulsion. In a secret room, appropriately furnished with a flag, a lantern, and a loaded revolver, the two bullies subject Basini to psychological and physical persecution which nearly ends in his death. Basini, who submits to this degradation with little protest, is a pathetic figure, the predestined victim. Apart from a few clever suggestions, Törless remains largely passive, but he is implicated by his occasional presence at the proceedings and by his

68. Kerr, "Robert Musil," pp. 240, 245; Jakob Schaffner, "Verwirrungen des Zöglings Törless," *Die neue Rundschau* 22, 2 (1911):1769–70; Oskar Maurus Fontana, "Robert Musil und sein Werk," *Prager Presse*, May 21, 1922.

69. *TE*, p. 440. Musil's effectiveness as a storyteller is apparent in the consistent appeal of his novel and in the success a half-century later of Volker Schlöndorff's film version.

70. While the portrayal is based primarily on Mährisch-Weisskirchen, Musil also drew on his Eisenstadt experience, and "W" is a secularized monastery school (as in Leopold Andrian's *Fest der Jugend* of 1895) rather than a military academy. Karl Corino ("Törless Ignotus," *Text + Kritik*, no. 21/22, [December 1968]:18–25) argues not only that the novel is based on Musil's personal experiences in 1895–1896, but that each of the characters can be identified with the aid of Gotthold Krebs, *Die k.u.k. Militär-Oberrealschule zu Mährisch-Weisskirchen. Ein Beitrag zur Geschichte des Militär-bildungswesens während der letzten fünfzig Jahren* (Vienna and Leipzig, 1906), which, ironically enough, appeared in the same year as *Young Törless*.

agreement to conceal Basini's theft from the teachers. More disturbingly
for Törless, he is upset by the responses of his own dawning sexuality to
Basini's nakedness and humiliation.

While it is Basini's persecution by Reiting and Beineberg that moves
the plot, the narrator's central interest is the inward experience of the
protagonist. Törless is distanced from the external action and portrayed
from the inside, as he attempts to relate the secure, regulated world of
his parents and teachers to the dark and threatening world of his peers.
His confrontation with power, magic, and sexuality is portrayed as a
creative moment of vulnerability, which has potential for destruction,
humiliation, or self-knowledge. The adult, bourgeois world of light,
order, and reason is challenged by a world that is associated with lower
or fallen status, with childhood solitude and fantasies, with the whore
Bozena, and with the irregular activities of his friends. The split in Törless's experience between his parents on the one hand and Beineberg
and Reiting on the other seems to go right through Basini, and ultimately right through Törless himself.

Musil saw this division in the self as the key to Törless's confusions,
and he defined it in terms of the incommensurability of "the world of
feelings and that of the understanding." He explained this in a letter to
Frau Tyrka by describing his own experience in looking at a painting:
"It is as though a person were in me with whom this picture speaks; this
person is drawn momentarily into the painting's circle, while my real
person . . . comprehends only the shadow of it. The ego is literally
split. . . . One sees mysterious movements without being able to distinguish them clearly."[71] This split was the fundamental notion behind
Musil's portrayal, but he was concerned more with mood and with the
imagery of perception and experience than with a systematic account of
the psyche. Some of Törless's confusions are specifically sexual, but
some are more broadly moral or refer to memories or varieties of diffuse
awareness. Törless's strange experiences of the second life of things
seem to correspond to something positive and enhancing within himself
which he does not yet understand. Gaining access to this primary symbolizing power within himself involves risk, because this inner self is
also the source of feverish dreams which break through the firm boundaries of life and threaten the comfortable healthiness of normal reality.
Törless's task is to confront his dreams without being overwhelmed by

71. From the *Nachlass*; quoted by Corino, "Ödipus oder Orest?" p. 155.

them, and without annihilating the creative, nourishing power of this hidden self. Yet he lacks a spiritual culture of his own, and he is not much helped by the Catholic piety of Prince H., by his mathematics professor's allusions to Kant, or by Beineberg's anti-intellectualism and crude Indian mysticism.

Törless finds intellectual form for his confused feelings when he discovers in mathematical symbols an attempt to express the incalculable elements of an otherwise normal reality. His sudden recognition in the woods of "how high the heavens actually were" reminds him of the function of infinity in mathematics: "Something that went beyond reason, something wild and annihilating, seemed through the work of some scientist or other to have been tamed and was now suddenly reawakened and made fruitful again." The mathematical notion of an imaginary number, the square root of minus one, expresses even more vividly to him the extraordinary human capacity to domesticate the world into linear, rational systems. This surd is "like a bridge, of which only the beginning and the end exist, and which one nonetheless so confidently walks over as though all of it were there." Imaginary numbers suggest the possibility of bridging two apparently disconnected realities, the possibility of calculating with unknown, irrational, and irreducible quantities. Yet unlike Beineberg, Törless is not looking for something supernatural but for something natural, something within himself.[72]

Törless's confused feelings eventually crystallize as a result of his intense sexual experiences with Basini. Törless's initiation into the mysteries of adolescent homosexuality is the first of many portrayals in Musil's art of a crisis of consciousness transformed by sexuality. The release of this tremendous energy overwhelms Törless at first, and his anxiety is compounded by the dramatic resolution of the conspiracy plot. By the time his mother comes to take him home, however, Törless is already finding a way out and growing beyond his crisis. His curiosity, passion, and sensitivity to experience are still with him, but he is no longer so vulnerable. He has discovered the transforming, intoxicating power of sexuality, but he feels no need to reify it in a particular person or situation. He is not hermetically sealed from his former confusions, but something inside him has come together to a whole. Far from shattering him, this experience refined his personality and added something positive to his maturity. He came to regard "it as inevitable that a person

72. Musil, *Die Verwirrungen des Zöglings Törless* in *Prosa*, pp. 69–70, 81, 90.

with a rich and varied inner life experienced moments of which other people must know nothing and memories that he kept in secret drawers. And all he himself expected of such a person was the ability to make exquisite use of them afterward."[73]

One need only consider contemporary reactions to the psycho-sexual dramas of Gide, Lawrence, and Freud to appreciate Musil's artistic courage in working out the logic of his story. At the time, Musil was annoyed by realists who took this episode to be a literal account of his own experience, "particularly since precisely what is most compromising is for the most part invented." Musil was offended by the notion that his book was a confession or a reformist tract, and it was only later that he appreciated the extent to which he had portrayed something typical. Moreover, his attempt at the time to minimize the autobiographical aspects of the novel was almost certainly informed by the possibility of legal suits against his family, even in "decadent" Austria. That *Young Törless* is autobiographical is not in doubt—setting the pattern for all his art in this respect—but the precise nature of the autobiographical basis in reality is muddled and, in the final analysis, unimportant. He did not intend the novel as an elaboration of the pathology of adolescent homosexuality, much less as a personal confession and self-justification. What concerned him was not the sensationalism of his story or its value as a case study, but "a connection between the moral and the intellectual."[74]

What Musil considered to be the preeminently autobiographical aspects of the novel were the interconnections of meaning within the mind of the protagonist and the structure of his growth and experience. Musil was trying to get at the sources of sexuality, love, and imagination, not at some particular object for them. He wanted to stress the positive value and situational determination of psychosis, at least in

73. Ibid., pp. 119. Törless is described as growing into someone who was inclined toward boredom if he was expected to show a "personal interest in particular instances of law and morality," for the only real interest such people feel "is concentrated on the growth of their own soul, or personality, or whatever one should call the thing within us . . . that is never there when we are writing minutes, building machines, going to the circus, or following any of the hundreds of other similar occupations."

74. *Prosa*, pp. 723–24. Musil had so little interest in the realistic material that he actually gave it away to two friends. Apparently Franz Schamann's "Mährische Geschichte" (1902) grew out of this and inspired Musil to write it in his own way. Cf. Fontana, "Erinerungen an Robert Musil," in *LWW*, p. 331. At the time, Musil thought that the characters in his novel were constructed out of combinations to such an extent that he doubted their psychological plausibility and realism: Musil, "Briefe," in *LWW*, pp. 276–77.

cases where the excitement is not overcome by the pathological.[75] In developmental terms, the immediate point of the story is Törless's acceptance of his own and his mother's sexuality. Törless accepts his homosexual experience and his hysteria as a learning process, an intensification of his situation and his feelings. His crisis leads to panic and flight as it had in the "Valerie-experience," but mother, whore, boy, and actress are all only correlatives for something else for which Musil, as well as Törless, can find no word. Törless moves beyond conventions about homosexuality and incest, Victorian or psychoanalytic, and he feels no need to judge in a lawful mode, whether social or scientific. Here sexuality appears as a release from normalcy, as a means for the general function of art as Musil understood it: "Springing the limits of the normal totality of experience. And this is the fundamental value in every art."[76]

There is a natural temptation to see the influence of Freud in Musil's treatment of sexuality and adolescence. It would not be too much to say that this is a story about a young man discovering his unconscious, and one could hardly ask for a more complete portrayal of the psychological basis of adolescent homosexuality. The relationships among the mother, Bozena, and Basini and the connection of these specifically sexual features with Törless's intellectual curiosity and development are elements that lie on the surface. Thus, it is not surprising that one critic argued that Young Törless "may in fact be the earliest novel of any sort in any language to show specific Freudian influence."[77] This is an instance of what might be called the fallacy of retrospective influence, since it is virutally certain that Musil knew nothing of Freud when he

75. Ibid. By 1906 Musil had a more sophisticated knowledge of academic psychology, particularly of French psychiatrists such as Charcot and Janet. He wrote to Paul Wiegler that he was convinced he might as well have written his story with any of their abnormalities as with the "relatively common one I chose."

76. *TE*, p. 674.

77. Cf. Harry Goldgar, "The Square Root of Minus One: Freud and Robert Musil's 'Törless,'" *Comparative Literature* 17 (1965):118. Goldgar's argument rests heavily on conjecture, since there is no mention of Freud in Musil's early diaries and Musil never discussed Freud in connection with his first novel. Goldgar's suggestion that Freud's theories of dreams (1900) and sexuality (1905) must have influenced a book which appeared in 1906 by a conscientious young psychology student does not square well with the facts. Musil wrote *Törless* in 1902–1903, revised it in 1904–1905, and began to take his psychological studies seriously only in 1905. Annie Reniers's conclusion that neither the novel nor the diaries justify attribution of Freudian influence is far more convincing. Cf. "'Törless': Freudsche Verwirrungen?" in *Studien*, pp. 26–39. The real point is that Freud is the most systematic, successful, and well-remembered of the psychosexual thinkers of this period.

wrote the novel. Based on the lack of evidence, one might just as well
(and probably also wrongly) call this the earliest application of Otto
Weininger's theories of bisexuality, which caused such a stir in Vienna
in 1903.[78] In fact, Freud, Weininger, and Musil all reflect a cultural preoccupation with sexuality and the meaning of masculinity and femininity. Musil's understanding almost certainly came from neither Freud
nor Weininger, but from his own lived experience of the culture and society of his youth.

The discovery of the unconscious was what Musil thought was unrealistic in his portrayal of Törless, but neither Musil nor Törless thinks it
is a Freudian unconscious. Törless's experience of a second, pre-rational
relation to things echoes a literary tradition from the romantics to the
symbolists of France and Austria. The unconscious is portrayed as a
condition of being, and the erotic, perceptual, emotional, and intellectual aspects of the unconscious are not conceptually determined. Schopenhauer, Hartmann, Emerson, Nietzsche, Maeterlinck, and the poets
had alerted Musil to issues which he made no effort to give systematic
form. He portrayed a process which allows for irrationality and disorder without discounting intellect. The mathematical symbols refer to a
sense of the self and its relatedness to the world which is not discursive,
but also not specifically sexual. Throughout Musil's work, a heightened
relation to the world and the self is often associated with sexuality, but
Basini might have been a woman or a dog; he stands simply as a symbol
for the irrationality of the world. Törless is trying to create his own spiritual culture out of the emptiness and terror of his inwardness and the
situations of his world as they present themselves.

Musil was critical of the tendency to make scientific and logical
thought the normative paradigm for all activities of the mind. He
rejected the identification of "the soul with consciousness and the as-
cription to it of the freedom of the will as its most excellent attribute."
He pointed to a second mode of generating language, which originates,

78. Otto Weininger, *Geschlecht und Charakter* (8th ed., Vienna, 1906; orig. pub.
1903). Weininger's theory of the mixture of male and female principles in every personality inspired Freud to comment that the young man had stolen the key to the castle.
Weininger explained homosexuality in terms of an excess of the feminine (bad, lower)
principle in the man. He made himself the most famous suicide of his generation in the
same year, when he judged himself too feminine and too Jewish. It is certainly likely that
Musil was familiar with Weininger by 1905, but Musil had already written the first draft
of his novel in the winter before Weininger's book came out. Moreover, moralizing about
male and female principles and determining the constitutional proclivity for homosexuality were not the goals of Musil's novel.

as it were, behind conscious intentionality, where sentences arise as though from nowhere. This is the source of what Törless calls "living thoughts":

The thought is not something that observes an inner event, but, rather, it is this inner event itself.
We do not reflect on something, but, rather, something thinks itself in us. The thought does not consist in the fact that we see something clearly, which has evolved itself in us, but, rather, that an inner development emerges into this bright region.

In this note from 1905 Musil joined Lichtenberg, Nietzsche, and Mach in his preference for the formulation "it thinks" rather than the conventional "I think" of Western thought since Descartes.[79]

In *Young Törless* Musil protrayed the liberating power of thoughts as moments in the inner life which have not yet frozen into fixed form. Törless experiences his flashes of understanding as momentary unities, "often no more than accidents, which pass again without leaving traces behind them."[80] Musil emphasized the contextual significance of these "living thoughts," which makes them independent of their logical value as propositions. Their spiritual significance lies in the lived context, as tentative expressions of growth and self-understanding. This attempt to address the complex interactions between thought and feeling established a new attitude toward the novel, which Musil later described in discussing *Young Törless*. He argued that "the evolution of the novel requires that the portrayal of reality finally become the serving means of the *conceputally strong* person, with the aid of which he can approach the understandings of feelings and the shatterings of thought which cannot be grasped generally and conceptually, but perhaps only in the flickers of the individual case."[81] Musil wanted to make it possible for a person who might have been a philosopher or a scientist in another generation to bring his intellectual gifts to bear on the concrete and individual situations of literature.

Young Törless portrays the breakdown of liberal thought and bourgeois normalcy, while attempting to overcome rigid concepts and feelings which are not flexible and open enough to experience. Törless's ex-

79. *TE*, pp. 104–105, 79. Cf. the much later formulation (*TE*, p. 310): "Depth: the point to which the light reaches."
80. *Prosa*, p. 142. Cf. *TE*, p. 43: "Every human being is a cemetery of his thoughts. They are the most beautiful for us in the moment when they arise; later we can often sense a deep pain that they leave us indifferent, where they once enchanted us."
81. Musil, "Über Robert Musils Bücher" (1913), in *TE*, p. 776.

perience challenges the narrowness of positivism and the perfunctory acceptance of Kant or mathematics as complete reductions of reality, while his homosexual experience provides the little touch of evil that saves him from a false healthiness. But the novel is not an attack on intellect or civilization. There is a gentle distancing from an adult social order that is portrayed as overexclusive, narrow in its judgments and concepts, oblivious to the problems of adolescents, and committed to a firm, unchanging notion of character. Against this is set an image of the adolescent self in process, isolated in a threatening peer-group during a precarious stage of development.

Musil was alert to the pathologies of both domination and revolt. Törless is by no means so alienated from the normal adult world as his friends are (his problem is not so much alienation as indifference and passivity—a kind of gnostic transcendence as though the plot cannot touch his soul), but neither is he willing to take up the Victorian position of moralizing about the waywardness of young boys. He embraces neither normalcy nor outrage, neither the society of worldly, repressed intellect in the service of social status and ambition nor the absolute craving for meaning without respect to rationality or limits. This refusal to acquiesce in either world established the basis for the emotional freedom required to cope with the free-floating life of the modern intellectual. *Törless* formulates the possibility of a revolt against bourgeois culture which does not produce something equally rigid and pathological, and stakes out a position of isolation and freedom, marked by Musil's enormous tolerance for ambiguity.

The subtlety of Musil's treatment distinguishes this work from the "school novels" of expressionism. The bleak atmosphere of the school is obviously no place for either love or self-realization, and the inadequacies of the instructors are clear enough. Yet there is no attempt to blame the episode on the school or to idealize the values and experience of the students. The real threat comes from Beineberg and Reiting, whose sadism and cynical manipulation point explicitly to the world outside the academy. In these skillful portrayals, the young Musil saw more deeply into his society than he knew. As he wrote in the thirties of these sons of the old and new imperialisms: "Reiting, Beineberg: today's dictators-in-embryo."[82] In this respect *Young Törless* is prophetic,

---

82. *TE*, p. 441. Cf. Musil's remark in the mid-1930s (*TE*, p. 374): "Would we then have thought that the putsch-officer would become the leading type in the world?! Beineberg had thought of it!"

in the precise sense of seeing the logic of the present with clarity, yet
Young Törless makes no attempt to grasp society as a whole: it reads
like a presentiment of German history because Musil is able to unveil
the relations among sexuality, irrationalism, and power in a microcosm
of *fin de siècle* Austria.

The Confusions of Young Törless portrays the emotional and intellectual development of a young man in terms of his attempts to get in
touch with unconscious energies and tap them, rather than allowing
them to overwhelm him. He is not in control of this process, but open to
it, both passively and courageously. This and not some ideological or
sensational issue is the central theme of the book. Musil was searching
here for a specifically modern spirituality, rooted in the particularity of
the context, in the responses of a sensitive adolescent to challenges to
his imperfectly formed image of reality. In this exploration Musil disturbed the conventional structure of bourgeois morality and perception
without offering any comfortable alternative. It is this honesty and balance in dealing with the ambiguity of moral experience in modern society which led Erich Kahler to see *Young Törless* as one of the first "existential" works in modern German literature.[83] Had Musil written
nothing more, he would have established his credentials, not only as a
skillful storyteller, but as a penetrating critic of human experience.

83. Erich Kahler, "Der Prosa des Expressionismus," in *Der deutsche Expressionismus*
(Göttingen, 1965), p. 175.

CHAPTER TWO

Between Science and Art: 1905-1911

Basic idea: . . . the agreement of the contemporary intellectual situation with that at the time of Aristotle. At that time
people wanted to reunite knowledge and religious feeling,
causality and love. With Aristotle these split; then research
began. . . . In a certain sense all the philosophical systems
from the scholastics to Kant have been only an interlude.[1]

etween the completion of *Young Törless* in 1905 and his marriage to Martha Marcovaldi in 1911, Musil resumed the line
of intellectual development which had broken off after the
"Valerie-experience." He continued his exploration of ethical experience, but he did so now in the context of his studies in philosophy and experimental psychology at the University of Berlin. Intellectually, Musil found himself midway between the exact sciences and
romantic literature; in practical terms, he was undecided between an
academic career and the much less secure prospect of becoming an
artist. He was that unusual case, a poet who loved science, and he
sought to relate his passion for scientific objectivity to his exploration of
the realm of the feelings. He wanted to learn to understand and form
the feelings without distorting what could be known of the factuality
and lawfulness of the world. Thus, his interest in romanticism, his
relationships with women, and his efforts to become an artist all developed during these years in tension with the sober positivism and
experimentalism of his academic work; and his respect for knowledge
and intellect remained after he had decided (by 1911) that he was an
artist.

Musil apparently hoped that philosophy would help to overcome the

1. *MoE, Anhang*, p. 1587.

division in liberal culture (and within himself) between science and art, positivism and romanticism. But he found that in his generation philosophy held a "characteristic position . . . between science and poetry, whereby it has the virtues of neither the one nor the other."[2] As he gained clarity about the tasks of science and art, the language of metaphysics dissolved to leave him stranded between his two passions. During the Berlin years Musil endured this split in his culture and worked out a sophisticated understanding of the relationship between science and art, between lawful regularity and metaphor. His dissertation on Ernst Mach in 1908 established his mature defense of scientific knowledge against the temptations of metaphysics, and the novellas of *Vereinigungen* (1911) accomplished a radical experiment in the metaphorical rendering of the relation of the feelings to the world. In these achievements Musil formed his image of the world and defined the intellectual categories of his creative project.

1. THE BERLIN YEARS

When Musil decided in 1903 to move away from the conventional social and professional expectations of his family, he chose Berlin as the place where he would at last give shape and direction to his life. No geographical location ever had the psychological primacy for Musil that one often finds among poets, but for the next seven years Berlin provided his first sustained experience of a cosmopolitan city. Like many intellectuals of his generation, Musil sensed that the center of German cultural and institutional dynamism was moving northward, and, until the war, Berlin played a much greater role in his life than Vienna. He later remarked that although "Vienna is the second largest German city," so many of its inhabitants live in Berlin that "there are not always enough who remain at home."[3] Berlin provided Musil with an opportunity to retreat from social reality, to resist the automatic process of professionalization, and to balance the competing elements of his personality. There he established his most important adult relationships, with Johannes von Allesch and Martha Marcovaldi, as well as the institutional and intellectual bases for his mature work, particularly through Alfred Kerr, Carl Stumpf, and Franz Blei. But the adventure of constituting a new world in Berlin was inhibited both by

2. *TE*, p. 105.
3. Musil, "Als Papa Tennis lernte" (1931), in *TE*, pp. 816–17.

the claims of his parents and by the painful resolution of his relationship with Herma Dietz. Even after his social reality began to take shape in Berlin—through the university and his literary contacts—he tended toward solitude, toward what he called the "inwardly intensified."[4] He left little record of his daily life and relationships, and his concrete existence is obscured by his emphasis on his intellectual development and on the literary transformation of his personal experience.

In Berlin Musil found himself alone once again in a world where no one knew him. One of his first literary attempts after his arrival portrayed a character named Grauauges, who was so solitary and purposeless that his landlady wondered if he might be a sex criminal. Like Musil's later characters, such as Vinzenz and Ulrich, this young man lacked a firm identity; living in the vacuum of a strange city, he felt the need to give his life form, "a meaning, a line, a goal":

Because without a theory of oneself—without an idea of what one believes— one is left entirely to one's drives; that is, without a theory of oneself, one also has no distinctive drives.

By the age of twenty-three Musil had already rejected promising careers in the army and engineering, and his work on *Young Törless* did little to further his third attempt to become a man of importance. What had once seemed like curiosity and growth began to take on the appearance of uncertainty, hesitation, and indifference in the face of the practical demands of adult life. He found himself unable to decide on a profession "because today it is virtually only those who have no profession who can be fulfilled." His alienation from normal social reality and conventional roles confronted him with the task of overcoming the disintegrating logic of decadence; as with Grauauges, this pointed to "an eventually 'absolute' art" as "one of the problems of his life."[5]

These feelings and the process of writing *Young Törless* might logically have led Musil to become an artist, but he could not decide between philosophy and literature. He suffered from the confusion of these two spheres, and he found his concept of philosophy expanding to encompass what "I have previously perceived as the essential in the artist." So alienated did he fill from his artistic identity at this time that

4. Cf. *Prosa*, p. 634: "Stepping out of the world of realities, the world of Bülow, of airplane flights, of the conservatives . . . into the world of symbols."
5. *Prosa*, pp. 554–63 ("Grauauges nebligster Herbst"); *TE*, pp. 63, 59.

he wrote a sketch in which he projected his poetic self, the author of *Young Törless*, into a younger brother whose death "brings a crisis in [the older brother's] life." For the older, colder, more sober brother who remained behind, there was the role and temperament of the philosopher "that defines a certain withdrawnness in his character, that style of hidden cynicism, which is the obverse of his understanding for everything." As early as 1905 Musil suspected that the academic study of philosophy could not provide the kind of growth he wanted, while as a writer he was demoralized by inner doubt and a lack of direction. As he put it in a letter to Gustl: "Has it never occurred to you that we believed ourselves to have immeasurable gifts and now hardly have faith even in our own mediocrity?"[6]

The years from 1905 to 1911 were marked by a delay of adult commitments and by intense personal and creative anguish.[7] This was the first stage of an extended creative crisis that lasted until the end of the First World War. In the second phase of his artistic moratorium, between 1911 and 1918, Musil resigned himself to the obligations of adulthood and resolved his problems by indirection. During the Berlin years, however, Musil's isolation and freedom from responsibility allowed him to focus directly on the central intellectual problems of his life. This protracted crisis of early maturity set in with the completion of *Young Törless* and was hardly deflected at all by the assurances of Kerr and the public that he was indeed an artist. Musil wanted to write, to prove himself as an artist, but he was uncertain about how to build on his precocious masterpiece. Precisely the resolution of his adolescent conflicts had left him without a firm identity or sense of direction. The problem of forward momentum was most acute for his creative powers, but it was intimately entwined with his uncertainty about his profession and those closest to him.

The most painful aspect of the early years in Berlin was his relationship with Herma Dietz. In a sense, she was the concrete symbol of his moratorium, of his break with Austria and his parents' expectations. Socially and aesthetically, she had also meant a break with the world Robert had shared with Gustl and Alice: "There is no deeper sadness than loving an unimportant person. One sees where the other ways of

6. *TE*, pp. 89, 63, 91.
7. This period corresponds roughly to Erikson's model of the psychosocial moratorium. Cf. Erik H. Erikson, *Identity: Youth and Crisis* (New York, 1968), pp. 21, 157.

one's friends lead and remains stopped nonetheless." Musil was prepared to resist the conventions of social status, but it was difficult for him to reconcile his relationship to Herma with the artistic identity he was beginning to forge. She could not provide the spiritual partnership he sought; yet there was an ethical quality in her that he loved, even though he knew it ruined. It is not certain when Herma followed Robert to Berlin, but it was probably about the time he finished *Young Törless* that their strange drama of fatality and mistrust began. Herma discovered that she was pregnant and that she had syphilis. It was possible that Robert had infected her himself, since he had been treated for syphilis several years earlier; and Herma never yielded in her insistence that she had not been unfaithful. But her doctors assured him that it was virtually certain that she had contracted the disease from, and become pregnant by, someone other than Robert. In his notes for *Tonka* at this time, Musil struggled with the contradiction between the objective probability that she had been unfaithful to him and the slight subjective possibility that he had infected her himself and was the father of the aborted child. Herma was hospitalized for an extended period, and she apparently died in 1907, when her name disappears from the diaries. Until the spring of 1907 Musil recorded his visits to her bedside, but his feelings of mistrust were always there "under the complicated feelings like a nail." Both his relationship with Herma and its grim resolution intensified his feelings of isolation, and Herma's democracy of death challenged his own spiritual and aesthetic elitism. Herma's death seems to have meant an inner maturation for Musil and a painful stage in the realization of his identity as a writer and as a human being.[8]

After the breakdown of his relationship with Herma, Musil's friendship with Gustl became an artistic task. Gustl was a model of the feminine, artistic type, and his life with Alice unveiled the confusing contradictions between sexual repulsion and love. Through letters and visits to Vienna, Musil maintained an intimate friendship with this couple during the Berlin years. He began a novel which was to have included Herma, Gustl, Alice, and Klages (the model for Meingast in *The Man without Qualities*). At this time, Musil worked out many of the details of the relationship between Walter and Clarisse, and his attempts to understand the tormented emotions of Alice shaped some of the insights

8. *Tag.* I, p. 105, II, p. 882, and passim; *Prosa*, p. 622.

for *Vereinigungen*. Moreover, the difficulties of this marriage spoke all too directly to the pain of Robert's relationship with Herma:

The relationship between Gustl and Alice shows again what madness it is to doubt the faithfulness of a woman. Alice's conduct has really been dubious for the longest time. And yet something really good will come of it, from the fact that Gustl finally allows himself to be deceived. There are, after all, still other values between a man and a woman than fidelity.[9]

Few insights can have been so painfully won for Musil as this.

Musil's first close friend in Berlin was Johannes von Allesch (1882–1967). Like Musil, Allesch was a provincial Austrian (from Graz) who had come to Berlin to study with Carl Stumpf. The two young men worked together in the laboratory and engaged in endless philosophical debates; and it was for Allesch's research that Musil invented the *Variationskreisel*. Unlike Musil, Allesch later continued in an academic career, helping to develop Stumpf's tone-psychology in the direction of Gestalt psychology and its application to the visual arts. It is an index of Musil's distance as a person as well as the conventions of his class that he continued to use formal address with Allesch until the war; but of all Musil's adult friendships with men, this was the closest and most durable.

Allesch was not only the center of Musil's scientific and philosophical life in Berlin, but a devil's advocate (very like Ulrich in *The Man without Qualities*) against the romantic enthusiasms of Gustl and Robert. Allesch and Gustl symbolized for Musil the conflict within himself between experimental research on the psyche and the artist's romantic soul. This split between science and art seemed sometimes to imply alternative cosmologies—for example, between Aristotle and Plotinus, or Descartes and Novalis—as well as different tasks and emotional styles. Allesch's sophisticated blend of positivism and urbane aestheticism exercised a great pull on Musil and apparently encouraged his shift away from literary sentimentality. After an initial period of mutual mistrust, Musil grew to appreciate Allesch's "Baconism of the feelings" and his insistence on the reality and solidity of the world: "Allesch is more many-sided. He [Robert] now recognizes in Allesch the type which until now has been missing from his life: the mobile, sensitive spirit. What he rejected in books as a snob." Nonetheless, Musil was inclined to see Allesch's preference for decadent French writers such as Huysmans as a

9. *TE*, p. 69.

stage he himself had outgrown. Ten years earlier it had been a cultural contribution to be decadent; now Musil doubted that this was adequate. He had grown more earnest and ethical. Allesch was the "type of the aesthetically sensitive. I am morally sensitive. Decisive since the time with Valerie. Earlier I went around with the aesthetes." [10]

Between 1905 and 1907 Musil began to establish himself in the literary world of Berlin. His personal contacts developed primarily through Alfred Kerr and the intellectual circle that frequented Paul Cassirer's art salon. Cassirer (the brother of the philosopher Ernst Cassirer) was the most important art-dealer in Berlin and organized the first showings of Van Gogh and Cézanne, making Berlin the capital of German art despite Kaiser Wilhelm's hostility. It was in these circles that Musil met Martha Marcovaldi and Franz Blei, the editor who invited Musil to write a story for *Hyperion* in 1908. Kerr also encouraged Musil to publish, arranging Musil's first journalistic essay with *Pan* in 1911. This world of artists and writers provided a social context for Musil's retreat from conventional reality and his resistance to an academic career. The urbane, liberal style of this quasi-Bohemian culture echoed the mood of Vienna ten years earlier, and its cynicism mirrored Musil's own inner crisis of motivation. The most readily available antidote to this mood was the wave of neo-romanticism that hit Berlin about this time.

Musil's introduction to the intellectual life of Berlin came very largely through reading the *Neue Rundschau*, the influential liberal journal he later helped to edit. It was dominated at this time by a neo-romanticism which had not yet been overcome by the revulsion against reason and science. The journal gave prominent attention to foreign writers such as Wilde, Schnitzler, Hofmannsthal, Key, Maeterlinck, Brandes, Hamsun, Ibsen, and Altenberg, all of whom contributed to the shift in German literature from social naturalism toward a more psychological and mystical art; it was in these pages that younger German writers such as Mann and Hesse were beginning to establish their reputations. These writers displayed a pre-Freudian fascination with dreams and the unconscious: their explorations of misty inwardness alternated with the fear that the unconscious could ultimately prove only to be a threat to liberal reason and progress. These articles repeatedly reflect the preoccupation of liberal culture with the return of the repressed and the inar-

10. Ibid., pp. 60–63, 92–93. Musil's friendship with Allesch also introduced him to an emphasis on relations with women which seek to satisfy the feelings, rather than Robert's emphasis on the "purely sensuous."

ticulate presentiment that human relations on the most fundamental
level are in crisis. Politics appears as morass, with Bülow's honeymoon
at an end and no hope for a liberalism caught between entrenched conservatism and the threat of revolution. It was within this grammar that
the expressionist rebellion began to emerge, and this context shaped
Musil's own search for a balance between intellect and soul.[11]

For Musil, romanticism meant both an ideology of self-development
and a soul-metaphysics with imprecise metaphysical moorings. He saw
German romanticism as a first attempt at his own task of working out a
balance between the conscious and the unconscious—a project which
had broken down almost completely after 1848. "The correct mixture
of conscious and unconscious is the ideal of the romantics. The annihilation of the unconscious under the too hot eyes of consciousness, its
fate." Musil wanted to explore in a more systematic way his distinction
between the Cartesian ego and the mystical ego. This required an examination of the historical process by which the soul was eliminated from
the thought of natural science. It also meant a critical self-examination:
"It is now to be asked to what extent the mystical formulation is justified. It grounds itself naturally before the historical already in personal
experience."[12] In these terms, the history of culture and the more recent
research in experimental psychology complemented each other and am-
plified personal experience.

In this way Musil derived a phenomenological method—grounded in
tradition, experimental science, and personal experience—that invited
him "to go to school with the romantics and the mystics. The only critical activity is thereby to reduce their ideals to the purely sentimental
content, i.e., to exclude what is possible only under a certain metaphysical viewpoint, such as Schelling's philosophy of nature." Musil saw mistakes arising when empirical responses to the world were translated into
firm conceptual structures which could not be justified by the facts. Un-
encumbered by the metaphysical certainties of the romantics, Musil set
out to explore love, religion, and soul on a purely phenomenological

11. The rage for neo-romanticism in the liberal periodicals of Berlin at this time would
deserve to be called fuzzy-headed, if that did not assume the availability of a clear idea to
which to reduce the nonsense. It is as though one were to have called Galileo confused
because he refused to settle for the old mechanics; nicely enough, Descartes's clear and
distinct ideas were simply wrong. The real problem with the neo-romantics was language,
an unctuous, precious, pregnant tone which gave historical specificity to their attempts at
psychology and spirituality. This was, however, a case of an hysterical pregnancy in which
the patient turned out actually to be pregnant.
12. *TE*, p. 82.

basis. Here the mystical and romantic traditions provided a huge fund of human feeling and experience. Aside from the romantics themselves, Musil found in Ricarda Huch's *Die Blütezeit der Romantik* one of his richest sources. He also read Plotinus and almost certainly other neo-Platonists, mystics, and Gnostics as well. This assimilation of the romantic tradition after years of work in the natural sciences helped him to focus a range of questions associated with death, creativity, and the ego-feeling. He was particularly drawn to the possibility of using the word *soul* without assuming any corresponding metaphysical reality:

Everything which is expressed by the word *soul* one does not understand with the intellect, in the way in which one always understands scientific philosophy with the necessary concentration. The thoughts in question are half feelings; one understands them when these feelings are awakened in the self.

Musil's interest in the romantic notion of the soul provided the intellectual and personal continuity between *Young Törless* and *Vereinigungen*.[13]

In this respect Musil's reading of Ellen Key was decisive. Her article in the *Neue Rundschau* in June 1905 touched him "very strongly—with the voice of my own past. Here is the way I used to think, the Valerie tradition." No work exercised a greater influence on Musil at this time, both as a summary of the romantic tradition and as a statement of fruitful directions still to be explored. A Swedish educator and feminist, Key emphasized the international character of romanticism and offered a summary of the spiritual culture of the West from the Greeks to Wilde and the French symbolists. She praised the Platonists, Stoics, and Epicureans for their demonstration of the freedom of the soul over externalities and the soul's capacity to form the given material of human nature. Underlying the notion of soul in both pantheism and Christianity, she found "the ancient conviction of the value of the human being and the value of life." She emphasized love as the greatest heightening of the soul and saw the liberation of woman in romanticism as crucial to the liberation of love. Although she criticized the anti-intellectual, impractical, and obscurantist tendencies of romanticism, her own vision stressed the primacy of feminine love over the serving means of masculine intellect. Her article was representative of the liberal preoccupation with romanticism, of an elite culture in search of its emotional moorings; and she concluded that socialism and anarchism would be possible only

13. Ibid., pp. 81–84, 249.

"when the soul is master in his own house." Musil later put Diotima's name next to his extensive summary of Key: "The art of living becomes religion. Perfection of the soul is only another name for religiosity."[14]

Musil interpreted all of Key's models as variations of "the ethical-aesthetic self": "Lessing's ideal of humanity and natural religion, Goethe's self-culture, Schleiermacher's self-realization, Nietzsche's Overman." Musil noted the similarity of these values in Spinoza, Rousseau, Carlyle, Ruskin, Emerson, Thoreau, Whitman, William James, and St. Francis of Assisi. He was attracted to the idea that "the task of the culture of the soul is to guide human beings in their use of spiritual energy," but he found Key's definitions contradictory, and he was not clear about the role intellect was to play in this process. Key tended to associate feelings or life-forms (e.g., intensity, simplicity, intoxication, spontaneity) with particular conceptual models of the world. She also tended toward the language of wholeness which finds its models in the pure madman, the child, and the animal: "Submission to the moment, yielding to the play of energies. This can be enviable to the adult. But it cannot be a model, since one cannot return a complicated constitution to a simpler one." Musil felt the power of these similes, and he was attracted to her attempt to carry over the strengths of the child to the adult, but he resisted her polemic against reason. He recalled that Nietzsche had already shown the limits of the narrowly rational type, but Key "seems to have no idea of the difficulties here." The romantics themselves had seen that the passage through adulthood required something more than simply a return to the innocence of childhood. Moreover, science offered Musil an empirical mode for understanding human limits and the real possibilities of combining Key's life-forms. Here Musil expressed his sympathy with neo-romantic *Lebensphilosophie*, but also his refusal to choose between Aristotelian logic and untrammeled enthusiasm.[15]

Musil wanted to bring his intellect to bear on romantic soul. At times he seemed to be experimenting in the realm of the feelings like a mad scientist of the early nineteenth century, trying to do for the inner world what airplanes had done in reality. He wrote as if he were trying to pick all the threads out of the psyche, but not as a psychologist: "I am simply drawn by certain things. . . . I am alert to processes in me and in others which elude most people." His regulative awareness was that each hu-

14. Ibid., pp. 91–99; Ellen Key, "Die Entfaltung der Seele durch Lebenskunst" ("The Shaping of the Soul through the Art of Living"), *Die neue Rundschau* (June 1905): 641–86.
15. *TE*, pp. 94–99.

man being seemed to experience the world in a different way, to have a distinctive—and often precarious—balance between the ego-feeling and the world:

> Distinguish people according to their feeling of the world. For one, everything is full, everything stands pressed closely together in the world; a stream of relations flows from one to the other. For another, life is something powerfully empty, with something unclearly flowing which merely draws itself together here and there without a central feeling.

Musil's own experience of life in these years was solitary and joyless, marked by feelings of routine and boredom—interrupted by moments of beauty which were sometimes revealed, especially in literature. He experienced himself as a person with no talent for happiness, but also as a poet: "The man who fundamentally loves only similes and for whom even incest is only a simile."[16]

Between 1906 and 1907, with the illness and death of Herma Dietz and his new relationships with other women, Musil's need for a spiritual partner came into focus. He was conscious of the relationship between his artistic identity and erotic dream, and he was tempted by the model of the heartless person who consciously masters love. But romanticism offered the ideal of the woman as poetess who shares "the same disease as he. Thus, they teach each other not to feel this." In his letters to Anna, Musil suggested new variations on the romantic model—for example, friends who do not share house and bed. He imagined a love relationship in which every gesture is significant: "Real love partners ought to play—it would serve them, a new form of love would arise." But the tension between romantic soul and biological reduction was explicit: "The animal dreams, the poor animal; it dreams so beautifully, in it dreams God, the human being, and grows ugly, because love is so much deeper when it grows over an abyss. But one must have experienced that." He could find no name for this friendship, for this intensity of going hand-in-hand, which has no content "except what the two unhappy, happy ones conceive, who may dream of their souls." Musil's search for spiritual partnership led to Martha Marcovaldi.[17]

16. *Tag.* II, pp. 916, 945, 912; cf. *Tag.* I, pp. 30–37. Musil thought of intoxication as the precondition of art, but in practice he was more like Brahms: "He does not create out of the fullness, he thirsts after the fullness." The goal of the artist was to achieve these heightened states out of which he gave himself to things. See also notes on Schopenhauer and Hartmann.

17. See the letters to Anna, *Tag.* II, pp. 909–917. "A friendship that gives itself entirely, which shivers with the other before so much beauty, which it can no longer master, and before the ugliness which lurks at the bottom of human beings" (p. 917).

Martha's own maturation as a person and as an artist had been an extraordinary drama of death, disease, and the decline of the bourgeois family. Almost seven years older than Musil, Martha Heimann was born in Berlin on January 21, 1874. Her father, a Jewish banker, committed suicide eight weeks later, probably in response to the financial collapse that followed the speculation of the *Gründerzeit*. At the age of twelve Martha went to live with her aunt (Henriette Alexander) and four cousins in the house that was to provide the model for the "enchanted house." Martha suffered a bout of scarlet fever at the age of fourteen, and her mother died in 1893. During her adolescence Martha was torn between the aggressive sexual attentions of the oldest cousin, Edmund, and the more sensitive, artistic Fritz (1870–1895). Fritz was the precocious child of the family, and Martha shared with him an interest in painting and drawing. They were married in early 1895, when Martha was twenty-one, but within the year Fritz had died of typhus. Returning to live with the Alexanders in Berlin, Martha found herself in another erotic triangle, this time between Edmund and Hans, a younger cousin who reminded her of Fritz. She also developed close friendships with Paul and Lucie Cassirer, and she was briefly engaged to Martin Cohn. When she did remarry in 1898, it was to an Italian businessman named Enrico Marcovaldi. She became a Roman Catholic, moved to Rome, and had two children: Gaetano, born in 1899, and Annina, born in 1903. When she and her husband separated in 1903, Martha returned to Berlin with her children, took up an independent residence, and resumed her study of painting at a school for women founded by Lovis Corinth. By the time she met Musil, Martha was in her early thirties, and her life epitomized the cutting edge of cultural change: cosmopolitan autonomy, modern art, sexual Bohemianism, and feminism.[18]

Martha and Robert founded their relationship on what they both felt to be the perversity of their sexual and emotional pasts. Martha helped Robert come to terms with the meaning of Herma for his life and his inability "to see through and hold onto this simplest human being." In their conversations together, Martha expressed the feeling that their "doubt and dissatisfaction" were "of more value than all earlier conventional eroticism." Their unhappiness and weariness of *globus intellectualis* focused on the beauty and incomprehensibility of the soul:

18. Cf. *Tag.* II, pp. 945–61, especially "Rabe," pp. 958–61. Cf. also Karl Corino, *Robert Musils "Vereinigungen"* (Munich, 1973), pp. 31–43.

"We have some mastery over it. But we do not know how we should use it. We know nothing of the capacity and limits of this power." The intensity of this new relationship drew Martha back toward her past and the need to be unfaithful with her former lover, Martin Cohn. This experience seems to have crystallized a self-understanding in Martha; inwardly something came together to a whole, a kind of self-knowledge beyond proof. This episode of infidelity sealed the relationship between Martha and Robert, although they did not marry until 1911.[19]

Musil later recalled that he had been capable of love only a few times in his life, but then very violently: in his homesickness in Eisenstadt, with Valerie, in his concern for his father's health, and with Martha. And he added: "The love for myself was cancelled out very early." Martha seems to have begun the restoration of his self-love, but it was only after his parents' deaths in 1924 that he fully worked this through. Musil confessed that he and Martha were vulnerable to the criticism "that our life has been built on the illusion of sexuality, on the typical overvaluation and will to overvalue. In fact, we both have a strong, inwardly directed sexuality, which can turn itself outward, however, as well, 'headlessly' (i.e., without soul)." But the very slight evidence suggests something like the model of the life-companionship that Musil described many years later:

One wants to have a life-companion even before sexuality is ripe and ready to be applied. Such people can be destined for one another.—Sexuality is one of the natural forces which they share in common.—They do not awaken it in each other; they receive it from each other.—It is good when they have not found each other as virgins.—They transform treachery into trust. . . . In general such communities are better which have been preceded by a divorce, among other things.

In Martha, Musil seems to have found such a companion, and their relationship was one of the few things he exempted from negative treatment in his diaries. While Agathe is definitely not a replica of Martha, the name Agathe first appears in the diaries around this time; and Musil referred to Martha in a letter to Allesch in 1910 as his "married sister Frau Heimann." Certainly their relationship bore to some degree on most of Musil's mature art.[20]

Musil's personal situation began to come into focus by 1907, but his uncertainty about his profession and his vocation as an artist continued.

19. *Tag.* II, p. 947.
20. *TE*, pp. 438-39, 450; "Briefe," in *LWW*, p. 278.

He became increasingly irritated by his work in philosophy, by "the endless multiplication of arguments" and by the "eternal scientific arguments with Allesch." Only his immense self-discipline enabled him to concentrate on his academic career and finish his dissertation: "Every day I am drawn more into the morass. I am like a mummy with a work tic!" Despite his bouts of depression and some disagreements with Stumpf, Musil completed his doctoral exams in February, 1908, and received his degree in March. As a vacation from his academic labors and as a kind of "spiritual shaking-up," he decided to draw together his insights on sexual jealousy. He wanted to explore "the uncertainty of the human being about the true nature of the self and the people closest to him" as a kind of literary exercise:

Now for those who have read "The Perfecting of a Love" there will hardly be a more incomprehensible contradiction than that between the intention and the execution. It is approximately as great as that between a plan to dash off a little story and the result that I worked on two novellas for two and a half years, and one can say: virtually day and night. I nearly condemned myself to go under emotionally for them. It approached monomania to devote such energy to what was finally such an unfruitful task (a novella may be treated more intensively, but quantitatively the achievement is slight), and I always knew this, but I did not want to give it up. Thus, there is in this either a personal madness or an episode of more than personal importance.

Whatever the broader implications of this "personal madness," these experiments in simile are enormously important for understanding Musil: both the young man who invested so much psychic energy in them and the established artist who wrote thirty years later that *Vereinigungen* was "the only book of mine in which I still sometimes read." In these novellas the crisis in Musil's personal development and his search to find his artistic voice came together.[21]

Except for Martha, Musil's friends and family had difficulty appreciating the intensity of his involvement with these two stories. His father felt it was time for Musil to take on the responsibilities of adulthood, and his plan to marry Martha made the press of necessity unavoidable. Musil had an opportunity to join Alexius Meinong on the faculty at Graz, and he was also considered for a position at Munich. It later seemed to him that he should have endured a boring assistantship

21. *TE*, pp. 90–91, 107, 118, 805–806, 809. Cf. Pike, *Robert Musil*, p. 60; Pike reports Annina Rosenthal's comment that "The Perfecting of a Love" was the story that meant most to her stepfather.

at Graz and lived through the revolution in psychology and philosophy as a professional, but he had "naive hopes" for furthering his literary career and had no idea "how dangerous it is in life not to take advantage of its opportunities." In January, 1909, he turned down the offer at Graz in order to continue working on *Vereinigungen*. But his hopes of starting a literary journal (*Das Pasquil*) with Blei failed to materialize, and Musil reluctantly agreed to his father's arrangement of a position as an archivist at the Technische Hochschule in Vienna. The luxury of being a student and postponing a career was over.[22]

Outwardly Musil seemed doomed to the social destiny of the Austrian mandarin. After a brief vacation in Italy at the end of 1910, he assumed his position at the archive in January, and on April 15 he and Martha were married. Musil liked to think of himself as having left the earth with Martha in 1911, but this became possible only after arranging her divorce and their conversions to Protestantism. They moved into an apartment on the Floriangasse, where Musil found himself encircled by a beautiful, dreamlike life with Martha, interrupted only by the little irritations of the children. But aside from his marriage to Martha, this was not at all what he had in mind. He felt the foreignness of the Viennese, and the bureaucratic routine of the Technische Hochschule seemed to mean the end of his hopes as a writer. "If something comes of Vienna, then I see myself succumbing to the grind altogether; if not, it is almost worse."

1905–1910 closed with a deficit of achieved goals. In 1905 Törless was finished. 1910, nothing, Vienna, bureaucratic career. What hopes have proved themselves not to be realizable for me! (Martha does not belong to this calculation; she is nothing that I have won, achieved; she is something which I have become. . . . Of that I do not speak.)

Musil's summary of these years accurately captures his mood of frustration, but it characteristically exaggerates his failure. The Berlin years had been crucial to his personal development and they had allowed him to think through the relationship of philosophy to science and art.[23]

22. *TE*, p. 445; *Tag.* II, pp. 893–94. Musil later recalled how naively he had assumed his rights to family property: "I put my claims on it, and the fact that I lived until my thirtieth year only for my education seemed quite natural to me. I was not a very agreeable son" (*TE*, pp. 448–49). Cf. *Tag.* II, p. 34: "At the age of thirty, one is, in the sense of high culture, a grown-up child."
23. "Briefe," in *LWW*, p. 277; *TE*, pp. 124–25, 132.

2. PHILOSOPHY AND SCIENCE

The age is past when the image of the world leaped spon-
taneously from the head of the philosopher.[24]

All spiritual courage today lies in the exact sciences. Not
from Goethe, Hebbel, Hölderlin will we learn, but from
Mach, Lorentz, Einstein, Minkowski, Couturat, Russell,
Paeno.[25]

Musil's dissertation on the Austrian scientist and philosopher Ernst
Mach (1838–1916) gave him an opportunity to clarify his own understanding of the relationship between philosophy and science. Like
Musil, Mach had come to philosophy from the physical sciences, and
the problems which were central to Mach's thought were precisely those
which troubled Musil: the relationship between psychology and physics, and the methodological separation of science from philosophy. In
1902 Mach had reawakened Musil's admiration for reason; he now
provided Musil's point of departure from the polemical oppositions
between idealism and materialism, romanticism and positivism. Musil's
Beitrag zur Beurteilung der Lehren Machs constituted his experience of
the methodological crisis of positivism and the rigorous basis of his
own approach to knowledge and philosophy. In order to understand
the context and meaning of his dissertation rather than the details of its
logic, we must attempt to reconstruct Musil's academic environment.
Here Musil's own comments are not very helpful, since he always mini-
mized the direct influence of other philosophers: "I have never looked
around in my intellectual environment, but always hid my head in
myself."[26]

When Musil began his technical training in philosophy and experimental psychology, the natural sciences were firmly established in Berlin
on an equal footing with the humanistic disciplines which had dominated the university in the early nineteenth century. With the arrival of
Stumpf's predecessor, Hermann von Helmholtz, in 1871, Berlin had
become a major center of positivism and experimental research in the

24. Robert Musil, *Beitrag zur Beurteilung der Lehren Machs* (Diss., Berlin, 1908),
p. 5.
25. Musil, *Nachlass*, quoted in Corino, *Robert Musils "Vereinigungen,"* p. 343.
26. *TE*, p. 440.

physical and life sciences. This was Musil's side of the university, and he seems to have been insulated from the historical, humanistic, and sociological disciplines. This apparently suited Musil, who completed an education that was a virtual reconstruction of the nineteenth-century evolution of positivism in philosophy, physics, and psychology. Musil came to philosophy from mechanical engineering, and his work at Berlin in physics and mathematics as well as philosophy and psychology represented the continuation of his determination to raise to the highest level of generality that passion for knowledge and precision which had ruled his father's life.

Austrian philosophers and scientists had played a large part in the development of European positivism, and Musil was not alone among Austrian writers of his generation in his informed and positive attitude toward science. The Austrian mandarin's commitment to objectivity and empiricism is important for understanding Mach, Wittgenstein, the Vienna Circle, and novelists such as Kafka and Broch, as well as Musil. These values were not peculiar to Austria, however, and it is misleading to associate Musil too closely with the distinctively Austrian brand of anti-Kantianism that had taken shape a hundred years earlier. Musil did not share the aggressive anti-Kantianism of Bolzano, and Musil's mentor in the critique of German idealism was Nietzsche rather than the Austrian-school philosophers. Musil's secular background was removed from the distinctively Catholic and Aristotelian approach of liberal priests such as Bolzano and Brentano, about whom Musil—unfortunately but significantly—left no comment. Moreover, for Musil, the seventeenth century represented, not the foundations of the Austrian Baroque, but the emergence of a cosmopolitan, European scientific revolution led by figures such as Kepler, Galileo, Descartes, and Leibniz. Whatever else the best minds of Musil's generation may have shared, they did not think that the criteria of universality, empiricism, objectivity, and public debate were achievements peculiar to the Austrian tradition.[27]

27. Leibniz, the great mentor of the Austrian tradition in philosophy, was, after all, a Protestant from northern Germany. Musil's own attitude toward Leibniz can best be understood, not in terms of Musil's Austrian background, but in terms of his admiration for the three great figures of the Leibniz revival in early twentieth-century philosophy: Russell, Couturat, and the German neo-Kantian Ernst Cassirer. This is by no means to deny the existence of an anti-Kantian tradition in Austrian philosophy; it is also true that students of German idealism are frequently unfamiliar with the tradition described by Roger Bauer in *Der Idealismus und seine Gegner in Österreich* (Heidelberg, 1966).

There was no clear break between a German and an Austrian tradition in nineteenth-century academic psychology. Herbart, a crucial figure of Austrian anti-Kantianism, was a German, a student of Kant, and Kant's successor at Königsberg. Moreover, Kant himself was centrally concerned with establishing the foundations of scientific knowledge, and by the 1830s, when the wave of German idealism had passed, many of the leading academic researchers—Helmholtz, Lotze, Fechner, and Wundt—were Germans. Even Brentano (1838–1917), who taught Freud, Ehrenfels, Husserl, and Stumpf, was German-born and -educated and learned his Aristotle from Trendelenburg in Berlin. Ernst Mach, although he was born in Moravia and taught at Prague and Vienna, did his work in relation to German physics and psychology. Moreover, British philosophy and psychology exercised a powerful influence on almost all Central European psychologists, particularly through the associationist psychology of the Mills. Finally, Central European psychologists from Freud to Musil looked to the French psychiatrists (especially Charcot and Janet) for an understanding of the insane and for research on hysteria, hypnotism, and the pathology of repression and automatic activities. Along with the contributions of the Russian Pavlov and the American William James, this blend of European scholarship constituted the basic framework of Musil's training in Berlin.[28]

Musil later compared his training under Stumpf to the Vienna Circle around Moritz Schlick: "How much more precise things were in the Stumpf school. This more sober and scientific atmosphere was, to be sure, an achievement of this teacher, who probably not simply by accident had the most important students."[29] Stumpf was a strong proponent of experimental research, particularly in the field of perception. Max Wertheimer, who began the systematic study of the perception of movement where none takes place, did his work in the Berlin lab shortly after Musil left; Köhler and Koffka, the most important popularizers of Gestalt psychology in the United States, were Stumpf's students, as were Allesch and Musil, both of whom advocated Gestalt psychology in the 1920s. But Stumpf was apparently more at home as a philosopher than as an experimentalist, and he deserves mention in the history of philoso-

28. See Edwin G. Boring, *A History of Experimental Psychology* (New York, 1929); Robert I. Watson, *The Great Psychologists* (New York, 1968).
29. *TE*, pp. 451–52.

phy as the man to whom Edmund Husserl dedicated his revolutionary *Logische Untersuchungen* in 1900.

Musil was sympathetic to the work of his colleagues in the Berlin laboratory. He later recalled that his enthusiasm for experimental psychology was quite un-Freudian: all his life he found himself "interested in the 'flat' experimental psychology, but not in Freud, Klages, or even phenomenology."[30] Experimental research seemed as legitimate in psychology as in mechanical engineering, but Musil was frustrated by the low yield of such research and as impatient with laboratory work as he had been in Stuttgart. He found himself in a period of psychology when the old assumptions seemed to have lost their fruitfulness, and just before new theoretical possibilities opened up. While he had some familiarity with Husserl, Freud, Simmel, and Bergson during this period, he was not strongly attracted to any of them. Many years later he explained his frustration with this intellectual situation in terms of his inability to find a valuable approach to ethics in either philosophy or psychology: "Important: that I always wanted to deal with ethics, but I found no approach that suited me. In other words, that I had studied too little. Scheler had found that approach."[31] In the absence of such an approach, Musil decided instead on a more abstract problem in the philosophy of science: a critique of Mach's views of causality and scientific language.

Mach's philosophy of science was a critical revision of an ossified nineteenth-century positivism. In *The Science of Mechanics* (1883), Mach assaulted the whole structure of Newtonian and Kantian assumptions underlying nineteenth-century physics. In place of the Kantian distinction between the phenomenon and the noumenal reality of the thing-in-itself, Mach argued that sensations themselves are reality. Similarly, he insisted that time and space are relations built up out of experience, that scientists have access only to relative motions in experience (that there are not two worlds, one in motion and one at rest). This argument helped to clear the way for the physical theory of relativity, but it was only part of a broader position which Mach elaborated in *The Analysis of Sensations* (1886).

---

30. Ibid., p. 477. Cf. also Johannes von Allesch, "Robert Musil in der geistigen Bewegungen seiner Zeit," in *LWW*, pp. 133–36.

31. *TE*, p. 445. Cf. Musil's extensive technical consideration of Husserl's *Logische Untersuchungen* in *Tag.* II, pp. 119–31.

The theory of sensations was an attempt to free the sciences from metaphysical problems, while at the same time securing the practical goals of positivism. The genius of Mach's approach was that it allowed him to establish the unity of the sciences in a way that would facilitate research, while eliminating the metaphysical priority of one science (physics, which was regarded as more "material") over another (psychology). By arguing that all sciences deal with sensations and not with things and forces, Mach invited the charge from physicists and materialists that his world was insufficiently substantial; by rejecting as outmoded the dichotomy between the physical and the psychical, he invited the charges of psychologists, idealists, and Christians that his was a thinly disguised materialism marching under a new banner. While Mach denied both charges, his methodological monism did threaten both extreme metaphysical positions. In relation to physics, Mach wanted to emphasize the accidental, historical, and psychological content of physical concepts, particularly those which physics tended to hypostatize, such as time, space, and energy. In relation to psychology, he was combating the tendency to divorce psychology from any connection with physics and biology and thus from any possibility of scientific investigation or significance.

If Mach seemed to endanger the status of physical concepts, his insistence that the individual, like other things, was merely a "relatively stable complex of sensational elements" drove the logic of scientific determinism right over the idealist position:

The ego must be given up. It is partly the perception of this fact, partly the fear of it, that has given rise to the many extravagances of pessimism and optimism, and to numerous religious, ascetic, and philosophical absurdities.[32]

In place of romantic revivals of individualism, immortality, and heroism, Mach offered liberal social reform and the steady progress of scientific and technological achievement; in this Mach stood firmly in the tradition of the Austrian mandarin, far removed from the anxieties of Weber and Heidegger about rationalization and technology. The inadequacies of Mach's terminology and his tendency to indulge in metaphysics against his own better judgment ought not to obscure the fact that in relation to his own time his work represented an impressive

32. Ernst Mach, *The Analysis of Sensations* (New York, 1959), pp. 24–25. This egoless position, which Mach had derived from Lichtenberg, obviously helped to shape Musil's concept of "the man without qualities." Cf. John T. Blackmore, *Ernst Mach: His Work, Life and Influence* (Berkeley, 1972).

effort to dispose of prejudice and outmoded concepts which could only be obstacles to precise scientific research.

For Musil, Mach's contribution lay "purely and solely on the safe ground of the exact natural sciences."[33] Since positivism had come to be more a philosophy than the actual attitude of the best practicing scientists, Mach's achievement was to save real science from the science of philosophers and sociologists.[34] In fact, Musil was even more faithful than Mach to the strictly methodological standpoint, embracing Mach insofar as he enhanced the project of modern science, but resisting him wherever he inhibited, obscured, or confused it. While Musil conceded that there can be no science without presuppositions, he saw in Mach the possibility of a science which "wants to be as presuppositionless as possible."[35]

Musil saw the appeal of Mach's epistemology in his pragmatic interpretation of the evolution of science. As the extension of the normal attitude of human consciousness, science generalizes from experience in order to establish continuity with succeeding experiences and assure mastery of the environment. Mathematics provides simple, economical abbreviations of these experiences, rather than explanations. According to Mach, the purpose in question is simply self-preservation and the practical activities that follow from it. Musil insisted that this interpretation of science did not necessarily imply epistemological nihilism or skepticism. He granted that practical necessity and historical accident lead to different formulations of reality depending on the occasion and the purpose, but not all responses are equally justified.

Thanks in large part to Mach's efforts, physics had moved toward "a more pragmatic and skeptical approach to scientific theories, as in the case of Maxwell, which insists that they be used simply as models, as visual images of the facts."[36] This view acknowledges that concepts such as mass, energy, space, and time "contain in their common usage

33. Musil, *Beitrag*, p. 9. Cf. Erwin N. Hiebert, "Mach's Philosophical Use of the History of Science," in Robert H. Stuewer, ed., *Historical and Philosophical Perspectives of Science* (Minneapolis, 1970), p. 196: "If the strict separation of science and philosophy which Mach's thought leads to is taken for granted by most philosophers and scientists today this was not so in Mach's environment." Nor in Musil's.

34. For detailed studies of Musil's dissertation see: Henri Avron, "Robert Musil und der Positivismus," in *Studien*, pp. 200–213; Jan Aler, "Als Zögling zwischen Maeterlinck und Mach," in *Probleme des Erzählens in der Weltliteratur*, ed. Fritz Martini (Stuttgart, 1971), pp. 234–90; and my "Robert Musil: An Intellectual Biography, 1880–1924" (Ph.D. diss., Harvard, 1972), pp. 136–65.

35. *TE*, p. 386.

36. Musil, *Beitrag*, p. 37.

more than empirical content" and that "the reason for this lies in historical, psychological, and economic motives."[37] In this emphasis on the
unverified element in physical concepts, Mach and Musil shared in the
attempts of Vaihinger, Poincaré, and Wittgenstein to create a more sophisticated approach to hypotheses and models. As Musil later emphasized, scientific hypotheses are formed by analogy (e.g., light moves
"like" a wave or "as if" it were in an ether). The heuristic value of such
hypotheses can be very great if the distinction between the facts and the
analogy is kept clear; the danger arises from taking analogies too literally, from the psychological need for physical images of mathematical
regularities, and from the tendency to defend the concept at the expense
of the facts.[38]

Mach's critical contribution was undeniable, but Musil was more reserved about Mach's anti-theoretical bias, his highly qualified view of
mathematics, and his extreme experimentalism. Although Mach's theory of the relativity of space and time had led the way for Einstein's
early work, Musil seems already to have sensed that Mach's epistemological relativism would ultimately be hostile to as sweeping a theory as
physical relativity. A similar pattern became apparent in mathematics
and psychology, where Minkowski's four-dimensional space and Wertheimer's Gestalt psychology set out from Mach's phenomenal critique
of Newtonian space, but went on to new theoretical structures. In such
matters Musil's instinct was to follow where Einstein, Planck, Minkowski, and Wertheimer led, protecting the interests of actual scientific
progress rather than Mach's philosophical position.[39]

Musil also parted company with Mach on a related question: the implications of the theory of functions for natural causality. Mach argued
that natural events are more complex than the notion of cause implies;
that individual events cannot be isolated from their complex network of
relations; and that the temporal reversibility of laws makes nonsense
of traditional formulations of causality. He insisted that the notion
of cause and effect had to be given up in favor of functional relations
that were simply abbreviations of observations and procedures. Musil
agreed that "the concept of function is the real vehicle of modern physics" and that the older definitions of "energy, thing, and causality" disappear, at least in their original form, but he argued that this emphasis

37. Ibid., p. 46.
38. *TE*, p. 436.
39. Musil, *Beitrag*, pp. 46, 111.

on functional relations was simply a recognition of the procedures of modern physics.[40] In describing the relationships in a given volume of gas, scientists observe not a unique event—the specific impact of one molecule on another at a specific point in time—but a statistical relationship among measurements taken at various times. The result is an equation which expresses the functional interdependence of temperature and pressure in a given volume, with time as an independent variable, a description of a reversible process in statistical terms. In such equations temporal sequence and causality do not come into question. This scientifically refined concept of function had a permanent impact on Musil's thought and art.

Mach was inclined to see this description of scientific theory as the death-knell of natural causality and metaphysics in general, but Musil insisted that this had nothing to do with philosophy, that it contained no anti-metaphysical tendency at all. Instead, Musil claimed, it argued for a rigorously methodological standpoint and the separation of the claims of physics and philosophy concerning such concepts as substance and cause, time and energy. What Musil resisted in Mach was the polemic against the very possibility of such concepts, when the obvious solution was for physics simply to make its definitions independent of philosophy: "This X may in the end be what you like, but for me, the physicist, it is only the function it discharges in my equations." If there are connections in nature, then it seemed wrong to Musil to exclude all possible ways of expressing these connections just because of failed attempts in the past. Harking back to Heraclitus, Musil summarized his own characteristic epistemological position: "The flux of phenomena reveals certain characteristics of the stream which justify the assumption of firm, regulative structures, even if these are not immediately visible."[41]

For Musil, the task of science was to ascertain regularities that lie in the facts, to master the realm of knowledge which he later called the *ratioïd*. He was determined to protect the legitimacy of this project, and he rejected Mach's view that the creative power of mathematics introduces a fictitious regularity:

Now, experience teaches with clarity the recognition of incredible regularities. This regularity, which seems at first to mean necessity, lies thus in the facts. And

40. Ibid., p. 73.
41. Ibid., pp. 73–74, 78.

it is naturally not eliminated by an idealization of the facts. . . . But it is, therefore, also a mistake to say that necessity is only introduced into the facts through
the idealization.

Musil concluded not only that Mach's view of function was indifferent
with respect to causality in nature, but that Mach was "in the sharpest
contradiction with himself." In passages drawn from all of Mach's major works except *The Analysis of Sensations*, Musil showed that Mach
explicitly assumed everything necessary to the concept of causality in
nature: the uniformity of the environment, the susceptibility of this environment to research, and the presumption of lawful and necessary relations.[42]

Musil did not want the theory of functions to lead to irrationalism or
to a radical empiricism that would undermine the development of scientific theory. In practice, Musil argued, the problem with the primitive
concept of cause was that it oversimplified both the process of observation and the complexity of physical events. Thus, the concept of cause is
used less and less in more sophisticated science, but the concept of function turns out to be a euphemism for everything essential to natural
causality. This was a problem of complexity and relativity, not fictitious
regularity; even Mach's recognition of the relativity of space and time
had made it possible to reduce these relations to general laws. Musil's
treatment of cause and function reveals a powerful sense of the complexity of reality and the partial nature of human knowledge. Given
Musil's statistical concept of function and his qualified view of material metaphors, Heisenberg's uncertainty principle and the problems of
quantum mechanics would hardly present insuperable theoretical difficulties. But Musil insisted that a refined concept of functional relations
was no threat to knowledge. The task of science was to order facts under laws, to postulate and verify regularities in nature, and Mach's functionalist approach had done nothing to bring this project into question.

Musil's critique of Mach was not an escape hatch into art and irrationalism, but a defense of scientific knowledge—in psychology as well
as physics and biology. When Musil finally decided to give up his scientific career, this was not at all because he doubted the value of the un-
dertaking. In fact, he cited "the concept of 'precision' " to account for
the fact that "I loved science absolutely passionately from my eigh-

42. Ibid., pp. 123, 120. For a fuller discussion of Musil's distinction between two
realms of knowledge (the *ratioïd* and the non-*ratioïd*), see his "Skizze der Erkenntnis des
Dichters," *Summa* (1918), in *TE*, pp. 781–85.

teenth to my 31st year, when I left the earth." Musil shared and admired the values of modern science, but what interested him most were the elusive connections among the emotional, the moral, and the intellectual, which resisted organization under laws. He wanted to apply the precision of intellect to the realm of the non-*ratioïd*, to the realm of "ethical and aesthetic relations, the realm of the idea." In any case, he was convinced that science would take care of itself. But he had nothing so generous to say about philosophy: "Only in philosophy does one not know from whom one should learn." Practically speaking, Musil saw two alternatives: either participate patiently in the experimental resolution of what had formerly been considered metaphysical questions, or become an artist.[43]

Musil's train of thought came close to the more radical conclusions of a slightly younger Austrian, Ludwig Wittgenstein. In the following decade, Wittgenstein dissolved the traditional role of philosophy and set science apart from what he called "the problems of life":

> The right method in philosophy would be this. To say nothing except what can be said, *i.e.* the propositions of natural science, *i.e.* something that has nothing to do with philosophy: and then always, when someone else wished to say something metaphysical to demonstrate that he had given no meaning to certain signs in his propositions.[44]

This deadpan irony of the *Tractatus*—describing philosophy as something which has nothing to do with philosophy—was more conclusive than anything Musil had to say on the subject, but it captured Musil's advice to science. Like Musil, Wittgenstein stopped short of the polemics against nonsense which dominated the Vienna Circle. Instead, he simply pointed to the region beyond the limits of natural science, about which philosophy had nothing to say.

In his departure from science Musil was aware that he was leaving the safe ground of knowledge, for "to poetry belongs essentially what one does not know."[45] His uneasiness is suggested both by his postponement of the decision to leave the university and by his later regret that he had not stayed to experience the revolutions in philosophy and psychology. But his decision recalls Erikson's observation about two other psychological revolutionaries, James and Freud, "that what 'you take for granted'. . . also determines what chances you can fruitfully take

43. *TE*, pp. 140, 105, and Musil, "Skizze," p. 783.
44. Ludwig Wittgenstein, *Tractatus Logico-Philosophicus* (London, 1960), p. 187.
45. *TE*, p. 810.

with it."[46] In Musil's case, his protected childhood, his easy acquisition of intellectual success, and his unqualified devotion to rationality and science gave him the confidence to depart from the academic mandarinate to explore motivation and the unconscious, sexuality and mysticism. If philosophy were nothing more than the propositions of natural science and if science had nothing to do with "the problems of life," then the obvious solution was to depart for art. On the other hand, Musil had no desire to break with the spiritual courage of Mach, Einstein, and Minkowski. He immersed himself in the language of inwardness not to distort the actual but to explore the outlines of the possible. His intellectual mentor, Ernst Mach, would have understood this project: "Poets and metaphysicians are always desirable insofar as they search for the *possible* world and find here and there something usable."[47]

3. METAPHOR AND SOUL

The defect of this book is being a book. That it has binding,

backing, pagination. One ought to spread out a few pages of

it between glass plates and change them from time to time.

Then one would see what it is.—People know only the causal

story. . . . This book is nothing of the kind.[48]

In *Vereinigungen* Musil continued the exploration of the mystical ego and the ethical self which he had begun in *Young Törless*.[49] He did so in the form of two literary experiments which constituted a departure from the conventions of prose realism and the concerns of academic psychology. If the determination of regularities among the facts was the task of science, then the portrayal of individualities was the task of art. In literary terms, these novellas meant a break with causal narrative to portray the flow of consciousness, perception, and the experience of the world in its density and relatedness. These metaphorical renderings of

46. Erikson, *Identity*, p. 25.
47. Mach's comment on Nietzsche in K. D. Heller, *Ernst Mach: Wegbereiter der modernen Physik* (New York, 1964), p. 71.
48. *TE*, p. 188.
49. Robert Musil, *Vereinigungen* (Munich, 1911); originally published by Georg Müller and later taken over by S. Fischer in Berlin. References to *Vereinigungen* and its predecessor, "Das verzauberte Haus," are from *Prosa*, pp. 147–228. The two stories of *Vereinigungen* (*Unions*) have been translated, along with Musil's later stories, as *Five Women* by Eithne Wilkins and Ernst Kaiser (New York, 1965), pp. 123–222.

mysterious spiritual union are concerned with the connections among love, self-knowledge, sexuality, and the world. Perhaps the most radical experiment in the sustained use of simile in modern prose, these stories "do not unfold, but turn back on themselves. Their essence and why they were not understood: a poem, not a story."[50]

In the wake of his studies in academic psychology, Musil was concerned with defining the boundaries between psychology and art. He carefully avoided every form of special-pleading for a poetical faculty of divine inspiration, intuition, or synthesis: "Reflective people are always analytic. For every metaphor is an unintended analysis."[51] Yet he insisted that art was something different from psychology, although literature did make use of science and knowledge, "to be sure of the inner world just as much as the outer."[52] Psychology wants laws and explanations, theories and proofs, while art gives experiences and understandings, values and images. Psychology penetrates beneath the surface of experience to the elements of psychic life which can be expressed as regularities. But the poet no more works with psychic elements than the painter works with atoms; he is interested in the living unities, in "the thoughts and feelings which lie on the surface."[53] Psychology, like any other science, organizes the particular under laws; art represents the individual and employs metaphor to convey the many-sided complexity of immediate experience and its world of meanings.

Vereinigungen meant a departure not only from the abstract reductionism of academic psychology but also from realistic narrative: "The clear turning—for in *Törless* it was already foreshadowed—from realism to truth."[54] Musil explained his turning from realism at the time in terms of the recognition of "another system of coordinates to which we relate everything spiritual [*Seelisches*]."[55] Artistically, this meant that the external action was only "a pretext for the reality one portrays."[56]

50. *TE*, p. 190.
51. Robert Musil, "Analyse und Synthese," *Revolution: Zweiwochenschrift*, no. 1, October 15, 1913: "One can naturally just as well say that every analogy is a synthesis, every understanding is one. Nonetheless, there are many literary people today who are hostile toward analysis and flatter themselves with synthesis."
52. *TE*, p. 808. Cf. Georg Lukács's formulation from 1911 in *Die Seele und die Formen*, p. 7: "In science the content affects us, in art the forms; science offers facts and their interconnections, but art offers souls and their destinies."
53. *TE*, p. 90.
54. *TE*, p. 809.
55. Ibid., p. 79.
56. Musil, "Über Robert Musils Bücher" (1913), in *TE*, p. 776. Cf. *TE*, p. 803: "Now one must naturally be able to narrate, if one claims the right not to tell stories, and I can do so tolerably well; but for me what I narrate is always of secondary importance."

The departures from psychology and literary realism were two aspects of the same impulse: "Let nothing happen (do nothing) which is not of spiritual [*seelisch*] value. I.e., also: do nothing causal, nothing mechanical."[57] This union of the ethical and the aesthetic led him toward a utopian art, whose characters "are born into a system of powers which we suppose only in the abstract extension of our lives."[58]

The two novellas of *Vereinigungen*, *The Perfecting of a Love* and *The Temptation of Quiet Veronica*, focus on decisive periods of self-discovery in the lives of two women. Each portrays a period of heightened awareness and instability in which the heroine finds a new sense of identity and relatedness to the world.[59] But what there is of plot in these stories is subordinated to spiritual events and the portrayal of a world of feeling. Musil himself was inclined to admit that the material he chose for his experiment was not very promising, perhaps not even defensible: "In the attraction to an animal there can also be something of the surrender to a priest, or an act of infidelity can be a union in a deeper zone of inwardness—thus has the basis of 'Veronica' and 'Claudine' been circumscribed."[60] No one who has read these difficult stories will be surprised by the primarily negative response to *Vereinigungen*'s appearance in 1911; even a sympathetic critic looked back on them as a failed literary experiment, as a decadent phase in the development of a master social-realist.[61] Charges of decadence, however, miss the point. Although Musil did not allow conventional prejudices to impede his portrayal of sexuality, these works have an ethical goal; the acts are only similes for the process through which two women recover that sense of balance between the ego and the world which constitutes the feeling of value.[62] Moreover, these stories represent a

57. *TE*, p. 812.

58. Ibid., p. 80.

59. Musil believed that the task of the novella was to portray such inner transformations. Cf. Musil's comments on the novellas of Walser and Kafka in "Literarische Chronik," *Die neue Rundschau* (1914), in *TE*, p. 684: "It is certain that one experiences great inner transformations only once or a few times: those who have them every few months (such types are thinkable) would not have a world-image so firmly anchored that its tearing-up could be of significance."

60. *TE*, p. 130.

61. Ernst Fischer, "Das Werk Robert Musils," *Sinn und Form* 9, 2 (1957), p. 856. Cf. Jacob Schaffner, "Vereinigungen," *Die neue Rundschau* 22, 2 (1911):1771. While the critical response was almost all negative, one expressionist review was enthusiastic: "Whoever has not experienced the poetry of Musil does not live today" (Alfred Wolfenstein, *Die neue Kunst* I [1913–1914]:219).

62. See Musil's fascinating analysis of alienation and the problem of sustaining the feeling of value in *Tag.* II, pp. 927–34. This rather technical analysis of the relations

decisive period in the evolution of Musil's style and artistic voice, and in the exploration of his own spiritual crisis. And recent scholarship has been more sympathetic to Musil's hope that his personal madness might represent an episode of more than personal importance.[63]

As early as 1905 Musil anticipated the problem of *The Perfecting of a Love* and of his own courtship with Martha: "Theme, that one ought to build marriage on infidelity."[64] The recurrent motif of his Berlin sketches was continuous with his first novel: "Sensuality is a power over all persons. But in itself it is, to a certain extent, nothing, but something out of which the most varied things (people) emerge."[65] Musil was interested in the impact of sexuality on heightened conditions of the soul, in the theme of *Fernliebe* (the absent or dead lover), in problems of disordered sexuality in both men and women, and in the problem of solitude in love.[66] The connections among love, animality, and the wish for the death of the loved one which appear in *The Temptation of Quiet Veronica* emerged out of his associations with Herma, Gustl, and Alice. But what crystallized this material was Musil's meeting of Martha—and his attempt to come to terms with her complicated past and the painful beginning of their relationship. Musil was preoccupied with the problems of jealousy, mistrust, the dissolution of ego-boundaries in love, and the unknown third or other who cannot be reduced to the particularity of one relationship. In these stories of gaining certainty in love and relatedness with the world, even a sex criminal can become a simile for what is not united in love.

A short, stylistically simple story that was close to the realistic technique of *Törless* despite its strange material, "Das verzauberte Haus" ("The Enchanted House") was written for Blei's *Hyperion* in 1908, and it was this story that Musil later revised into *The Temptation of Quiet*

---

among the objective world, perception, feeling, and intellect distinguishes between external events and inward processes, for example, in the case of a suicide. "Naturally, the human being goes under also as a result of causal chains which belong only to the external world." But in this loss of self-certainty and contentment, the external causes may also be accompanied by processes of disintegration that transcend real events.

63. See Dorrit Cohn, "Psycho-Analogies: A Means for Rendering Consciousness in Fiction," in *Probleme des Erzählens*, p. 276; Corino, *Robert Musils "Vereinigungen,"* p. 1; Frank Kermode, Preface to *Five Women*, p. 11; Hans Geulen, "Robert Musils "Die Versuchung der stillen Veronica,"" *Wirkendes Wort* 15 (1965):186–87; Lisa Appignanesi, "Femininity and Robert Musil's 'Die Vollendung der Liebe,'" *Monatshefte* 65, 1 (1973):14–26.

64. *TE*, p. 101.
65. Ibid., p. 102.
66. Ibid., pp. 97–112.

Veronica. Actually, this was only one of four preliminary stages for the novella in *Vereinigungen* which Musil had originally intended to call *Der Schutzengel.*[67] The guardian angel (or demon) gradually disappeared from the story, but it was the germ of the novella and the key to the problem of perspective. The demon had an educative role and was particularly concerned with problems of sexuality and self-awareness: his only appearance in "The Enchanted House" is the high point of Viktoria's reverie, a moment of unspeakable tenderness and self-knowledge.[68] At the same time, the guardian angel was a symbol for what was problematic in Musil's attempt to portray another person, particularly a person of the opposite sex. While the theme of the *Schutzengel* faded from *Vereinigungen*, this invisible mentor came to correspond to the lack of perspective in these stories.[69] Musil's attempt to solve the problem of perspective with a radical experiment in simile confronted him with the task of balancing "the dissipating, formlessly intellectual and the compressed, empty formality of rhetorical invention."[70]

What concerned Musil most as a writer was "the passionate energy of the thought. When I cannot work out some particular thought, the work immediately becomes boring for me: this is true of almost every individual paragraph." This intellectual passion was different from scientific thought; the striving for a certain individual truth went more slowly and often dissolved into "a disordered, amorphous complex":

Now, exact thought is limited and articulated by the goal of the work, the limitation of what is demonstrable, the separation between the probable and the certain, etc., in short, by methodological requirements which arise from the subject. This ideal arrangement is missing here. Instead, [the thought] arises through the images, the style, the mood of the whole.[71]

The extreme nature of the literary device he had chosen as the vehicle for his intellectual insights made the autonomy of his gift of language all the more frustrating. He was forced to police his metaphors with great

67. Cf. Corino, *Robert Musils "Vereinigungen,"* pp. 78–80, 129, 161. See also p. 134, where Corino suggests that Musil's later notion of the other condition may have come from Freud's description of ecstatic states in *Studien über Hysterie* as "the second condition."
68. *Prosa,* p. 157.
69. *Tag.* II, p. 943: "These stories have no central point of perspective."
70. *TE,* p. 117. Musil commented at the time on what had been lost after *Törless:* "That sureness of language, which touched on a great deal without many words. The delivery" (ibid., p. 131).
71. Ibid., pp. 116–17.

care, to organize their unity with excruciating self-consciousness. In the process, Musil was victimized by his own genius for language: the fact that he took two and a half years to write seventy pages expresses the pain of his creative crisis in these years and anticipates the meticulous approach to writing which later plagued *The Man without Qualities.* But he had set himself an important and extremely difficult literary experiment, and he executed it with far greater success than he or anyone else would have granted at the time.

The central stylistic problem was the sustained use of simile; this was the constitutive problem of *Vereinigungen*—the most extreme expression of Musil's understanding of metaphor as the key to art, as opposed to the unequivocal language of science. In *The Perfecting of a Love* Musil employs the comparative constructions "like" or "as if" (*wie, wie wenn, als ob*) 337 times. Almost as frequently, Musil cancels adjectives, adverbs, and substantives with *un-* or *-los* (224 times), while actually negating whole sentences or phrases 208 times! Perhaps most Musilian is the use of the subjunctive 151 times.[72] Nearly every line of this novella is negated or relativized in some way, in order to describe emotions by analogy and simile as "not-this, but like-that, which would be as if. . . ." Musil offers these comparisons and paradoxes as a means of describing inner states with great care. The more one studies these stories, the more one becomes aware of the precision of Musil's ambiguity and vagueness. It is clear why the primacy of the rhetorical might become a torment for someone who was constructing a forty-page prose poem with the precision of a mathematician. The exacting standards of language Musil set for himself in *The Perfecting of a Love* then became his model when he began the revision of "The Enchanted House" into *The Temptation of Quiet Veronica.*

The Perfecting of a Love is perhaps Musil's most beautiful piece of writing, a long prose-poem in which the metaphors reveal an inner state and its slow transitions. Musil called this the method of the shortest step:

I had to follow the way which led, within almost 24 hours, from a deep attachment to infidelity. Psychologically there are hundreds of ways. . . . Then the decision shaped itself in me to choose "the maximally laden path" (the way of

72. Jürgen Schröder, "Am Grenzwert der Sprache," *Euphorion* 60 (1966):311–34: "The 'unseparated and not-united' is no longer separated and not yet united; it knows no exclusive oppositions and binds up everything" (p. 316).

the shortest steps), the way of the most gradual, imperceptible transitions. That has a moral value: the demonstration of the moral spectrum with the continual transitions from something into its opposite.[73]

This method of portraying contradictory relationships and feelings, in combination with simile and subjunctive, gives the novella its Hermetic quality. As in *Young Törless*, however, Musil offers no metaphysics, but a process of perception and a new balance between the ego-feeling and the world: "Precisely what is essential in life, the fine perceptions, the touch of the Holy Spirit, has only to do with this hardly perceptible shift."[74]

Claudine's brief separation from her new husband gives her the opportunity to come to terms with her feelings about her marriage and her promiscuous past. Her journey to visit her daughter and her seduction by a stranger she meets on the train are emblems of a spiritual event, objective correlatives for the gliding logic of her psychic life:

1. What is essential in Claudine's past is that in her unhappiness she did not yet feel anything final and fully serious. Her condition is not yet stabilized, and she does not yet master it, as long as she does not acknowledge the dynamic nature of her balance. . . .
2. The whole is a way to certainty in love. Climbing out of mistrust and jealousy. At the end she achieves her certainty, the consciousness of this fine, strong person and cries for happiness because she must purchase it at this price.
3. Claudine's mistrust in her love is naturally already more fine and more love than ordinary happiness.[75]

Her experience with the stranger is not directed against her husband; it is a simile for her inward confrontation with her own finitude, with a life which she spent "passively, a captive in her own being, committed to one place, to a particular city, one habitation, and one sense of herself." Through her experience she realizes an "awareness of some ultimate integrity deep within her, never clearly defined, yet always present," which is independent of her external identity.[76] Her spiritual journey reclaims her past and brings to consciousness the connection between the impersonality of the sexual drive and her struggle to give the self form and meaning.

While portraying Claudine's process of coming to self-understanding, Musil underscored the contingency of human experience and rejected

73. *TE*, pp. 811–12.   74. *Tag.* II, p. 932.   75. Ibid., p. 930.
76. *Prosa*, p. 1972.

the reification of good and evil in external acts. The metaphorical language does not allow Musil a direct object for the mystical union he portrays, but her pilgrimage implies both a deeper union with her husband and an acceptance of the world out of a new center of meaning. Claudine "recognizes that the happiness of emotional balance is a quality of Gestalt":

A complicated, balanced-out object of a higher order. If one loses the tension for a moment, it goes into endless holes. One defends himself against the world. . . . Every other person sustains this tension in a different way, and the way each does it is for every other person an abyss. Love means having a companion on this dangerous path. Love means acknowledging the dangerousness of the way and feeling the incomprehensibility of the coincidence with another.[77]

For Musil, the descent into inwardness offered no certainties, but in it lay the awareness of the arbitrariness of any particular way of being on which any possibility of self-understanding and union could rest.

Formally, *The Temptation of Quiet Veronica* echoes *The Perfecting of a Love*. While Musil's use of simile to represent the floating world within is sometimes a disturbing element in *The Perfecting of a Love*, the reiteration and extension of images predominate still more in *Veronica*, particularly in the central sections which portray Veronica alone. Once again the story begins with the physical closeness of the lovers and a conversation which reveals the imperfection of the relationship. Again there is a separation which focuses on the woman's process of coming to self-knowledge in two solitary nights of spiritual crisis. The story is her opportunity of self-knowledge, the crisis in her ambivalent relationships with two brothers. Though Demeter seems superficially animalistic, she decides it is the priestly Johannes who is really like an animal because of "that emptiness at the point where other people possess themselves."[78] As in "The Enchanted House," Veronica's crisis leads to spiritual union with her distant lover, Johannes, but this time she does not give herself to Demeter. At night she feels the sensuousness of her body alone, a tenderness for Johannes, and a solitary delight:

What is really her problem? Her happiness, her manifestation, the singing person in her . . . that ought to arise out of the fragments. It was inhibited before (through the dog, Demeter, her insipid life . . .) and is swallowed up afterward again. What does she want? With the dog, with the rooster, with the fight [between Demeter and Johannes], with the conversation with Demeter a yearning

77. *Tag.* II, p. 931.   78. *Prosa*, p. 204.

shapes itself in her for a hardly imaginable and yet somehow or other circumscribed class of experiences. As if in God and yet impersonal experiences.[79]

Musil's portrayal of Veronica's intense experience of the world recalls
his remark about Alice Donath's mad lucidity: that in her mental illness
"this incredibly heightened symbolism must have been remarkable. Everything stands in relationships which healthy people cannot see."[80]

These portrayals of spiritual union raise questions of Musil's relationship to traditional metaphysics and scientific psychology which are difficult to specify with precision. Karl Corino lays great stress on Musil's
anxiety in the face of a sustained study of Freudian psychoanalysis, yet
Musil was content to describe Veronica with such scientific precision
that he nearly transformed his novella into a case study. Musil wanted
an eclectic, complex vision of the psyche that avoided rigid metaphysical formulations and academic psychology. It was for precisely this reason that Musil turned to simile to express and describe what did not
lend itself to systematic treatment. The Hermetic symbolism of these
spiritual unions is not meant to be finally decoded. Moreover, a distinction must be preserved even between Musil's own crystalline observations on his novellas and the esoteric compression with which he wrote
them. The terms of spiritual union, whether with God, lover, self, or
world, are not given metaphysical specificity. Musil had no interest in
doctrines, systems, influences. He simply presented his protagonists in
search of their demons, communion, and self-realization within the limits of the language bequeathed to him by the tradition.

The key metaphysical issue is Musil's understanding of the word *Seele.*
Corino attempts to clarify Musil's meaning by arguing "the strong influence of Meister Eckhardt, Nicholas of Cusa, Leibniz, Novalis, Tieck,
Schopenhauer, Nietzsche, Weininger, Maeterlinck, Altenberg, Kerr, and
Rilke, to mention only the most important names."[81] Kaiser and Wilkins see Musil's usage in relation to Meister Eckhardt's *scintilla animae,*
"which is the point of union of the soul with God, the point of continual re-creation or rebirth." But they wisely point out that "for Musil
this point or spark is neither a psychological nor a metaphysical concept, but rather an autonomous poetic symbol."[82] Relevant to the usage
of *Seele* in *Vereinigungen* are all the meanings in the tradition which
inform and limit it, as well as that profound disillusionment with lan-

79. Ibid., pp. 645–46.
80. *TE,* p. 126.
81. Corino, *Robert Musils "Vereinigungen,"* p. 395.
82. Kaiser and Wilkins, *Robert Musil,* p. 96.

guage which shaped Musil's whole experiment. At the same time, Musil was careful to avoid the cult of feeling that dominated the irrationalism of his day: "Soul is an interaction of feeling and understanding. . . . But no one should deceive himself: in this pairing the element of growth lies in the understanding."[83]

Even the most careful abstraction of a systematic soul-metaphysics from *Vereinigungen* is in danger of being trapped in a language which is more literal, rigid, and unequivocal than Musil intended. His debt to traditional metaphysics from Leibniz to Novalis is undeniable, but he was also writing after Nietzsche and Mach, and a systematic formulation of such language as substance, cause, and soul seemed absurd to him. Here Musil's separation of science from philosophy applies to his own art—this x (whether matter or soul) may be whatever you like, but in my equation (simile) it functions thus: "In this way the whole of the story becomes a functional field of dependent and unknown quantities, which only mutually define each other and become more precise."[84] Musil is calculating with unknown quantities, while maintaining his refusal to hold something as a constant from which to understand everything else. His world of simile, relations, functions, and unfixed values has only a direction, not a rigid, programmatic content. It hardly seems appropriate to provide a systematic, metaphysical exegesis for a work which is so self-consciously a departure from conventional metaphysics, such a radical experiment in multivalent meanings. It seems odd to take literally the most metaphorical work of an author who wrote twenty years later:

> God means the world by no means literally; it is an image, an analogy, a figure of speech, which he for some reason or other must make use of, and naturally always insufficiently; we dare not take him at his word; we ourselves must work out the solutions which he yields to us.[85]

Musil did draw back from the extreme position of *Vereinigungen* to a more extensive, situational mode which made the social realism of *The Man without Qualities* possible. But realistic narrative remained for him a secondary aspect of the work of art, and he never gave up the view that "only as analogy (*Gleichnis*) does reality appear freed from its

---

83. Musil, *Nachlass*, quoted in Corino, *Robert Musils "Vereinigungen,"* p. 340. Cf. Musil, "Über Robert Musils Bücher," in *TE*, p. 779: "If one stays clear about this, one does not fall into the fallacy of the reputedly great feelings in life, whose sources the narrator need only find in order to fill his jug."
84. Schröder, "Grenzwert der Sprache," p. 322.
85. *MoE* I, chap. 84.

individualized, rigidified, and abstract one-sidedness" to reveal things in their "interrelation and juxtaposition."[86]

Musil's ethical view of art protected him against moral sterility and sentimental banality, but he was painfully aware of the esoteric quality of these stories. He had come a long way toward understanding the conflict in himself between his logical and lyrical tendencies, but he had hardly begun to come to terms with the most obvious criticism of *Vereinigungen*: that his art was not in touch with politics and social concerns, but dealt only with "a narrow circle of hypersensible people." Two years later, Musil portrayed the views of his critics in a satirical conversation about his works: " 'The twentieth century thunders above all with events, and this man knows nothing decisive to report about the appearances of life or the life of appearances!' . . . And he flexed his biceps."[87] The blindness of a psychologically undernourished criticism ought not to obscure what Musil was able to see and portray, but his withdrawal was beginning to dry up the springs of his art. *Vereinigungen* had taken two and a half years to write, and after the move to Vienna in 1911 Musil seemed unable to make progress with his other literary ideas. Despite the critical sharpness and originality of his early views, what was missing was the lived reality of human beings working and thinking together. The abstract clarity of his formulations, as well as the boredom, isolation, and social indifference of the Berlin years, expressed the security and passivity of the *haut bourgeois* intellectual, but the freedom and precocity of his student years had been a liability as well as an advantage: "I began aggressively and oriented myself by pressing the image of the world into the highly incomplete spaces of my ideas."[88]

Musil's commitment to intellect and his attempt to move from a psychological to an ideological art both pointed to the wider concerns of the twentieth century.[89] Between the poles of scientific law and metaphorical inwardness lay the untouched realms of politics, society, and shared culture. After 1911, the banal but life-giving challenges of adulthood began to bring home to Musil the connections between his own experience and the historical situation of European society.

86. Jörg Kühne, *Das Gleichnis* (Tübingen, 1968), pp. 193–94.
87. Musil, "Über Robert Musils Bücher," in *TE*, p. 778.
88. *TE*, p. 456.
89. Cf. *Tag.* II, p. 939.

CHAPTER THREE

Ideology and Civilization: 1911-1924

The pressures of the coming scientific, objective age of civilization, when all people will be wise and moderate, already weighed on this generation, whose last flight was sexuality and war.[1]

etween 1911 and 1924 Musil was drawn into the breakdown of the European order which had been established around 1870. For Musil's generation of intellectuals in Central Europe, the collapse of the nineteenth century fell into three phases: elite consciousness of cultural crisis on the eve of war; destruction of traditional and liberal institutions in the mass upheavals of war and revolution; and disillusionment after Versailles, as Europe sank back into conservative routine. Musil diagnosed this process as a revolt against civilization. He believed that the pre-war irrationalism, the ecstatic politics of 1914–1919, and the post-war despair were all expressions of the breakdown of traditional ideologies, whether Christian, liberal, or Marxist. The existing ideologies had failed to respond creatively to the realities of modern life and to the massive expansion of objective relations in European civilization. Musil shared the revulsion of the slightly younger expressionists against the rigidity of the traditional-bourgeois social order and its ideologies, but he was also committed to the promise of the Enlightenment and the tremendous potential of science and technology. He saw his own generation as a first attempt to forge a genuinely modern culture, to create the concepts and values through which Europeans could understand and cope with their experience in modern civilization. He believed that the failure of his

1. MoE, Anhang, p. 1593.

generation to work out an evolutionary solution, to find a new balance between intellect and feeling, had led in a direct line to the war.[2] The return of the repressed in war and revolution undermined the social basis of the traditional-liberal intellectual, but the great expectations of 1919 failed to bring a new order into being. By 1924, Musil was a survivor, left to report on his generation's experience.

After 1911 Musil's inner development figured less prominently in his life situation than before, as the style of the neurotic evaporated in the mature, practical mastery of his roles as archivist, journalist, editor, soldier, and administrator in the Austrian ministries of foreign affairs and defense. These were the years between the publication of *Vereinigungen* and the restoration of his artistic reputation, between his marriage to Martha and the deaths of his parents, between the slide to war and the end of the revolutionary era. Musil calculated the years torn out of his life as four and a quarter (doubled) in the army and three and a half in the ministries. Adding the three years in the archives before the war, he calculated a total of ten and three-quarters (or, really, fifteen) years in the service of the state.[3] For a decade he published no literary works, and it was not until 1924 that he was able to devote himself exclusively to *The Man without Qualities*. The practical experience of these years, however, established the broader context of Musil's mature work, and in the essays of 1911–1924 he began to develop a way of thinking and feeling commensurate with the complexity of modern civilization. In his reflections on politics and culture, Musil mediated between romantic idealism and modern life and sought to fill up the vacuum in German culture between science and rhetoric.

I. ETHICS AND ESSAYISM: 1911–1914

We Germans have no books about people—aside from the great attempt of Nietzsche; no systematizers and organizers of life. Artistic and scientific thought hardly even come into contact with each other among us. The questions of a middle zone between them remain unsolved.[4]

2. Ibid., p. 1592.
3. Musil, "Curriculum Vitae," in *MoE, Anhang*, pp. 1610–11.
4. Musil, "Anmerkung zu einer Metaphysik," *Die neue Rundschau* (April 1914), in *TE*, p. 651. Cf. ibid., p. 129: "What one writes in such a diffuse way must be elements, at least by-products, of a broad and not accidental striving."

In the literary and political journals of pre-war Germany Musil developed his characteristic vision of the predicament of European culture. He believed that the intellectual despair of his generation revolved around the polarity between science and mysticism, and he saw the essay as the literary form appropriate to this situation, the form of the thinking poet mediating between science and art. Since his early student years Musil had been disturbed by the contradiction between a philosophy which was out of touch with lived reality and an art which was lacking in clarity and ideas. Essayism allowed him to retain both the scientist's precision and the artist's search for values in the midst of spiritual crisis. The objectivity and lucidity of the French *moralistes* provided the most obvious model, but Musil wanted to enlarge this concept of the critic to include two nineteenth-century writers who had anticipated his own spiritual project: Emerson and Nietzsche.[5] The essay provided a way to bring the mode of *Vereinigungen*, the interpenetration of thought and feeling in a unique personality, into constructive relation with broader social and cultural issues. Between 1911 and 1914, Musil's search for ethical guidelines in his articles and diaries centered primarily on spiritual issues, but he grew steadily more conscious of the political and social context of his reflections. In the realms of literature, sexuality, religion, and politics, he sought to free the emotions from outmoded and inadequate concepts. Essayism allowed him to explore the possibilities of a new balance between the concept and the flesh, between intellect and soul, to do for the realm of the feelings what science had already accomplished in the realm of physics: "To examine once again all inner possibilities, to invent them anew, and at last to carry over the virtues of an unprejudiced laboratory technique from natural science into morality."[6]

The anxiety and malaise of the Berlin years climaxed in Vienna between 1911 and 1913. Despite the conventional surface of his life at this time, Musil was living in inward rebellion. His work at the archive drained his artistic energies, and he seems to have shown little interest in the intellectual life of Vienna. His diaries include little direct comment on Viennese social and political life, but all of his literary sketches from this period were dominated by his dissatisfaction with bourgeois

5. Cf. ibid., p. 120.
6. Musil, "Politisches Bekenntnis eines jungen Mannes: Ein Fragment," *Die weissen Blätter* 1, 3 (November 1913):239.

society and his consciousness of unlimited human possibilities.[7] He
imagined an ideological novel, *Südpol*, as a satiric imitation of the
Divine Comedy in which "nationalists, state fanatics, idealist philosophers, etc., are punished by being forced to live out the true consequences of their assertions."[8] Although the ideas for *Südpol* and *Die
Anarchisten* (later *Die Schwärmer*) grew out of the Berlin years, Musil
seems to have been particularly impressed by the inauthentic existence
of the Viennese. More personally, he suffered from frustration with his
work at the archive, exhaustion from his fruitless attempts to continue
writing, and a diffuse anxiety keyed to fear of death and his uneven
relations with his parents.[9] The absence of diary entries for most of
1912 suggests that he may have suffered an extended period of depression and writing-inhibition. At least twice, in the autumn of 1911 and
in the spring of 1913, Musil's emotional distress led to serious illness,
and on the second time he decided to see a psychiatrist.[10] For more than
two years Musil had been frustrated in his hopes of becoming a writer,
and his whole situation must have argued powerfully for a change of
scene and occupation.

From the time he left Berlin, Musil had been determined to return to
the city, which he saw as the center of German culture and of his own
hopes as a writer. By 1910 the balance of cultural power had shifted
from Vienna to Berlin, and the new art movements of Munich and
Dresden were focusing on the German capital. For Musil, Berlin represented his student years, Martha's family, his frienships with Allesch,
Blei, and Kerr, and his connections with the literary world. Although he
remained in Vienna until the summer of 1913, he visited Berlin as often
as possible and kept in touch through the *Neue Rundschau* and the
Berliner Tageblatt. In 1911 Kerr arranged for him to do an article for
Pan, but Musil's real opportunity came through Blei. In January, 1913,
Musil's essays began to appear regularly in Blei's new journal, *Der lose
Vogel*, and in the spring Musil took an extended vacation in Berlin to

7. *TE*, pp. 132–46. Musil's ideas for a novel taking place on another planet included
bringing Martha together with her other husbands, a collective suicide and reconstruction after death, and a variety of other situations to satirize conventional assumptions
about sexuality and religion. See also *Nachlass*, H. 7, p. 11.
8. *Prosa*, p. 567.
9. *TE*, p. 137. The diary from 1911 reports a diagnosis of angina pectoris. At about
this time Musil's mother was trying to convince the couple to move to Brno, and Musil
was deeply concerned about his father's worsening health.
10. Musil went to Dr. Otto Pötzl (1877–1962), whose blend of classicial, experimental, and Freudian training Musil seems to have found congenial.

visit Allesch. It was probably on this trip that he conferred with Samuel Fischer about a permanent position with the *Neue Rundschau*. Although he returned briefly to Vienna, he continued to contribute articles to a number of German literary and political reviews throughout 1913. After a long Italian vacation in the fall, he moved to Berlin to become an editor of the *Neue Rundschau*.[11] Musil later remarked that had he not begun to write for *Der lose Vogel* he might have fallen away from literature entirely and become a gentleman-diplomat on the model of Andrian-Werburg.[12] Instead, 1913 was the year when he climbed out of his social destiny as an Austrian mandarin and formulated the fundamental spiritual and cultural assumptions that informed his project as a *Dichter*.

Nearly all of Musil's important pre-war essays appeared in 1913, in *Die neue Rundschau, Die Aktion, Die weissen Blätter, Revolution,* and most frequently of all, in *Der lose Vogel*. With the exception of the *Neue Rundschau,* all of these German periodicals were founded just a few years before the war in response to a new generation of writers and a relatively limited audience of cognoscenti. Politically, they ranged from the moderate liberalism of the *Neue Rundschau* to the millenarian anarchism of Franz Pfemfert's *Die Aktion,* the most militant of the journals of early expressionism. Kerr, Blei, and Paul Cassirer were anti-Wilhelmine democrats and opponents of social imperialism, but the younger writers of Germany tended to be anarchist, syndicalist, and revolutionary, looking to the visions of Luxemburg, Liebknecht, Sorel, Lenin, Landauer, Mussolini, and Mehring. The modes of political opposition varied, but all the new journals shared a critical attitude toward positivism, whether capitalist or socialist.[13]

Musil's work for these journals represented the fruition of his hope of

11. Fischer's decision to hire Musil was a conscious attempt to make contact with the younger generation and to compete with the flood of new periodicals that had begun to appear in Germany around 1910. See Fontana, "Erinnerungen an Robert Musil," in *LWW*, p. 325.

12. *TE*, p. 446. It was during this summer that Musil wrote "Fliegenpapier Tanglefoot," finding an image of the individual's social destiny in a fly's frustrated struggle to resist sinking into fly-paper.

13. An excellent reference for the outpouring of periodicals in Germany around 1910 is Fritz Schlawe's *Literarische Zeitschriften*, parts 1 and 2 (Stuttgart, 1961–1962). For a thoughtful discussion of German periodicals see Harry Pross, *Literatur und Politik: Geschichte und Programme der politischen Zeitschriften im deutschen Sprachgebiet seit 1870* (Olten und Freiburg im B., 1963). Musil's pre-war essays have received relatively little attention. The most recent study of Musil's essays and attitudes toward society (Hartmut Böhme, *Anomie und Entfremdung* [Kronberg Ts., 1974]) emphasizes the period between 1918 and 1923.

becoming a freelance writer, but it also marked a considerable departure from his earlier disdainful attitude toward journalism and political
literati. As late as 1910, he had stated the *Dichter*'s prejudices quite
clearly: "Feuilletonism, even that in *Die neue Rundschau* or *Pan*, is
loathsome." Even Kerr tended to subsume mere literature under a larger
project of propaganda, while Musil saw literature as the "creation or
working out of possibilities . . . for an intellectual-emotional goal." At
the same time, Musil sensed that something was missing in his aggressively apolitical contempt for literati. He confessed that he could
not maintain an altogether clear conscience about his asocial view of art
in relation to Kerr, Blei, and the liberal-democratic critics of social imperialism. The social direction of *Pan* challenged his aestheticism, and
he found in Kerr's affinity with Heine and the Young Germans the "sole
antipode which sometimes threatens my righteousness." Thanks to the
encouragement of Kerr and Blei, Musil began to incorporate a new social awareness into his thought, to bridge the gap between art and society. He was searching for a mode of criticism which would be consistent with the rigorous integrity of his own artistic vision, and it was a
defense of the tradition of decadent art since Flaubert that initially drew
Musil into the political arena.[14]

Musil's attempt to relate his art to broader social issues grew out of
Pan's quarrel over censorship with the president of the Berlin police. In
"Das Unanständige und Kranke in der Kunst," Musil not only reiter-
ated the conventional case for artistic freedom, but made an aggressive
argument for the moral value of perversity in art. He argued that "art
not only ought to portray the immoral and the repugnant, but may also
love them." In fact, the representation of perversity was central to the
ethical task of art: "In truth, there is no perversity which would not
have its correlative health and morality, as it were. This presumes that
for all the elements of which it is composed there are analogies in the
soul that live virtuously in other people." Moreover, the German mania
for "healthy" art actually interfered with art's contribution to the moral
health of society:

Art too seeks knowledge: it represents the indecent and the morbid in terms of
their relationship to the healthy, and that means nothing other than: it furthers
the knowledge of the decent and the healthy.

It was inappropriate to apply categories of social utility, health, and morality to the artist's search for knowledge. The artist himself was not

14. *TE*, pp. 120, 128–29, 133.

pathological, but he portrayed the deviant in order to "further the register of what is inwardly still possible." The one-sidedness of bourgeois morality had so diminished man and so narrowed his possibilities that the only route to understanding the fully healthy was the exploration of the perverse, of those regions not yet reduced to mechanical formulations of mental health and illness. While insisting that the artist's exploration of spiritual possibility did not belong to the realm of practical reality, Musil acknowledged the progressive social implications of such an art. The danger was that conservative repression might smother the healthy impact of art on the growth and maturation of social life: "People must learn to think differently in real life in order to understand art. One defines as moral some purpose of the community, but with an increasing number of permissible side roads."[15]

Although Musil published nothing for the next two years, he continued to explore this ethical perspective in his Vienna diaries between 1911 and 1913. His notes reveal a search for an approach to morality which would open up a richer, more complex spiritual life. The close connection between his ethical thought and his essayistic mode is apparent from a note on *Anna Karenina* in 1911. Musil thought of portraying a figure who had grown up in Christian morality to see if he would arrive at Musil's own morality. He wanted to embody this Christian culture "softly, undogmatically, and attractively in a mother whom one can love." But the thought breaks off with Musil's characteristic conclusion that he "has no morality. Reason: for me everything becomes fragments of a theoretical system. I have given up on philosophy, so the justification falls away. There remain only: insights." But these insights hinted at the pieces of a theoretical system which he had no desire to freeze into a fixed form. In his undogmatic approach to ethics, Musil rejected the categories of good and evil, altruism and egoism, as moralistic oversimplifications which were, at most, justifiable for the regulation of social life. In place of these formulations, he suggested the more neutral and empirical language of "ego-petal" and "ego-fugal" in order to emphasize that all moral life goes out from its centers in the emotional balance of individuals.[16]

In Austrian culture, Christianity offered the obvious alternative to Musil's own intense inwardness: "Love thy neighbor as thyself: there is no clearer certainty of the feelings." He admired Christianity as "edu-

15. Musil, "Das Unanständige und Kranke in der Kunst," *Pan* (March 11, 1911): pp. 303–310.
16. *TE*, p. 137.

cation to shared, active life," but for him the gulf between the ethical condition and integration into the commonality was too great. In this respect, he saw his preoccupation with feelings as psychologically unhealthy rather than immoral. Intellectually, Musil could recognize the value of integrating the ethical self into shared, practical life; emotionally, he felt the appeal of participation, duty, and the feeling of being justified. In reality, however, he found himself cut off from meaningful participation in the life of his society. Moreover, despite the appeal of Christianity, he was convinced that "the mistakes begin as soon as one tries to force this happiness on others."[17]

Musil believed that bourgeois culture had too narrowly defined morality from the perspective of altruism and duty, as an ethos of coercive individualism: "An exclusive morality of duty, without bringing it into relation with the condition of feeling of the individual, is not enough. . . . For an exaggerated consciousness of duty can be just as sick as the lack of it." The sign of health was the congruence of duty and the condition of feeling in the individual. Eschewing Nietzsche's tendency to moralize, Musil explored the meaning of altruism in the bourgeois-Christian world. In his elaboration of the relationship between the ego-fugal and the ego-petal, he concluded that "the decisive thing about the value of this whole possibility would be whether one could be ego-fugal without doing damage to the personality." Alert to the pathologies of both authority and rebellion in a morally repressive society, Musil argued for a sense of duty and communal action which would express an inner balance and growth. In this way, social action might be a creative expression of health rather than a pathological lurch toward duty or undigested ideals.[18]

In "Moralische Fruchtbarkeit," an article for *Der lose Vogel*, Musil rejected the style of moralizing which depends on verbal polarities. He argued that a mature ethical vision, which had grown up to the precision and clarity of scientific language, would have to admit that there are in reality no fundamental or absolutely final moral oppositions, but only practical, impure combinations; that formulations like good and evil correspond to an earlier, pre-scientific condition of thought which

17. Ibid., pp. 137–38.
18. Ibid., p. 138, and cf. p. 113. Musil saw in Altenberg a balance to the model of Christ in moving toward an image of humanity "in which everything can happen." This balance yielded the notion of one who "accepts all teasing about his excess of goodness, because he knows that he is good on his own account, not out of duty, but rather out of the value of feeling."

depended almost entirely on polar oppositions. Musil denied the appropriateness of such terms as egoism even in cases of extreme pathology. Even the sex criminal or murderer is attempting to express his emotional pain and to have an impact on others, and the concept of egoism would apply only to "an automatism without accompanying consciousness." What is ordinarily called egoism turns out to be "an emotional relation to the environment, a relation between I and Thou which is difficult at both ends." Even the act of love contains within it an element of assault, and vice versa. Hate and love blur into one another as expressions of moral aggressiveness, sustained by the human need for impact on others: "Altruism and egoism are possibilities for the expression of this moral imagination, but together they are nothing more than two among the many forms which have never been counted."[19]

Musil recognized the practical need for such distinctions in law, which has to concern itself with punishing antisocial acts. But moralists make the mistake of assuming that the inner lives of criminals and saints correspond to such distinctions. Even utilitarians cannot bear to think how adventurous morality really is; instead, they give up on empiricism in the moral realm in favor of duty. For Musil, every attempt to make duty a stranger (a force from the outside with appropriate dignity) was an evasion of the real terror of moral life, which is something much more fluid and solitary than that:

Morality begins in earnest only in the solitude which separates each from the other. The incommunicable, the encapsulation in the self, is what makes people need good and evil. Good and evil, duty and failure to be dutiful are forms in which the individual establishes a balance between himself and the world.

These are helpful oversimplifications of the real relations, but "no one does more harm to morality than those good-*vs.*-evil urchins, who in insipid horror over the form of a phenomenon reject what lies behind it." It is not hard to understand Musil's sense of debt to the author of *Beyond Good and Evil* or the difficulty of bringing this intense ethical inwardness into relation with practical obligations in society. Musil never lost sight of the repressive and distorting elements in social action and ideology, but social issues and the need for shared, active life increasingly became more important in his thought.[20]

19. Musil [Anon.], "Moralische Fruchtbarkeit," *Der lose Vogel*, no. 8–9 (1913): 283–84.
20. Ibid., p. 285. In place of firm oppositions between good and evil, Musil preferred to think in terms of what deserves to be opposed and what deserves to be supported.

In his concern for loosening the bonds of a repressive culture, Musil placed great importance on the changing roles of women in European society. But his articles in *Der lose Vogel* emphasized the revolutions in dress, emotions, and private life, rather that the more conspicuous battle for political suffrage. Much as he admired the courage of feminists in Sweden and elsewhere, he had a low opinion of the spiritual significance of political leaders and generals, whether male or female. The fundamental importance of the changing role of women lay:

> not in the realm of the emancipation of the woman but, rather, in the emancipation of the man from traditional styles of eroticism; and the path sketched by ideology runs: from the passive enfranchisement of women to sensuousness and from there to a refined humanity.[21]

The dualism between male and female had become just another instance of the rigidity of bourgeois morality, and Musil looked to changes in clothing as a way to open up the tremendous variation of personality that was hidden beneath the impersonal distinction of sex.[22] He recalled the range of feminine types in European history from the daughters of Wotan to Athena, and he looked to the recovery of possibilities lost since the last sexual investigation of the divine had been undertaken in the Middle Ages. In the nineteenth century's reduction of the feminine to a single norm, "whole countries of the soul have been lost and submerged; European experiences and personalities are here to be found again."[23]

For Musil, the rigidity of masculine and feminine stereotypes was central to the crisis of European culture. Although his critique of repressive moralities of duty anticipated Freud's *Civilization and Its Discontents*, Musil was already moving beyond Freud's assumptions about women and eroticism. Musil saw that the structure of bourgeois morality rested on a narrow and exclusive definition of eroticism, which Freud himself tended to assume as a biological given. The European house of sentimentality was founded on the woman's attachment to the man in all things, at the expense of both the individual and society:

> It is already a pleasure not to be the exclusive thought of a woman, but a central element in her interests. . . . A time could come when . . . the bipolar erotic would seem a sin or a weakness, almost as mindless as obliviousness toward the loved one in unfaithfulness.[24]

21. Musil [Anon.], "Penthesileadie," *Der lose Vogel*, no. 1 (1913):24.
22. Musil [Anon.], "Erinnerung an eine Mode," *Der lose Vogel*, no. 1 (1913):17–19.
23. Musil [Anon.], "Penthesileadie," p. 24.
24. Ibid., p. 25.

Here the author of *Vereinigungen* began to envision the social implications of his art, drawing into question the economy of guilt, sex, and civilization which informed Freud's work.

Musil looked forward to a new openness of erotic relations and emotional realization, perhaps in triangles or even "in completely multipolar relations." As if it were not enough for Musil to challenge the bourgeois conception of marriage, he suggested a surprising implication of the death of bourgeois-Christian culture when he found his view anticipated "in the balance called for by Christianity between married love and love of neighbor":

> And so, when finally eroticism—which today is actually in opposition to the commonality and degenerates under a cowardly feeling of shame—allows the limits to fall away, rejects every artificial feeling of shame, in order again to seek for something more inward and personal, when the reliance of the ego on conquest requires no locked and protected places of retreat, the inclusion of all human relations in the sexual will be possible.[25]

For Musil, the precondition for understanding this possibility was a fuller understanding of the emotional disease of European culture.

Blei's *Der lose Vogel*, which appeared for only a year in 1913, provided an ideal vehicle for Musil's ethical thought; more than any other journal, it expressed Musil's own sense of generational and ideological identity. Restricting itself to a small group of contributors, the journal carried poems by Brod, Werfel, and Walser, and unsigned essays by Alain, Blei, Musil, Scheler, Suarès, and a few others. *Der lose Vogel's* search for new modes of spirituality was marked by an affection for the French tradition from Montaigne to Péguy and by a rejection of all doctrine and dogma. In religious terms this meant an openness to grace and mysticism; in political terms, a disenchantment with existing institutions in the wake of the Dreyfus Affair, the Russian Revolution of 1905, and the ossification of liberalism and socialism in Central Europe. One unsigned review recommended books and authors which suggested the kind of audience the editors had in mind. The recommended authors ranged from Confucius and Lao-tse to Buber and Kierkegaard, but the most striking aspect of this review is the emphasis on essayism as a distinctive literary mode appropriate to a period of transition which lacked a dominant philosophical system. The reviewer mentioned Georg Lukács's *Die Seele und die Formen* (1911) as the model of this type, and added Musil, H. Reisinger, Andrey Bjeley, and French writers such as

25. Ibid., p. 26.

Claudel, Gide, and Suarès. According to the reviewer, essayism or "the intellectual poem" was the most flexible and appropriate genre for the finest minds of this generation of spiritual uncertainty.[26] For Musil, essayism was the intellectual counterpart to his personal struggle to mediate between social responsibility and the emotional economy of the individual.

In "Essaybücher" (a review of Hermann Bahr and Franz Blei) Musil distinguished the essay from flowery rectorial addresses and left-over professional writings:

> Its thoughts rest firmly and inseparably in a substratum of feeling, desire, personal experience, and connections of ideas, which gain and yield sense only in the psychological atmosphere of a unique spiritual situation. They make no claim to universal validity, but affect us like people who impress us and yet elude us without our being able to make rational sense of them, and who infect us with something spiritual that cannot be proven. They may even contain contradictions; for in the essay what has the form of a judgment is only a momentary formulation of something that can be grasped in no other way.

This definition, which anticipated the formulations of *The Man without Qualities*, seemed to Musil to offer a solution to the contemporary intellectual situation. Distinguishing the essay from the universality of philosophy and from conventional scientific standards of proof, Musil insisted on its contextual and personal significance: "One sees this in philosophical attempts to extract conceptually something scientific from great essayists: for example, from Emerson or Nietzsche."[27]

As the representative mode of the generation, essayism also revealed the predicament of a period of ideological uncertainty. In his discussion of Bahr's *Inventur*, Musil diagnosed the characteristic disease of the essayist: the syndrome of radical skepticism, intellectual despair, and irrational faith. Musil cautioned against the temptations of this learned skepticism that moves too easily from ignorance in a limited field to exaggerated skepticism about all knowledge. After making earnest but unrealistic claims on intellect, the essayist could discover complexity and contradiction—and then liberate himself to despair or irrationalism. Musil believed that even the best minds of his "age of spiritual [*seelisch*] reform" spoke irresponsibly about reason and knowledge, and he rejected the temptation "to make oneself more stupid than one is in order to descend to the desired height of feeling." In a culture that took for granted the polarity between corrosive reason and artistic feeling, the

26. Anon., *Der lose Vogel*, no. 1 (1913):36–37.
27. Musil, "Essaybücher," *Die neue Rundschau* 24, 9 (September 1913):1316–17.

task of the essayist was demanding: "The person who thinks artistically is threatened today by the person who does not think artistically and by the artist who does not think." Musil refused to succumb to the intellectual despair of so many pre-war intellectuals who saw in the loss of a specific world-view grounds for giving up on thought altogether. He argued that the long alternation between epistemological certainty and radical agnosticism, between the "conceptual Gothic of the scholastics" and the "godly, clever Bishop Berkeley," was nothing more than a relative quarrel over a question of limits: "Radical skepticism . . . has never been seriously believed by any theoretician; it would have gone against all his favorite habits." Musil saw great signs of intellectual promise in what looked to others like cultural decay, and he judged it the worst kind of capitulation to despair just at a time when these limits were being established "without pathos and apparently with success." Despite his intelligence, Bahr displayed the typical tendency of the age to rush from insights to easy solutions not genuinely won, doing so by means of "a slight exaggeration of everything which is alogical and a slight understatement of everything that is understanding."[28]

This criticism was no mere academic matter; it bore directly on the capacity of intellect and knowledge to guide and shape the ethical life. Musil agreed with Bahr's analysis of Mach, Vaihinger, and James, which led to the conclusion that "in certain matters intellect does not suffice, inwardly we cannot live by it alone." But Bahr's encomiums to goodness or the whole man did not begin to touch on the complexity of the task which confronted the intellect in this realm. The man "who is good without constraints" was at best a goal, and "what is recommended to us today" as an alternative to degenerate literary types in the guise of "the good, symmetrical, healthy human beings—even in literature which counts as serious—is terribly cheap." The skepticism and agnosticism of this age of spiritual disorder seemed to have an odd symptom: "Its answers do not lack certainty, but rather that uncertainty which a sharply inquiring intellect would bring to them." The false skepticism of the age, its intolerance of science, and its resistance to intellect in the realm of the feelings all led consistently to premature dogmatic formulations. For Musil, essayism was not only a means of mediating between science and art, but also a way of doing combat for both in the name of the future.[29]

Many of Musil's contemporaries, in their craving for metaphysics and

28. Ibid., pp. 1316–18.
29. Ibid., pp. 1318–20.

religion, were inclined to blame science and reason for cultural despair and disorder. The liberal intellectuals of Germany had already made cultural decline into a commonplace, as poets and Gymnasium graduates stood in line to denigrate the destructive impact of science and to praise intuition and Rousseauist feeling at the expense of mere reason. Although Musil did distinguish essayism from science, what was distinctive about his position was that it bore a positive relation to science at all. He was not the typical graduate of a humanistic Gymnasium; he had no classical languages, and he was good at mathematics. His entire education and training until his early thirties had taught him disdain for "all moral and *geisteswissenschaftlichen* subjects."[30]

For Musil, science was not a threat to tradition; it was itself a tradition, on its way to creating a new civilization. While his contemporaries saw only the burnt-out remains of a demolished past, Musil looked to the sixteenth and seventeenth centuries as a fruitful beginning. He saw the achievements of Copernicus, Kepler, Galileo, Newton, and Leibniz as the spiritual watershed of the modern world. The model of the mathematician represented that glorious boldness of reason which had created modern civilization:

> The rest of us lost our courage after the Enlightenment. A minor failure was enough to turn us away from reason, and we permitted every barren enthusiast to inveigh against the intentions of a d'Alembert or a Diderot as mere rationalism. We beat the drums for feeling against intellect and forgot that without it— aside from a few exceptional cases—feeling is a thing as dense as a blockhead. In this way we have ruined our imaginative literature so badly that every time one reads two German novels in a row, one must pause a moment to vomit.[31]

As an antidote to German culture's abuse of science and intellect, Musil invited anxious literary metaphysicians to adopt the model of the mathematician:

> There is no denying that outside their subject mathematicians are banal or silly minds, that they themselves have left their logic in the lurch. There it is none of their business, and they do in their field what we should do in ours. Therein consists the significant lesson and model of their existence; they are an analogy for the spiritual man to come.[32]

Science had created the basis for a new world, and it was senseless to reproach it with being soulless. The scientific understanding had simply

---

30. *TE*, p. 141.
31. Musil, "Der mathematische Mensch," *Der lose Vogel*, no. 10-11-12 (1913), in *TE*, p. 595.
32. Ibid.

done "in a realm of interest of the second order what we ought to have done in the questions of life."[33]

Musil saw great promise in the spiritual pluralism of his age, and he believed that science and technology had already created a civilization more universal than anything previously imagined. Science and technology were transforming and unifying the world, yet liberal intellectuals could only lament that peasants in Bavaria and electricians in Berlin did not share the same culture. The real problem, Musil argued, was not science, but the sheer scale of modern social and political institutions. What his contemporaries called cultural decline was actually only disunity and pluralism; despite its universality, science had had little unifying effect because of the uneven growth of modern culture. The achievements of science simply drew attention to a pre-existing social and cultural variety and to the failure of Europeans to come to terms with the conditions of life in the modern world. The huge scale of modern institutions and social life had "released a formless excess of feeling," which was no longer contained by universally shared values, symbols, and rituals.[34] What remained, as the typical pattern of modern life, was a senseless alternation between the routine of meaningless work and escape into hysterical leisure.

The development of science had imposed professionalization and specialization on socially and culturally various human beings in the absence of corresponding emotional and spiritual growth. Thus, the normal situation among Musil's educated contemporaries was the "existence of powerful specialized brains in the souls of children"; while amassing tremendous professional expertise, they continued to live "the life of that spiritual [seelischen] village from which they happen[ed] to come."[35] Musil found this condition of cultural multiplicity and the corresponding isolation and insecurity of the individual to be in a particularly advanced stage in Austria. For Musil's generation the divine logic of history had collapsed into technological civilization and a maze of competing partial ideologies. Musil understood the despair this inspired in his contemporaries, but he wanted to emphasize the positive dimensions of a situation normally perceived as simply negative. The recognition of the failure of all existing ideologies, philosophies, and moralities was the precondition for the creation of a new culture. As the

33. Musil, "Politisches Bekenntnis," p. 240.
34. Musil [Anon.], "Das Geistliche, der Modernismus, und die Metaphysik," *Der lose Vogel*, no. 2 (1913):74.
35. Musil, "Politisches Bekenntnis," pp. 240–41.

paradigm of modern liberal culture, Austria symbolized what was positive in this situation: "For today's inability to judge is tomorrow's lack
of prejudice."[36]

Musil rejected the conventional explanation of the decline of religion
in terms of the rise of science; instead, he emphasized the rationalization and centralization of state power and the failed response of the
church to science, the state, and bourgeois reason in general. The pro-
longed struggle between church and state "began with the church allowing itself to want to rule the state in the state's way" and "ended with
the church being ruled in the church's way, that of invisible spiritual
penetration." The church had succumbed so completely to this process
(particularly in Austria) that baptism, once the pure expression of the
otherworldly resistance of the church to the state, had now become the
epitome of bureaucratic procedure and paper-registration. While the
state grew powerful with the victory of reason, the church was left help-
less, hanging on to its dogmas in a literal way, but "for a long time now
without the least understanding of the enormous not-yet-outlived value
of their unreason." Although medieval scholasticism won Musil's admiration for making the human being the goal of metaphysics, this attempt had collapsed under the pressure of modern science. The Aristotelian system had been worn out from two thousand years of use: "It
might easily have been replaced by a new one. But the church found
nothing appropriate for that."[37]

The breakdown of scholasticism was only one aspect of the spiritual
watershed of modernity. The cosmopolitan intellectual culture of Central Europe in the sixteenth and seventeenth centuries also represented a
time when it had not yet been discovered that science and religion were
inimical. Kepler, Leibniz, and even Galileo were not yet aware that only
Aristotelians and bad mathematicians could be Christians. Similarly,
Musil very much doubted that St. Francis of Assisi would have been attracted to the notion that truths of feeling ought to stand in opposition
to science. Science was concerned only with regularities, with what re-
curred in the midst of change. It cared nothing for the unique, the accidental, the pure event, which was still virgin territory for a reason

36. Musil [Anon.], "Politik in Österreich," *Der lose Vogel*, no. 6 (1913) (again in *Die
Aktion*, July 1913), in *TE*, p. 591.
37. Musil [Anon.], "Das Geistliche," pp. 72–73. Musil's analysis suggests a familiarity with German sociology of culture. He was aware of the work of Naumann, Scheler,
Simmel, Sombart, and Rathenau, but it is not clear how much he knew about Troeltsch
and Weber before the war.

"which would give new and bold direction to the feelings, . . . an intellectual skeleton of support to a way of being human which has not yet taken form."[38]

Musil was as critical of the false application of reason in philosophy and theology as he was of barren enthusiasm for feeling in literature and religion. Both shared the dominant rigidity and anxiety of a bourgeois culture cut off from flexibility and growth. The characteristic fault of bourgeois reason was its misapplication of the model of natural science; in its drive for uniformity, bourgeois reason had lost track of the capacity to create value and enhance life. In its yearning for truth, concept, and abstraction, it had lost respect for the flesh, for the concrete lives of individual human beings. Bourgeois metaphysicians built bridges to a cheerless land: "In Kantian terms: they are transcendental, and the transcendent remains pure boredom." Bourgeois metaphysics had failed to be empirical, to respond to the concrete individuality of lived experience.

This insight did not drive Musil into the arms of vitalism and irrationalism. The rigidity and sterility of bourgeois thought was not a proof of the much-lamented lack of feeling in the age, but a symptom of the "formless excess of feelings" that underlay it. "Nothing is more pernicious than simply to demand more feeling from our rational age, for that means a feeling which has too long remained underdeveloped and unarticulated." Under the circumstances, an outpouring of unformed feeling could only be pathological, and the vague offerings of German cultural prophets and liberal priests were pathetic, when not actually dangerous. Musil rejected the complaints about the soullessness of materialism and mere science and the claims of an "emotional knowledge" with which to round out the world image. This petit-bourgeois mentality could manage nothing more than "an Oversoul who reads the newspaper and manifests a certain understanding of social issues." Although the German mandarin and his less successful colleagues, the prophets of cultural despair, have justly earned a special reputation for such harangues, Musil did not consider this approach peculiar to Wilhelm's Germany. He saw it as a general phenomenon of European bourgeois culture in 1913, though its fullest expression came in the following decade.[39]

On the eve of the war, Musil found his culture filled with neo-roman-

38. Ibid., pp. 75–77.
39. Ibid., pp. 74–76.

tic literary searches for God. He was interested primarily not in the political implications of this activity, but rather in the quality of spirituality it expressed. He believed that the cut-rate spiritualisms, monisms, and idealisms that buzzed about him were made possible by a culture which had lost its capacity for dealing with the things of the spirit:

In a world so at home with the mundane, so busied with the this-worldly, there is naturally something good-naturedly defenseless in relation to the purveyors of holy teaching. They enjoy the irresponsible position of house chaplain in the castle of the robber barons.[40]

Even writers who undertook valuable explorations of emotional life seemed to move too quickly from the experimental, from borderline experiences and mystical intuitions, to the affirmation of "hypothetical indemonstrables." These yearnings were "not God, but disinherited, unchanged religious feelings in search of a new master."[41] Loaded down with concepts, creative literary moments became "not legends of new spiritual discoveries [Seelenbesitz], but, rather, allegories of what has long since grown old."[42] The religious yearnings and metaphysical cravings of this time seemed to Musil to express a failure of will in liberal culture, a loss of hope, sheer anxiety in the face of being human.

Musil's most detailed reflections on bourgeois neo-romanticism and the mystical awakening in liberal culture came in a review of Walther Rathenau's Zur Mechanik des Geistes. Musil wrote his discussion of Rathenau shortly after meeting the famous businessman/philosopher (who later became the model for Arnheim in The Man without Qualities). Musil respected Rathenau and saw his book as one of the more serious attempts of its kind, but he began his review with a reminder of "the responsibility which the otherworldly has to the mundane."[43] Musil's principal criticism of Rathenau's metaphysics was his narrow conception of human nature. Rathenau's ethical ideal was a blend of love, magnanimity, independence, strength, loyalty, and firmness. Musil admitted that this might be valuable if it were portrayed in connection with lived reality, rather than abstractly, as a list of commonplaces, but at best this was only one cultural type, which hardly glimpsed the riches of even the European tradition. Rathenau's moral vision seemed to have

40. Musil, "Die Wallfahrt nach innen," Die neue Rundschau (April 1913):588.
41. Musil, "Die Wallfahrt," p. 588.
42. Ibid., p. 590.
43. Musil, "Anmerkung," in TE, p. 647; cf. TE, p. 166. At this first meeting Rathenau put his arm around Musil, as he often did with men he liked—foreshadowing the scene between Arnheim and Ulrich.

no place in it for the variety of humorists, fools, madmen, and evil geniuses who had extended the range of spiritual life in the West, to say nothing of the multitude of other types in the ancient world of Greece, Egypt, and East Asia. It seemed odd to settle for the model of one spiritual type which came out of a tradition which had lost faith in itself. Nonetheless, Musil found value in Rathenau's examination of mystical experience.

In his empirical response to his own mystical experience, Rathenau had managed to describe "the experience of soul or love" which Musil called "the fundamental experience of mysticism." This unique experience (*Erlebnis* rather than *Erfahrung*) resisted the normal categories of language, but Musil was struck by Rathenau's masterful description of this experience, which arises "through a nameless power of concentration, an inner gathering and union of the intuitive powers":

Desire dissolves itself; we are no longer ourselves and yet for the first time ourselves. The soul which awakens in this moment wants nothing and promises nothing and remains nonetheless active. It does not require law; its ethical principle is awakening and ascent. There is no ethical action, but, rather, only an ethical condition, in the context of which an immoral action or way of being is no longer possible.[44]

In this description of Rathenau's account, Musil offered his clearest prewar statement of his own spirituality, the yield of his decision to reduce the metaphysics of the romantics to its purely phenomenological content.

Musil was conscious of the impossibility of describing such conditions of awakening to someone who has never experienced them, and he knew that this mystical sense of participation in a new existence is shattered the moment one attempts to formulate it in words. He saw three possible responses to the discovery of this condition: one may simply accept it as the strange and fragile experience that it is; or, like the medieval mystics, one may assume the permanent possibility of God which corresponds to the accessibility of this condition, an option Musil did not consider very lively in 1914; or, one may attempt to see the world from the perspective of this heightened spirituality. The value of Rathenau's book lay in his effort to do the last of these, but he fell

44. Ibid., pp. 648–49. Cf. *TE*, p. 168: "One thinks, one must believe in the suprasensuous [*Übersinnliche*]; it exists, one says to oneself, as soon as one is in this magic world, secretly [*heimisch*] like a child." This follows a very brief description of his fairytale experience with a heavenly bird one night in May of 1914. Cf. "Die Amsel," in *Prosa*, pp. 521–35.

into the typical fault of the metaphysical pundits of the age: disguising himself behind an aura of mystical awakening, Rathenau offered a rational system like any other, which "distinguishes itself from scientific understanding only through the fact that it renounces its virtues of methodology and precision." Rathenau employed the magical method of transforming a legitimate insight into an unquestioned piece of a system. What arose was the worst of both worlds: a pseudo-system, and "a certain vacuum of the feelings" which lost track of the spiritual content. As usual, medieval verbiage crowded out the original experience and insight, freezing the flesh into the reassuring totality and unity of a system. Once again Musil found himself caught between the solitude of the ethical condition and the dishonesty and confusion of contemporary moralities, metaphysics, and ideologies.[45]

Musil applied a similar analysis to the politics of Central Europe. Although he was not a Karl Kraus or a Maximilian Harden, Musil understood that the political situation of Europe in 1913 no longer permitted the luxury of aloof indifference. In his "Political Confessions of a Young Man" he frankly acknowledged his privileged position near the pinnacle of a highly stratified social order. This had allowed him until recently to be apolitical and to see politics as a specialty of secondary importance. He had always perceived politicians and bureaucrats as servants in his house, who saw to it "that the dust did not get too deep and that dinner was ready on time." One did not expect that this work would be done particularly well, but as long as the situation did not become catastrophic there was no real point in getting involved. He looked with loving irony on the inadequacy of rich people, kings, and unbelievers who lived in a Christian state; and he found himself enjoying this spectacle because of his appreciation of "the great inner disorder itself."[46]

The absurd political and ideological contradictions of his day seemed to him the result of the recent speed-up of human evolution, and he was aware that members of his class found the accompanying tendency toward democracy and mass society profoundly disturbing. Although Musil was not indifferent to the negative effects of this leveling process, one day it occurred to him that "You yourself are already . . . a creature of democracy, and the future is only to be achieved through an intensified and purer democracy."[47] Musil was conscious of belonging to an

45. Musil, "Anmerkung," p. 650.
46. Musil, "Politisches Bekenntnis," p. 238.
47. Ibid., p. 239.

elite which was virtually an aristocracy itself, and yet was the product of
two hundred years of democratization. Even in science, once a legitimate bastion of elitism, the genius of one generation hardly exceeded
the average of the next; not only did a larger number of people participate in this process, but the aristocratic selection of talent had become
increasingly less important.

Musil saw the principal obstacle to democracy in the ideological
rigidity of all existing parties. Although he admitted that in practice he
would vote for the Social Democrats or Liberals, he defined himself politically as a "conservative anarchist." In this he expressed his critical
attitude toward "the flatness of contemporary parties." The ideologically defined parties of Germany and Austria were trapped by irrelevant
theories they themselves no longer took seriously. Neither fighting for
their ideals nor responding to empirical reality, they settled for abusing
the few meager ideas which had been bequeathed to the opposition. The
socialists were at least open to the future, but even they shared in the
same irresponsible system of long-windedness and petty *Realpolitik*.
The disjunction in Germany and Austria between imperial bureaucra-
cies and constitutionally weak parliaments invited political parties to
indulge in ideological symphonies. Since no one ever followed through
on these ideologies, "they gained the appearance of meaning and the
sacred, which among other things is also a sin against the spirit." Fragmented by ideological differences, these parties were incapable of responding to real problems:

> I am convinced that none of them has an economic program which could be
> carried out, and that one should not even bother to give thought to improving
> one of them. They will be blown away as soon as the wind comes up, like a lot
> of shit which has piled up on the still ground. They will be falsely formulated
> questions, to which no Yes or No ought to be given any longer, as soon as a
> yearning passes through the world. I have no proof for that, but I know that,
> like me, a lot of people are waiting.[48]

This was Musil's most expressionist statement on pre-war politics and a
trenchant justification of the apolitical intellectual. The hopeless political and institutional situation of Central Europe offered him no foot-
hold for meaningful political action.

Unike most of his contemporaries, however, Musil did not blame capitalism for this situation. Much as he despised many of the cultural

48. Ibid., pp. 241–43.

manifestations of capitalism, Musil was inclined to resign himself to a
capitalist-democratic version of mass society. He understood the revulsion against money, but he wondered what person or institution would
be more trustworthy than market relations. "Even money does not divide itself according to justice, but it divides itself at least according to
luck and accident, and it is not the stabilized hopelessness that the all-
powerful state would be."[49] In this Musil rejected the conservative critique of culture and capitalism and anticipated his reservations about
communism in the post-war period. This analysis cut Musil off from
meaningful practical action, but he believed his task as an intellectual
was to clear away the dead wood of ideology which stood in the way of
progress.

For Musil, Austria was the pure type of the purposelessness and vac-
uousness of European politics in 1913. He saw the apparent passion for
politics and the endless quarrels among the nationalities as a "pretext,"
for behind all this activity there "staggers the emptiness of the inner life,
like the emptiness in the stomach of an alcoholic." His description of
Austria in 1913 foreshadowed his portrayal of the state without qualities—Kakania—as the most modern state of all:

> There is something uncanny in this obstinate rhythm without melody, with-
> out words, without feeling. Somewhere in this state there must be hidden a se-
> cret, an idea. But it cannot be determined. It is not the idea of the state, not the
> dynastic idea, not the idea of a cultural symbiosis of different peoples (Austria
> might be a world experiment)—probably the whole thing is really a result of the
> lack of a driving idea, like the spinning of a bicycle that does not go forward.

While Musil did not join the ideological frenzy of Germans, liberals,
and nationalists of all sorts against the Habsburgs, he was hardly a sentimental Austrian of the old school. Neither did he consider the Austrian state any more immoral than its neighbors. He simply noted that
its state of political stalemate, confusion, and purposelessness was more
pronounced than elsewhere, enough so that its politicians could no
longer take their own quarrels quite seriously.[50]

The old regime was in a serious state of dysfunction. Like the rest of
Europe, Austria seemed unable to respond; it lacked the focus of human
and political purpose that could transform it. This cultural boredom
and political listlessness expressed a spiritual disorder in which

49. Ibid., p. 243.
50. Musil, "Politik in Österreich," pp. 589–90.

one treasures catastrophes, since they take the responsibility upon themselves, and one needs misfortune, since it generates violent gestures, behind which people disappear and become conventional. One lives political life like a Serbian epic, since heroism is the most impersonal form of action.[51]

Within less than a year the Serbian epic took the responsibility upon itself, providing an epoch of heroism, violence, and impersonality to unleash the formless excess of feeling that Musil had feared. For the remainder of his life, the complex problems of Central Europe became the focus for Europe's malaise, cruelty, and collapse.

2. THE REVOLT AGAINST CIVILIZATION: 1914—1919

Many a writer of a basically contemplative type has been
driven to participation in the life of the community by the
social conditions of his time.[52]

If a *future* is to be hoped for at all, it can come only from
selflessness or equivalent qualities and institutions.[53]

August 1914 opened the door on an age of violence which demolished the world from which Musil came. But the war also gave more universal meaning and substance to the inwardness of his spiritual journey. The "five-year slavery of the war" provided him with the central project of his mature thought: understanding the spiritual preconditions of what he perceived as a massive revolt against civilization.[54] The passions of Germans for the nation in 1914 and for a new European order in 1917—1919 were the two experiences around which his political thought revolved; and the negation of these two possibilities at Versailles ended the period of his preoccupation with politics. Although Musil was neither a politician nor a political thinker, his aloof, aesthetic posture toward society became impossible in practice between 1914 and 1919: the outbreak of war drew him into the life of the German nation with a violence that surprised him even then, and the disaster of Austria and Europe became his firsthand experience and professional responsibility.

51. Ibid., p. 592: "Necessity and the hero go together like sickness and fever. Every violent act has therefore something pathological about it, a limitation of consciousness."
52. Georg Lukács, *Studies in European Realism* (London, 1964), p. 12.
53. *TE*, p. 236.
54. Ibid., p. 213.

Viewing the outbreak of war in Berlin, Musil was struck by the sudden passion of civilized men for violence and death: "People throw themselves in front of trains because they are not allowed to go into the field. . . . Psychotics are in their element, live themselves out to the full."[55] Even Musil, with all his ironic distance, felt that everything had been changed and that his inner balance had been dramatically shifted toward more primitive emotions and a passionate sense of the nation. He was deeply impressed by the power of that moment and its revolutionary force against the entire existing order. He felt this sense of brotherhood with other Germans as an idealistic vision of community and a real physical presence of emotional commonality. The upheaval went on too long to leave anything positive behind, but even the resentment and resignation of the post-1919 period could not make Musil forget that initial religious experience. One may wonder how this critical intellectual and urbane Austrian mandarin could have found himself caught up in German nationalism and the outbreak of war. Musil wondered himself, and *The Man without Qualities* was in part an attempt to make sense of this fact.

In his last article for the *Neue Rundschau* in September 1914, Musil emphasized that the war represented a fundamental departure from fifty years of European peace. This break in the moral lives of Europeans was particularly shocking for liberal intellectuals. Musil felt himself torn between his place in a European minority whose "most valuable spiritual [*seelischen*] achievements over the past thirty years were directed almost entirely against the prevailing social order and the feelings on which it depended" and the sudden appeal of the nation to values that had no place in their vision of a higher form of humanity: "Loyalty, subordination, duty, and simplicity." The whole world had been simplified into screams of German and anti-German, and Musil was conscious that all Germans felt inwardly devalued by the hatred of Europeans. He was also convinced of the inadequacy of his own elitism in the face of national solidarity, and he tried to come to terms with the discovery of intellectuals throughout Europe that they were possessed by an atavistic feeling of which they had been unaware, of identification with the nation and willingness to sacrifice for the tribe.[56]

Musil resisted the temptation to indulge in the patriotic justifications

55. Ibid., p. 169.
56. Musil, "Europaertum, Krieg, Deutschtum," *Die neue Rundschau* (September 1914), in *TE*, pp. 595–97.

of German preceptors such as Thomas Mann, Meinecke, and Scheler. He did not pretend that German *Kultur*, any more than Hofmannsthal's international Austria, embodied a messianic redemption from the money and worldliness of the West. Still less did he suggest that the chosen state or nation would redeem the world in war. Moreover, he reminded his German audience that friends and loved ones in other European countries were experiencing the same feelings. He was convinced, however, that nothing could ever be the same again, and he remained skeptical of intellectuals who claimed after the first moment of passion to have regained their balance. His own response to this mystical sense of national unity set the terms for his analysis of the war and the "age of violent acts" which "began rather by surprise in the summer of 1914."[57] The mass release of unformed feelings in 1914 confirmed Musil's analysis of the cultural crisis and provided the key to his later reflections. Without attempting to give ideological justification to this explosion of passion, Musil scanned the posted lists of losses as he left for Austria: "dead . . . dead . . . dead."[58] The last flight of his generation.

For Musil, daily life in the war was the extreme instance of the dissolution of the personal into duty, function, and collective action. He found nothing heroic in this war, and the Austrians executed the project with enough ineptitude and indifference to save him from any inclination to romanticize it. Musil was called up immediately, in August, to assume command of a company at Linz. From there he was transferred to the Italian border in South Tyrol, where he found the collective life of the army unbearable. He was struck by the lack of energy and discipline in the Austrian army, and he found himself surrounded by people who had never read a book. His sober, clinical notes capture the routine of warfare—artillery fire, airplanes, horses, flies, supply wagons, interrogation of prisoners. Musil found no mystique of personal heroism in all this, nor did he savor "life more madly . . . the way the poets tell it." But in this impersonal submission to the duty and routine of war, he found that he was "freed from a bond . . . the bondage to the will to live, terror before death. One is no longer encumbered. One is free. It is lordliness (*Herr-lichkeit*)." This attitude seems to have served him well during his year of active combat on the Southwestern front after Italy entered the war in 1915. Serving as a reconnaissance officer on a number of dan-

57. Musil, "Der Dichter und diese Zeit" (1936), in *TE*, p. 907.
58. *TE*, p. 169.

gerous missions, Musil won the admiration of those who worked with him, and he received a bronze military-service cross in recognition of his bravery. By the end of 1915 he had become a battalion adjutant and had the opportunity to participate in planning battles. His duties at the front ended in March, 1916, when he was hospitalized with a stomach ulcer, apparently from the bad food, a casualty commensurate with his disabused view of modern warfare.[59]

If the war could not inspire Musil, it did stimulate his critical intellect and his sense of humor. He conceived and partly wrote a drama entitled *Panama*, a satire on the confused values, rigid hierarchy, and vacuous protocols of the K.u.k. army. It expressed the irritation of the bourgeois officer at the incompetence and corruption of an aristocracy for whom war was the preeminent social occasion, a kind of extended polo match. Despite his sympathy for the human type of the Austrian officer, Musil could not resist satirizing the aristocracy's self-important maneuvering of divisions in a manner which managed to be oblivious both to victory and to the lives of the men in the divisions. Although Musil never published this play, *Panama* remained for him a catchword for the military spirit, crystallizing the corruption and illegitimate influence that predominated in Austria.[60] For a time he actually considered these ideas as the basis for a two-part novel, to be called the *Double Turning: I. Anarchist; II. Panama*. But the short manuscript he left behind suggests both that drama was not his natural medium and that the war did not capture the best of his imagination.

Musil's finest stories of the post-war years grew out of his sketches and personal experiences during the war. The Tyrolean countryside provided the setting for insights about love, death, and mysticism, and also about the meaning of the feminine, just at a time when he had assumed his most masculine role. He associated his mystical experiences with the countryside, with animals and peasant women, and with the proximity of death; but he found on his return to the city that the feeling was gone again. The atmosphere of the Italian front was less brutal and degrading than trench warfare in France, and Martha was able to visit Musil from time to time in Bozen, just north of Trent and Verona.

59. *TE*, pp. 471–72, 176–87.
60. *Panama*, forty-one pages, as typed from the manuscript in the *Nachlass* in 1967. The original manuscript (Dinklage numbering 51–82) was probably written up in that form in 1919.

During this alternation between the front and visits from Martha, Musil was preoccupied with the likelihood of his own death and with his intense love for Martha. He felt freed from personal caution in war and aware of a newly won youth in their reunions:

With the hope for the eternity of a relationship, love is unshakeable. Who would allow himself to be led into infidelity and sacrifice eternity for a quarter of an hour? That can occur only when one calculates mundanely. Love seen from the perspective of the man of the world.

No question where the greater power of happiness lies. Constancy. Courage in battle.

One can love at all, only if one is religious.

Unfaithfulness kills the heavenly blessedness; it is a breach of the sacrament.

The tension between his mystical love for Martha and his daily exposure to the earthy rhythms of the peasant women drew him toward another possibility: "Since he loves ecstatically, he can give free rein to his lower desires." Once again there appears the dichotomy of *Vereinigungen* between the mystical and the instinctual in love, but his notes leave the impression that although he thought a great deal about infidelity, he remained faithful to Martha.[61]

The other aspect of his mystical awareness during this period was his sense of release from the fear of death. He put this nicely in *Die Amsel* in a metaphor which echoes the last scene of *Grigia*: "It is as though the anxiety before death, which obviously always lies like a stone on human beings, were rolled away, and there now blooms in this nearness to death a strange inner freedom."[62] These feelings crystallized in an experience at Isonzo where he missed by inches being killed by airplane fire. He referred to this in his diary as the "experience of God at Isonzo," and he later portrayed this moment in *Die Amsel* as the physical presence of the divine.[63] In his proximity to death during the war, Musil seems to have found release from life and reconciliation with the anxieties about death which had troubled him before the war.

After his release from the hospital in 1916, Musil became the editor of the army newspaper for the Southwestern front, the *Tyroler Soldatenzeitung* (later *Die Soldatenzeitung*). In less than a year Musil trans-

61. TE, pp. 172–73; *Prosa*, p. 658; cf. *TE*, p. 472. Musil later compared his lifelong preoccupation with monogamy to that of "a little girl with her doll."

62. Musil, "Die Amsel," in *Prosa*, p. 528.

63. TE, p. 186. Cf. *TE*, p. 188: Musil saw the war as something the Europeans needed, a realized desire, a female angel.

formed a routine propaganda organ into a significant vehicle for political and social criticism.[64] His editorial position emphasized a critique of social privilege and the rejection of what he saw as destructive nationalism. Although both the foot-soldier's view of social privilege and the anti-irredentist line conformed to the propaganda functions of the paper, they also expressed the heritage of the mandarin and established convictions which Musil continued to hold in the post-war era. Musil served in this capacity until the paper folded in April, 1917, after covering a crucial period in the war: the turnip winter of 1916–1917. Although Austria, with the assistance of the Germans, was still holding on to the Italian front, the signs of war-weariness and internal collapse became more serious after the death of Franz Joseph in November. While the new emperor, Karl, struggled to arrange a separate peace, the Germans launched their submarine warfare, Russia suffered the first round of its revolution, and the United States entered the war.

It was in this context that Musil summed up his position of "critical patriotism" in an editorial for the last number of *Die Soldatenzeitung*. Assuming his characteristic position as mediator between Red and Black, he insisted that the tasks of reconstruction after the war could not be solved by subservience to old elites or by fanatical adherence to fixed ideas. Without recommending a specific constitutional solution to the problem of nationalities, Musil argued that the best interests of Austria would be served by a debate which stayed close to the facts, and he added that the proper function of a responsible press was to clear away the social and political obstacles to the emergence of more effective leadership. A patriotic Austrian press would open the way to the "serious, disciplined, autonomous people" who "as a result of the whole structure of political and social life . . . have too rarely found their way to public influence."[65]

After brief military duty near Trieste, Musil was transferred to Vienna, where he first encountered civilian reaction to the war. Puzzled by civilian indifference to the soldiers' sacrifices, he concluded that the age would be impossible to understand if one had met only officers and

64. Cf. Dinklage, "Musils Herkunft," in *LWW*, p. 231. Dinklage quotes from an army command memo of January 1917: "That [*Die Soldaten-Zeitung*] 'knew how to achieve an impact that was unique among military newspapers in Austria Hungary.'"

65. Anon., "Vermächtnis," (*Die Soldaten-Zeitung*, no. 45 [April 1917]), in *TE*, pp. 269–72. Musil received the Knight's Cross of the Franz-Joseph Order on March 29, 1917, and later in the year he was promoted to the rank of captain. Ironically enough, in light of Musil's frequent criticisms of the aristocracy, his father was awarded a patent of the lower nobility on October 22, 1917, though Musil declined to use the title himself.

troops.[66] Eduard Donath was trying to secure him a regular civil-service position, but meanwhile Musil was assigned to another military newspaper. The propaganda weekly *Heimat* had been created by the press section of the war ministry for the express purpose of coping with the challenges of defeat and collapse. Musil joined the staff of the press section in the spring of 1918, just after the first number appeared, and stayed on after the dissolution of the paper until the complete liquidation of imperial institutions in December, 1918. This work brought Musil into contact with other writers and friends, but it also taught him to despise the ineffectuality and anti-intellectualism of the Austrian bureaucracy. His friends Blei and Albert Paris Gütersloh, along with Franz Werfel, seemed to Musil the only people of intelligence in the press section.[67]

Nonetheless, Musil continued to meet his responsibilities; his friends left in October to resume their literary contacts in Vienna and Prague, but Musil stayed on through the November revolution. Karl Otten later recalled the tenacity of Musil's sense of duty: "Sometimes Musil said—it was toward the end of the year 1918—that he would now go into the war ministry. When I asked him what was left to do there, since the war, along with the monarchy, was already over, he replied with impassive irony: '*Ich löse auf* [I am closing up shop.].'"[68] On January 15, 1919, Musil took a position in the archive of the press section for the office of foreign affairs in the new Austrian Republic. He stayed in the foreign office until April 1920—an ideal position from which to observe the year of the Paris Peace and international revolution. He saw the brutal conflicts of this year as an "*experimentum crucis Gottes*," as the culmination of a trauma so fundamental that it could be justified only by the construction of a new European order.[69] He expressed his hopes for the post-war order in an article for the *Neue Rundschau* in early 1919, a public statement on *Anschluss* and the League of Nations which must be seen in relation to his private reflections on the war and the new diplomacy.

At the end of 1917 Musil examined in his diaries the diplomatic possibilities of responding to the war and the new enthusiasm for peace. He already sensed that the messianic hopes for Wilson and Lenin might col-

66. TE, p. 246.
67. Ibid., p. 194. When Gütersloh was called to the foreign office, Musil remarked on the absurdity of hiring this sensitive poet to write letters to Clemenceau.
68. Karl Otten, "Eindrücke von Robert Musil," in LWW, p. 361.
69. TE, p. 229.

lide with the old nation-state politics of Europe to produce an ambivalent peace:

There are two possibilities: a power peace, or dissolution of the state into a European community. If one leaves aside altogether what "ought" to be, it is these two possibilities which remain. . . . One must want one of the two possibilities or one will achieve only something half-assed.

He argued that a creative peace could come only from a sober calculation of self-interest, and not from the "peace psychosis" which was sweeping Central Europe much like the war psychosis of 1914. The sense of finding a brother in every German had been lost in the actual conduct of the war, and by 1917 Germans were ready to project this same inner need on a European sense of brotherhood. Musil felt that the peace psychosis in Germany and Austria did very little for peace because it undermined the bargaining position of bureaucrats like Czernin, who had to translate the vague feeling of war-weariness into purely practical considerations of the limits of power.[70]

The mindless passion of the peace psychosis seemed to Musil only another symptom of a situation which lay at the basis of the war itself. Nothing had been more characteristic of this war than the breakdown of substantial rationality: "Since 1916 all states have wanted to end the war. But the idea of war aims was missing. There are only two goals: victory, or the unknown." Musil was conscious that after so many years of extreme sacrifice the psychological need for victory was enormous, unless it could be replaced by some other goal. But he was convinced that even in the war-weariness of 1917, Europeans still lacked an image of peace powerful enough to make the effort worthwhile. Peace had not yet captured the imagination concretely and creatively enough, leaving the danger that peace would mean only moral and political collapse. Somehow shape and limit had to be given to the diffuse passions Europeans had experienced since 1914.[71]

Musil emphasized that the sudden departure of civilized Europe for war in 1914 had meant not a diminution but, rather, an enhancing of the inner powers of the individual. The passionate response to the outbreak of war seemed to be explained only by the assumption "that it was a matter of a catastrophe as a final explosion of a European situation which was long since prepared." He was convinced that the expla-

70. Ibid., pp. 855–56.
71. Ibid., pp. 855–59.

nation of the spontaneous enthusiasm which had broken out everywhere in Europe in 1914 lay, not in capitalism or nationalism, but in
"the lack of higher life-content":

> An enormous depression lay over Europe and was probably felt most oppres-
> sively, to be sure, in Germany. Religion dead. Art and science an esoteric occa-
> sion. Philosophy carried on only as epistemology. Family life to the point of
> yawning (to be honest about it!). . . . Almost every person a precision worker.
> . . . What value is there in such a life? This person of 1914 bored himself literally
> to death! That is why the war came over him with the intoxication of an adven-
> ture, with the glamor of undiscovered, distant coasts. That is why those who
> had not believed before called it a religious experience.

The failure to give meaning to the peace before 1914 led to the release
of a formless excess of feeling: "One can reduce the war to a formula:
one dies for ideals, because they are not worth living for. Or: as an
idealist, it is easier to die than to live." In this, Musil summarized his
understanding of the war as a revolt against civilization.[72]

Germany represented for Musil the extreme case of the revolt against
the conditions of life in modern civilization. The exaggerated intensity
and discipline of Germany's response to the war was its characteristic
solution to the need for more effective forms of collective organization.
The war had meant the breakdown of "civil courage," but it also represented a transition from the narrow individualism and elitism of liberalism to the collective efficiency and organization which Musil called
"machen Wir" or "MW." In its militarism Germany had expressed its
fundamental "religion and ethos." Musil argued that "MW" was "the
highest achievement that a state can create." Here Musil touched on the
problems of will and collective action which lay at the heart of the political thought and action of his generation—of Sorel, Lenin, Stalin, Mussolini, and Hitler. Musil saw the German officer as the "only human
model of value and charm that Germany has created." He saw Germany
as the land of "MW," of "the imperative gone mad," as the most remarkable of modern collectivities, which unfortunately left nothing but
a grey, drab existence to the individuals within it. It seemed to him a
shrewd instinct, and much more than propaganda, to demand that the
Germans give up militarism, for militarism was not merely an unpleasant vice but the very identity of Germany as a nation-state. German
"MW," however, was only the extreme expression of a European expe-

72. Ibid., pp. 857-58.

rience. The Germans could be convincingly asked to sacrifice their identity as a nation only if all Europeans were actively committed to values
which would make peace more meaningful than war.[73]

In its spiritual revolt against modernity, Germany had formulated the
basic organizational problem of modern society. Although it was tied to
a legacy of ideological and political atavisms, German "MW" marked
significant progress beyond institutional and social individualism. The
difficulty arose when the organizational needs of the state intersected
with the emotional needs of the individual in a failed culture, as they
had in August, 1914. In Musil's view, this unfortunate coincidence of
institutional and cultural problems established the terms for the fascist
era. Sixteen years later, he saw Hitler as *the living unknown soldier.*"
The collapse of civil courage in 1933 appeared simply as the continuation of the war by other means. In the atmosphere of the Berlin streets
when Hitler assumed power, Musil saw a parody of the August day that
brought the old Europe to an end: "It was the war mood with guaran-
teed victory, the blatant release of a profound need; as it were, a small,
successful repetition of 1914." The war had provided the recipe which
counterrevolutionary movements simply took over: the need for discipline and the need for crisis.[74]

In March, 1919, in "Der Anschluss an Deutschland," Musil drew the
practical consequences of his interpretation of the war and formulated
what he took to be the task of the Paris Peace. Although the war had
been an unprecedented disaster for European civilization, it presented a
rare opportunity to break with the past and forge a new European system. He argued that the principal obstacle to the creation of a human
world was "the state—not as an administrative organism but as a spiritual-moral essence—and it is the task of the impulses that have
grouped themselves around the idea of a League of Nations to escape
from the prison which locks human organization into states." All the
moralizing about criminal states and war guilt had simply failed to take
into account the antisocial structure and function of the state: "To be an
almost completely self-enclosed system of social energy, with an infinitely greater number of life relationships internally than externally." Thus,
"every state is quite naturally recognized by the inhabitants of the oth-

73. Ibid., pp. 858–59. As Musil put it twenty years later (ibid., p. 909): "What we
experienced in the war was our impotence as individuals and our dependence on a mass
. . . with which we obeyed orders into which we had no insight, but whose justice we sum-
marily acknowledged."

74. Ibid., pp. 361–62, 357.

ers as a criminal, but seems to its own inhabitants . . . to be the embodiment of their honor and moral maturity." The spiritual-moral essence of the state lagged behind the spirit of its inhabitants and acquired for itself those rights of immorality which it denied to the individual.[75]

Within the larger task of overcoming the state and creating a European community, Musil argued that the immediate task for Austria was to overcome its own defunct state-idea and unite with Germany. The myth of Austria had been bought at the price of anachronism after Sadowa, and the state it produced was nothing to regret: "It was an anonymous administrative organism, dominated by illegitimate influences for the lack of legitimate ones." Moreover, Austria's failure to cope with the modern world was no reason for a tiny group of German bureaucrats and peasants to cling nostalgically to a fragment of the Habsburg domains. Musil recommended union with Germany as a constructive response to the dissolution of the Empire, a gesture against the endless multiplication of states, and a way-station in the development of a European or even a world community. This would be necessary

even if tomorrow the world movement coming from the East should bring a new form to transform borders, or if in the West the limitations of yesterday should be victorious again. In both cases enormous tasks would be presented, which would require purposefully united energies for solution.

Resuming his position as a German intellectual and a member of the European *internationale* of the spirit, Musil recommended *Anschluss* as a constructive element in what he believed to be the possibility of a creative peace.[76]

The Peace of Paris was an enormous disillusionment for Musil, representing in substance and symbol the victory of the limitations of yesterday. It excluded Germany and Russia, multiplied the number of nation-states, and achieved precisely that unfortunate confusion of national *Machtpolitik* and starry-eyed idealism that Musil had feared in 1917. Musil acknowledged the crimes of the central powers in Belgium and at Brest-Litovsk, but he believed that Versailles had to be judged in rela-

75. Musil, "Der Anschluss an Deutschland," *Die neue Rundschau* (March 1919), in *TE*, pp. 598–600. Cf. Robert Musil, *Briefe nach Prag* (Hamburg, 1971), p. 125. Richard Coudenhove-Kalergi, a prominent supporter of the European idea, later praised Musil's vision in having advocated "the Pan-European idea from the beginning, when most people looked upon it as utopian." According to Coudenhove-Kalergi, Musil doubted the viability of a German Austria and felt strongly that England should be included in a United Europe, despite the difficulties created by her empire.

76. Ibid., pp. 603–607.

tion to Wilson's "Trojan Horse" and the immensely greater opportunities of 1919. Clemenceau proved to be as uncomprehending as Ludendorff of Wilson's visionary ideals, and Musil faulted Wilson only for not drawing the consequences and simply leaving.[77] Instead, Wilson had given legitimacy to the kind of contradictory peace Musil had anticipated. For Musil, "the peace treaties" were "less forgivable than the declarations of war. For the war was the catastrophe of an old world, the peace treaties the obstacle to the birth of a new one."[78]

The combination of punishment and piety in the Versailles Treaty heightened still further Musil's sense of identification with the fate of the German nation. Musil rejected the notion that the morality of Germans and their state was fundamentally different from the rest of Europe, "and no one has a right to reproaches, except a Bolshevik, and he ought not to praise his day before nightfall." Clemenceau and Lloyd George, like Bethmann Hollweg, had committed the inexcusable mistake of conservative statesmen: they had failed to respond to the opportunities that lay in the events. Instead, they had created a French alliance system in the name of the League of Nations:

The question of guilt is different with the French, the Czechs, etc. We had to reckon with the old and apparently incorrigible Europe [at Brest-Litovsk]. . . . We knew of no way out in a desperate situation; they refused to make use of a creative situation. The Czechoslovakian state is much more immoral than the old Austrian one.

The entente had acquiesced in the ambitions of the new nationalities just enough to create an impractical state structure for Central Europe. Versailles had created a punitive peace with enough show of liberal idealism to be unstable and hypocritical, while leaving revision and *revanchism* to the highest bidder: "*The task of Germany* would now be . . . the overcoming of the state, the critique of the state."[79]

The year 1919 was, of course, not only the year of Versailles, but also the height of the revolutionary period in Central Europe. Musil's distaste for ideologies and mass action ill-suited him for the class antagonisms and social chaos of the post-war period, but he was not so indifferent to the politics of the revolutionary period as some commentators have suggested. Not only was he working for the imperial and republican governments throughout this period, but Vienna was a difficult place in which to remain indifferent to revolutions in Budapest, Munich, and Berlin, let alone in Vienna itself. The transition from em-

77. *TE*, p. 220.   78. Musil, *Briefe nach Prag*, p. 25.
79. *TE*, pp. 220, 227, 241–42.

pire to rump-republic seemed to him hardly to be a revolution at all; much as in Germany at the end of 1918, the Empire simply abdicated to a socialist and democratic leadership which seemed only reluctantly to accept the responsibilities of power. In practice, Musil tended to be sympathetic to the Republic and the socialists, who took the leading role at first, but the disorder of the far left and the mass resentment against the old elites made no sense to him. He was troubled by the relegation of his social stratum after the war to the status of pariahs, and he was determined to make a constructive contribution to the peace. His reflections in his diaries are directed primarily at a critique of narrowly ideological politics, whether the ideologies served the purpose of manipulating masses of people or expressed exalted visions that reality could not bear.

Musil was sympathetic to the efforts of left-wing intellectuals to press the revolution far enough to make a clean break with the authoritarian institutions of Central Europe. He signed a manifesto of left-wing intellectuals in Berlin, and he was deeply moved by the murders of Kurt Eisner and Gustav Landauer.[80] Musil admitted that the "rule of the councils in Hungary has in all probability brought with it an enormous quantity of filth, meanness, corruption, etc."[81] But, as in his condemnation of Noske's bloody reaction in the name of socialism, Musil reserved his harshest criticism for the reactionary terror which he associated with France and the entente: "The man of French imperialism, of the Hungarian White Terror! The most disinherited person."[82] Musil refused to allow his revulsion at the violence and manipulation of the revolutionaries to disguise an ideology of the old elites:

> The aristocratic argument against the masses, directed against Bolshevism, is of course false. For neither in it nor in any sort of democracy does the will arise from an amorphous mass. They are ruled by a political caste, and that will always be so. The question is only whether a better technique could not be found.[83]

Musil realized that for evolution "something must happen," and he insisted that Bolshevism was "reviled too much, and we have the guilt of not bringing any enlightenment on this count."[84]

80. See TE, pp. 222, 860. The Activist Manifesto and the list of its signers were printed in "Politischer Rat geistiger Arbeiter, Berlin: Programm," in Das Ziel: Jahrbücher für geistige Politik, ed. Kurt Hiller, vol. III, no. 1 (Leipzig, 1919):219–23. See also Jürgen C. Thöming, "Der optimistische Pessimismus eines passiven Aktivisten" in Studien, pp. 214–35.
81. TE, pp. 221, 216.   82. Ibid., p. 196.   83. Ibid., p. 214.
84. Ibid., pp. 217, 221.

Nonetheless, Musil had grave doubts about the expressionist style of revolutionary politics in 1919. He saw a form of pessimism in the pathos of the call for the New Man, which means "one does not possess it, otherwise one would not invoke it in this way." He was convinced that this romantic approach to politics would only compound the disaster of the old order: "In memory of those who also wanted another human being: the revolutionaries. In much, thankful for their holy zeal, but they believe that the New Man is simply a liberated old one." Musil mistrusted the emotional type of the radical, who "either burns for the untouchability of any hair on a human head or condemns thousands to death with a single stroke. He is necessary. As necessary as war and social injustice. No more and no less. He can perform nothing. He can only initiate achievements. The conservative man must perform. On him rests all responsibility." Musil shared in the common predicament of the mandarinate in his moral revulsion at anarchism and his conviction that the traditional elites had the training and discipline to offer something to the new order.[85]

For Musil, the important distinction between conservatism and radicalism was temperamental and ethical rather than ideological. His own commitment was to civilization, whatever his own anarchist impulses. The dualism between his conservative temperament and his desire for social change resolved his political practice in the direction of the Republic and the government socialists:

> The enormous burden of radical politics is the certainty that they will not be able to reconstruct after the destruction. However enraged one may be over the philistinism of the government socialists and over the crimes which they have committed, this one thing must be granted them: they looked into the abyss.
>
> As an individual I am a revolutionary. That cannot be otherwise, for the creative individual always is. But in politics I am an evolutionist.[86]

Musil epitomized the predicament of the liberal intellectual, caught between conservative pragmatism and revolutionary zeal. Disillusioned with the old Austria and weaned from political romanticism by the war, Musil took up the intermediate position described by his fellow Austrian, Karl Mannheim:

> Socially, this intellectualistic outlook had its basis in a middle stratum, in the bourgeoisie and in the intellectual class. This outlook, in accordance with the structural relationships of the groups representing it, pursued a dynamic course

85. Ibid., pp. 221, 290.   86. Ibid., pp. 216–17.

between the vitality, ecstasy, and vindictiveness of the oppressed strata, and the immediate concreteness of a feudal ruling class whose aspirations were in complete congruence with the then existing reality.[87]

When the political order which had sustained this reality in Austria and Germany collapsed, Musil sought to shape the tradition of mandarin liberalism creatively toward the future. He sympathized with the monarchists in their emphasis on order and their ability to criticize the other ideologies, but found the decisive weakness of their position in the lack of any real monarchs. On the other hand, the ideologies of the other parties seemed mainly to be gimmicks to market to the masses, leaving a few powerful people to rule behind the disguise of an idea. He saw the Christian Socialists as cynical opportunists; and he believed that parliamentarism had burned itself out as a spiritual movement after 1848 and really had very little to recommend it. It seemed to him absurd to defend the failed institution of parliamentarism in the name of equality and democracy, and the struggle among the atavistic programs of the parties seemed to him less important than the indifference of the voters.[88]

Musil believed that socialism had already made clear by 1919 that it was not serious about revolution, and he found in it nothing of value which was not already present in Christianity and liberalism. The emotional appeal of socialism, Musil argued, resided mainly in two axioms: that all men are equal, which seemed to him merely untrue; and the injunction to love thy neighbor as thyself, which he found was never realized except in the exaggeration of loving thy neighbor more. It made more sense to him to replace these abstractions with the practical notion of acting with solidarity, against the oppressors or on behalf of the oppressed. While this conception had originally given socialism its momentum, he believed that an analysis of this problem in class terms no longer gave the true picture:

A huge body of human beings ruled by a caste of kings, feudalists, and financiers, or financiers and politicians, closed interest-groups with very little knowledge of each other. ... The organization of communication did not keep up with the obstacles to flow between groups. ... That is the true picture. Not the one thrown up by socialism of a bourgeois layer which monopolized all material and spiritual goods for itself. They have no way to make use of the spiritual goods, and the material ones have few real connoisseurs.

87. Karl Mannheim, *Ideology and Utopia* (New York, n.d.), p. 221.
88. *TE*, pp. 194–95, 214.

Musil believed that socialism was destroying itself with its ideological fixation on a poorly formulated class-conception of politics. The socialist line toward the small owners of shops and homes seemed to him a brutal misunderstanding of capital and a grotesque distortion of the nature of the oppressors. Moreover, he was convinced that the simplistic distinction between the exploiters and the oppressed obscured the real problem of bureaucracy, which socialism revealed even more clearly than capitalism: "The capitalist and the Bolshevik are only quite imperceptible variations on the recent type of human being."[89]

The stalemate of class forces in Austria, between the quelling of the Bolsheviks in early 1919 and the resurgence of the bourgeois parties in 1922, gave Musil an opportunity to put into practice his commitments to democracy and institutional reform. During these four years of "functional democracy" and class coalition, Musil served the Republic as a bureaucrat and consultant in the ministries of foreign affairs and defense, giving substance to Mannheim's question about the possibilities of this liberal type during the collapse of the old order: "It remains to be asked, however, whether in the political sphere, a decision in favor of dynamic mediation may not be just as much a decision as the ruthless espousal of yesterday's theories or the one-sided emphasis on tomorrow's."[90] This political role of mediation corresponds to the function of the representative writer, who thinks through the limits of consciousness of his own class without moving beyond it:

I am dissatisfied. Dissatisfaction with the fatherland expressed itself gently and ironically in The Man without Qualities. But I am also convinced of the inadequacy of capitalism or the bourgeoisie, without being able to decide for its political opponents. Certainly the intellectual has a right to be dissatisfied with politics. But the intellectual who knows no compromise will seem too individualistic to ordinary people.[91]

In his practical service and mediation of ideologies, Musil certainly went beyond uncompromising individualism, but politics was not his demon. He served the state out of a sense of the necessities of the hour, but intellectually he had moved beyond the whole structure of ideological debate. While he functioned as a liberal, he no longer had much in common with the conventional liberalism of the nineteenth century. Though he did not think of himself as a political philosopher, his dis-

89. Ibid., pp. 195, 209–210, 214–15, 247.
90. Mannheim, Ideology and Utopia, p. 158. Cf. Otto Bauer, The Austrian Revolution (London, 1925), pp. 246–47.
91. TE, p. 477.

tance from politics and his critique of ideologies allowed him to see the revolutionary era with unusual clarity. Perhaps his keenest political insight in 1919 was his observation that: "Today, revolutionary energies express themselves only in the conservative parties. . . . The reason for this is that the bourgeois parties have stronger ideologies, the atmosphere of ideology. On the other side, there is only the romanticism of revolution."[92] Since the socialists had made clear that they no longer took their own talk of revolution seriously, conservative ideology was ready to use the language of oppressor and oppressed for its own purposes. Conservative ideology was on the offensive, even though it had nothing relevant to say to the modern world. The clericals and the conservatives had managed to take over the aura of revolution, while the real resistance to modernity lay not with big capital but in the lower middle class, in the reactionary parties of Germany and Austria.[93]

When the promise of the post-war period collapsed into domestic and international stagnation, Musil moved away from immediate political issues toward a broader investigation of the development of European institutions and ideologies. Though he continued in the Austrian bureaucracy until 1922, his intellectual preoccupations after 1919 centered on an analysis of the crisis of European civilization and on his own artistic development. It was only the absolute demand of the historical situation and not a passion for politics which drew Musil into the practical sphere. For longer than he would have liked, he had devoted his quantum of seriousness and self-transcendence to politics, but he did not share the dominant view of the twenties that the state could meet the demands of the spirit. Yet Musil's remark that he was "apolitical out of indifference to external circumstances" hardly does justice to the disciplined practice of these years.[94] More to the point was his ob-

92. Ibid., p. 223.
93. Ibid., pp. 233, 218. Cf. C. E. Williams, *The Broken Eagle* (London, 1974), pp. 155-67. Williams calls Musil a fascist sympathizer and a fanatic without explaining what he means or giving evidence for this judgment. Although Williams does not do so, it would be possible to demonstrate a striking correspondence between the political observations of Hitler and those of Musil. Musil was extremely critical of Versailles, identified with the idea of a Greater Germany, and pointed to the extremity of social and national conflict in Central and Eastern Europe which made harder movements than liberalism, such as communism and extreme varieties of conservatism, likely. The correspondence in views between a liberal intellectual and the leading fascist of the twentieth century is a matter worth examining more carefully, and it says a good deal about Musil's insight into Central European politics. But to call him a fanatic or a fascist on the basis of his political service between 1914 and 1922 is to fly in the face of the facts.
94. *TE*, p. 451. This is the sort of quotation that commentators on Musil have tended to emphasize.

servation that he "believed the age had finished with its catastrophes. My relationship to politics may be understood from that."[95] Politics became a peripheral concern for Musil after 1919, but his mature achievements as a critic of culture and ideology are hard to imagine apart from his personal experience in the war and the revolution. It was in the ecstatic politics of war and revolution that Musil evolved his disabused, functionalist view of the state and crystallized the critique of ideology that he had begun to develop in the pre-war years. The five-year slavery was over; in December, 1919, Musil wrote to his friend Allesch that he hoped soon to return to Berlin to resume his career as a writer.[96]

3. GERMAN CULTURE AS SYMPTOM: 1919–1924

German history as a paradigm of world history. (More visible because the organism was new.)[97]

Title: A German ideology is sought. . . . Attempt at an ideological anti-ideology. One that is optimistically resigned.[98]

As a writer and a poet, Musil identified not with states but with the historical continuity and unity of German language and culture. This was the only meaningful sense he could give to the idea of the nation, and it was in this sense that he saw himself as both a German and a German *Dichter*. The idea of an Austrian culture—which took credit for Leibniz, Goethe, and Schlegel, while remaining aloof from the bad Prussians—seemed to him a patriotic distortion of the concept of culture. He was conscious that this conception of the German nation united him spiritually with Noske and Bismarck as well as Goethe and Cranach, but he was convinced that "Austrian culture" was grotesquely irrelevant to the challenges of modern civilization, a useless myth perpetuated by his own class. In "Buridans Österreicher" Musil satirized the good Austrian of 1919 who, finding himself trapped between a Danube Federation and a Greater Germany, "discovers Austrian culture":

Austria has Grillparzer and Karl Kraus. It has Bahr and Hugo von Hofmannsthal. In any case also the *Neue Freie Presse* and the *esprit de finesse*. Kralik and Kernstock. It does not, to be sure, have some of its more important sons—those who fled spiritually abroad just in time.

95. Ibid., p. 455.   96. Musil, "Briefe," in *LWW*, p. 279.
97. *MoE, Anhang*, p. 1592.   98. *TE*, p. 222.

In the context of the pre-war dispersion, one thinks of Wittgenstein, Blei, Rilke, Lukács, Broch, Stefan Zweig, of Musil himself and his friend Allesch. But Musil pressed the point further to recall that even those members of his generation most identified with Vienna had already fled Austrian culture spiritually. Karl Kraus had refused to write for the *Neue Freie Presse*, while Hofmannsthal, Altenberg, and others published in Germany:

All the same; all the same, there remains—no, there does *not* remain an Austrian culture, but, rather, a talented country which generates an excess of thinkers, poets, actors, waiters, and hairdressers. A country of spiritual and personal taste; who would quarrel with that?![99]

Musil wanted to avoid confusing culture and personal refinement with the political fortunes of states. Instead of using Austrian culture as a compensation for the defeat of 1866, Musil preferred to respond to the political situation of 1919. He argued that a state could have energy or health, but not culture. At most the culture of a state meant the publishing houses, newspapers, universities, research institutes, organizational energies, and finances made available for cultural ends—and it was precisely in these respects that Germany had decisively outstripped Austria, not only in 1918, but in the decade before the war. Austria had a great many cultivated people, but it did not have the resources to launch a modern culture.[100] Germany, on the other hand, had the social and economic basis for a vital modern culture, but it suffered more severely than Austria from the problems of modern civilization. For Musil, the genuine opportunities and challenges of the spirit lay in Germany; it was there that cultivated Austrians could best contribute to the health of European culture. In its misery and despair as the pariah of Europe, Germany epitomized the problems of Europe as a whole, and Musil was determined to cast his lot with those with whom he had suffered the hopes and disillusionments of 1914 and 1919: "So that our people will be ready on the next day of utopia, we must prepare them. . . . 'Our people' must mean: the part of humanity accessible to us."[101] It was the plight of the ordinary German in modern civilization that preoccupied Musil in his major essays of the post-war years.

When the entente proved to be a more substantial obstacle to *Anschluss* than the cultivated classes of Vienna, Musil drew the obvious

99. Musil, "Buridans Österreicher," *Der Friede* (Vienna, 1919), in *TE*, p. 835.
100. Ibid., p. 836.
101. *TE*, p. 219.

inference and decided to move to Berlin. In April, 1920, he left his job in
the Austrian foreign ministry and went to Berlin for three months to try
to arrange a permanent situation. It was natural that he should have
attempted to resume his ties with the *Neue Rundschau* and Samuel
Fischer, the leading publisher of Weimar, but Fischer was not financially
able to offer him an editorial position, and Musil reluctantly returned to
Vienna. There, during the post-war period, he enjoyed the best material
circumstances of his adult life. Julius Deutsch invited him to join the
defense ministry as a consultant for the re-education of Austrian officers
to the methods of a democratic army, a position ideally suited to Musil's
abilities and convictions.[102] Moreover, this prestigious post left him
master of his own time and provided a steady income between September,
ber, 1920, and February, 1923. During this period Musil was also a
regular contributor to the *Prager Presse*, writing book reviews and
theater criticism for this Czech newspaper.[103] The combined income
from these two positions finally gave Musil economic freedom and
allowed him in November, 1921, to purchase the apartment on the
Rasumofskygasse which became his only bastion of economic security
after 1924.

102. Musil was able to apply his education in psychology and his experience as an
officer and a propagandist to refashion the officer corps on the model of labor leaders
rather than *haut bourgeois* monarchists and social snobs. As the neutral coordinator of
the party specialists who worked with him, Musil was expected to make effective Bauer's
conception of the state as a mediator in a stalemated equilibrium between the mass parties
of the middle class (Christian Socialists and German Nationalists) and the working class
(Social Democrats). Musil's work convinced him of the central importance of education
and propaganda in the modern, democratic state, and the need to create the ideological
and institutional preconditions which would allow democracy to work.
Cf. Robert Musil, "Ein wichtiges Buch," *Der neue Merkur* 7, 1 (1923–1924):165–67.
In this review of Leopold von Wiese's *Soziologie des Volksbildungswesens*, Musil emphasized the importance of reorganizing the gymnasia and the military academies, "the comprehensive task of spiritual organization" (p. 166). For Musil, idealism made no difference unless it led to the practical application of intellect to institutional structures. For
the details of Musil's bureaucratic service to the Austrian Republic see Dinklage, "Musils
Herkunft," in *LWW*, pp. 236–38.
Cf. also Robert Musil [Ing., Dr. phil., Fachbeirat im Bundesministerium für Heeres-
wesen], "Psychotechnik und ihre Anwendungsmöglichkeit im Bundesheere," *Militärwissenschaftliche und technische Mitteilung* (Fortsetzung der M. A. u. G.), LIII. Jahrgang,
1922, 6. H., (Vienna), pp. 244–65. This article is a sophisticated yet simple presentation
of the state of applied and industrial psychology and its potential for military organization and efficiency. Very little of modern advertising would have surprised the author of
this article, but his main concern is to show his military colleagues the practical implications of psychology for the efficient loading of a gun or the creation of a modern, democratic army (including intelligence tests and the like). When Musil talked about modernization, he knew what he meant, and he preferred that propaganda and techniques of
manipulation be used *by* democracy rather than against it.
103. Musil wrote more for the *Prager Presse* than for any other periodical: see Musil,
Briefe nach Prag.

Although Musil continued to publish his most important work in Germany—with *Die neue Rundschau, Der neue Merkur, Die literarische Welt,* and the Rowohlt Verlag—practical considerations forced him to spend the Weimar years in Vienna. As a critic and defender of democracy, as a writer for Fischer and Rowohlt, and as a veteran of the blossoming of modernism in pre-war Berlin, Musil belonged to the liberal culture of Weimar. He shared its tendency to write for an audience that did not yet exist and its opposition to fanatical nationalism and prophecies of despair. Kurt Hiller called him one of "the representative humanists of contemporary Germany" (adding, "There are certainly not many of these"), and writers such as Thomas Mann and Alfred Döblin admired his work.[104] But Musil lived on the periphery of Weimar culture and became in practice a figure in the cultural world of Vienna. His closest friends—Blei, Gütersloh, Fontana, Alfred Polgar, Robert Müller, Karl Otten, and Franz Csokor—were primarily figures of Vienna rather than Germany. They gathered regularly at the ultimate coffee-house of the Viennese intellectual, the Café Central: as Csokor put it, "The coffee-house was for us what the Agora was for Socrates."[105] Except for visits to Berlin and one brief stay there between 1931 and 1933, Musil lived in Vienna until 1938. By necessity rather than preference, his world was not the raucous modernism of Berlin but the quieter world of Vienna. There he lived as the prototype of the homeless modern man, not quite belonging in Berlin or Prague or Brno or Vienna.

It was not only geographically that Musil was driven to the periphery. Although he "stood for years in the struggle of the intellectuals or whatever one should call it in Germany," he experienced his "life in contemporary Germany as an outsider, and I know that even within contemporary literature I am fought, misunderstood, and undervalued as an outsider."[106] It may be an exaggeration to think of Stefan George or Thomas Mann as an outsider, but it is certainly an accurate term for Musil.[107] It was difficult to find an audience for a writer who had kind words for the Vienna Circle and Oswald Spengler, Peter Altenberg and

---

104. Ibid., p. 82.

105. Franz Theodor Csokor, "Gedenkenrede" in *LWW*, pp. 351–54.

106. *TE,* p. 288. See also Musil's review of Alfred Schwoner's *Wertphilosophie eines Outsiders* in *Prager Presse,* Morgenausgabe, December 18, 1923, p. 4. Musil wrote this review under the pseudonym "Matthias Rychtarschow."

107. Peter Gay (*Weimar Culture* [New York, 1968], p. xiv) describes the chaotic, experimental culture of Weimar as "the creation of outsiders, propelled by history into the inside, for a short, dizzying, fragile moment." Musil was an outsider even in this culture of outsiders.

Georg Lukács; and Musil's critique of all forms of ideology was as unwelcome to most intellectuals as it was to the German middle class. Musil mistrusted the ideological style of the Weimar intellectuals, marked by expressionism, the disillusionments of war and peace, and contempt for the average German. He believed that the imperfect and practical world of politics could not bear more than a little of the ideal and fanatical world of the spirit.[108] But if Musil found the political intellectuals too contemptuous of the ordinary German, this ordinary German was unlikely to read Musil at all. Though his livelihood depended on his ability to appeal to a popular audience, at least within the middle class, Musil maintained an unfashionable rationalism and refused to appeal to the special interests of any group or ideology. In a decade when outsiders everywhere were organizing themselves into political parties, movements, institutes, and international key-clubs of every variety, Musil remained aloof. His pragmatic view of politics, his concern for culture's independence from the state, and his determination to achieve a dispassionate view of modern civilization all constrained him to keep his distance and his intellectual independence. But his personal isolation, his lack of institutional commitments, his peculiar position between Germany and Austria, and his sympathy for both science and art ideally suited him to think through the experience of his generation in Central Europe.

Musil's discussion of the ideological confusion of post-war Germany, like his pre-war analysis of Austria, began with the assumption that embarrassing political situations always have a cultural basis. The vitality of reactionary forces in Germany after 1919 seemed to him only an extreme instance of Europe's failure to come to terms with the conditions of life in modern civilization, and he saw the cultural despair of the twenties and the resurgence of nationalism as virtually identical phenomena: "Only a time of cowardice can be spiritually nationalist and conservative; it is defensive because it has given up hope."[109] The soul of this neo-Biedermeier world was the ordinary German burgher; it was this good, moral person who had most passionately supported the war and unveiled the vacuity of his morality. Musil believed that the illusion of the nation had flowed into the vacuum left by the collapse of

108. Cf. *TE*, p. 210: "Left to itself, spirit is a feud without end." Cf. István Deák, *Weimar Germany's Left-Wing Intellectuals* (Berkeley, 1968), and Harold Poor, *Kurt Tucholsky and the Ordeal of Germany* (New York, 1968).
109. Musil, *Der deutsche Mensch*, p. 25.

the other ideologies, primarily as a spiritual compensation for the lost individual. Christianity, socialism, and liberalism had all succumbed to national-imperialism; and the vitality of nationalism simply expressed their failure to inform the moral lives and practical activities of their adherents. After suffering the collapse of the mutually contradictory illusions of the war psychosis and the peace psychosis, the average German burgher found himself in the midst of a period of ideological conflict and confusion. In the spiritual collapse of the post-war years, this ordinary Germany looked again to the idea of the nation as a means of giving form to the emptiness of his existence. In "Die Nation als Ideal und als Wirklichkeit" (1921) Musil explored the problem of German nationalism as a paradigm of the inadequacy of inherited ideals to the conditions of modern life.

He argued that the ideal of the nation—whether formulated as race, as commonality of spirit, or as the state—was a typical case of the confused relation of the individual to his ideals. What impressed him about the anti-Semitic racism of *völkisch* ideology was not simply that it was an intellectual and moral perversion:

A good part of our national idealism consists of this sickness of thought. . . . What is taken in [Germany] to be idealism [is] that regressive need for ideas, which refers every thought back to older, eternal, supposedly sublime ones instead of thinking it out.

We stabilize our ideals like Platonic-Pythagorean ideas, immoveable and unchangeable, and if reality does not follow them, then we are in a position to claim precisely this as a proof of their ideality, of which reality is only their "impure" realization.

Similarly, the illusion of a commonality of spirit within the nation sought to find in the realm of ideas a surrogate for the empirical reality of social conflict and division. But dangerous and dishonest as the delusions of race and shared spirit were, they took on their practical significance in relation to the idea of the state: that good old conservative idea of Central Europe which gave body to the passions of modern nationalism. In Musil's view, the Prussian ideal of the state as the realization of the ethical individual was not only the vehicle for the peculiar atavisms of German ideology, but an atavism itself, which had won the favor of virtually every political ideology of the inter-war years. The tendency to make the state an institution for spiritual fulfillment rather than for merely practical functions was "simply a holdover from the age of the authoritarian state, which saved itself in the proverbs of the preceptors of the young German Empire and which is unfortunately on its way to finding new life in socialism." The state—like race, nation, the Kaiser, and the sublime moral law—had become a means of compensating for the emptiness of the emotional and moral life of the individual, displacing personal gratification into a surrogate "higher" realm.[110]

Musil argued that in reality the state was not the vehicle for the ethical realization of the individual, but, rather, the model for everything that was problematic about ethical action in the modern world. The ethical ideal of the state threatened the individual and culture and disguised the real conditions of ethical action. The obverse of the mystical attitude toward the state (and its invariable complement in modern civilization) was total indifference to its reified functions. While the apotheosis of the state was reserved mainly for crises and special occasions, the normal relation of the individual to the state was *Gewährenlassen*— apathy and indifference, "let it do as it pleases": this expression of the impotence of the individual was "one of the formulas of the age in general." And, in fact, things happened whether the individual liked it or not—the atrocities in Belgium during the war or the starvation of Central Europeans afterward. Even the agents of these actions simply let them happen: "Naturally, we did it; we let it happen; 'it' did it without being hindered by us." This impersonal context for social action in the modern world could not be overcome by goodness of heart, but only by "cold-blooded organization." To those who thought differently, Musil suggested that they simply open the morning newspaper and try to empathize: "They would go mad."[111]

The apathy and brutality of modern man were not proofs of moral decline but symptoms of a new situation, of the separation between the person and the public function:

The active counterpart to this "let-things-happen" is the summary, general, routine treatment of human cases; the legal act is the symbol of the indirect relationship between the state and the human being. It is the odorless, tasteless, weightless life, the button that one presses—and if a human being dies because of it, one did not do it, because one's consciousness was consumed by the complicated task of operating the button; the legal act, that is the judgment of the court, the gas attack, the good conscience of our torturers: it creates the unholy division in the human being between the private person and the functionary, but

110. Musil, "Die Nation als Ideal und als Wirklichkeit," *Die neue Rundschau* (December 1921), in *TE*, pp. 612–19.
111. Ibid., pp. 610–16.

this indirectness of relations is apparently under contemporary conditions an unavoidable hygiene.

Resonating the cultural tensions of the world of Weber, Kafka, and Himmler, Musil stepped back from the temptation to lend ethical grandeur to the functions of the state. He was convinced that the moral problem of the modern citizen would not be solved by mystifying these impersonal and indirect relations. Instead of a political idealism which evaded the structure of political action and found confirmation in its unreality, Musil preferred an idealism that came to terms with the complexity of reality in order to shape it toward the future.[112]

The idea of the nation was a special instance of the general task of contemporary morality, that of building "itself up from the shapelessness which European civilization and the enormous growth of its relations have given to human beings." Musil emphasized that no morality adequate to modern reality had yet been created. The project of coming to terms with technological society had only just begun, but he trusted in the potential of human beings to respond creatively to it. He doubted that "a race of machine-builders and salesmen is to be helped by myth, intuition, and classicism," but he saw hope in the pluralism of his culture and "the energies which rage even in the misuse of civilization." It would be enough if the all-powerful state and the all-knowing prophets and philosophers would simply leave it "to human beings, insofar as it is somehow compatible with living together, to find the way for themselves and to follow their own interests."[113] In his two most extensive essays of the post-war period, *Das hilflose Europa* and *Der deutsche Mensch als Symptom*, Musil offered a more systematic treatment of the assumptions underlying this view of European morality. But even as he extended and clarified the assumptions of his pre-war essays, Musil resisted systematic form. His insights suggested a whole which he was not in a position to state: "I renounce system and precise proof. I want only to say what I think and make clear why I think it. I reassure myself with the fact that even significant scientific works have been born out of such necessity."[114] Nonetheless, Musil's essays display a consistent method and a fundamental vision of the nature of the problem.

Musil approached the analysis of ideologies in the same spirit in which Mach had analyzed the outmoded concepts of nineteenth-century sci-

112. Ibid., p. 616.
113. Ibid., pp. 619–21.
114. *TE*, p. 213.

ence. Threading his way between the metaphysical positions of materialism and idealism, Musil attempted to clarify the disjunction between
the objective development of European institutions and the chaos of
conflicting ideologies.[115] While his approach was similar to Mach's in
its empirical critique of frozen concepts, Musil was conscious that social
knowledge differed from natural science. The enormous impact of lawful patterns in social life was characteristic of modern society, but the
search for regularities did not adequately reflect the decisive importance
of the accidental, the unique, the individual in the historical world.
Whatever functions and regularities could be discovered in modern civilization, the central problem remained of giving form and inner direction to the spiritual life of individuals within this civilization.

Musil's understanding of the word *ideology* was somewhat idiosyncratic. One ordinary meaning of the word in the nineteenth century was
that of a coherent, systematic vision of the world. Often understood as
an historical philosophy or cosmology, an ideology discovered objective
values in true knowledge of history; by discovering the central goal of
the historical process, ideology could read moral instruction off the objective facts of history. After Marx, social thought began to see ideology
from a materialist point of view, as false consciousness, as a surface epi-
phenomenon which concealed more fundamental realities of interest
and nature. Musil rejected both definitions of ideology. On the one
hand, the important fact about ideology for the student of society was
not its relative accuracy as a portrayal of historical destiny; if theories
were based on knowledge, then they were either true or false and did
not need to be infused with the quality of emotion. Common to all objective ideologies of necessity (before or after Marx) was the determination to confuse matters of fact with the search for spiritual values. On
the other hand, Musil shared Weber's view that the materialist reduction of ideology missed the point when it saw ideology merely as a
symptom of more fundamental determinants.

Musil's critique of culture and his use of the novel to portray the metaphysics of everyday life set out from the assumption that ideology is
something at once less exalted and more important than conventional
views of it suggested. For Musil, an ideology was primarily neither a

115. Musil listed the host of contradictory ideologies which assaulted the confused
individual of Weimar: "The activists, dadaists, expressionists, anarchists, nihilists, communists, monarchists, neo-Catholics, Zionists, etc." (*TE*, p. 234).

scientific theory nor a symptom of social life, but, rather, "the intellectual organization of the feelings." An ideology forms, shapes, and simplifies the emotional life of the individual by giving objective coherence and interconnection to the inner life. Without these shaping patterns of the inner life, the subjective life of the individual would be a mass of random and incoherent feelings. These ideological bonds and conventions exist on a variety of levels, but they ordinarily have the support of a highly articulated thought-system. While Musil admitted that "an order of the feelings" based solely on impulse and habits derived from tradition could be imagined, this would not be an ideology in the strict sense: "Experience teaches that never—whether one searches in history or ethnology—has there been such a life order without 'teaching.'"[116]

By organizing and simplifying the feelings, ideology plays a dominant role in all aspects of everyday life. Without these assumptions before the fact, no assimilation of ordinary experience would be possible. Most decisions are based not on individual judgments of truth or value but on commitments made years before. Moreover, once practical activity ceases, life would become a meaningless void were it not for ideology, which gives the human being a feeling of being justified and threads past actions through the emptiness of leisure hours and on to the next activity. Thus, the function of ideology is to provide an identity which is both limiting and energizing: "Principles, guidelines, models, limitations are energy accumulators." The power of ideology to define is perhaps most apparent in love, where "only the seizing of the little woman arises from an internal impulse"—the rest is convention and ritual, externalized and regulated by ideology.[117]

Those who discussed ideology as though it were merely a matter for speculative philosophy or a symptom of market relations did not begin to grasp the daily implications of the problem for the ordinary human being:

The human being is . . . a far less disinterested metaphysician than is commonly admitted. A dull accompanying feeling of this strange situation rarely leaves him. Death, the tiny-ness of the whole world, the questionableness of the illusion of the ego, the senselessness of existence which grows more pressing with the

116. Musil, *Der deutsche Mensch*, pp. 31ff. Musil's definition of ideology made explicit that transition in the early twentieth century from objective cosmologies to subjectives ontologies, which was apparent in the work of Weber, Sorel, Bergson, Wittgenstein, and Tillich, among others.

117. Ibid., p. 33.

years: those are questions which the average person turns away with scorn, and which he nevertheless feels surrounding his whole life like the walls of a black room.

Musil's ideal type of this ordinary man in modern civilization, in both his essays and his art, was the professional. This, the type he knew best from his own experience and his social place in the mandarinate, was the principal attempt of the modern world to replace the function of ideology: "Today the primary bond is the profession. With the professional label and a little modifier such as talented or untalented and amusing or not, respectable or not respectable," an identity is exhausted. Even when a professional has a hobby, like stamps, tennis, or women, he almost certainly organizes it "as an amateur profession, just as methodically and exclusively as the real one."

Outside of these bonds, the human being collapses like a blown-up balloon; or when an external impulse seizes him, he deforms himself immediately in this direction. Busy-ness, the encapsulation in the profession, the tumult of the leisure hours cover over a profound anxiety which would otherwise be there.[118]

The passionate ideological quarrels of the 1920s expressed not an argument over facts or the practical interests of competing groups, but an attempt to overcome the isolation of the individual and the emptiness of emotional life. "The unhappy sectarianism of our time is an evil, dreamlike superstructure for the fear of death, the separation of the individual from the generality and the horde."[119] In a time of fragmented ideologies, the individual was lost, disoriented, torn apart by a confusion of competing partial communities in politics, religion, profession, and leisure.[120] The intensity of ideological conflict in the early 1920s seemed to Musil to demonstrate the inability of any one ideology to give form to this situation and the lives of individuals. And, like Max Weber, Musil was unwilling to evade the complexity of social issues simply in order to provide reassurance for the feelings.[121] There was no longer a single

118. Ibid., pp. 32–34. Cf. Hölderlin (quoted in *TE*, p. 291):"There are no longer any people in Germany today, but only professions."
119. *TE*, p. 263.
120. Cf. ibid., p. 296: "State, nation, church, profession, class, sex, etc. The individual cannot belong entirely to any one of these associations, because they stand in contradiction to one another. Even here it is a matter of the war among the apparatuses." By apparatus Musil meant the whole system of group influences and institutions in which culture is imbedded: "Tradition, custom, morality, in sum, ideology" (ibid., p. 297). "Not the poem that I read, but that I read it is apparatus."
121. Like Max Weber, Musil was convinced that a closed totality was not an appropriate response to the complexity of modern life. They were once invited to speak on the

reigning ideology, no longer an objective thought to correspond to the emotional need of the individual for universal agreement and positions of rest. Instead of complaining "about our soullessness, our mechanization, calculation, irreligiosity," Musil invited his readers instead to see "this problematic of the contemporary age for once as a new problem, and not as a failed solution." [122] He believed that the correct response to this situation lay, not in another ideology, but in the creation of the social, institutional, and educational preconditions in which an ideology could have an effect. Here the primary function of the intellectual was the task of spiritual organization, the analysis and ordering of a structure in which meaning could be awakened. [123] Within this context, Musil treated ideologies essayistically, not as total explanations of history and cosmology, but as "experimental intellectual principles for giving form to the inner life." [124] Thus, his attempt at an anti-ideological ideology of civilization was both critical, in its description of the failure of the existing ideologies, and creative, in its search for tentative, essayistic modes of giving intellectual organization to the feelings.

In opposition to the pieties of German culture about character and morality, Musil emphasized the relative formlessness of the moral German. The average German was rushed from the diffusion of childhood into the firmness of profession, rules, newspapers, and moral conflicts; the schools took the soul and quickly put it into final form for the world. But Musil believed that only environment and upbringing separated the tender Rilke from South Sea cannibals. Musil stopped short of a pure milieu-theory—leaving room for the determination of a tran-

---

same occasion regarding the questions of the day; but neither was able to offer much satisfaction, since they shared in refusing to pretend to have total solutions: "Therein lies a great deal about the position of the professorate in Germany" (*TE*, p. 192).

122. Musil, *Der deutsche Mensch*, pp. 34–35. Musil found a remark from Hume appropriate to the ideological conflict of the 1920s: "'Quarrels compound themselves as if everything were in doubt, and they are carried on with an intensity as if everything were certain'" (*TE*, p. 287).

123. Ibid., pp. 622–37.

124. Musil, "Geist und Erfahrung: Anmerkungen für Leser, welche dem Untergang des Abendlandes entronnen sind," *Der neue Merkur* (March 1921), in *TE*, p. 664. A substantial portion of this essay is devoted to a critique of Spengler's historical method, his self-enclosed view of cultures, and his irresponsible use of the analogical method. In general, Musil found in Spengler the characteristic weaknesses of German thought in the 1920s, but Musil expressed his admiration for Spengler's attempt "to press the whole of world history into new forms of thought. That it does not succeed is not only Spengler's fault alone, but also lies in the lack of any preparation" (ibid., p. 659). Cf. ibid., p. 667: "And Oswald Spengler, I declare openly and as a sign of my love that other writers do not make so many mistakes because they lack the necessary reach to touch both shores and bring so much together."

scendent ego in a term such as "temperament," which was independent
of culture—though it was not yet possible to give a scientific account of
these few determinants which lie within human beings.[125] But he believed that the war had demonstrated in an enormous mass experiment
that "not only hidden neuropaths, but also the good average person"
was capable of shockingly immoral activities, "that the human being is
ethically something almost formless, unexpectedly plastic, capable of
anything."[126] Musil was conscious that his theory of the moral formlessness of man in modern civilization was offensive to almost everyone.
Yet for him it offered both an accurate description of the situation and
the most creative way of overcoming the old ideologies, whose corpses
lay in the path of spiritual growth. Because the old ideologies no longer
effectively gave form to the inner lives of Europeans, the situation could
not be resolved by exhortations for "more responsibility, goodness,
Christianity, humanity, in short, by any more of what there had been
too little of before."[127] One would simply have to begin with the assumption that the good was not a constant but a variable function.

   Musil saw the war as the culmination of a process which had intensified around 1870 with the growth of an urbanized and technological
society. At about the time the European nation-state system had been
forged, the direction and creativity of the liberal tradition had been lost.
For nearly fifty years, European development had been marked by genuine success in practical matters and a naive complacency about progress. Failure to respond creatively to the rapid industrialization of the
last third of the century had led to confusion, bordering on despair, in
matters of the spirit. Academic philosophy had given up on the problems of human life and had left them to a second-rate newspaper indus-
try, to a popular philosophy which sought for false and superficial syntheses of universal knowledge. At the same time, the conventional
forms of giving meaning to existence—the schools, the churches, bourgeois morality—had been unable to speak directly to the problems of
urban life. In the midst of an age of fulfillment, when technology was
realizing the primitive dreams of mankind, the individual was left alone
and directionless in an enormously fragmented spiritual world. Civilization had meant a gain in reality, and a loss in the dream. This lost per-

125. Musil, *Der deutsche Mensch*, p. 19.
126. Ibid., and Musil, "Die Nation," p. 620.
127. Musil, *Das hilflose Europa oder Reise vom hundertsten ins Tausendste* (Munich,
1921), in *TE*, p. 637.

son of the pre-war years, who wanted to know that there was "something like heaven over him," was "overtaken by the war." Musil believed that "the war broke out like a disease in this social body," and he interpreted the war "as the crisis of this 'mere civilization.'"[128]

Musil saw the passionate response to the outbreak of war as part of a general phenomenology of social experience, "as a revolution of the soul against the existing order; in many ages it leads to religious awakenings, in others to warlike ones." Such upheavals expressed not simply the collapse of a single ideology ("for example, the bourgeois now or the Catholic in 1618"), but, rather, "the periodic breakdown of all ideologies" when they find themselves in faulty relationship to life.[129] This ideological collapse did not mean the exhaustion of a metaphysical principle, but simply that the objective development of European civilization since 1870 has moved beyond the concepts provided by the old ideologies. The failure of ideologies to influence the practical life of Europe as it rushed toward war was one symptom of this breakdown. Ideologies had become sublime abstractions, out of touch with practical reality. They were also out of touch with the inner lives of individuals, and the passion for war expressed the failure of ideologies to give meaning to the peace. Moreover, the traumatic experiences of the war and the revolution remained unassimilated, just as Europeans remained unchanged: "We have seen much and understood nothing" because "we did not have the concepts with which to take in what we experienced."[130]

Musil's analysis of the war as the breakdown of all ideologies was fundamentally opposed to the view that there is an essence or destiny, "a real efficacious spirit, a mysterium" working in human history. If the Germans were particularly devoted to the notion of a fixed moral character, they were equally committed to historicism, "to the assumption of the type, the epoch, and the like." These two Biedermeier notions of moral character and historicism had become the central conventions of German ideology. In place of them Musil proposed his theory of the moral formlessness of man and a view of history under the aspect of accident and statistics. From Ranke and Hegel to Oswald Spengler, the Germans had been fond of interpreting history as the working out of a higher destiny, principle, spiritual idea, or type. Musil argued that it

128. *TE*, pp. 294, 215, and Musil, *Das hilflose Europa*, p. 635.
129. Musil, *Das hilflose Europa*, p. 636.
130. Ibid., p. 623.

was possible to do this for the Greeks or the Middle Ages primarily because 95 percent of the historical facts had been lost or forgotten.
Looked at more closely, however, cultures and epochs turned out to be
products of induction and abstraction rather than pre-existing forms or
inevitable destinies. Moreover, these cultures, types, and epochs over-
lapped and interpenetrated in a manner much more disorderly than
German historicism cared to admit. Musil's historical world of statistics
and accident is not very poetic; it is complex, clinical, and stripped of its
compulsive power.[131]

Musil believed that the discovery that there was no inevitable destiny
hidden in history was just as liberating as the discovery of the malleabil-
ity and formlessness of human nature. On both counts, European man
found himself free to respond to an open and uncharted situation. His
contemporaries in Germany wanted to hold onto the older, more sublime view of history, and Spengler and Hitler were only the most famous members of his generation to salvage the notion of historical destiny, whatever the intellectual or human costs. Musil understood this
need to derive moral purpose from the inner logic of the historical process, but he considered it to be a distortion of the facts and a failure of
will. Like Nietzsche, Sorel, and the early Marx, Musil believed that man
makes his own history. The limits to this freedom lay not in historical
necessity, but, rather, in the far greater weight, objectivity, and impen-
etrability which the social products of individuals had taken on in the
past century. It was not so much the people who had changed as "the
impersonal (or supra-personal) products of their social life together."[132]
At the same time, the rationalized social system which was so bitterly
lamented in the twentieth century offered a basis for the individual to
express himself and have an impact. Musil's rejections of historical determinism and the internal determinism of character interfaced in the
relativistic formula, "People make their clothes, but clothes also make
people," and, similarly, "One must not always think that one's essence
does what it is, but rather that it becomes what—for God knows what
reasons—it does."[133] For Musil, history unveiled itself as a confused
tangle of the external, accidental situation and whatever human beings

---

131. Ibid., pp. 624–25. Cf. Ernst Robert Curtius, *Der Syndicalismus der Geistesarbeiter in Frankreich* (Bonn, 1921), p. 3. Musil was defensive about this analysis (by a mind
he admired) which reduced all German interpretations of the war to a characteristic position.

132. Musil, *Der deutsche Mensch*, p. 20.
133. Musil, *Das hilflose Europa*, p. 627.

happened to bring to bear on it, and he believed that very slight inward change in the European mentality might have sweeping consequences for the character of European social life.[134]

Musil considered it a relief to find that he was bound by no necessity; in the midst of the prophets of cultural despair, he found that "the world is full of an untrammeled will to the new, full of a driving idea of making things different, of progress."[135] Ordinary people were not in a position to wait for philosophers and historians to provide a clear overview of the complexity and variety of modern life, yet the inadequacy of the old categories and ideologies did not mean a decline, but a new situation, an immaturity: "We are only just now stepping out of our booties; we are a *Frühzeit*."[136] The German habit of seeing even the present in historical terms simply expressed cowardice about making direct judgments and intellectual poverty in depending on grand schemes which no longer corresponded to the complexity of the new situation. Musil's anti-historicist brand of optimism argued for tolerance of uncertainty in general and for confidence in individual judgments in practice. This seemed to him the most creative philosophical response to an era which he described as "the age of facts."

Musil believed that the proper philosophical response to this situation was a patient, tentative empiricism. The facts "in their totality are still somewhat disunited for the philosophical vision. Philosophy has fallen a bit(!) behind the facts, and that led to the belief that paying attention to the facts was something anti-philosophical: it is, however, the right philosophy for our age that we have no philosophy."[137] Whatever the field, Musil rejected the popular view that it was a merely negative characteristic of the modern world that it had no philosophy: "Formulated positively, the skepticism of our age means: it believes only in facts."[138] The popular rage for a premature synthesis and the literary condescension toward mere empiricism both evaded the simple fact that all the old philosophies had proved inadequate. Like Ulrich in *The Man without Qualities*, Musil thought it was nonsense to see an honest, creative empiricism as merely cynical and evil. "It is an underwater-

134. Musil, *Der deutsche Mensch*, p. 20. 135. Musil, *Das hilflose Europa*, p. 625.
136. Musil, *Der deutsche Mensch*, p. 40. 137. Ibid., p. 39.
138. Ibid., p. 36. As a model of the modern evolution which acknowledges only "what is, so to speak, really real," Musil pointed to the progression from faith in God, to proof of God's existence by reason, to belief in God in the absence of disproof, and finally to "our own age, which would believe in him only if it could encounter him regularly in a laboratory."

swimming in an ocean of reality, an obstinate hold-your-breath-just-a-bit-longer, threatened, to be sure, by the danger that the swimmer will never come to the surface again."[139] The modern age of empiricism renounced philosophy in the old, systematic, deductive style not because it was incapable of philosophy but because it rejected what did not agree with the facts. Musil emphasized the huge extent of historical time required to work out a new way of thinking and the "after-effect of the old" which still remained in the preference for "great deductive systems" over the less exalted tasks of science.[140] He pointed out that it was not only the German idealists such as Fichte, Schelling, and Hegel who had given up on empiricism. The French version of bourgeois ideology since Descartes had also allowed itself to be trapped in the straitjacket of a narrow rationalism. By the late nineteenth century, the initial impulse of the seventeenth and eighteenth centuries had exhausted itself in positivism, when rationalism had at last "become despicable and ridiculous."[141]

Musil argued that the reaction to this failure of "the rational-constructive" was "a need for the irrational, for the fullness of facts, for reality." In the late nineteenth century, this turning from abstract rationalism to the irrationalism of the merely factual took two main forms, historicism and pragmatism. Historicism was a last attempt to salvage the dignity of philosophy in a side-office. It had the virtue of a spirit of reconciliation and an openness to facts, but it lacked the intellectual categories to cope with "an hourly growing mountain of facts." Swamped by lifeless facticity, it offered "a gain in knowledge, and a loss in life, a spiritual [seelischer] miscarriage." Historicism tried to take over for philosophy in an age of pragmatism, and found itself "burdened with two kinds of bad conscience: a practical one, which mocked the untimeliness of an historical philosophy; and a philosophical one, which groaned because it could not go on without a great ordering point of view."[142]

While historicism tried to preserve a veneer of philosophical dignity for the age of facts, the real vanguard of the revolt against rationalism was pragmatism. By pragmatism Musil meant the typical attitude toward life in the modern world, most fully expressed in the models of the politician and the businessman. This attitude, of course, had roots in the attempt of modern science to master the realm of the *ratioïd*, to dis-

---

139. Musil, *Das hilflose Europa*, p. 632.   140. Musil, *Der deutsche Mensch*, p.38.
141. Musil, *Das hilflose Europa*, p. 629.   142. Ibid.

cover what is stable, regular, measurable, repeatable in apparently quite dissimilar events, "such as the falling of a stone in a straight line and the orbiting of the planets." What science and the fact-oriented thought of the modern businessman and politician carried over from the old speculative philosophy was the search for the "unambiguous" and certain, which is the essence of scientific lawfulness. The spiritual presupposition of capitalism was very simple: "Whoever wants to build on stone in human affairs must make use of either force or desire." The key to both methods was the dependability of a calculation grounded in the lowest common denominator. What made capitalism such a masterful human system was its ability to rely on desire rather than force. Capitalist speculation worked on the principle of "I let you win, so that I can win more, or I let you win more, so that I can win anything at all; this cunning of a reflective parasite is the soul of all reputable business." Moreover, capitalism had achieved this on a completely impersonal scale, which provided an extraordinarily dependable principle of order in the absence of any generally valid one. Its formula was simply: "Money is the measure of all things. Its negative formulation is: the human act bears no measure in itself." To those who were offended by this "organized self-seeking," Musil pointed out that capitalism was "the most energetic and elastic form of organization which human beings have so far achieved." Not surprisingly, modern politicians did their best to extend this pragmatic principle of the lowest common denominator, but the greater unreliability of the political sphere meant that politicians still resorted to more vulgar forms of force.[143]

Among the intellectuals of the 1920s Musil identified two main centers of opposition to this pragmatic man of facts: those who denied the facts and those who wanted to be less rational. Protests were most often directed against the narrow rationalism of the positivist era and the objective routine of capitalism and bureaucracy. Musil believed that the protest against positivism and Darwinism had no serious implications at all as a critique of reason, since these had been simply premature syntheses, a caricature of science, "a transitional case which means nothing."[144] On the other hand, the protests against the pragmatic man failed to define the opponent correctly. Although the businessman and the politician depended on calculation, regularity, and probability, they were not at all paradigms of rationality "in the sense of a preponderance

143. Musil, *Der deutsche Mensch*, pp. 44–48.
144. Ibid., p. 41.

of the intellectual. In their activity is a great deal more of the irrational, even the anti-rational."[145] The critics of pragmatism came closer when they defined the problem as the evil of calculating with human beings as objects, but "they date the fall from innocence too late."[146] The problem, according to Musil, was not the evil of intellect but, rather, that "objectivity cannot found a human order, but only a factual one."[147] The goal of Musil's art was to explore the realm where predictability and regularity broke down, to investigate the unique, the individual, the incalculable—the realm of the non-*ratioïd*. But the recovery of the personal had nothing to do with the rejection of reason, science, or empiricism.

Musil believed that German literary and philosophical culture had defined itself too much in opposition to the great revolutionary period of the modern world. In its vulgar clichés about mere knowledge and mechanistic thought, German culture had forgotten that "once and for great men" the "passion of turning . . . to the witness of the understanding and the senses" had been a "powerful abstinence movement of the soul."[148] The difficulties involved in applying the model of the natural sciences to the human realm had been used in Germany to justify a cowardly escape from intellect and facts. German classicism had been only too quick to see the limitations of the new scientific spirit and its failure to make connection with life. Musil admitted that those among "our poets, artists, philosophical pathetics" who welcomed the new spirit "were the worst"; and he agreed that "Goethe's love for the individual and the concrete was the right reaction to it."[149] The classical generation of humanists had seen themselves in personal relation to the cosmos, "an order at rest with a closed book of laws," and they would certainly have found the "disorder and ugliness" of the modern world "unbearable."[150] Nonetheless, Musil denied the irrationalists and neoromantics of the 1920s the support of the Goethe who "admired Kant, loved Spinoza, did research in the natural sciences, and stood on much better terms with the understanding than the little Goethe-souls of today."[151] Moreover, German classicism's supreme indifference to "math-

145. Ibid., p. 50.   146. Ibid., p. 51.
147. Musil, *Das hilflose Europa*, p. 638. Musil was commenting on one of his favorite discussions of the culture of the 1920s: Walter Strich, "Der Fluch des objektiven Geistes," *Der neue Merkur*, 3. Jahrgang, H. 7, 1920, pp. 494–504. See below, Chapter IV, section 1.
148. Musil, *Das hilflose Europa*, p. 631.
149. Musil, *Der deutsche Mensch*, pp. 41–43.
150. Musil, *Das hilflose Europa*, p. 630.   151. Ibid.

ematics, English philosophy, political economy, spinning looms, and business affairs" had bequeathed a backward, petty-state, and Biedermeier style to the German spirit:[152] "What was just a small dead space in Goethe's field of vision, a hundred years later blots out an important section of the horizon."[153] The Goethe cult had become a shabby excuse for the failure of German culture to come to terms with reason, science, and the industrial revolution.

Musil agreed that the human being is "not merely intellect, but also will, feeling, unconsciousness, and often mere factuality, like the clouds wandering in the heavens." But the appeal to intuition had become the blank check of German culture, and Musil was convinced that its abuse in politics was unlikely to lead to the liberation of the soul. Those who see in man "only what is not influenced by reason must in the end see the ideal in an ant-state, against whose mythos, harmony, and intuitive certainty of action everything human is most probably nothing."[154] Even when they did not follow this logic as far as fascism, these soulful skeptics and intuitionists invariably saw intellect as the enemy. The view common among intellectuals that the intellect destroyed the soul was a mistake, and the opposition between the two was false: "It can then be nothing other than a matter of the wrong relationship between intellect and soul. It is not that we have too much understanding and too little soul, but rather that we have too little understanding in questions of the soul."[155] What was needed was not more emotion or a theory of world history but a fluid, open style of thought which brought its concepts into relation with the experiences of everyday life, an exploration "of the reasons, connections, limitations, the flowing meanings of human motives and actions—an explication of life."[156]

152. Musil, *Der deutsche Mensch*, p. 42.   153. Ibid.
154. Musil, "Geist und Erfahrung," p. 665.
155. Musil, *Das hilflose Europa*, p. 638. See also Musil, "Geist und Erfahrung": "It is an unholy misunderstanding to set the spirit [*Geist*] in opposition to the understanding [*Verstand*]: the humanly essential questions are merely confused by all the scribblings about rationalism and irrationalism; the only possible yearning where one does not lose just as much as one gains is supra-rationalism [*Überrationalismus*]" (p. 658). Efraim Frisch, the editor of *Der neue Merkur*, described Musil's review of Spengler: "'That is a supra-rational standpoint, which seeks to establish itself here, even if in the sober context of the advantages of empiricism in relation to false intuitionism'" (quoted in Guy Stern, "Musil über seine Essays: Ein Bericht über eine unveröffentlichte Korrespondenz," *Germanic Review* 49 [1974]:60–82). See also Guy Stern, *War, Weimar, and Literature: The Story of the "Neue Merkur" 1914–1925* (University Park, Pa., 1971).
156. Musil, *Das hilflose Europa*, p. 640.

CHAPTER FOUR

Der Dichter: 1918-1933

This is the homeland of the *Dichter*, the realm where his
intellect reigns. . . . The task is always to discover new
solutions, connections, constellations, variables, appealing
models of how one can be human, *to invent* the inner person.[1]

By 1918 Musil was ready to return to the project of the thinking
poet which he had formulated in his pre-war essays. Between
1911 and 1918 he had been inwardly inhibited and outwardly obstructed from realizing his mission as a *Dichter*,
but the experience of the war helped him to break through his creative
inhibition and prepared him for the tasks of intellect in the realm of the
non-*ratioïd*. His maturity as a creative writer between 1918 and 1933
was important primarily for the process of conceiving and writing *The
Man without Qualities*, but this novel is only the most conspicuous
product of his most creative period. Moreover, Musil's significance lies
not only in his individual works, but also in the understanding which
informs them: he emphasized "the utopian assumptions" of his work,
that the "individual works are always occasional!"[2] Just as strongly as
Musil resisted systematic philosophy and reductionist psychology, he
argued *for* a theoretical literature. In his brilliant "Ansätze zu neuer
Aesthetik" (1925), Musil quoted Béla Balázs as wise counsel to the
poets of German culture:

"By that I do not mean to say that the artist must necessarily be 'learned,' and
I also know the common (all too common!) view of the value of 'unconscious

---

1. Musil, "Skizze der Erkenntnis des Dichters" (1918), in *TE*, p. 784.
2. *TE*, p. 478.

creation.' Still, it depends on what level of consciousness one creates 'unconsciously.' "[3]

Musil's characteristic predicament as a writer was to find himself in a middle zone between the "so-called intellectual" and the "so-called man of feeling."[4] Resisting the drives for unified formulas and positions of rest, Musil offered a more flexible model of the mutuality of thinking and feeling.

This chapter examines three overlapping levels of Musil's creative maturity. In his plays—*Die Schwärmer* (1921) and *Vinzenz* (1923)— and in his theater criticism, Musil explored the mystery of individuality in relation to the fixed roles of bourgeois culture. In the novellas and stories of the mid-1920s, particularly in *Drei Frauen* (1924), he overcame the problems of *Vereinigungen* and found his way to the purity of the symbolic story. In the process, Musil formulated his mature aesthetics and his phenomenological reduction of the romantic tradition in terms of "the other condition" (*der andere Zustand*). He also gave new clarity to his understanding of the novel's function of mediation between the ideological art of his dramas and the formalism of the novellas. The war had provided the framework for his conceptions for a novel and after 1918 his sketches evolved with steady intensity, until by 1924 he was ready to write. Since Musil devoted the remainder of the decade to *The Man without Qualities*, the range of his creativity is most apparent in the early 1920s.

The extraordinarily productive years between 1918 and 1924, which firmly established Musil's stature and reputation as a *Dichter*, represent a crucial period of maturation.[5] As he emptied himself into his art, Musil seems almost to have died inwardly—working through the feelings of doubt and despair which had inhibited his writing before the war.[6] This struggle to become humanly mature culminated in 1924 with

3. Musil, "Ansätze zu neuer Aesthetik," *Der neue Merkur* (March 1925), in *TE*, p. 667.

4. Musil, "Literat und Literatur," *Die neue Rundschau* (September 1931), in *TE*, p. 700: Here Musil suggests the model of "a person whose intellect plays with his feelings or whose feelings play with his intellect."

5. The moment of public recognition was short-lived. In 1923 a number of his friends wrote admiring reviews in an attempt to lift his work out of obscurity. He was awarded the Kleist Prize for *Die Schwärmer* and the "Kunstpreis der Stadt Wien" for *Drei Frauen*, and in 1923 his peers elected him vice-president of the "Schutzverband deutscher Schriftsteller in Österreich" (of which Hofmannsthal was president), but to the general public he remained an esoteric literary figure.

6. Envisioning an introduction to a possible edition of his essays in 1921, Musil wrote: "I hardly need say that I am publishing the work of a dead man. One will see that,

the deaths of his parents, the loss of economic security in the inflation, and the task of writing his novel. It was only then that he allowed himself finally to confront "the astonishing question: how did I come to be myself, etc.?"[7] What seem to have died in Musil were the pathos, anger, and rebellion which had dominated earlier conceptions of his novel. In his struggle for self-acceptance between 1921 and 1924 he gained access to a prose voice touched by the deepest sources of his creative energies, the not-yet-outlived power of his own unreason. Despite the bitterness and isolation that marred the years after 1924, he found his way to the ironic voice which allowed him to sublimate his antagonistic relation to the world. With the objectivity of the scientist and the disabused irony of the poet, Musil unveiled the emptiness of the old world and pointed to the spiritual structure of the world to come. He saw his work as the novel of the coming generation and consciously took his place as the lost voice of a lost generation, among the posthumous writers of German culture: "I dedicate this novel to German youth. Not to the youth of today . . . but to the youth which will come in time and will have to begin precisely where we stopped before the war."[8]

I. THE CREATIVE PERSON AND BOURGEOIS CULTURE

A formulation of Balázs comes close: ". . . this soul of which Musil makes us aware signifies the absolute solitude of the human being. But the struggle of the soul with its isolated solitude is actually nothing other than its outrage against the false connections (*Vereinigungen*) among human beings in our society."[9]

The goal of Musil's art was the ethical person, the motivated human being who creates meanings out of himself. In writing *Die Schwärmer*

---

according to his own definition, he was already dead when he wrote down many of his ideas" (*TE*, p. 290). Cf. also *TE*, pp. 474–75: Musil later recalled the intensity of his fear of death as a child and as a younger man. He found that as one grows older one hangs less frantically on to life, and he wondered to what extent a positive, metaphysically influenced relationship was added: "Turning with the death of my mother."

7. *TE*, p. 456.
8. *MoE, Anhang*, p. 1597.
9. Musil, in a letter to Josef Nadler (December 1, 1924), in "Drei Briefe Musils," in *Studien*, p. 287.

Musil developed a model of this type which he considered schematically valid for all his work. The creative person is characterized by his intense awareness of isolation and of the mystery of individuality. Musil described this person as "undefined, beyond truth and right, and metaphysically restless"; he is experienced by others as "asocial," as an "unfeeling dreamer" who is "exclusive, passive in relation to what exists as well as the improvements, contemptuous of reality, and opposed to both ideals and illusions." This type of the other person was the guiding paradigm for the protagonists of Musil's plays—Thomas and Vinzenz—and the point of departure for the sequence of heroes for his novel—Achilles, Anders, and Ulrich. While the outlines of the type remain throughout the 1920s, there is a clear evolution from the seriousness of Thomas and the rebelliousness of Achilles to the ironic hero who emerges in Vinzenz and Ulrich. Musil defined this creative type in opposition to the normal or uncreative person, who was "defined, true, righteous, sympathetic, social, metaphysically secure, inclusive, active, real, and committed to Sunday-ideals, illusions, realities." The enemy of the creative person was all the authorized conditions of the soul which had become rigidified in the conventions of bourgeois culture under the guidance of the mandarinate and the norms of bourgeois morality.[10]

Musil's favorite analysis of the predicament of bourgeois morality was Walter Strich's "Der Fluch des objektiven Geistes." According to Strich, the curse of the objective spirit was not modern science, but the capitulation of the individual to externality: "Irreligiosity lies, above all, in the self-serving security of society, in the typical spiritual symptom of the bourgeois *cum grano salis*: in the belief in morality and works." The characteristic phenomenon of bourgeois spirituality was the agreement to value security, routine, and achievement over the immediate experience of life. Thus, what was individual or personal had been sacrificed to an abstract common basis. In his will to facts, logic, proof, good works, the demonstrable in every respect, modern man had lost track of "the blessing of the indemonstrable" and no longer felt "the wonder of the personal possession." Like Musil, however, Strich was convinced that most complaints against the impersonality and objectivity of bourgeois culture were symptoms of the situation rather than solutions, compulsive reactions to the mechanization of modern life rather than

10. Musil, *Nachlass*, "An 6," and in *TE*. Cf. *Tag*. II, pp. 1102: "All my apparently immoral people are 'creative.'"

inward transformations. The overwhelming impact of impersonal social functions was a given; but the individual was still confronted with the task of being human, of making his own values rather than relying on an abstract common basis or the myth of the demonstrably good action.[11]

Musil was convinced that modern European man had lost track of the capacity to think and act regarding his ego and had settled instead for the bonds of objectivity. Evading the terror of the ethical, European man had escaped into the shelter of the moral law and socially given roles. Bourgeois culture and morality, the preoccupation with the *ratioïd* inspired by modern science, and the need for security had virtually cut modern man off from access to religion, ethics, and mysticism. The situation of the 1920s recalled Luther's problem: "It is the protest of the feelings, of the will, of what lives and changes, of everything human which separates itself from theology, knowledge, the firm and rigid repression." Musil believed that the revolt of the soul against rigidity, whether intellectual, moral, or institutional, had been "the drivewheel of all mysticism."[12] This search for a personal relationship to experience was by no means something merely negative and otherworldly. Ages of religious awakening were characterized not only by "the intense preoccupation of the human being with God, but also with life, a burning factuality of 'being here.'"[13] It was the religious man who had the audacity to take himself, his actions, and his meanings seriously. But ethical experience—love, presentiment, contemplation, humility—had the disadvantage that it was hard to communicate, "entirely personal and almost asocial." In the 1920s all that remained of real ethics led a precarious existence in art, in essayism, and in the chaos of private relations.[14]

Musil saw the continuity of the ethical not in the uniformity of finished values, but in the ethical activity, the inner movement out of which values are created. Historically, Musil was thinking of the great ethical thinkers, mystics, essayists, poets, saints—of all those who have new ethical experience, who are "other" people. In addition to the

---

11. Walter Strich, "Der Fluch des objektiven Geistes," *Der neue Merkur,* 3. Jahrgang, H. 7, 1920, pp. 494–504. Musil's notes on Strich describe Christ's "If not me, then my works" as a despairing concession to rationalism; the belief in mysterious acts was simply a negative rationalism, just as occultism was materialism, but simply with a different concept of matter (*Tag.* I, pp. 362–63).
12. Musil, *Das hilflose Europa,* pp. 638–39.
13. Musil, "Der 'Untergang' des Theaters," in *TE,* p. 740.
14. Musil, *Das hilflose Europa,* p. 639.

teachers of mankind, Musil included within the ethical "all the anonymous forces that transform conventional morality."[15] The "other" person echoes the criminal and the saint in his indifference to the conventionally authorized conditions of the soul, in the intensity of his
focus on the logic of his own inner motivation. The type of the "other"
person decides slowly; he offers an ethical example, but not in a tangible and inspiring way. He renounces the human need for totality, for
conditions of rest and remote philosophical forms, and satisfies himself
"with partial solutions. He has the movement, but not the infinitely
distant point."[16] This model of the ethical in the creative person was an
antidote to a period of metaphysical collapse and to a society suffering
from the reduction of the individual to function, convention, and lack
of inner motivation.

The distinctions between science and the person, between the *ratioïd*
and the non-*ratioïd*, lay at the basis of Musil's distinction between morality and ethics. He believed there was a profound connection between
the civilized character of morality and scientific understanding. The
brilliant successes of natural science had led, understandably, to the
view that "human beings should attempt to employ the same method in
moral relations—in the broadest sense—although there it grows more
difficult daily."[17] Musil wanted to clarify the connection between science and morality in a way that isolated the generalizing function of
scientific intellect in the realm of the *ratioïd*, but did not sacrifice precision and empiricism. The *ratioïd* realm is characterized by monotony,
lack of ambiguity, repeatability, regularity, "by the concept of the firm
and fixed as a fundamental underlying fiction in things."[18] The natural
inclination of the Enlightenment had been to apply the methodology of
the *ratioïd* in the sphere of morality by searching for constants and regularities, for "character, law, normality, goodness, imperative, the assured in every respect."[19] Under the aegis of science, civilized morality
was preoccupied with the normative, with the binding force of law and
the concept of the universal good: "The moralist brings a pre-existing

15. *TE*, p. 279. Cf. *Tag.* I, p. 490: What Musil valued in contemporary ethics was the
capacity "to see with new eyes" and to make oneself independent of the old bonds.
16. Musil, *Nachlass*, U 17, B33.
17. Musil, "Skizze," p. 782.
18. Ibid. This led to the morality of repetition, the morality of "if, then" (*Tag.* I,
p. 482).
19. Ibid. Musil was fascinated by problems of probability and statistics, particularly in
the context of the Enlightenment's attempts down to John Stuart Mill to systematize everything under laws (*Tag.* I, 460–69).

and inherited fund of moral precepts into logical order. He brings to the values no value, but, rather, a system."[20] Morality is the typical mode of the philosopher, whose insights tend to be ordering instruments to gratify his central drive for logical organization and coherence. In this respect Musil saw the mandarinate as the shaping cultural group within the German bourgeoisie: "The morality of duty came into the German people through the universities."[21] Musil consistently satirized this moralizing function of the German professor in figures such as Josef in *Die Schwärmer*, the academic stereotypes in *Vinzenz*, and Agathe's husband Hagauer, but he also associated the righteous morality with novelists such as Galsworthy, Undset, and Thomas Mann.[22]

Musil believed that the material of ethics and aesthetics would not submit to rational systematization and law without fundamental distortion: "If the *ratioïd* realm is that of the domination of 'the rule with exceptions,' the realm of the non-*ratioïd* is that of the domination of the exceptions to the rule."[23] Scientists had little to say about the realm of the non-*ratioïd*, since its "facts consist of experiences (*Erlebnisse*), which are not known to them in the necessary multiplicity and variety."[24] In its effort to organize facts under law, Western thought since the eighteenth century had been dominated by a concern with the kind of experience (*Erfahrung*) "which under specifiable conditions is available to everyone." Musil called this kind of experience trivial and argued that this form of empirical thought "naturally narrows the spirit."[25] Musil's inclusion of ethics in the realm of the non-*ratioïd* implied both the importance of aesthetics for ethics and a move away from logical system toward experience—a rapproachement between the ethical and the aesthetic that was closer to Schiller than to Kant.[26] But for Musil, the real clarification of the problem of knowledge came with Dilthey's distinction between *Erfahrung* and *Erlebnis*, a purely epistemo-

20. *TE,* p. 278.
21. Musil, *Nachlass,* "An 5" U39.
22. *Tag.* I, p. 679. Cf. the excerpt from Heinrich Gomperz in *Tag.* II, p. 302: Gomperz saw morality as "the crystallized formulation of the egoistic-unfree way of valuing" which generalizes itself to the altruistic; he opposed this to an ethic of inner freedom that is indifferent to what happens in the external world.
23. Musil, "Skizze," p. 783. Musil paraphrased Kassner's formulation of this dynamic ethic as "acting not from principle, but out of a situation" (*Tag.* I, p. 482).
24. Musil, "Geist und Erfahrung," p. 659.
25. Ibid., p. 656.
26. Cf. Musil's notes on Strich (*Tag.* I, p. 363): "Kant's idea of general validity had nothing to do with validity for all. But Schiller protested against even this slight element of the rational, just as Luther protested against morality."

logical and quite unmagical distinction between two groups of empirically accessible facts: those which submit to lawful regularity and those which do not. Musil admired Dilthey's attempt to bridge the methodologies of the *ratioïd* and the non-*ratioïd* without reducing them to each other, and he preferred Dilthey's more sober language of *Verstehen* to the ecstatic language of intuition. The task of the *Dichter* was to apply his intellect (and not some magical faculty of intuition) to understanding the individuality and meaning of unrepeatable and irreducible combinations of experience in the realm of the non-*ratioïd*, to explore those experiences which could not be reliably repeated by everyone in a laboratory.[27]

In Musil's thought the *Dichter* replaces the philosopher, just as the creative person replaces the normal, moral human being. The *Dichter* speaks on behalf of the exception in an unfirm world with unfirm values. He explores ethical experience—i.e., experiences in the understanding of feeling—to master experiences which are not accessible to others and to create "the good as such."[28] In this venture the *Dichter* takes upon himself the spiritual tensions of the whole civilization; he is "the human being in whom the desperate isolation of the individual in the world and among people comes most strongly to the surface."[29] Both the *Dichter* and the creative person suffer on behalf of the normal person the real bases of a situation which the latter ordinarily does not feel. The normal person lacks the consciousness of his own experience and is in this sense pathological, egoistic, *unzurechnungsfähig*, and unable to assimilate new experience. While normal people hold the world together and moralists communicate their shared values, the movement of humanity since Homer has come "from the variations," and it is these that the *Dichter* is responsible for exploring and creating. It was Musil's gift to notice the variations, to portray the creative person and

---

27. Musil's distinction between the *ratioïd* and the non-*ratioïd* emphasized the object of knowledge rather than the faculties of knowing. He insisted on the value of intellect in both realms and resisted formulations of the scientist and the poet along the lines of reason vs. feeling, outside vs. inside, intellect vs. intuition. But he also knew that poetry arose out of a relationship between subject and object: "There are people who understand only what they love and people who understand what they do not love: the first understand with spirit, the second with ratio" (*Tag.* I, p. 482). Cf. also *Tag.* II, p. 1165: "The spirit transforms the other things, not the things the spirit. That means: we understand only what is ours." In these passages Musil was struggling to come to terms with *intuition*, a word that he felt was overused in his culture.

28. Musil, from the *Nachlass*, "Ich messe der Dichtung eine Wichtigkeit bei . . . ," quoted in Roth, *Robert Musil: Ethik und Aesthetik* (Munich, 1972), pp. 555–58.

29. Musil, "Skizze," p. 784.

his relation to the norm, to explore the inner self on behalf of the whole civilization. This meant the proclamation of "a formless, homeless life," in a world in which "everything is inauthentic," and the attempt to move beyond this to the invention of the person.[30] Despite his isolation, however, Musil sensed that the model of Zarathustra, of "the solitary one in the mountains," somehow contradicted his temperament.[31] He believed that the nineteenth century had made too much of genius, that people are not very different from each other in rank, and that genius is, psychologically, almost a weakness.[32] Despite his individualism, Musil checked himself with truth, knowledge, realism, and the objective spirit. He opposed the cult of personality in modern literature because it obscured the real tasks of the spirit in a way that never happened in physics: "The structure *of the world* and *not of his predispositions determines the poet's task, that he has a mission!*[33]

Musil's attempt to reconcile objectivity and the person in his art isolated him in a culture which was normatively divided between scientific intellect and poetic feeling, and socially split between the mandarinate and the expressionist rebels. While the mandarinate had obviously left a deep impression on him as an intellectual and as a person, Musil was disappointed with the scientist as a human type: "The physicist had his heroic age with the Encyclopedists. Today all these people live a bit like castrati, harem people, since they are in no way bound to life by their professions."[34] Yet the social prestige of the scientist and the university professor had risen since 1848 in the same measure that the *Dichter*'s status had declined. Musil believed that the *Dichter* had lost track of his own *raison d'être*, while the mandarin's social success had corrupted his commitment to the autonomous values of a spiritual elite.[35] If the mandarin was held together only by the bonds of profession and social status, then the modern artist seemed to Musil to be nothing until he was swallowed by a movement. Musil set himself against the trendiness of modern literary culture because this passion for "isms" was too much an evasion of intellectual independence and the higher claims of literature:

30. Allesch, "Robert Musil," in *LWW*, p. 138.
31. *TE*, p. 303: "What sort of position must one take, however, to be finished with a world which has no firm point?"
32. Ibid., p. 299.
33. Musil, "Skizze," p. 784.
34. *TE*, p. 228.
35. Cf. Musil, "Monolog eines Geistesaristokraten," in *TE*, pp. 844–46.

Confronted with the choice between impressionism and expressionism, I would decide for the dead Dilthey . . . who saw the mission of the great poet in a line with the prophets, thinkers, sages, founders of religions, and other great image-makers of the human spirit.[36]

Musil had developed in relation to impressionism as a young man, and he saw expressionism as something that had arrived after his identity had been formed.[37] This generational experience of cyclical trends made him suspicious of literary ideologies, but his own mode—the thinking poet—also made him critical of these movements. For Musil, the failures common to impressionism and expressionism were lack of ideas and unwillingness to think things through. Both literary ideologies had encouraged opposition to intellect, emphasizing the need to speak to "the heart or to some similar organ."[38] Impressionism had tended toward an undifferentiated receptivity to experience which left only random feelings and impressions. Its naive epistemology ignored "the fact that there is no report of experience which does not presume a spiritual system with the help of which the report is 'created' out of the facts."[39] Musil's ambivalence toward the impressionism which had been dominant in Austria when he was a young man echoed his blend of enthusiasm and reserve toward Mach. It is clear that Musil valued much of what is described as impressionism, and he saw his own work as an attempt to evolve out of this position. But he did not believe that expressionism's cult of personality, feeling, intuitionism, and willfulness was the correct response. Expressionism's invocation of great ideas "such as suffering, love, eternity, goodness, inordinate desire, whore, blood, chaos, etc." turned out to be "no more valuable than the lyrical activity of a dog barking at the moon."[40] Although he shared a great deal of expressionism's awareness of the tension between emotional truth and the dead forms of bourgeois culture, Musil rejected the tendency in con-

36. Musil, "Symptomen-Theater I," in *Theater: Kritisches und Theoretisches* (Munich, 1965).

37. Cf. Musil, "Stilgeneration und Generationsstil," *Berliner Börsen-Courier*, 1922, in *TE*, p. 838: "Around 1900, people already believed that naturalism, impressionism, decadence, and heroic immoralism were various sides of a new soul; around 1910, people came to believe (what only a few of the participants such as Alfred Kerr had already known) that this soul was a hole, of which nothing was real but the sides; and today from the generation-soul there is nothing left over but a few individual souls. . . . There are reasons to believe that it will not turn out any differently with expressionism."

38. Musil, "Der 'Untergang' des Theaters," in *TE*, p. 736.

39. Musil, "Literat und Literatur," p. 704.

40. Musil noted that in the artistic programs of the post-war period, God was characteristically often sought in chaos (*Tag.* I, p. 359).

temporary drama toward an emotional escapism which set the *Dichter* in opposition to intellect, empiricism, and the practical requirements of modern life.[41]

Musil wanted a creative, critical tension with reality which required the flexible use of intellect to mediate between cooption and pathos. In expressionism he perceived a false dynamism which claimed to set the spirit in motion, but actually only repeated the same motions: "The language of the feelings is conservative, even when the feeling is not."[42] The cycles of expressionism, between messianic hope and desperate cynicism, confirmed for him the sterility of a literature of great feelings without enough intellect or patience to sustain it. He saw the expressionists as too much the victims of their own passions, dogmas, and trends, without that leaven of intellect, irony, and self-criticism which might have nurtured growth in both literature and life. By making a cult of intuitionism, they threw themselves into an assumed deeper language of life without trying first to understand it: "Naturalism offered reality without spirit, expressionism spirit without reality; neither is spirit."[43] Musil felt no personal stake in the quarrel between impressionism and expressionism, since his task remained the creation of the inner self, the intellect's exploration of the realm of the non-*ratioïd*. Nietzsche, Dilthey, and the symbolists all pointed in this direction, toward a task which was irrelevant to the constraints of cultural fashion. In a period of critical and artistic confusion, Musil recalled that "there is a system, a synthesis, which is more important than poets, more comprehensive and enduring than tendencies: literature."[44] But Musil was only too aware of the price of social and cultural isolation that the poet often had to pay, particularly in the modern world. It was with both pride and bitterness that he looked to figures such as Büchner, Hebbel, Nietzsche, Stendhal, Flaubert, Dostoevsky, Wilde, and Rilke—and wondered: "Why must a few poets always be 20–100 years ahead?"[45]

41. Musil's development parallels the emergence of expressionism in many respects. Wilhelm Bausinger ("Robert Musil und die Ablehnung des Expressionismus," *Studi Germanici* 3 [1965]:383–89) argues that despite Musil's hostility toward expressionism, it makes sense to think of him as an idiosyncratic variation on the broader phenomenon, as a critic from within. It is obvious that Musil's definition of this amorphous historical phenomenon may not fit with the changing critical definition of the term. Musil had in mind a dramatist such as Anton Wildgans, while a more recent critic might be thinking of Franz Kafka. It *is* clear that Musil would not have used this term to describe himself.

42. Musil, "Bücher und Literatur" (1926), in *TE*, pp. 612–13.

43. Musil, "Geist und Erfahrung," p. 666.

44. Musil, "Bücher und Literatur," p. 695.

45. *TE*, p. 456.

Musil's vision of the poet and the realities of bourgeois culture in the
1920s intersected in his relationship to the theater, both as a dramatist
and as a critic of the Vienna stage.[46] Whatever the occasional achievements of specific poets, directors, or actors, Musil concluded that the
theater had become the most rigidified of bourgeois cultural institutions, victimized both by the routine of cultural convention and by the
demands of the marketplace. Film had access to undreamed-of technical
freedom and the chance to create a new audience; the novel was relatively formless and less dominated by the problems of selling tickets;
theater seemed to have the worst of both worlds. Trapped by money
and convention, it sought to maintain the favor of a socially and culturally limited group of people who were interested only in repeating
past performances. Musil was convinced that even "our critical points
of view are little more than a dramaturgy of enjoyment, a business-dra-
maturgy, a dramaturgy of exhaustion and weariness." This led to a cult
of performances, and he saw Vienna as a city of actors and critics rather
than poets and directors.[47]

Musil disliked any art which depended on standard metaphors, images, and emotional scenarios, instead of building life further. He saw
the theater of his day as an arena of manipulation which worked for
effects and drew on the emotional habituation of the audience rather
than the creative power of the poet. A theater which repeated the emotions and actions of some other world and could not believe in the authentic individuality of the destinies it enacted was not likely to serve
the real needs of the spirit. The preference for heroic gestures, sublime
rhetoric, and formalized action had lost touch with lived reality, with
the structure of the dramatic as human beings lived it in the 1920s:
"Without doubt the most important decisions are brought to completion between people more often in a silence or in a word than in a
scream or the visible action of the body."[48] In the theater culture of the
1920s such an observation sounded like an invitation to the undramatic
and uneconomical, but Musil believed that the poet's task was to see
new things, to notice the way human beings actually experience their
lives:

The spirit . . . has the unpleasant quality that it has not come into the world for
the theater, but also for other tasks. It has its own events. . . . Even the church

46. Cf. Musil's theater reviews collected in Musil, *Theater*, ed. Roth; also Asta Lepinis, "Der Kritiker Robert Musil" (Ph.D. diss., Yale, 1970).
47. Musil, "'Untergang,'" p. 730.
48. Musil, "Symptomen-Theater II," in *TE*, p. 721.

does not consist of nothing but saints, but what a strange quality of it it would be, if it saw the saints only as unpleasant surprises.[49]

Musil believed that the problems of the theater were symptomatic of the crisis of bourgeois culture as a whole—a crisis of the values and institutions of the eighteenth century. He understood this process in terms of Friedrich Paulsen's categories of the three stages of social organization and cultural leadership through which the German people had evolved: "The ecclesiastical-Latin ideal of education with the clergy as the leading group, the courtly-French ideal of the noble, and finally the bourgeois-Hellenistic-Humanistic ideal in whose final stages we presumably find ourselves."[50] In the eighteenth century the theater had been part of a vital social experience, helping to focus the transforming cultural energies of the ideology of *Bildung*. But *Bildung* had "lost its social nimbus," not simply because of the emancipation of the working class, but because of the spiritual ossification of the educated classes and their mandarin elite. This situation of cultural decline in the midst of social heterogeneity gave the theater its quality of sheer spectacle. Musil believed that in an age without valid rules for the feelings or authentic bases for action, people were all too likely to seek release in the spectacle of great gestures. His preference for inaction over pseudo-action, for authentic feelings over manufactured ones, made him seem like an unfeeling man of reason and a bad dramatist. He wanted to lead his culture back to the preconditions of drama, but he wondered how to "lead a people whose ideal is the strong man without many words, the reserve lieutenant"; this heroic type of the leader was hailed by critics "in whom the spirit now clamors like the noise in class when the teacher unexpectedly has to go out."[51] Given the disintegration of the motivating power of culture, the poet was left to create a drama which reflected the new spiritual situation:

In place of the tragic contradiction of the individual *to* the law must step the revealed contradictions *in* the laws of mundane existence; in that lies the distinction between the Enlightenment, which believed in the autonomy of the moral law and reason, and the age of empiricism, for which the world is an unending task with progressive partial solutions.[52]

This vision informed Musil's attempt in *Die Schwärmer* (*The Visionaries*) to turn modern theater away from tragic drama to investigate the

49. Musil, "Das neue Drama und das neue Theater," in *TE*, p. 742.
50. Musil, "'Untergang,'" p. 734.
51. Ibid., pp. 740–41.
52. Musil, "Symptomen-Theater II," p. 737.

bases of motivation.[53] As the major connecting link between his early and late art, *Die Schwärmer* expressed Musil's conviction that "life ought to be motivated in the extreme, and thus also the drama."[54] In dramatizing the tension between the creative person and the inauthenticity of normal reality, Musil focused primarily on the basic form and value in bourgeois culture—marriage—and secondarily on the other main form of the encapsulation of the ethical-aesthetic self—the profession. The plot involves nothing more than an exchange of lovers, but the real substance is the explication of the creative person and the problems of leading a motivated life. The figures gather at the home of Thomas and Maria to discover the truth about the adventures of Anselm and Regine. As in "Das verzauberte Haus" and again in *Vinzenz* and *The Man without Qualities*, the house is the central spiritual symbol. Here it stands for the world of the creative person, for the will to be different, for the antagonism toward the normal, uncreative person and the world of ordinary reality: "There are people who will always know only what could be, while the others, like detectives, know what is. The former conceal something that is in motion, while the latter are firm." The play is a reckoning after ten years with the figures who shared these values in their youth.[55]

Anselm and Thomas (the opposing types of the adventurer and the hard worker) share an awareness of the isolation and formlessness of human beings, and of the yearning for union that arises out of this. Since their youth they had acted out of raw energy and ruthlessness, while Regine's husband, Johannes, had broken under the stress of their vision. He had committed suicide, acting out the symbolic gesture of their generation because he lacked "that stupid drop of credulity with-

---

53. Kaiser and Wilkins describe *Die Schwärmer* as "a Lesestück" which is "far too long for the stage" (*Robert Musil*, p. 102). Despite the length and difficulty of the play, it has steadily risen in the judgment of critics since Musil's death. It has had some success as theater in German and French; although it has never been translated into English, it is an American critic who has praised it most highly: "After the dust has settled around *The Man without Qualities*, Musil's only serious play, *The Visionaries*, may one day be considered his finest work" (Pike, *Robert Musil*, p. 71). Virtually all of the recent students of the play agree in emphasizing its importance: see Gorden Eastridge Birrell, "The Problem of Ethical Responsibility in Robert Musil's 'Die Schwärmer'" (M.A. diss., Stanford, 1965); Annie Reniers-Servranckx, *Robert Musil* (Bonn, 1972), p. 197; Sibylle Bauer, "Ethik und Bewusstsein," in Bauer and Ingrid Drevermann, *Studien zu Robert Musil* (Cologne, 1966). The most careful and extensive discussion of the play (Günther Schneider, *Untersuchungen zum dramatischen Werk Robert Musils*, [Frankfort, 1973]) emphasizes how little attention had been given to Musil's dramatic work.

54. *TE*, p. 466.

55. Musil, *Die Schwärmer*, in *Prosa*, pp. 306, 324–25.

out which one cannot live, or admire a single friend or find one."[56] Regine's infidelity to her second husband, Josef, expressed a deeper inner fidelity to Johannes, whose ghost was always with her, while Anselm acted out of the need for love and the fear of being alone. Thomas, meanwhile, has succumbed to the normalcy of marriage and profession, though he cannot bring himself to take either role seriously.[57] He embodies a characteristically Musilian version of the creative person, with a bias toward the intellectual and toward passive observation; yet he is in constant spiritual activity in his awareness of the conflicting ethical possibilities of his social world. Anselm acts out the sense of the unfirmness of values and reality which Thomas only thinks; he is the anarchist, lover, charlatan, and religious type, who escapes into other people from the truths that Thomas bears consciously and passively. Anselm's need for other people is both what makes Thomas seem inhuman to him and what mitigates his manipulations of other people. Yet Anselm's romantic case for the liberating power of evil is compromised by his real motive: convincing Thomas and Maria to give him the dossier which the detective Stader has gathered on his secret evil.

Regine and Anselm appear as the disturbers of bourgeois normalcy, particularly of the outwardly conventional marriage between Thomas and the beautiful, motherly Maria, who is Regine's sister. Anselm sees himself as a magician, trying to bring Maria and Thomas back to life. Thomas is convinced that Anselm will lead Maria to a profound disillusionment, but he refuses to interfere in her destiny. At the same time, he sees that the facts which Stader and Josef want to reveal about Anselm do not touch the real issues. Thomas's willingness to respect the autonomy and feelings of those around him is maddening to the other characters, who are still committed to their rights and to the illusion of controlling other people's lives. Maria (in her appeals for Thomas to make sense of their marriage) and Josef (in his appeal for Thomas to verify the facts) both seek external comfort from the real ambiguity of the ethical. Even Anselm has lived a life that evaded what he and Thomas both once knew:

56. Ibid., p. 355.
57. About his own professional achievement, Thomas remarks: "In my entire life I have never come to know anything so shameful as success" (ibid., p. 309). About his marriage: "When people are married for so long and always go on four feet and always take double breaths and go every stretch of thought twice and the time between what is essential is always twice as filled with side issues: then one naturally yearns sometimes like an arrow for a completely air-thin space" (ibid., p. 316).

That we stand in the middle of a reckoning, which contains nothing but unknown quantities, and it goes forward only when one uses a skiff and assumes
something as constant. A virtue as highest. Or God. Or one loves people. Or one
hates them. One is religious or modern. Passionate or disillusioned. Warlike or
pacifist. . . . One simply walks in and immediately finds his feelings and convictions ready-made for his whole life and for every imaginable special case. It is
hard to find one's feelings only if one accepts no other presuppositions than that
this escaped monkey, our soul, balled up on a pile of clay, whizzes through
God's unknown infinity.

The cold clarity of this vision, and Thomas's willingness to let Maria do
as she wishes, are unbearable for his wife; much as he loves her, he is
unwilling to lock himself in a cage of eternal love. His willingness to let
go of their whole former life together leads her to the accusation that
women love more deeply. Thomas replies that this is because women
love men: "With a man the world breaks in to you." [58]

   This world of the creative person is confronted by Stader's scientific
version of external reality and by Josef's moralistic version of normalcy.
Stader, who represents the detective bureau of Newton, Galilei and Stader, had once been Regine's servant. He has risen to a position of importance in technological society, while transforming his artistic temperament by the methods of the *ratioïd*. He sees his detective work as a
faithful emulation of Thomas's scholarly views, and his passion for reducing the accidental and personal to the purely lawful echoes
Thomas's critique of Anselm's exaggeration of the personal. In this, Stader is Musil's first comic figure (foreshadowing aspects of Vinzenz, Ulrich, and Stumm von Bordwehr), a parody of Thomas's convictions
about science and modern civilization. Stader announces the new age
when male and female have become variants of synthetic hormones, an
age when spiritual questions must be brought into relation with mathematics and experimental technique. In his passionate speculation in the
lowest common denominator, this Viennese detective advocates the
methods of the *ratioïd* in the realm of the non-*ratioïd*: "Oh, it is a pleasure to spread out the hidden essence of a person so playfully before
oneself." He is impervious to Regine's insistence that an act can mean
something entirely different inwardly from what it seems outwardly.
Stader is beside himself with the success of science in reducing everything accidental to functional relations, but Thomas cannot bring him-

   58. Ibid., pp. 330, 379, 384. Thomas wonders if Maria has never really hated him,
"like a knife that is always lying in your way?" To her reaction that this would be the end
of love, he replies: "No! The true beginning!" (ibid., p. 317).

self to take his own writing or Stader's discipleship entirely seriously: "I am a child of the times. I must be satisfied to place myself on earth between the two stools of knowledge and ignorance."[59]

Thomas's attitude toward Stader's shiny half-truth is loving and ironic, but his confrontation with the moral man, Josef, engages his person and his outrage. He has no interest in demonstrating Anselm's immorality or pathology, or in teaching people like Regine "not to make claims and to have respect for the firm principles of existence":

THOMAS: Josef, that is precisely it: this is what she does not have, this respect. For you there are laws, rules, feelings which one must respect, people to whom one must pay heed. She is through with all that. . . . In the midst of an enormously good order, against which she did not have a single solid reason to complain, something remains unordered in her—the germ of another order which she will not think out. A little piece of the molten core of creation.

It is, of course, just this which draws Thomas to Regine, but it is also what allows Josef to insist that all this talk merely justifies Anselm's chicanery:

THOMAS: Yes. I know it. And that is what I want to do. You demand ideals; but also that one make no extreme use of them. You allow widows to remarry, but declare love to be eternal, so that remarriage occurs only *after* death. You believe in the struggle of life, but soften it with the injunction: Love your neighbor. . . . You are for property *and* good works. You declare that one must die for the highest good, because you already presuppose that no one lives for it even for an hour.[60]

When Josef leaves in anger, the pathos builds between Regine and Thomas, who are now left alone in the house. The spiritual world of their generation looks ever more desolate and lonely. Regine speaks of her own flight into unreality with Johannes and of her contempt for Maria's flight with Anselm into reality, while Thomas worries that he is just a prisoner of success. The special affinity between Thomas and his "wild sister" foreshadows Ulrich and Agathe, but Thomas's sense of the purposelessness of the lives they have led is echoed by Regine, who is apparently on the verge of suicide. They are both conscious of the tension between the illusion of unlimited possibilities that people cherish in their youth and the roles to which they so quickly and apparently happily submit. The rhythm is all prefabricated, as impersonal as the rising and setting of the sun, processing the marriages in summer and the sui-

59. Ibid., pp. 334, 388.
60. Ibid., p. 393.

cides in the fall. To Regine's pleas for counsel in her despair, Thomas can only invite her to "love these contradictions" and confess that perhaps he will "think differently later. I simply want to go forward." Regine wants Thomas to go with her, but he mistrusts the illusion to which the attempt to evade one's loneliness leads:

THOMAS: One simply wanders about this way. Antagonistic toward all those who go their defined ways, while you are on the undefined beggar's journey of the spirit through the world. Nonetheless, you belong to them somehow. Don't say much when they look at you severely; stillness; one creeps along behind one's skin.[61]

To Regine's accusation that he is an unfeeling man of reason, Thomas replies:

THOMAS: No, no, Regine, if anyone, then precisely I am the dreamer. And you are a dreamer. Those are the apparently unfeeling people. They wander, look on at what the people do who feel at home in the world. And carry something in themselves that the others don't notice. A sinking in every moment through everything into the bottomless. Without going under. The creative condition. (*Regine kisses him quickly and runs out before he can catch her.*)[62]

Despite the pathos, Musil's point is not that everything is meaningless, but rather that the individual need not automatically live out preordained roles. He is free to make his own meanings, free to make his life motivated in the extreme, to decide for himself. For Musil, submission to the life one happens to be leading is always an ethical failure, as is any attempt to justify it on general grounds—whether social or biological—which do not unfold and justify themselves inwardly as one's own grounds.

Die Schwärmer assaults the impulse to acquiesce in a pre-established cluster of prejudices, assumptions, and roles, which lead a life of their own without interference from the human being they possess. While rejecting external forms of reassurance or security, Thomas attempts to maintain the tension between the half-truths of insanity and capitulation, of suicide and reduction to a role, of alienation and domination. In the creative person there is something that is always activated which is simply dormant in other people or firmly encapsulated in marriage or profession. Balázs argues that Musil was portraying the struggle of a deeper identity against the merely accidental forms of human existence,

61. Ibid., p. 400. Cf. *Tag.* I, p. 635: "Be strong without God, without sense: but it is no pleasure."
62. Ibid., p. 401.

the soul which is always there and yet never participates in experience. In *Die Schwärmer* this awareness is expressed through Thomas's firmly male intellect and his ability to love contradictions. His critique of both normalcy and rebellion creates a context in which the soul can break its bonds with moral firmness. This critical impulse reveals social roles as deceits and illusions which are not naturally given; and it liberates the individual to be something other than what he does. But it also leaves him with the starkest possible consciousness of his isolation. In the culture of the early 1920s the impulse to solidarity ("Alone, we are mad; together, a new humanity") and the creation of more authentic human relations was very fragile. Musil's inability or unwillingness to resolve these contradictions into a firm position reflects the intellectual situation of his generation. *Die Schwärmer* offers no final position, but only a perspective on the inward experience of his culture's failure in the early twentieth century.

In *Vinzenz und die Freundin bedeutender Männer* Musil blended the half-truths of Anselm and Stader into a protagonist less serious than Thomas, a kind of rough draft of the ironic man without qualities. Vinzenz and Alpha are farcical precursors of Ulrich and Agathe; they reflect on their ecstatic experience together twenty years earlier, while tormenting the men of importance. These stereotypes without names, who live out their roles as scholar (historian), musician, politician, and reformer, are revealed as emotional cripples who give up their souls for their professions, and get them back only in spasms of irrationality. Vinzenz represents the transformation of the creative person from the discontented and deeply serious Thomas to the apparently superficial hero with no defined relation to the world and no pretensions. He has relinquished Thomas's need for status and achievement; his job as an insurance actuary points both to his acquiescence in modernity and to his transcendence of the mandarin need to be a man of importance. His only role is to leave everyone with the impression that he is totally dissolute or perhaps criminal. At the end of the farce he admits that he is not really a confidence man at all, but lives his life "like every other respectable person, without the consciousness of being its cause and without melody, direction, intoxication or depth." He is not a bad man at all, but only a point of resistance against the fixed cluster of biases and compulsions that seem to satisfy normal people for a lifetime: "My only superiority is that I have no proper profession, which is why I can perhaps see through things a bit more freely than others." Here Musil created a hero outside the mandarinate, but he is a man without qualities who cannot take the roles of rebellion seriously, either. He is content with the profession of impersonality, "calculating the formulas according to which people must die." As a person, he lacks the defect, mania, or secret perversion that would give his life a mission or seriousness. The comic power of the ironic hero frees Vinzenz from the roles offered by his society, but Musil cannot resist a touch of satiric wisdom in the end:

VINZENZ: ... If one does not find his own life, one must go and live behind a foreign one. And then it is best not to do it out of enthusiasm, but simply for money. There are only two possibilities for an ambitious man: to create a great work or to become a servant. For the first I am too honorable; for the second, just adequate.[63]

Musil's meanings were too inward to be at home on the stage as it was conceived in the 1920s, yet he shared the problems of the best dramatists of the previous half-century. The undramatic quality of his work seemed to him only a faithful attempt to touch the reality of the flowing meanings and ambiguities of life:

Even in personal life, the external conduct of mood is nothing more than a passing and expressively poor translation of the inner, and the essence of the human being lies not in his experience and feelings, but, rather, in the sticky, silent external and internal argument with them.

His brief involvement with the theater as a critic and playwright was enough to remind him that in his generation the main vehicle of the spirit was not the theater but the novel. The novel left more freedom for the spirit, both formally and substantively. The preoccupation of theater with heroic action and feeling left too little room for the truths of impersonality which were made more apparent by the structure of modern life, however much sentimental theater liked to evade them: "Great passions are never only personal, but, rather, contain something objective, and it is this which makes the love of Dante greater than that of an unhappy maiden who drowns herself." Musil's theater audience was not receptive to such insights.[64]

Musil found his greatest artistic fulfillment in the forms of the novella and the novel, but his experience with theater marked the initial phase in his development of the ironic voice and the satirical emplotment. He discovered that the old tragedies were dying out, and with *Vinzenz* he began to move away from anger and pathos. As Peter Berger has ob-

63. Musil, *Vinzenz und die Freundin bedeutender Männer,* in *Prosa,* pp. 402–444. Musil published this play in 1923, the year he left the mandarinate for the second time.
64. *TE,* pp. 742, 721.

served, comedy is a signal of transcendence.[65] With the magical powers
of the clown behind the laws, Musil's dark walls began not to seem so
grim as they had looked before. In the early 1920s Musil's comic vision
was balanced tenuously between hysterical and redeeming laughter, but
even then his irony was never quite a nihilistic guffaw, never merely cynicism or sarcasm. His despair drove deep, until it found the refreshing
bath of irony and almost Dadaist laughter.[66] His high valuation of intellect may have drawn him toward the comic; it certainly kept him aloof
from expressionism. Musil lived in an age of social and cultural breakdown, and his irony was critical rather than reasurringly comic in the
sense of confirming the existing social order.[67] The liberating power of
invective was there as a form of combat and creativity, but it mellowed
steadily in the 1920s from Juvenalian to Horatian satire, from self-
righteous rage to a gentler wisdom.[68] Even in Thomas and Vinzenz, urbane self-irony is already present, not as a failure of will but as a form
of love. In Musil's novellas of the 1920s, the magical powers of combat
spilled over into the still more magical world of symbolism. Here a new
seriousness became possible again:

> He who does not understand irony and has no ear for its whisperings lacks *eo
> ipso* what might be called the absolute beginning of personal life, lacks the bath
> of regeneration and rejuvenation, the cleansing baptism of irony that redeems
> the soul from having its life in finitude though living boldly and energetically
> in finitude.[69]

Musil had begun to find his way to the satiric magic and ironic objectivity that made it possible for him to write a great social novel; he had
also found his way to the absolute beginning of his own personal life, to
the novella, and to the crystallization of his aesthetic vision.

2. SYMBOLISM AND "THE OTHER CONDITION"

> The world in which we live and ordinarily react, this
>
> world of authorized conditions of the intellect and the soul, is
>
> simply a necessary substitute for another, to which the true
>
> relation has been lost.[70]

65. Peter Berger, *The Precarious Vision* (New York, 1961), p. 212.
66. Musil associated the new humor of *Vinzenz* with Dada and Brecht (*TE,* p. 270).
67. Hayden White, *Metahistory* (Baltimore, 1973).
68. Robert Elliott, *The Power of Satire* (Princeton, 1966).
69. Sören Kierkegaard, *The Concept of Irony* (New York, 1965), p. 338.
70. Musil, "Geist und Erfahrung," p. 662.

Musil believed that modernism's frantic reactions against intellect were "nothing but a regularly repeated attempt to come closer to 'the other condition,' which, in its various forms as church, art, ethics, eroticism, enters into our existence with enormous power, but has grown completely confused and corrupt." [71] In reaction against modern science, these cultural forms were ordinarily understood as the search for another world or as the affirmation of feeling at the expense of intellect. In Musil's terms, however, "the other condition" referred not to another world but to a lost relation to this one and, concomitantly, to the recovery of a suppressed half of the self: "The understanding is not the only means of orientation and understanding; there are older ones. Sympathy belongs in this context. Sometimes the older forms break through. Those are mystical moments." [72] Musil believed that the more deeply the artist penetrates the realm of the non-*ratioïd*, "the more the element of the understanding retreats in relation to the experience (*Erlebnis*)." [73] For Musil, the novella was the most effective form for the presentation of the *Erlebnis*, of those moments which break through the normal condition of being, not into another world but into a new relation to the same world. In the symbolic magic of *Drei Frauen* and "Die Amsel," Musil gave this vision its most intense poetic expression, and in the notes and essays of the mid-1920s he gave focus and clarity to his understanding of this fundamental polarity of human experience.

In his own generation, Musil saw Rilke as the model of the poetic, admitting that the lyric was "the innermost wellspring of a literature, even if one considers it false to make that a question of literary rank." As the greatest German lyricist since the Middle Ages, Rilke had mastered a new realm of the poetic:

With Rilke the stones and trees do not become people—as they have everywhere that poems have been made—but the human beings become things or nameless beings and only then thereby win their last humanity, moved by an equally nameless breath. One can say: in the feeling of this great poet everything is simile and—nothing any longer only simile.

The ocean is no longer angry in the tradition of the pathetic fallacy, nor am I like the ocean, but I *am* the ocean. Rilke was the poet of the generation of essayists, because he developed a new relation to things, of union and separation, which has nothing to do "either with philoso-

71. Musil, "Ansätze," p. 675.
72. *Tag.* I, p. 390.
73. Musil, "Geist und Erfahrung," p. 658.

phy or skepticism, or with anything else except experience." It was precisely the fluidity of the world and the self which opened up new possibilities for understanding the relatedness of things, the meanings in small: "And even that, this relatedness of the smallest in the greatest, is Rilke. . . . A firm world and within it the feelings as what move and change: this is the normal picture. But actually both, the feelings and the world, are unfirm, even if within very different limits." Musil believed that Rilke had found the poetic voice of the age of the formlessness of human beings. All his poetry was a matter "of the feeling as totality, on which the world rests like an island. . . . He was in a certain sense the most religious poet since Novalis, but I am not certain whether he had any religion at all. He saw differently. In a new, inner way." Musil might have been describing the author of *Drei Frauen* and "Die Amsel," for his own art was an attempt to transform the dead world of univalent meanings into a world of love and meaning, to gain access again to a lost relation to the world.[74]

In *Drei Frauen* Musil demonstrated his mastery of the symbolic tale within the novella, of those moments that break up the normal patterns of ordinary life. Here Musil was able to narrate simple, realistic stories in which events and things assume an extraordinary intensity and inwardness. Here he brilliantly fulfilled the project which he had begun in *Vereinigungen*, a project Frank Kermode compares to Rilke's "sense of a world in metaphysical collapse, a universe of hideously heaped contingency, in which there are nonetheless transcendent human powers. . . . Musil believed that the heightening of consciousness which makes possible the ordered perceptions of good fiction has something in common with erotic feeling; and meaningless contingency is the enemy of novels as well as love."[75] In the poetic mode of relating to the world, meanings emerge through the mutual relations of words and sentences, pages and paragraphs, and these fluid, moving meanings take shape according to laws different from those of scientific univalence. Poetry gives the words their freedom again, but not arbitrarily:

The word of the poet is like the human being who goes where he is drawn; he will spend his time in an adventure, but he will not spend it without sense; and he will have mastered powerful exertions, for the mastery of the half-firm is in no way easier than the mastery of the firm.[76]

74. Musil, "Rede zur Rilke-Feier" (January 16, 1927, in Berlin), in *TE*, pp. 885–99.
75. Frank Kermode, Preface to Musil, *Five Women*, pp. 9–10.
76. Musil, "Literat und Literatur," p. 707.

In the three love-stories of *Drei Frauen* Musil found his way to the recovery of dream speech. As with Kafka, his voice and vision nearly transcended the normal connections with language, opening the door on a world to which most people find access only in sleep or in love. It is the poetry of those times in life when everything slows down perceptibly, and what rarely happens can happen. This world of the release of the soul from the normal condition of being is precarious, leading not only to the divine but into a dark and threatening world of the animal, the magical, and death. Autobiographically, these novellas reflect the process by which Musil gradually came to terms with his own past and his relationship to death. In *Grigia* his old self of the war, science, and practical mastery is shattered by the departure from accustomed roles and dies in the seductive landscape of the Tyrolean Alps; here the tension between mystical epiphany and sexuality is resolved in self-burial. In *The Lady from Portugal* Musil portrayed his own return from war, from the male role to the reconstitution of his relationship to Martha and to his art; here the death of the hero is borne by a *Stellvertreter*, a cat.[77] In *Tonka* another human being dies for him; here Musil came to terms with the most painful ethical experience of his life, his relationship with Herma Dietz.[78]

As in *Vereinigungen*, the spiritual situations of these stories turn on the notion of *Fernliebe* and the portrayal of a heightened condition of being that is related to sexuality and death, love and religion. Here, however, the protagonists are men, in fact, stereotypically male, bearers of the European traditions of practical mastery over nature, warfare, and scientific knowledge. All three heroes find themselves at stages of isolation or inactivity, when they are more vulnerable than in their normal condition. Stepping outside the bonds of family, profession, and social convention, these types of the mandarinate find themselves in a new relation to the world. In each of these stories, the hero achieves this heightened state through a woman, and in each Musil successfully objectifies the symbolic process of consciousness in the flow of things and events.[79] The moment of vulnerability leads Homo to infidelity, disintegration, and death, while Herr von Ketten finds his way to self-knowledge and love. For the young scientist in *Tonka*, this vulnerability sets

77. Cf. the final lines of *The Lady from Portugal*, in *Prosa*, p. 264: "'If God can become a man, he can also become a cat,' said the Portuguese Lady." The death in the cave was replaced in this medieval tale by a new wholeness in the castle of inwardness.
78. Cf. Erich Heintel, "Glaube in Zweideutigkeit," in *Vom "Törless,"* pp. 47–88.
79. Reniers-Servranckx, *Robert Musil*, p. 160.

the stage for his departure from the conventions of his social world and his own narrowly enclosed and confident sense of identity and reality.

While he was writing the stories of *Drei Frauen*, Musil also published his only important lyric poem: "Isis und Osiris" (1923).[80] Although it is not a major achievement, this poem underscores the role Egyptian mythology and the theme of incest play in Musil's work. The echoes of Egyptian mythology and the imagery of neo-Platonic Hermeticism can be found in *Vinzenz*, *Grigia*, and *The Lady from Portugal*, but the connection is explicit in this modern variation on the Egyptian myth of incest: the female/male, mother/son, sister/brother godhead. In "Isis und Osiris" Musil expressed a magical androgynous vision of the union of male and female, passing through tenderness to a moment of profound terror and anxiety, released in a final vision of resolution: "And he ate her heart, and she ate his." The pagan rituals of dismemberment and cyclical renewal through the ingestion of the male generative organ, as well as the love feast of the hearts, give the poem a brutal and frightening quality. Musil was aware of the destructive and regressive elements of sexuality which were tied to the mother/son relation, but in *Grigia* and "Isis und Osiris" he was also attempting to work through the functions of disintegration and destruction in the logic of sexuality itself. Moreover, the threatening elements of "Isis und Osiris" come not only from within or from projections of the dominant female, but also from the tension with society and the brother-clan, as well as the cyclical annihilation of individuality through nature.

Leon Titche sees this poem of death, dismemberment, and resurrection as a *unio mystica* in the unity of the personality.[81] The sister eating the brother echoes the Christ myth and announces the union of male and female in the personality as the goal of Musil's mature art. At the same time, the poem attempts to come to terms with the dominant, annihilating mother and the suicidal and murderous will within the male personality. In *The Temptation of Quiet Veronica* and *Tonka* the older female emerged as a negative figure, set off against an inhibited love-relation; particularly in *Tonka*, one sees the choice of a partner felt to be inferior and her destiny as victim and whore of male guilt and destruc-

80. Musil, "Isis und Osiris" (*Prager Presse*, April, 1923), in *Prosa*, p. 597. Musil later noted that this poem "contains the novel [*MoE*] *in nucleo*. The novel has been charged with perversity. Reply: The archaic and the schizophrenic express themselves artistically in the same way, despite the fact that they are totally different. Feelings for a sibling can be perverse, and they can also be myth" (*TE*, p. 355).

81. Leon L. Titche, "Isis und Osiris," *Kentucky Foreign Language Quarterly* 13 (1966):165–69.

tiveness.[82] In *Grigia* Musil experimented with the absolute separation of spiritual and physical love, where the threatening image of the female appears as the danger of loss of control, madness, and self-destruction. This mediumistic function of the partly mundane, partly divine Grigia recurs again in Clarisse, just as Clarisse echoes the aborted savior-myth of *Tonka*. But the resolutions of *The Lady from Portugal* and *Tonka* point (along with "Isis und Osiris") toward Musil's newly won inner wholeness, which was crystallized by his mother's death in 1924. His father's death followed within months, but it was this last awakening to his mother which helped him to come to terms with death and with the balance of the male and the female in his own personality.

In "Die Amsel" Musil moved beyond the negative vision of his mother and found his way to acceptance of the alogical, the a-*ratioïd*, the *anima* within himself.[83] The title of the story echoes the names Alpha and Agathe, while the two male figures—Aeins and Azwei—continue the anonymous impersonality of Homo, Ketten, the young scientist, and the man without qualities. From a psychoanalytic point of view, the story is the artistic resolution of Musil's ambivalence toward his mother, but this is also one of the most irreducible of Musil's works. The three epiphanies recounted here were based on Musil's own experiences between 1914 and 1924, but neither the narrator nor the protagonist attempts to say what they mean. In the first experience, he was led away from his whole former life by a bird; in the second he experienced the physical presence of a God he did not believe in. The final indignity drew him so far back into his childhood that when he sat in his bedroom, spiritually his feet no longer reached the floor; this experience left him feeding worms to a blackbird which he took to be his mother.

Reasonably enough, Aeins wants to know the meaning of these stories: "Good Lord—replied Azwei—it all simply happened just that way; and if I knew what it meant, then I would probably not even need to tell you the stories."[84] One may call them stories of emotional maturation, of the recovery of childhood or self, but they are as irreducibly mystical as anything Musil ever wrote. It was precisely in the age of the breakdown of the story—so well described by Walter Benjamin as the loss of a coherent context of tradition in which the story can have meaning—just at the most extreme point of this breakdown of commu-

82. Corino, "Ödipus oder Orest?" pp. 185–89.
83. Musil, "Die Amsel," in *Prosa*, pp. 521–35; although it was published in *Nachlass zu Lebzeiten* (1936), it first appeared in the *Neue Rundschau* in 1928.
84. Ibid., p. 535.

nicability, that the story returned again in symbolic form. Here in the absolute story, the parabolic fable, the meaning really is not known; the narrator has no counsel, except the attempt to give expression to his experience. The symbolic novella becomes the aspect of intensity and directness within the mode of ironic objectivity. This is the storyteller who really *is* ignorant. His symbolic immediacy is the other pole of his divine laughter.

Even in these portrayals of mystical ecstacy, Musil chose what his friend Allesch (the model for Aeins?) called "the pure way of objectivity."[85] Musil believed that art was "a gift of grace" and "in every way a human exception," but he was convinced that only tremendous discipline would allow the grace of poetry to come into the world.[86] Banal reduction to profane thought was the enemy of poetry; but Musil's wide reading throughout the 1920s in psychology, anthropology, cultural history, and physiology makes clear the deep commitment to objectivity which underlay his art. These stories, in particular, touch most obviously on the concerns of psychology, on that borderline between psychology and art which led Musil to characterize "Klages, in part Freud, Jung" as pseudo-poets.[87] As before the war, his own work was so close to psychology that he often felt the need to formulate this distinction aggressively.

Musil conceded that psychological reductionism often had major successes, almost entirely conquering certain areas of experience, "as in the case of psychoanalysis."[88] Musil respected Freud as a fellow master of the inner life, and he believed that the psychoanalytic movement had contributed to civilization by making it possible to talk about sexuality.[89] In the late 1930s Musil wondered if Freud's influence had really gone far enough in convincing people to value the unconscious. Moreover, Musil recognized in Freud the reminder that experiences of intuition belong on a scale which ranges from faith to pathology, from the condition of the believer, of the lover, to serious cases of mental illness. However, Musil found the symbolism of psychoanalysis primitive, and he mistrusted the ideological and anti-scientific mentality of the movement.[90] In Freud's own work, he saw scientific discoveries "of great

85. Allesch, "Robert Musil," in *LWW*, p. 142.
86. Musil, "Bücher und Literatur," p. 695.
87. *Tag.* I, p. 787.
88. Musil, "Geist und Erfahrung," p. 658.
89. *Tag.* II, p. 1193.
90. Ibid., p. 1194. Musil's most extended public discussion of psychoanalysis was his playful "Der bedrohte Oedipus," in *Prosa*, pp. 502–504. Here Musil teased about psy-

significance confused with impossibilities, one-sidedness, even dilettan-tism."[91] Moreover, like the German historians, Freud tended to empha-size the compulsive power of the past and the fixity of character. Musil resisted Freud's instinct for positivist reduction, and he believed that the tendency toward a therapy which was moral and enhanced the norm cut against the liberating power of Freud's original insights. While Musil grew to respect much of Freud's creative work, Freud remained one psy-chologist among others—and a fellow artist whose visions Musil did not prefer to his own.

Musil was more sympathetic to Gestalt psychology and often empha-sized its achievements, pointing to Wolfgang Köhler's work on percep-tion as an instance of progress toward the resolution through experi-ment of previously insoluble speculative issues in epistemology. He believed that Gestalt psychology had demonstrated that the reduction of a perception to its elements, much less to only one of them, always leaves something important behind. Gestalt offered a principle of co-herence that resisted system and meaninglessness alike. Here the form-ing power of the poet or the essayist found confirmation in the scientific study of perception: "That the whole mediates a fuller spiritual expres-sion than the elements in which it is grounded, for a figure has more physiognomy than a line, and a configuration of five tones says more to the soul than the amorphous one after another of these five." The concept of Gestalt cut against the disintegrating vision of a tangle of meaningless facts suggested by Mach. While resisting reductionism, it confirmed the reality of meaningful situations, the uniqueness and im-mediacy of non-statistical experience. While avoiding the search for a fundamental underlying substance, it valued the shaping and direction of the process. The Gestalt was not completely irrational, but it always contained an element of individuality which could not be reduced to more general categories. In a sense, Gestalt replaced system. It was a whole or a totality, "not a summarizing totality; but, rather, in the mo-ment when it arises, it sets a special quality into the world, which is other than its elements." The human capacity to form the world into Gestalts was like sleep at night, which overcomes the destructive ana-lytical processes of the day, and the artist was peculiarly responsible for forming the stuff of life. This notion of a dynamic principle of order

choanalytic argumentation and the limitations of Freud's model in a late-nineteenth-cen-tury social context. "Although nasty and one-sided," Musil's critique made "no claim to scientific objectivity."

91. *Tag.* I, p. 749.

which is not strictly conscious or entirely unconscious suggested to
Musil a vision of the ego in flow between control and acceptance, somewhere between captain and passenger in life. This, he believed, was
much like the relationship between form and content in the work of
art.[92]

Musil was impressed by the confirmation of the meaningfulness of
Gestalt in the work of the psychiatrist Ernst Kretschmer, who also influenced the physician/novelist Alfred Döblin. Kretschmer's *Körperbau
und Charakter* seemed to validate the artist's instinctive wisdom that
the external *is* the internal, or as Nietzsche put in, in a certain sense the
body *is* the soul: "The motto is, roughly: Why does one paint devils
thin, and jolly men fat?"[93] Moosbrugger, like Franz Bieberkopf in Döblin's *Berlin Alexanderplatz*, follows Kretschmer's typology of a particular kind of criminal personality. Musil was also influenced in a more
general way by Kretschmer's important psychiatric textbook, *Medizinische Psychologie* (1922). He found in the term "Sphäre" (spheres)—
a half-rational, half-emotional region at the end of consciousness—a
possible antidote to the temptation to take the psychoanalytic metaphor
of the *Unterbewusstsein* too literally, "since consciousness is a condition but not a region."[94] In general, Kretschmer's discussion of symbolizing, sublimation, and dreams was more sympathetic than Freud's
to the autonomous power of the artistic imagination, closer to Jung,
and more confirming of Musil's identity as a poet.[95] Kretschmer's analogy between the symbolizing power of the poet and the primitive's identification of the picture with the soul seemed to be confirmed by the an-
thropologist Lucien Lévy-Bruhl's explanation of primitive mentality in
terms of the notion of mystical participation in things and in other people.[96] Lévy-Bruhl argued that this capacity for magic and related modes

92. Musil, "Literat und Literatur," pp. 712–15.
93. Musil, *Briefe nach Prag*, p. 50.
94. Musil, "Literat und Literatur," p. 708.
95. Musil's first serious reading of Jung seems to have come at about the time he was
completing *The Man without Qualities*. Cf. *Nachlass*, Mappe VII/13. At that time he read
Jung's long introduction to Richard Wilhelm's 1929 edition of *Das Geheimnis der goldenen Blüte*. Musil's notes show that he was particularly interested in Jung's conceptions of
anima and *animus*: the male spirit as *logos* in the man and *animus* in the woman, and the
female spirit as *eros* in the woman and *anima* in the man. Musil noted that this was very
close to his own notion but that he did not fully understand the Jungian terminology. He
did point out that Jung's terms were a good description of the Ulrich-Agathe relationship.
96. Cf. Lucien Lévy-Bruhl, *Primitive Mentality* (Boston, 1966), and *How Natives
Think* (New York, 1966). Cf. *Tag.* I, p. 499, and *Tag.* II, pp. 319–22, on Karl Ludwig
Schleich, "Die Physiologie des Ichs": This article discusses the physiological basis of the
ego-feeling and the functions of the two halves of the brain.

of thought implied no practical incapacity or lack of intelligence; it constituted a different relation to the world which followed its own logic and principles of coherence and relatedness. This openness to the logic of primitive thought raised the question of the loss of this relation to the world in modern man.

Musil was puzzled by the fact that his contemporaries tended to look upon the huge mass of modern knowledge about myth and primitive experience as though it had no personal implications: "There is no thought that these countless remainders of the dreams of humanity, which were overcome by waking thought and shattered, could ever be made again into a whole, that they could set off again into something new." Musil recognized that this could not simply be carried off self-consciously and synthetically, but he rejected the prejudice of European man that myths "belong to a stage of consciousness which we have left behind." The attempt to disclaim any relation to mythical thought led to the split in contemporary culture between a prosaic reality and a yearning for the irrational:

The spiritual [*seelische*] double existence which we lead between a too unlyrical and a too lyrical condition which is no longer bound to the truth of reality is one of the reasons why the arts today are felt to be so artificial and life so mechanical; that is, neither of them relating to the full needs of the human soul.

Musil believed that the novel might help to forge a link between the poles of escapism and meaninglessness in literature and life. In his enthusiastic review of Döblin's epic poem *Manas* (1927), Musil announced his own project in *The Man without Qualities:*

There are not many questions which are so important for literature as this: in what way one could give back to it the intoxication, the divinity, the verse, the feeling of being more than life-size, without plaster-of-Paris monumentality and without artificially obscuring the achieved illumination of our spirit.[97]

Two other books influenced Musil's understanding of this primitive symbolizing power: Ludwig Klages's *Vom Kosmogonischen Eros* (1922) and Martin Buber's *Ekstatische Konfessionen* (1909).[98] Like Goethe, Klages taught "the reality of images," but his distinctive contribution was to discuss what he called cosmogonic eros, particularly in connec-

97. *Prosa*, p. 616.
98. Cf. *Tag.* II, pp. 419–36, and Dietmar Goltschnigg, *Mystische Tradition im Roman Robert Musils* (Heidelberg, 1974). See also Musil's notes on Harnack's view of *eros* and *agape* in early Christianity: *Tag.* I, p. 506, and *Tag.* II, pp. 325–27. The range of Musil's readings in the history of culture is very striking in the 1920s (e.g., *Tag.* I, pp. 485–88).

tion with pagan traditions. His analysis of the ancient concept of eros, as a mediator between God and man, evolved the distinction between earthly and heavenly love, between sensuous attraction and ecstatic enthusiasm of the soul. Klages rejected what he thought of as the abstract, rational love of Christianity or Platonism and emphasized the connection of love with looking, gazing, seeing, with the moment when the individual stands in the beam of eros. This book had a powerful influence on Musil's own refinement of the notion of love, its varieties and their relations to biological drives and spiritual conditions. Similarly, Buber's *Ekstatische Konfessionen* provided Musil with a wealth of crosscultural sources on the history of mystical experience. While granting that these unspeakable mysteries of the soul might turn out simply to be madness, Buber invited his readers to listen to these experiences and to what they say of the needs of the soul. He argued, *à la* Mach, that neither the world (a bundle of sensations) nor the self (a bundle of sensations) is a unity; it is, rather, the moment of mystical ecstacy which unveils the unity of the self and the world. For Buber, freedom meant going beyond the realm of differentiated life to the *Erlebnis* of the ego. The ecstatics from the great religious traditions were not, in Buber's view, simply stammering, but, rather, attempting to salvage timelessness in time with images from memory.

The tension in Musil's own experience and in the history of culture between waking thought and dream-logic, between practical mastery and mystical ecstasy, led him in the early 1920s to postulate a fundamental polarity in human experience. Maintaining the phenomenological perspective of his pre-war essays, Musil evolved his theory primarily in his diaries and notes, but he gave it clear public expression in 1925 in his masterful "Ansätze zu neuer Aesthetik." His mature formulation of the structure of human experience begins with an account of "the normal condition of our relationship to the world, human beings, and the self":

We have evolved—if one were to describe this condition in relation to the other—by means of the *sharpness* of our intellect to what we are: lords of an earth, on which we were once a nothing within the vastness of space; activity, boldness, cunning, deceit, restlessness, evil, a talent for the hunt, love of war and the like are the moral qualities for which we may thank this ascent.[99]

This description of the human genius for mastery and survival echoed the positivist visions of Darwin, Mach, Freud, and Weber. These achieve-

99. Musil, "Ansätze," pp. 672–73.

ments of human civilization and science, as well as the philosophical pictures of the world which accompanied them, were, in Musil's view, refinements and elaborations of a particular condition of being, of a characteristic way of relating to the world. This practical, manipulative relation to people and things was rooted, according to Musil, in a deep-seated mistrust, which expressed itself equally in the measurements of science, in the calculations of capitalism and politics, and in the sharp-eyed hunter sighting down the barrel of a gun. While Musil challenged the validity of making this relation to the world normative, he was quick to remind idealists, moralists, and romantics of the enormous positive value of this capacity for evil: "There is evil that is good, just as there is evil that is evil."[100] The principle of this evil was simply the capacity to calculate in terms of the lowest common denominator, in terms of what is firm and predictable in the world, in the self, and in other human beings. The laws of the normal condition set limits for everyone who seeks to have impact in the world, and those who seek to renounce evil in the name of goodwill should remember that "without his evil qualities there is nothing left over of the human being that we are but a formless heap":

Even morality itself is in its own nature completely riddled by the sharp and evil basic qualities of our spirit; even in its form as rule, norm, command, threat, law, and good as well as evil, this quantifying computation reveals the forming influence of the metric, calculating, mistrusting, annihilating will of the spirit.[101]

In opposition to this normal condition Musil identified another spiritual condition which he believed was "no less demonstrable historically, even if it has left a less powerful imprint on our past." It has left its traces in all historical cultures, and Musil believed that it was the source of all religions and ideologies:

It has been called the condition of love, of goodness, of withdrawal from the world, of contemplation, of envisioning, of the approach of God, of escape, of will-lessness, of turning inward, and many other sides of a fundamental experience, which returns in equal agreement in the religion, mysticism, and ethics of all historical peoples.

Despite its continuity throughout human history, the fleeting quality of this experience seemed to imply that it was illusory, epiphenomenal, irrelevant, or even pathological. Its inability to create a stable world-pic-

100. Musil, *Der deutsche Mensch,* p. 55.
101. Musil, "Ansätze," p. 673.

ture out of itself had always left it defenseless or even uninteresting in the eyes of the normal condition. While morality, idealism, ideologies, and religions all bore traces of this condition, it had yet to mix itself correctly with the normal condition: "This condition is that in which the image of each object does not become a practical goal, but a wordless experience." It was made still more inaccessible to language by the fact that it is "never of much duration except in cases of mental illness":

> In the absence of a few thorough studies as a foundation, one must eschew further comment today on the meaning and essence of this other condition, for our knowledge of it was, until recently, roughly like our knowledge of the physical world in the tenth century.[102]

Standing at the source of moral and religious insight, this condition of being was the motor of the spiritual evolution of mankind. Historically, however, its fate was either to die in institutions or to come into the world with such violence as to mutate into something else. The church (as "the ruin of the other condition") and the great revolutionary moments of mankind were the most obvious instances of this process. Thus, a major problem for Musil was to clarify in what way this exceptional condition of being could be brought into relation with the normal condition. In the early 1920s he emphasized its fleeting and unstable quality:

> It is not a matter of making the *other condition* the bearer of social life. It is far too fleeting. I myself can hardly even remember it today. But it leaves traces in all ideologies, in the love of art, etc., for it touches the life of these phenomena which are caught up in rigidity.[103]

But increasingly, Musil became preoccupied with the forms and varieties of this condition and the ways in which it was brought into relation with the rigid forms of normal life.

Musil's distinction cut across the doctrinal quarrels among Christianity, liberalism, and socialism. All of these positions appeared as dogmatic reductions, bureaucratic normalizations, and abstract commitments to non-verifiable formulations. Musil wanted to focus attention on questions that all of these positions had lost track of: the process of living itself and access to the ethical condition. In his search for the sources of ethical energy, Musil was not rejecting science, morality,

102. Ibid., pp. 673–74, 683.
103. *Prosa,* p. 707; *TE,* p. 284.

or public law. He was drawing attention to other faculties and to the need to balance those already developed. The condition of love was, in Musil's view, the nourishing and transforming power of the spiritual history of mankind, but he was convinced that it had never been properly brought into relation with the normal condition of being. In modern civilization, it sometimes seemed as though people had entirely lost track of this relation to being: "The bureaucrat in the state, in the church, in socialism: the hereditary enemy. Simply the personification of a human quality, of the inability always simply, immediately to be."[104] The rigid forms of morality and institutions followed necessarily from human limitations, but Musil wanted to argue against the tendency for these to become normative. Musil wanted a flexible morality, and he saw the historical study of the other condition in poetry, essay, philosophy, and social life as an important step in this direction.

A phenomenological clarification of the other condition required first of all that Musil come to terms with the epistemological primacy of the scientific version of the normal condition in modern thought. Setting out from assumptions that would have satisfied a positivist, Musil was prepared to attempt a scientific and biological account of the ecstatic condition. Thus, for example, he saw the biological basis for this distinction in the polarity of the drives for survival and sex, which emerges throughout the history of civilization in the tension between power and sexuality, knowledge and love. But Musil believed that these drives had differentiated themselves enormously in the evolution of civilization. At the same time, the drive for survival and its practical requirements had made the rationality of domination the normative mode for understanding the world. This was most apparent in the widely shared conventions about language which assumed the dualities of subjective/objective, emotional/rational. Here the artist and the scientist were in agreement, but Musil was convinced that these conventions of language were derived from the Cartesian version of the normal condition, which conceded the primacy of the scientific version of truth and left the artist to a cult of feeling that distorted the other condition and the real tasks of art.

Musil argued that the normal condition of being was by no means more objective, rational, or unfeeling than the other condition. Its distinguishing marks were pragmatism, a narrow focus of attention, and a

104. *TE,* p. 285.

192]

Der Dichter: 1918-1933

goal-orientation. The hunter may be an egoist, but he ought not to think too much about himself; he is not without feelings, but if he allows himself to be subject to moods, this will prove dysfunctional in the hunt. In ordinary life, people who are exclusively preoccupied with ambition and wealth might be looked upon as victims of the survival-instinct gone wild. The drive for struggle and mastery presumes the reality and importance of the ego, and it sustains the normal condition of being long enough to achieve the rational coherence of modern science and the certainty of a firm world. The drive for reproduction, on the other hand, goes beyond the individual and is more fragile. Yet, according to Musil, the other condition is not more emotional, more subjective, or more illusory than the normal condition. It is a different relation to the world.

In the other condition, "the border between the ego and the non-ego is less sharp than otherwise," and this experience is accompanied by "a certain inversion of relationships." This participation in things is intensely personal, "like a harmony between subject and object," but the "stronger element of subjectivity" is not like ordinary egoism. The ego is actually eliminated, canceled out in objective relations; the normal sense of the ego and possessiveness dissolves into a true *object*-ivity which is self*less*. Thus, the other condition has aspects both of "a heightened subjectivity" and of an "extinguishing." Musil believed that not only people but also things change completely "depending on whether one observes" them "with sympathy or not, and one can describe our science precisely as an observer without sympathy, for that is the essential core of the demand that it not be fantastical." This sympathetic relation of the observer to the world has not proved very useful for practical purposes and has therefore received little attention from philosophers since Descartes. The other condition, the condition of love, does not sustain itself long enough to be able to develop a comprehensive vision of totality. It has therefore always been forced to remain in a side-office of philosophy, emerging in the endless struggle between religion and the state—or, as Musil sometimes put it, in the struggle between mysticism and theology, since the church had long since put itself at the service of the state. Thus, all the rational, coherent, practical, moral views of the world—science, the church, the state, socialism—had come effectively into alliance by insisting on the metaphysical exclusiveness of a particular condition of being. The normal condition creates the rational world, with its rules and assumptions, "but since 'love' appears with people only periodically or accidentally, it does not create a total world but only sustains the exception."[105]

Musil distinguished between two modes of the other condition, which were roughly equivalent to the distinction between the Dionysian and the Apollonian. In the motory (or Dionysian) form of ecstasy, the personality was dissolved into the action of the muscles in dance, conflict, song, or mass political action. In the sensory (or Apollonian) mode of ecstasy the motory nervous system was eliminated, leading to contemplation: "The automatic nervous system continues. Complete elimination: Death. Thus the relationship between death and ecstasy." Musil argued that the ego lay on the border between these two ways of experiencing the world: the active and the passive, the motory and the sensory, the Dionysian and the Apollonian: "If one of the two aspects predominates, the ego is snuffed out. . . . This is where the metaphysical solution offers itself: the ego is something unnatural, in ecstasy it dissolves itself." The happiness of the Dionysian form of ecstasy arose from the dissolution "of the intellectual, voluntaristic normal relation between the ego and the (physical, social) world." This active form of ecstasy left its most direct historical record in wars, revolutions, and the like, but Musil's own interest was primarily in the contemplative form of the ecstatic relation to the world. In this distinction between the two forms of the dissolution of the ego, Musil formulated the dualism of *The Man without Qualities* between the ecstasy of violent action in Clarisse, Moosbrugger, and European society, and the Apollonian ecstasy of Ulrich and Agathe. This distinction between the orgiastic and the contemplative paralleled the distinction between the "man of action and the other man," which was "partially equivalent to the distinction between male and female."[106]

In attempting to explain the origins of the condition of love or contemplation, the biological reduction presented itself. Musil conceded that the reproductive drive (or, variously, sexual need as such) was probably the historical precursor of the other condition, but he believed that in the condition of love, desire fell away: "What then distinguishes the primitive love-affect from pure sexual desire? Obviously the presence of contradictory affects." Thus, sexual convention was a regressive oversimplification of civilized emotions and the suppressed half of the self. Musil believed that civilized people were characterized by the com-

105. Musil, *Der deutsche Mensch*, pp. 50–53.
106. *TE*, p. 284.

plexity and number of their emotions, which no longer allowed them access to simple, undiluted impulse. Social evolution had so differentiated and complicated the emotions over millenia that the normal way of describing primitive drives no longer had meaning for civilized life. Twentieth-century Europeans tended to expect from themselves emotions appropriate to meeting a blood enemy in the forest or finding the woman on returning to the cave. The contemporary experiences of love, anger, hate, envy, anxiety, revulsion, and shame were mixtures rather than pure emotions, although they had their antecedents in primitive relations and animals. By reducing the complexity of modern experience to the fundamental drives of aggression and sexuality, the positivist was at one with the average European man, who believed that without killing men and mastering women he had not yet begun to confront life's problems. The refusal of contemporary Europeans to be honest about the mixture of violence, lust, tenderness, shyness, and countless other emotions that entered into sexual relations expressed itself most dogmatically in convenient prejudices about the duality of male and female. Musil believed that the conventional typologies of male and female had relatively little to do with the confusing blend of emotions and experiences that constituted actual men and women: "Masculine is the movement of the arms; feminine is the falling into the arms. The man is masculine with feminine additive; the woman feminine with masculine." The rest is social convention.[107]

Sexual convention attempted to encapsulate the other condition in the normal condition through the biological reduction. The other main attempt to regulate this condition in the Western world was the church, which institutionalized the theological reduction. But Musil did not believe that this human capacity for love and contemplation could be reduced to a single, fixed, rational version of normal reality, whether theological or biological:

It has no sense, for the theologians have given it merely a pseudo-sense. It is also a drive, a need, a suppressed half of the person, which seeks again and again to realize itself.

This other half is, however, biologically incomprehensible, for a world in the condition of contemplation would go under, if not from purposelessness, then from defenselessness. The available theories of this are extremely simple: the lost condition of being God's child, the lost paradise; they contain the admission that with worldly means the condition is not to be achieved.[108]

107. Musil, *Der deutsche Mensch*, p. 58.
108. Ibid., p. 64.

The church and sexuality were the two main ways in which European civilization had sought to give expression to this suppressed half of the self.

Musil had a special stake in the functions of the church, because it was this apparatus which still had majority control over the spiritual life of Europeans, although it was beginning to give way to what Musil thought of as the other great annihilating movement, socialism. Although the church was profoundly implicated in the simplistic "veneration of the male-ideal" still dominant in European culture, it had managed to make "being good into something ridiculous, unmanly." While preserving the rigid, traditional social conventions of the masculine, the church marketed a notion of the good which was so without courage, risk, creativity, or heroism that it virtually forced a man to be "antimoral" except where special family influences worked against it. Thus, the normal male gained access to the good only out of weariness, cynicism, and the prejudices of middle age. In a culture whose religious and moral life was dessicated, barren, and dead on its feet, the average male had access to the other condition only through sexuality.

The structure of European culture was such that the one time when the normal person was likely to be affected by the good in the sense of the other condition was early in life, at the life-stage when people often fall in love. It was not the sheer falling in love that Musil had in mind, but a condition of being which sometimes accompanied it. This condition of love seemed to be the most commonly shared experience of the other condition. The experience of wanting to give, communicate, overflow was related to the condition of poetry and was something other than the convention of falling in love:

> Now, instead of saying: he was in love, somehow eccentrically, one can take this other point of focus seriously and construct a complete orientation to the world from it.
>
> All conflict, ambition, all relations become a nothing, "because it is all a matter of something else."
>
> One does not want to possess the loved one, but, rather, to live with her in the newly discovered world.

This ecstatic condition of love was ordinarily quickly assimilated into the assumptions of the normal condition, usually through marriage. Conventional romanticism was stamped by the logic of rationalism and capitalism, by the compulsive, possessive way in which it sought to order these feelings and the love object into the normal world:

Be mine: gives the connection among love-rationalism-capitalism. The other point of view requires that one not treat even one's insights as property; one does not treasure them in the ego; but, rather, they are the common property of the loving people. It is possible that thereby an entirely different growth of thought would come into being. Certainly, one weakens oneself, in that one "does not hold onto oneself," but also one entices oneself to a supra-heightening. It has something dynamic, something of the necessity of inner movement, in order to remain in balance.

In this description of the condition of love, of the loss of ego and possessiveness in the heightened love-relation, Musil defined the experiment he attempted in *The Man without Qualities.*[109]

From these assumptions Musil tried to describe the canceling out of sexual desire in the condition of love: "In love, desire is weakened, but the surging essense which surrounds it is expanded. The lovers are united in God, as they used to say, or as one might say today: in the world." Insofar as the tradition reported feelings of sexual desire or discomfort, Musil suspected that these were associated with "the failure of the contemplative to arrive." Not only was sexual desire canceled out, but many negative feelings, such as envy and hate, seemed to be incompatible with the condition of love. They simply did not arise. Musil could imagine a blissful (*selig*) love, anger, regret, shame, anxiety, but not envy, hate, selfishness, social uncertainty, or jealousy:

Why are these feelings missing? Envy, biologically speaking, is frustrated struggle of life, likewise hate, selfishness, in part even jealousy. Then one could assume: feelings of struggle are missing. This would clarify the feminine in the contemplative love of the man. And justify the characterization: condition of love.

Here Musil was not attempting to moralize about emotions or sexuality, but simply characterizing the experience of this state of being and what facilitated it. This ethical relation to things involved a blurring of the normal conception of ego and world which transcended morality in the ordinary sense. In place of good and evil there appears "the pair enhancing-diminishing"; and in place of the normal concept of the useful appears the highest value of enhancement: "The contemplative has no conscience, because this reaction is simply not possible for someone in continuous ethical action." In this condition "one can philosophize, but not add." In the contemplative condition, the individual is released

109. *TE,* pp. 281–82.

from struggle, worldly ego, and feelings of vanity, possessiveness, and degradation.[110]

For Musil the path to the mystical condition of contemplation was fundamentally tied up with understanding the condition of love: "The person in love is selfless and heightened self. It is not egoism by twos, but, rather, another relationship to the world, another feeling-tone of things." Even in coitus there is the feeling of "the incredible singularity of this experience, that one is not an ego, but rather dual!" What interested Musil was the spiritual union of lovers: "Spiritual [*seelische*] union in broad daylight with the duality of bodies. The impression that the differences of the persons disappear, the great congruence, is illusory; but the canceling of the ego-emphasis is reality." The puzzle for Musil, which so complicated his writing and rewriting of *The Man without Qualities*, was sorting out the relationship between sexual and spiritual union:

> Has a remainder of the mystery been preserved in connection with sexuality, or does sexuality create the illusion of a mystery? Both answers have been tried. Christianity as the extension of this "godly" love, love of neighbor in God. Nietzsche: Christianity gave Eros poison to drink. Klages: Polyandrous bonds.
>
> Not whom one loves, but that one loves is the main thing. [Don] Juanism: on the other hand degeneration into the sexual.

Musil was convinced that all religions and moralities were attempts to sustain these feelings and attitudes in everyday life, although they normally degenerated into the bureaucratic regulation of authorized feelings. Instead of furthering the other condition, conventional attempts to encapsulate it ordinarily cut the human being off from the sources of these feelings.[111]

Although this condition had always been too fleeting to constitute anything so permanent as a world view, Musil was convinced that it was not merely accidental or pathological, not an abnormality facilitated by illness or extreme situations; instead, it was a condition that could be achieved by the use of human faculties. While he wanted to avoid conventional theological assumptions, it seemed to him unavoidable that the other condition had traditionally been associated with "the hypothesis of the presence of God," and that "even the earthly, erotic state of love leads many people who believe nothing at all about the beyond far

110. Musil, *Der deutsche Mensch*, pp. 58–60.
111. *Prosa*, p. 707.

into this realm." It seemed obvious at first glance that the normal attitude serves the organization of social life, while the other condition
serves union with God. In the mid-1920s, however, Musil was prepared
to eschew giving this profane religiosity any such justification or meaning at all: "It has no goal, for it has always concealed an unreal and
unattainable one." It is, then, presumably an experience (*Erlebnis*) in
and for itself, completely self-authenticating and self-justifying without
words. Musil decided to call this experience "the other condition" because he was as convinced of its reality as he was of the impossibility of
giving it an appropriate name in the cultural situation of the 1920s: "In
all the characterizations, as love, goodness, irrationality, religiosity . . .
there is hidden a side of the truth, and for the whole truth, there is today no thought available to us." One could at best make forays from
this condition into normal reality in the spirit of philosophical essayism,
without deluding oneself about having captured the whole truth in a
word or in a system. It was this image of the structure of experience
which informed Musil's resolution of metaphysics and the novel in *The
Man without Qualities.*[112]

3. METAPHYSICS AND THE NOVEL

When it flattered me that philosophers and scholars sought

my company and preferred my books to others, what a mis-

take! They were not valuing my philosophical content (signifi-

cance), but, rather, they thought: here then was a poet who

understood theirs![113]

Actually, the history of my life must be very interesting, as

a result of the fact that I am a very disciplined writer, a

severe writer, but my ascent exhibits every sort of burden.[114]

Like Lukács, Benjamin, and Broch, Musil believed that the novel was
the mode appropriate to the philosophical situation of his generation:
"Novels are the Socratic dialogs of our time. In this liberal form, life

112. Musil, *Der deutsche Mensch*, pp. 63, 52. Regarding the hypothesis of the existence of God, Musil adds that the other condition is clearly "independent of this presupposition."
113. *TE*, p. 469.   114. Ibid., p. 461.

wisdom has fled from the wisdom of the schools." [115] Since his student years in Berlin, Musil had set himself against an academic philosophy whose ideas never came into relation with lived experience. On the other hand, in relation to the normal conventions of literature, Musil was embarked on an art form which seemed too intellectual, too conceptual, too abstract. Musil wanted to bridge the chasm between a conceptual art that gives form to sensation and experience and a formal art that shatters the systematic rigidity of normal reality and conceptual metaphysics. At the same time, he wanted to write a novel which would come to terms with his own life and the historical experience of his generation. [116] Throughout the 1920s Musil struggled to bring his impulse to abstract, conceptual reflection into relation with a formless mass of detail and literary insight. The yield of this solitary process was the great representative novel of his generation.

In an attempt to clarify his peculiar position between metaphysics and the novel, between concept and experience, Musil formulated two extreme views of the task of art. On the one hand, art is committed to the constant reforming of life, disturbing the balance of the emotions and the fixed conceptual structures of the intellect. This mode, which tends to dominate in literature, is concerned with the ordering of experience (*Erfahrungen*) under concepts, and in this respect Musil conceded that literature was relatively more intellectual than music. The second extreme formulation of art, most apparent in the formalism of music and poetry, breaks through all concepts into a moment or *Erlebnis* which cannot be reintegrated into concepts. The danger of the more intellectual or discursive mode was that it might rigidify into sterility, while the striving of a formal art for the creation of another world made it too much like an old drunk who is good for nothing once he is sober. Confronted by this dichotomy between a too prosaic and a too lyrical art, Musil wanted a novel that moved between sobriety and intoxication.

Musil agreed that the goal of every art is to break free from the normal total experience, but he believed it was a mistake to interpret this as a conflict between feeling and intellect. The techniques of mod-

115. *Prosa,* p. 722. Musil appropriated this remark from Friedrich Schlegel; it was even more apt for Musil's generation than it had been a century earlier.

116. See Ibid., p. 721: "Should it not be superfluous to write more than one novel, if the artist has not become a new person?" (This is also from Schlegel.)

ernism in poetry, painting, and music were all directed at the attempt
"to free the human being from the understanding and set him again in
an immediate relation to creation." But the ideologs of irrationalism in
modern art forgot that concepts are required not only for the understanding but for the senses and feelings as well. The human response to
sounds, tastes, smells, images is possible only within a structure of
assumptions and meanings. Both thought and feelings are regulated by
pre-established abbreviations of experience. This need for practical formulations goes so far in human beings "that without preformed, stable
pictures, and those are concepts, nothing remains at all but a chaos, and
since, on the other hand, concepts are again dependent on experience, a
mutual relationship arises which is like a flow and a vessel, a balance
without opposition, for which we have still not yet found a correct
description, so that it is fundamentally as mysterious as the surface of
a well." Literary art was relatively more responsible for the task of
ceaselessly reforming experience, but his project was concerned with the
senses as well as the intellect; it meant opening up the preformed structures of thought and sensibility to give human beings fresh access to
their experience. The novel is an artistic form peculiarly responsible for
the interaction between concept and experience, but even music is integrated into the person in some fashion, so that one must eventually ask
what it means. On the other hand, the novel is not directed only at the
intellect and analysis: "Even on a page of prose which really deserves
this name, one can recognize that before the meaning a general excitement is communicated. Sensation and meaning have then in literature
simply another weighting." All art is implicated in the process of breaking through concepts in order to reform and renew our image of the
world.[117]

The second extreme view of art points in the direction of the other
condition, and contains a value of pure actuality and incitement which
breaks out of the normal ordering of experience: "When the formal
relations of an art suddenly emerge in isolation, there arises . . . that
terrible wonder in the face of an irrational world." While the expres-

---

117. Musil, "Ansätze," pp. 676, 679. Cf. ibid., p. 676: "It is not thought, but the need
for practical orientation which drives to formulas. . . . But then opposition may also not
be directed against thought, as almost invariably occurs in such connections, but must
attempt to liberate itself from the practical and factual normal condition of human beings.
Nonetheless, if this happens, nothing remains but the dark realm of the other condition,
in which everything provisionally ceases. This is the true and apparently unavoidable an-
tithesis."

sionists tended to look upon intellectual art as late and decadent, Musil argued that it was formal art which came later. Instead of seeking a conceptual form for totality as in more primitive art, modern art focused on the formal techniques which liberate a different relation to the world. But this ordinarily led to the opposition between reality and aestheticism:

The concepts of purposeless beauty or of beautiful things which continue to play an important role in our view of art have something of a holiday mood about them; if I am not mistaken, the root of it lies in the beginning of the reign of Christianity, when art suffered under the jealousy of true believers and was pushed by its defenders into a life at one remove.

Normally, this other experience was treated simply as enjoyment, leisure, recreation, interruption, but Musil set himself against the view that art and literature were simply interruptions of real life. He found it remarkable that we tend to value these experiences "as elements of another totality, as elements of another experience which stretches into another dimension from that of ordinary experience; for this is presupposed by all attempts, which posit as attainable another inwardness, a world without words, an unconceptualized culture and soul." Musil believed that the transition between these two modes, when an object moves from the sphere of worldly observation into the creative relation, was particularly apparent "in art forms which unite both attitudes, as, for example, the novel."[118]

Musil shared with the finest literary critics of his generation the conviction that the novel brought most fully to consciousness the predicament of an objective world so extensive and complex that subjectivity can find no home in it. Whether as the transition from the epic to the novel (Lukács) or as the decline of the story (Benjamin), literary critics drew attention to an historical process whose culmination was the novel of this generation. In notes written in 1930–1932, Musil described the most recent phase of this process as the crisis of the novel, a theoretical formulation with obvious implications for the novel he was writing. He agreed with Lukács and Benjamin that the crisis of literary forms was not a recent catastrophe of language peculiar to his generation; he emphasized its enduring, stationary quality in a long, slow evolutionary process which had begun in the seventeenth century. Since the 1890s, however, the decline of the story had been such that "one can no longer

118. Ibid., pp. 670, 682–83.

with a naive conscience take individual destinies so seriously as before. Still with Balzac. With Zola still an attempt."[119] Within Musil's generation, it was Thomas Mann who was best able to retain this naive relation to the epic material of the story, but for Mann, as well as the other novelists of the generation of 1905, the roles of explanation, interpretation, and reflection predominated in a way that drew into question the mere particularity of the individual. "*The poet today* tells people stories which he must first explain"; this meant "a turning away from the primitive sense of the story."[120] Even with a classical storyteller like Thomas Mann, the modes of the historical and the scientific seemed to compromise the importance formerly attached to individual destinies.

Musil argued that the epic is concentrated on a report of experience, but it was no longer clear what sort of report would be both novel and entertaining:

Should we say that we can no longer endure the extended portrayal of a human destiny? To sing the kiss which Mr. A. gives to Miss B. (the engagement and the break-up) presumes great meaning and dignity for this event. Elevated portrayal assumes the sublime life and the desire for such a life. We have become prosaic (i.e., we have become *unbürgerlich*).

In his search for something new and pleasing to report the novelist seemed to have no way out: "What is new is narrated by the newspapers; what is pleasing to hear we look upon as kitsch." In a prosaic world without meaning, the novelist was left with information and manufactured emotion, the *reductio ad absurdum* of the objective and the subjective. He might offer explanations as a kind of shadow-science, but, unlike the storyteller, he would not have immediate access to counsel in the traditional sense. Like Lukács and Benjamin, Musil understood this new situation in ideological terms, as the loss of closed totality and given, concrete structures of meaning. He argued that the story is possible and meaningful only within the context of ideology, i.e., of connections of language in relation to which the story can speak: "Communists and nationalists and Catholics still enjoy hearing something narrated. The need is immediately there again when the ideology is firm. When the object is given." To this unfirm world, Musil added the unfirm hero; the bad conscience of the problematic hero was the

119. Musil, "Aufzeichnungen zur Krisis des Romans," in *TE*, p. 861.
120. *TE*, p. 399.

bad conscience of the novel, which amounted to the bad conscience of love. The crisis of the novel was summarized in these obstacles.[121]

From the end of the war onward, there is a fundamental continuity in Musil's determination to write a novel which would be at once autobiographical, essayistic, and a reflection on the ideological problems of his age. On the other hand, Musil was never able to finish his novel, leaving in doubt what the "final form" was to have been, or whether Musil himself knew. Shortly after the war, Musil was working with material for seven novels, and a different sort of novelist would have found fulfillment in writing and publishing all of them. He kept sifting and reforming this material to find the structure he needed. Eventually, all of his conceptions, except the experimental moral-satiric novels of science fiction, found their way into *The Man without Qualities* in some form. But the difficulty of determining the place of these disparate elements within an unfinished literary whole has enmeshed the critical discussion of the novel with the history of its evolution to an extraordinary degree. Kaiser and Wilkins have actually argued that the novel should be read as a reflection on itself, as a narcissistic recollection of its own process of becoming: "It is Ulrich's Karma that he has to suffer under the consequences of the acts which he committed or wanted to commit in his earlier incarnations."[122]

The continuity in Musil's development makes it possible to see each insight in his creative process as a prelude to *The Man without Qualities*, but it was the war that provided the frame for his diffuse ideas. By 1918 all of his projects had come to center around a few ordering ideas, which were to be the basis for his masterwork. While there are no sharp breaks among these conceptions or the stages in which the material developed, it is possible to delineate three main periods of evolution, based on Musil's conception of the hero. Roughly speaking, the Achilles period (the years just after the war) emphasized the hero's relation to the age as a whole, to the war and ideology (in *Spion, Panama, Katacombe*). The Anders period (the mid-1920s) began to draw more on the material of the love-story and the autobiography (from the *Archivar, Der Teufel, Der Krähe*). Finally, in the late 1920s came the crisis of holding all this material together, when Ulrich was introduced and the first volume was brought to completion.

121. Musil, "Aufzeichnungen," pp. 863–64.
122. Kaiser and Wilkins, *Robert Musil*, p. 169.

Musil's idea of a quasi-autobiographical novel about an archivist or a priest originated in the pre-war period in Vienna, in his attempt to come to terms with the cultural dominance of Roman Catholicism. He wanted to use this setting to work in "all unused philosophical and literary plans," but the consistent motive was "to justify myself and to explain myself." This conception was to emphasize the generational theme and evolve into a mystical love-story. The version he called *Der Teufel* (or *Der Antichrist*) was to be about a hero who became a theologian after completing his doctorate in philosophy. Despite his free relationship to the church, he is enlisted by a bishop who sees him as an ally in the battle against science. His first approach is to go at religion rationally, and he discovers "307 proofs for the existence of God and 311 counterproofs. He gives up on rational discussion, proves God to be merely possible, and draws the consequences." Assigned to the parish of St. Ulrich, he finds himself oppressed by the baroque atmosphere of contemporary Catholicism and by the gruesome mediocrity of the Christian Socialists. The post-war situation provides the context for the confrontation of Catholicism and Bolshevism and the meeting of "the woman, dark like the Stefanskirche." In this search for a modern religiosity Agathe introduces the theme of mysticism, which is taken up in the post-war notes under the titles of *Der Krähe* or *Der Grieche*. The struggle of the hero against the age of Christian society, the conceptions of the love-story and of the God of possibility, as well as the idea of the sex criminal, all emerged out of the pre-war period, but the war got the novel under way, and most of Musil's notes on these ideas date from 1915 to 1920. By the end of the war Musil seems to have been less interested in autobiographical themes and more concerned with the ideological constituents of the age. Here the earlier conceptions of the hero blend into Ulrich's first unambiguous precursor, Achilles.[123]

In dealing with the political issues of the war and the post-war era, Musil evolved the more aggressive activist hero of *Spion*. Like Musil himself and like the earlier autobiographical heroes, Achilles was to be "a modern philosopher, since [philosophy] reflects what is dissatisfied and unsatisfying in the age." Musil also imagined him as the extreme type of the rebel and planned to let him "do all the things which I am inhibited from doing by reason and conviction." Achilles was to be the

123. *TE,* pp. 240, 179, 176, 181.

healthy, complete hero who nonetheless acts out all possible anarchistic, criminal, and pathological impulses because of the inadequacy of his age and the impossibility of meaningful action within his society. His alter-ego was Moosbrugger: "Releasing all the criminals one has in oneself. The rage of Moosbrugger—stabbing somebody in the stomach, etc." Musil conceived Achilles as the representative of the generation since 1880, which was perceived by the liberal fathers in a patronizing way as both degenerate and utopian. Intellectually, Achilles was to be a figure so far ahead of his time that he was not even noticed by his age, like an adventurer in a fairytale who sees the meaninglessness of the lives people are leading around him, but can offer only possible solutions, which no one shares, or acts of rebellion, as principled insanity.[124]

This "hero of the age" was set off against the main social/ideological/psychological types: the scientist, the humanist, the poet, the businessman, the big-businessman, the lower bureaucrat, the ministerial bureaucrat, the priest, the soldier, the technician, the politician, etc., and each of these was paralleled by a corresponding female figure. Musil wanted to develop all the various philosophical key-clubs of the day in relation to particular personality types, "at least one hundred figures, the main types of contemporary people," to show the variety of responses to the intellectual and emotional confusion of modern life. Much of his time and effort in the 1920s was devoted to studying and working out from historical reality such figures as Liechtenstein, Rathenau, Klages, Kerschensteiner, Förster, and Key. Musil wanted to construct characters "entirely out of quotations," yet he did not intend a comprehensive synthesis of the age, but, rather, "the conflict of Achilles with the age. Not synthetic, but broken up by him." The real goal of the novel was not the solution to the philosophical debate but "the founding of the realm of the spirit."[125]

Although the ideological conflict with the age seems to have been central to the conception of *Spion*, Achilles's relationship with his sister Agathe was already fundamental to the novel. Achilles was to be the

---

124. Ibid., pp. 233, 249, 253, 242, 190.
125. Ibid., pp. 257–58, 226. Musil's plan to construct characters entirely out of quotations recalls Benjamin's project in "Paris: Hauptstadt des neunzehnten Jahrhunderts." For a discussion of Musil's attempt to reproduce the ideologies of particular historical figures see Götz Müller, *Ideologiekritik und Metasprache* (Munich, 1972).

strong, masculine, logical type, while his sister was more in touch with
the primitive and the mystical; she was "the human being in whom the
older stage is less repressed." The handsome Achilles had been burdened with the needs of sentimental and respectable women, while
Agathe married a not very spiritual person. This theme, already in
Achilles, seems to have predominated in the Anders period, when Musil
conceived the meeting of the siblings as the first event of the novel, preceded only by a brief preliminary sketch of the constituents of the age. A
huge amount of Musil's *Nachlass* dates from the Anders period, when
Musil was able to concentrate all his energies on the novel. Anders was
bored with the game of "antiquated sexuality," and wanted to find his
way beyond this to a relation to the woman as sister. For this he chose
his real sister. "The sibling love (*Geschwisterliebe*) must be strongly defended. . . . The autistic component of his personality flows together
here with love. It is one of the few possibilities of unity available to
him." This love-story was to express their rejection of the whole bourgeois world, as well as their own previous experiences with love and
sexuality.[126]

In 1926 Musil reported on the progress of his novel, then called *Die
Zwillingsschwester*, in a published interview with his friend Fontana.
The material for the Parallel Action had not yet developed overwhelming proportions, but the novel was already recognizably *The Man without Qualities*. It was to take place between 1912 and 1914, ending with
"the mobilization, the world and thought so divided that it still cannot
be put together today." Musil had already decided on the basic scenario: playing the dreams of Austria-Hungary and Prussia-Germany off
against each other as an historical context for the ideological themes.
He imagined a committee in each of these German states planning a ju-
bilee for the year 1918: the seventieth year of Franz Joseph's reign, and
the thirtieth for the upstart Wilhelm. To the ironic situation of the
search for salvation on the eve of 1914 was added the competition of
two empires for recognition in the year of the last judgment, when they
would expire together. The Austrian plan to market its vision of a world
experiment of peoples against the Prussian idea of power and technology became the basis for the Parallel Action in *The Man without
Qualities*. Musil made clear, however, that this was not to be an historical novel in the conventional sense, since he had no interest in the ex-

126. Ibid., pp. 237, 263.

planation of real events or a description of historical facts: "The facts are always interchangeable. I am interested in the spiritually typical; I would even say: the ghost of the events."[127]

The young hero of the novel was to provide the focus for the central question of the work: "How should an intellectual [*ein geistiger Mensch*] relate himself to reality?" This figure was to be "schooled in the best science of his time, in mathematics, physics, technology," representing not just the local situation of Austria in 1913 but the general predicament of the intellectual in the modern world. This was consistent with Musil's commitment to portray nothing in his "historical novel" which would not still be valid for the 1920s. The Parallel Action was to be the setting for the hero's confrontation with the great businessman (Arnheim/Rathenau), on vacation in Vienna from Berlin. Arnheim falls in love with the second Diotima in the salon where the Parallel Action takes place, and "a soul-novel evolves which has to end in emptiness." A second plot develops when the hero returns home and meets his sister at the funeral of their parents:

The Siamese Twin is something extremely rare biologically, but it lives in all of us as a spiritual utopia, as the manifest idea of our selves. What is only longing for most people is realized for my character. And soon the two live a life which corresponds in proper society to an old-fashioned marriage. I place both of them in the midst of the complex of the "troubles of the day"; no genius, no religion, living "for something" instead of "in something," merely objective relations in which our idealism evaporates.[128]

The flight of the siblings from social reality was to reflect the failure of community and a corresponding escape into love and mysticism:

But this attempt to sustain the experience, to freeze it, fails. The Absolute cannot be held onto. I conclude from this that the world cannot exist without evil; it brings movement into the world. The good alone makes rigidity. I offer for that the parallel of the couple: Diotima and the business genius.

Musil did not elaborate the exact details of his conclusion, but he did make clear that, after the failure of the love affair, the hero is thrown back on himself, and the themes of the Parallel Action must be worked out to the finish. Both end in the war:

The young man comes to the conclusion that he is an accident; that he can penetrate to his essence, but cannot achieve it. The human being is not complete,

127. Oskar Maurus Fontana, "Was arbeiten Sie? Gespräch mit Robert Musil," *Die literarische Welt* (1926), in *TE*, pp. 785–88.
128. Ibid.

and cannot be. Like an actor, he assumes all the masks without losing the feeling of the accidental character of his existence. He, too, like all the characters in my novel, is liberated from making a decision by the mobilization. The war came, had to come, is the sum of all the contradictory streams and influences and movements which I portray.[129]

Fontana wondered how Musil would be able to avoid the essayistic and formless in a novel with so much intellectual material and so many characters. Musil offered two answers: "the ironic perspective, whereby I lay value on the fact that for me irony is not a gesture of condescension but a form of struggle"; and the development of living scenes and fantastic passion to counter the essay. The concern with the details of plot misses the extent to which Musil's irony is constitutive for the whole novel, while the scenes are important not so much as guides to the ending as for their lived passion. One creates the structure of meaning, the other the moment of living thought. Although the story is constructed so that everything culminates in the mobilization, this is not the main point. The point of the novel lies not in the outcome but in the process of dissolving an old morality which could no longer help, while moving toward the shape of a new one: "It is an attempt at a dissolution (*Auflösung*) and the intimation (*Andeutung*) of a synthesis." The essayism and reflection of the novel were fundamental; Musil later remarked that if the first volume was too long, it was the plot and not the thinking which had gotten out of control. He was not attempting a piece of beautiful narrative on the model of Thomas Mann, but a new form for integrating the intellectual and the aesthetic:

> I want to offer contributions to the spiritual conquest of the world. Also through the novel. I would therefore be very grateful to the public, if it would pay less attention to my aesthetic qualities and more to my intentions. Style is for me the exact working-out of an idea. I mean the thought in the most beautiful form I can achieve.

It is strange, indeed, that precisely with this author, the critical literature should have become so absorbed by the issue of plot.[130]

The fundamental structure of the novel was clear by the mid-1920s; but the actual working-out of this project turned out to be an overwhelming task, particularly because the material related to the Parallel Action kept expanding. Between 1924 and 1933 Musil hardly existed apart from his struggle with his endlessly unfolding novel. Financially,

129. Ibid.   130. Ibid.

Musil was almost completely dependent on publisher's advances from Ernst Rowohlt, and as early as December, 1925, he was already late with the novel and running into conflicts with his publisher. During the second half of the decade, he and Martha lived a life of relative anonymity and financial insecurity; although Musil always had a home and food, it seemed to him indecent that his existence so often hung by a thread. It was only the dedication of Martha and a few close friends that brought Musil through this period at all. Repeatedly, their confidence in the overriding importance of his work and their gift for practical intervention in his affairs sustained an artist whose life corresponded very little to the popular image of the *haut bourgeois* man of letters.

Musil found it irritating that poets were expected not only to write but, in addition to this, also to live. His bitterness in these years about his life situation and his resentment toward more successful contemporary poets are understandable; but Musil did write very slowly, and he was fortunate to have a publisher who would stay with him for so long. Moreover, to a certain extent he failed to be rich, secure, and famous because he was not morally or temperamentally at home with what this involved. He wanted to be recognized and appreciated, but there was clearly something repulsive for him about the conventionally successful bourgeois artist. Though he would have preferred to live more comfortably and believed himself outrageously undervalued, his place as an outsider was the natural consequence of his values, his pace of writing, and his decision to be nothing but a poet. In a sense, his lack of recognition confirmed his identity as a *Dichter*, as someone who thinks out of the spirit of his age but "so much ahead of its tempo that he feels himself in opposition to it."[131] Moreover, along with the bitterness and anxiety of these years, there are also witnesses to his ironic smile and his wisdom as a human being. His confidence about his own genius might seem like arrogance in an ordinary person; but if one compares Musil's actual accomplishments to his culture's conventions about genius, the reports of those who knew him leave the impression of remarkable modesty.

In 1928, worn down by worry, smoking, overwork, and emotional collapse, Musil accepted Balázs's advice to see an Adlerian psychiatrist named Hugo Lukács, who was apparently able to free Musil from his writing block. Musil's main problem was almost certainly that he was

131. *MoE, Frühe Studien*, p. 1593.

overwhelmed by the sheer mass of detail and his tendency to be too abstract and self-critical to allow his novel to flow. Musil called this "the cowardice of a neurotic," but this project would have been too much for an ordinary coward.[132] Corino argues that the therapy helped Musil resolve his conception of the novel beyond the neurotic character of Anders: "The tendency to want *everything to be different* [*anders*] is a significant trait of the neurotic, bound up with a tendency toward devaluation and negativity." This supports Kaiser and Wilkins's argument that 1928–1929 marked the transition from the Anders period to Ulrich, representing a new stage of self-consciousness and a name that "means nothing other etymologically than 'master in one's own house.'"[133]

Whether or not Lukács helped Musil resolve the substantive issues of the novel's conception, he did suggest practical techniques for overcoming his anxiety about writing and his tendency to be overwhelmed by detail. Musil seems to have gotten the thread of his novel back by 1929, and he wrote to Allesch that despite his nervous breakdown he was not yet "down on all fours."[134] But he suffered terrible inhibitions in coming to terms with the final draft. By February, 1930, he was barely hanging onto life, and both he and Martha doubted that he could go on any longer. The financial situations of both Musil and the Rowohlt Verlag grew so desperate by March that Musil actually tried to change publishers, and only Allesch's intervention with Rowohlt saved the situation. In the midst of all these pressures, Musil insisted that the creative process must have its own way; and the yield by the autumn of 1930 justified his perseverance and the loyalty of his friends.

The publication in Germany of the first volume of *The Man without Qualities*, coinciding with Musil's fiftieth birthday, was the climax of Musil's career as a *Dichter*, and it unleashed a flood of public praise and unanimously enthusiastic reviews. Much to Musil's surprise, he had written a novel which seemed to speak to the deepest needs of the age, which in its departure from literary convention seemed to offer the form precisely appropriate to the novel in 1930. Franz Spunda summed up the critical response in his expectation that *The Man without Qualities* would prove to be "a turning point for the novel in general," which "can become for us what Proust is for the French." While he granted that one might be "frightened by his icy coldness or reject Musil's con-

132. *Tag.* II, p. 1182.
133. Corino, "Ödipus oder Orest?" p. 209; cf. pp. 193ff.
134. *TE*, p. 293.

cept of the novel," he insisted that one "must admire precisely the un-
canny brilliance and clarity of his spirit."[135] Even with the fate of
Musil's hero left undecided, Spunda was convinced that this was a great
and unique work of art. As Efraim Frisch emphasized in his review for
the *Frankfurter Zeitung*, Musil wrote out of the experience of a generation which had lived through two eras and drew into one volume the
double perspective of those who were then about fifty.[136] But the first
volume of *The Man without Qualities* was also acknowledged as the
voice of the younger generation of intellectuals, who were soon to go
into exile.[137]

The work met with similar enthusiasm abroad. *The Times Literary
Supplement* hailed it as "the prose-epic of the Habsburg Monarchy
hastening to its decay," praised its analysis of the ideological origins of
the war, and eagerly anticipated the second volume.[138] In the *Revue
d'Allemagne*, Paul Jacob emphasized Musil's kinship with the French
and his unique place in German literature. As Jacob correctly judged,
Musil was not, for all his similarities to Schnitzler, the ripe fruit of a
dying world, but a man who had grown beyond it. "Even the pitiless
condemnation of European civilization in Mann's *The Magic Mountain*
is still bourgeois by comparison with the hardness of Musil's novel."
Jacob saw in Musil's transcendence of the ideological limitations of his
age, of the bourgeoisie as well as its opponents, "the only form of heroism in our age" and acknowledged him as "one of the great poets of our
tragic epoch."[139] The world was now aware of the project under way in
Vienna, and the response to *The Man without Qualities* brought Musil
a moment of undisputed triumph—even in Vienna.[140] Musil's friend
Ernst Blass, writing in the *Prager Presse*, expressed the hope that Musil's influence would now be broad as well as deep. Placing himself
among those intellectuals for whom Musil "is acknowledged as a
leader," Blass concluded that "the decisive word will fall in the coming

135. Franz Spunda, "Der Mann ohne Eigenschaften," *Die neue Literatur* (February
1931):87–88.

136. Efraim Frisch, "Der Mann ohne Eigenschaften," *Frankfurter Zeitung*, December
20, 1930.

137. Karl Baedeker, "Robert Musil und ein junger Mann seiner Zeit," in *Studien*,
p. 330.

138. Anon., "An Austrian Novel," *TLS*, November 19, 1931, p. 914.

139. Paul Jacob, "Robert Musil," *Revue d'Allemagne* (June 1932):517.

140. Cf. *Tag.* II, pp. 1074–75. Addressing a celebration for Musil at the PEN Club in
Vienna in March of 1931, Fontana counted his friend "as a good Viennese and at the same
time as a distinguished foreigner, since Musil is above all things at home in the region of
the spirit."

decade." [141] In fact, critical response to *The Man without Qualities* far exceeded Musil's expectations, but there was a bitter irony in Blass's prediction that Musil's position in German letters would be decided in the 1930s.

This hour of public recognition was gratifying, but it could not break the logic of Musil's life situation. Even the critical praise for the book reminded Musil of how forgotten and undervalued he had been, and even in 1930 praise for the book was too often accompanied by incomprehension and indifference toward the *Dichter* who had written it. On a more practical level, Musil was conscious that the signs did not augur well for completion of the second volume. Rowohlt nearly went out of business at this point, and he warned Musil that advances could continue only until early 1932, but Musil's friends and the attention which the first volume had won saved him again. In November, 1931, Musil's dream of moving to Berlin was realized by a group of contributors who agreed to support the continuation of his project. This freed Musil temporarily of financial worries and allowed him to be closer to Rowohlt, Allesch, and his friends in Berlin, but the moment was in no respect propitious—least of all, politically. Wolfdietrich Rasch, who knew him in Berlin, recalled that "the critical culmination of the situation in Germany in 1932 was for him a confirmation of his conviction that since 1913—the year of his novel—nothing had changed decisively, no solution to the great questions had succeeded." [142] Musil had arrived just in time to exchange a last line with a nation on its way to a repeat performance.

In a time of political anxiety and economic uncertainty, Musil struggled under pressure from his publisher to finish Book II. The second book proved not to be as easy to finish as he had expected, and Musil had great difficulty deciding which of the sketches from the early and mid-1920s still belonged in his conception of the novel as it went to print in 1930. By 1932 he doubted "whether I can finish the whole thing, or whether I will have to break off at a point that lies not very far beyond what is already completed." [143] While he gave lack of money as the main obstacle, he was also wearing thin under countless pressures that were ill-suited to the completion of his project. Musil saw that his problem of finishing the novel went deeper: "There are people who re-

141. Ernst Blass, "Robert Musil zum 50. Geburtstag," *Prager Presse*, November 6, 1930, p. 8.
142. Wolfdietrich Rasch, "Erinnerungen an Robert Musil," in *Studien*, p. 365.
143. Musil, "Vermächtnis, I" (1932), in *TE*, p. 800.

spond in such cases: why did he let things go so far? Answer: I would not be I, had I not let things go so far."[144] In response to the pleas of his publisher and his own financial desperation, Musil agreed to publish a fragment of the love-story of Ulrich and Agathe. This solution disappointed critics who had been excited by the first volume. For Musil, the publication of the second volume in 1933 was forced and artificial, and he suspected that it represented a dead end: "For unless something unexpected happens, I will not be in a position to finish this work."[145] The simultaneous appearance of the partial rendering of Musil's "Ins tausendjährige Reich" and Adolf Hitler's half-truth of the Third Reich presented with appropriate irony the relationship of this lost poet to German history. In the summer of 1933 Musil voluntarily removed himself to Vienna, where once again the financial support of friends allowed him to continue his work. But the decline of his physical and emotional strength made all the more difficult the task he had set himself, and the arrival of Hitler in Vienna in 1938 confirmed the prescience of Musil's fear that his novel would never be finished.

Musil's death in 1942 bequeathed to the critics the author's own neurosis about how to finish his novel. One impulse has been to stress those indications that Musil meant to finish his novel essentially as he had conceived it in 1924. Another has been to emphasize his preoccupation with the issues of the second book and the extent to which these broke off from the original conception. The historical fact is simply that Musil never resolved this question himself. Here one is led to the bottomless well of textual criticism or speculations on Musil's spiritual condition in old age, but the preoccupation of the Musil literature with decisions Musil was unable to make himself overestimate the tragedy of his inability to finish the novel. Musil once remarked that he wanted to end the second book in the middle of a sentence with a comma, so that the novel would not appear finished and absolute, but this is a stressful vision for a critic. Perhaps the most unfortunate aspect of a criticism which tries to finish a story that was not told is that it implicitly undervalues the work of art as Musil actually published it: "Volume I closed roughly at the high point of an arch; on the other side, it has no support. . . . Today the structure of a work of art matters more than its course. One must learn to understand the pages, then one will have books."[146]

144. Ibid., p. 801.
145. Musil, "Vermächtnis II" (1932), in *TE*, p. 802.
146. *MoE, Anhang*, p. 1598.

CHAPTER FIVE

The Man Without Qualities

T*he Man without Qualities* explores what Musil took to be the typical ideological difficulties of his generation. The explicit setting is Vienna 1913, and Musil's brilliant portrayal of Austrian elites suggests that his central theme is "the cultural and moral decline of the ruling classes before the First World War."[1] For Musil, however, the old Austria was simply "an especially clear case of the modern world," a model for the larger theme of the transition from traditional-bourgeois society to modern, pluralistic, mass culture.[2] Moreover, he was concerned not so much with politics as with the spiritually typical, not so much with the decline of Austria as with the birth of a spirituality commensurate with modern science. Kakania is a paradigm of European culture in Musil's generation, and the implied setting for this adventure of the mind is the flow of European culture in the first third of the twentieth century. Musil explores the manifold relations within this culture between knowledge and love, male and female, evil and good, power and intimacy, intellect and feeling. The mode of portrayal is impersonal, objective, ironic—allowing the contradictions to speak for themselves and showing the interdependence of

1. Eduard Zak, "Gegen den Strom," *Neue Deutsche Literatur* 4, 10 (October 1956): 122. The counterclaim that politics and science were "minor interests" for Musil is still less satisfactory: see Kaiser and Wilkins, *Robert Musil*, p. 297.
2. *MoE, Nachlass*, p. 1577.

the characters within the structure of a culture in crisis. The assumption of Musil's portrayal is that only by driving the dissolution of dead ideology to its limit, to the pure whiteness of leveled-out, devalued reality, can the constructive possibilities of a new culture be liberated.

Ulrich, the man without qualities, lives in the historical reality of prewar Austria but he is also the extreme case of modern consciousness, intensely aware of the fluidity of the world and of his own identity. His disinterested objectivity makes him an ideal ironic hero, free to bring his scientific audacity to bear on the forms of culture. His inability to take his own qualities personally allows his intellect to play with his feelings and to suspend the conventions of social reality. At the same time, Ulrich functions as a "kind of statistical midpoint" for a huge cast of characters who display the nuances of ideological variation and analogy.[3] Around Ulrich, Musil weaves a tapestry of conversations, knit together by thematic associations of clusters of characters, all of whom touch on the central thread of a culture in dissolution and transition. The inability of these figures to cope with this transition foreshadows their escape into meaningless action, but the ironic critique of ideologies and social roles is also a part of the search for authentic feeling and action.

Socially, the novel turns on the polarity between controlling and rebelling groups. The aristocrats, Stallburg and Leinsdorf, remain in the background as patrons of the search for a viable accommodation to industrial society. The main burden falls to the representatives of capital and culture, Arnheim (the German industrialist) and Diotima (the priestess of liberal culture), who have one last chance to salvage bourgeois society. They resist the counsel of the men of reality: Diotima's husband Tuzzi, a foreign-office bureaucrat, and the genial General Stumm, who waits in the wings with the military solution. Thanks to his father's influence, Ulrich (who is Diotima's cousin) becomes the secretary of this hopeless search to impose order on cultural chaos. Set against the attempts of the Parallel Action to justify normal consciousness and bourgeois order are a variety of challenges, symbolized by Moosbrugger, a homicidal maniac on trial for stabbing a woman to death. His fate is particularly important to Clarisse, whose painful marriage to Ulrich's friend Walter introduces the generational theme. Ulrich's mistress Bonadea is also fascinated by this sex-murderer; and

3. Dieter Kühn, *Analogie und Variation* (Bonn, 1965), p. 9.

Moosbrugger provides a metaphor for the political irrationalism of
Clarisse's friend Meingast and the Germanic-Christian visions of Hans
Sepp. The advocates of order and rebellion alike suffer from lack of
content for meaningful action, and they share a common grammar of
political irrationalism. The disorder and pluralism that emerge in this
drama of ideological breakdown heighten the need for redeeming action and order.

Instead of acting out the social roles available to him, Ulrich sets
himself the task of exploring the presuppositions of meaningful action.
While he follows both the Parallel Action and the Moosbrugger controversy in a desultory way, these options hold steadily less promise for
him as Book I unfolds. Against his impulse to be a man of importance
and have an impact on the world, Ulrich feels drawn toward the suppressed, inactive side of his being. His search for a more meaningful
relationship to the world is portrayed in Book I through his movement
beyond conventional eroticism. The last ten chapters of Book I constitute a convergence in which the Parallel Action and Moosbrugger are
emptied of value for Ulrich, while his relations with women bring him
to a point of decision.[4] This convergence opens the way to his adventure
with his sister Agathe in Book II. Although the other motifs and characters continue in the second book, the conversations between Ulrich and
Agathe clearly become Musil's main preoccupation. In this alliance in
search of the truth, they seek to reconcile intellect and feeling in order to
discover the presuppositions of ethical action.

The Man without Qualities is not an attempt to tell a real story with
a beginning and an end. Book I stresses irony and the constant reforming of concepts, while Book II presses toward the second extreme formulation of art, as a release from the normal ordering of experience.
But the political imbecility of the Parallel Action and the retreat of the
siblings do not stand in isolation. The two books of the novel share a
concern with the ideological predicament of modern consciousness,
with the duality of force and love in human affairs, and with the varieties of heightened consciousness and their relations with normal reality. The polar structure of the novel is also present within each book,
part, chapter, and page. Both critique and utopia belong to the process
of reforming the inner life, and Musil's values of science, spirit, intellect,
and flexibility are continuous throughout. This novel, however, is not a

4. Kaiser and Wilkins have contributed most to understanding the significance of this
turning within the structure of the novel.

systematic presentation of a complete model of the world. Its meaning lies not in a final yield of truth or narrative resolution, but in the transforming process of reading itself. This exegesis of the text of a failed culture eschews firm order, and its open ideology offers at most a way of proceeding under particular historical circumstances. Musil does illuminate patterns and relations within the flow of culture, but to see this novel as a fixed totality—whether as a story or philosophy—would make it simply another abstract version of the stabilized hopelessness that it seeks to overcome. Musil offers a complex texture of analogies, shattered moments, and reawakened meanings, always fluidly moving the process forward. His essayistic mode seeks to stay in touch with both intellect and feeling, while giving partial solutions to lived experience. *The Man without Qualities* captures the spiritual predicament of a generation, but it gives its meanings with a richness and indirection which underscore the incommensurability of *Dichtung* and criticism. This chapter can only highlight three main themes. While Musil intertwines his motifs throughout the novel, these issues correspond to the archetechtonic structure of its three parts: science and the self; the forms of culture in crisis; and the sources of the ethical.[5]

I. SCIENCE AND THE SELF

What has arisen is a world of qualities without a man, of experiences without someone to experience them. . . . Probably the dissolution of the anthropocentric way of relating, which has held the human being for so long at the center of the universe, but has now been disappearing for centuries, has finally made its way to the self.[6]

What one still calls personal destiny today is threatened by collective and ultimately statistically comprehensible processes.[7]

---

5. A single chapter discussing *The Man without Qualities* must inevitably leave out a great deal. The most compact German edition of the novel is more than 1,000 pages long, followed by 600 pages of published *Nachlass*. Since 1959 approximately thirty books (mostly in German) have been devoted entirely or primarily to *The Man without Qualities*, not including biographies, comparative studies, and innumerable articles and dissertations.
6. *MoE* I, chap. 39.
7. *MoE* II, chap. 8.

The Man without Qualities presents a world in which science and technology have vastly outdistanced the way people live and their assumptions about reality and morality. From the outset, Musil reminds his reader that the cosmos of Goethe is simply no longer there.[8] Against the main trend of his generation, Musil asserts the value of the achievements of intellect and science and examines the impact on consciousness of the transition from houses and horses to skyscrapers and trucks. Setting out from the assumption that the structure of modern life has created peculiar difficulties for ethical action, Musil establishes the discrepancy between the individual's pretense to identity (wearing his initials significantly stitched on his underwear) and the tendency for responsibility to lie outside the self. The complex relations of energy and time in modern physics do little to satisfy the normal assumptions about physical reality, identity, and causality. Self-sufficiency and morality are dissolved by the reduction of personal destiny to the regular patterns of statistical and institutional functions. Technology, pluralism, specialization, and the compartmentalization of feelings and values give to modern life a quality of the inessential and accidental. Science undermines the firm sense of reality and ego—and establishes the utopia of objectivity in which Musil writes.

The novel illuminates the tension between the structure of scientific reality—which most people manage to forget in all their really important decisions—and the possibility of being poetically produced—a possibility which seemed to have evaporated from modern life altogether. By forcing the reader from the outset to doubt his own ordinary reality and to suffer the scientific space in which he lives, Musil challenges himself to make the form of the novel victorious within this situation, or in spite of it. He creates obstacles for himself to be poetic, just as his ironic hero creates obstacles for himself to be good. Musil gives up the conventions of plot and heroic action, just as Ulrich wonders how anything he does in such a tangle of forces can make a scrap of difference. In exploring the tension between truth and subjectivity, Musil drew the consequences of Schlegel's short text of romantic phi-

---

8. The meteorological description of the opening paragraph is not only a parody of epic style, but also a poetic heightening and parody of scientific style. The most detailed of many discussions of the first chapter is Günter Graf, *Studien zur Funktion des ersten Kapitels* (Göppingen, 1969). See also Ulf Schramm, *Fiktion und Reflexion* (Frankfort, 1967). Schramm argues that Musil is unable to bridge the chasm between science and the individual, and he criticizes Musil for being what he was: a point of transition between the old philosophical dignity and the pure immediacy of modern art.

losophy: that all science must become art, and all art science. *The Man without Qualities* presents a world dissolved by science and reconstituted by metaphor, but these are aspects of a single process. Metaphor is not a mode for a thought which might just as well have been conceptually expressed, nor is it a sentimental escape from the objectivity of science. There are not two worlds, one made meaningless by science and one made sublime by symbol. The beauty of metaphorical language and the irony of scientific objectivity are constituted in a single gesture.

Ulrich, who suffers consciously what the others live unconsciously, is the vehicle for Musil's inquiry into the motivated life.[9] He represents the highest degree of scientific sophistication and intellectual self-consciousness possible for a European of his generation. Bringing the values of the engineer and the mathematician into the realm of morality, Ulrich discovers that the language of the feelings has not kept pace with modern developments, that "in all things concerned with high ideals, mankind behaves in a way that is considerably more old-fashioned than one would expect from looking at his machines":

Who can be interested any longer in that age-old idle talk about good and evil, when it has been established that good and evil are not "constants" at all, but "functional values," so that the goodness of works depends on historical circumstances, and the goodness of human beings on the psycho-technical skill with which their qualities are exploited? The world is simply comical if one looks at it from the technical point of view.[10]

Ulrich notices that the truths of thought and freedom of thought have developed together, while the feelings have lacked both the strict school of truth and the corresponding freedom of movement. He wonders why men who live by the sliderule in professional life never dream of applying their intellect to the rest of life; why people live only their professions with passion, intensity, precision, and objectivity; why the man of intellect demands something new and functional in the way of an automobile or surgery, while leaving all the really important matters to his wife and to men he does not respect who spout "thousand-year-old phrases of the sword and cup of life."[11] Ulrich wants to do for the feelings what science has done for the physical world. He wants to risk the

9. Neil Bolton calls this a search for "valid guidelines for authentic action": "Robert Musil and Phenomenological Psychology," *Journal of the British Society for Phenomenology* 6, 1 (January 1975):54.
10. *MoE* I, chap. 10.
11. *MoE* I, chap. 62.

values of truth and freedom in the realms of emotion and private life, but also in those realms which pass for morality when they are merely conventional arrangements for dealing with practical problems. He jams the old metaphors and values of Europe up against a new way of thinking appropriate to the age of technology, which had then only just begun.

The man without qualities is living in the midst of the Second Industrial Revolution, and he estimates the individual's potential for impact as virtually nil. He is introduced as the observer, looking out from his house at the fantastic speed and dynamic force of modern society. In the face of all this senseless activity, he reserves his energies like a sick person, not out of indifference, but out of the conviction that he cannot possibly have any impact. The massive scale of institutional and technological realities is opposed by a subjective cultural confusion so great that no individual insight can possibly have any real penetration. Any exertion would simply be canceled out into something average. In this hopeless tangle of forces, the power lies with the average, and old Napoleonic notions of heroism must go the way of old-fashioned notions of responsibility. Ulrich has all the faculties of the traditional hero, but he sees no reason to add to this whirlwind of unmotivated activity. Preferring inaction to senseless activity, he decides to take a year's vacation from life to inquire into the right way to live.

As an Austrian mandarin, Ulrich has the right combination of scientific, psychological, and artistic values to think through this historical situation, but he also lives the socially based ambivalence of the critical intellectual who seeks recognition and security within the old order; he is critical yet accepted, the fool in a social order about to go under. He is the beneficiary of the achievements of bourgeois-industrial civilization in his father's generation. As the son of a generation which had been assimilated to the eighteenth-century state without making a revolution, Ulrich benefits from his father's connections in the aristocracy and himself belongs to a kept elite. His father's model of male bourgeois values amounts to a combination of social ambition and professional achievement. As a typical liberal of the 1870s, the old man's accomplishments as a legal scholar earned him a seat in the Austrian House of Lords, and he has a deep respect for the social foundations on which he has constructed his success.

Ulrich began by emulating his father's values in his attempts to be a man of importance as a soldier, engineer, and mathematician. But as he became aware of the falseness of ambition, achievement, and recognition in his time, he lost his appetite for the bait that was offered to him. Ulrich's inability to find meaningful employment for his highly developed qualities seems to his father simply decadent, a symptom of the ravaged senses of the spoiled child. Ulrich is also, then, the *haut bourgeois* aesthete, the young man who has everything except a sense of identity and purpose. His youthful friendship with Walter represents this generational experience of rebellion against bourgeois values, and the two appear in the novel ten years later as hostile brothers. Walter believes that science and intellect are the enemies of soul, art, and great feelings, but he is also deeply embedded in the bourgeois values of social status and professional success. Ulrich, on the other hand, has lost his father's sense of mastery, ambition, and piety toward the social order, but he retains the commitment to science and intellect. Intellectually he differs from his father only in his shocking intention to apply these faculties to feelings and morality.[12]

In the ideological confusion of modern culture, Ulrich can find no guiding idea to justify sustained and coherent action in the world. The chaos of this pluralistic culture is mirrored in the unstable feelings of the individual, who is vulnerable to random impulses from his environment.[13] Kakania, in its multinational cultural pluralism and institutional confusion, is a paradigm of modern culture. It is "the most pro-

12. The absence of a mother in this account and Ulrich's similarity to Musil deserve comment. Ulrich's mother is hardly mentioned. She died young, perhaps as a symbol of the precocious execution of the feminine in Ulrich's family and personality. This scenario is, of course, a shuffling of Musil's own experience: Ulrich's sister lives and his mother dies, while Musil's sister died and his mother lived. Here, as in other matters, Ulrich is an ideal type and not an autobiographical rendering. Ulrich's mother came from a Rhenish industrial family, adding the perfect touch to the model Central European bourgeois: Austrian *Wissenschaft* enhanced by German money. There are other important differences between Ulrich and Musil. Ulrich attended the *Theresianer Ritterakademie* in Vienna, his father's social connections were more elevated than the Musils', and Ulrich was educated in the cosmopolitan atmosphere of Belgium rather than in a military academy on the road to Russia. Ulrich is a fictional character, artificially constructed with an eye to the typical. Moreover, Musil was writing from the historical distance of two decades. Nonetheless, the imperceptible transitions from narrator's voice to inner monolog highlight the close identification of ironic narrator and ironic hero; and there are of course similarities between them.

13. Bolton calls Musil's novel "a quest whose aim is to maximize the human potentiality for feeling." He argues, however, that Musil mistrusted modes of authenticity that exclusively emphasized feelings and spontaneity (Clarisse) without giving any thought to "the difficulties of fulfilling oneself rationally, that is, in accordance with objective criteria." Bolton formulates Musil's solution as "a suspension of belief in the reality of social reality, a refusal to act on the basis of emotions of dubious intellectual status, a determination to reduce the arbitrariness of the life of feeling" ("Robert Musil," pp. 52–54).

gressive state of all," where one is "negatively free, constantly aware of the inadequate grounds for one's own existence."[14] Living in a contradictory culture, Ulrich refuses to pretend that the broken pieces of culture and the fragments of preformed feeling which correspond to them have fallen together into a whole. As an Austrian, as an empiricist, and as a member of the decadent younger generation, Ulrich has developed an extraordinary tolerance for pluralism, yet he wonders if it is possible to live happily without a limit. He wants the freedom to choose, but he wants his life to have the coherence of an idea.

Ulrich wants to be master in his own house, and Musil uses his house as a symbol of the self, trapped in the tangle of prejudice. Musil describes it as "a hunt or love castle of times past," a little baroque castle with "a partially kept-up garden from the eighteenth century or even the seventeenth century," surrounded by an iron-grating fence. Ulrich is living in an order constructed under Maria Theresa or even earlier and only modestly remodeled by bourgeois overlays. There he lives somewhat cut off from the modern world, replacing the hunt with science and keeping love more or less the same. His inability to decide how to furnish his house reflects the eclecticism and pluralism in which he lives. With each decision he notices that he might just as well do everything differently—and he begins to dream instead of to decide. He asks only that arrangements be useful and comfortable; otherwise, he is content to leave it to the specialists, who are confident that they will be faithful to the limitations of convention, prejudice, and fashion. Ulrich is convinced that feelings in the modern world are no longer "'firm enough for houses. ... Today almost everyone feels that a formless life is the only form which corresponds to the multiplicity of desires and possibilities.'"[15]

Ulrich is unable to take personally the jumble of qualities his culture bestows on him, to accept them as his ego, as his *Eigen-schaften.*[16] His

14. *MoE* I, chap. 8.
15. *MoE* I, chap. 2, and II, chap. 24. Throughout the novel Musil uses architectural structures as fundamental unifying symbols. Ulrich's father's house represents the bourgeois tradition of masculine discipline and achievement, while Diotima's apartment symbolizes the feminine supervision of bourgeois culture. The homes of the Fischels and Walter and Clarisse symbolize both the torment of bourgeois private life and the revolt of the bourgeoisie against itself. Public structures represent, variously, traditional piety (the church), the chaos of knowledge (the library), the chaos of feelings (the insane asylum), the world (street), the history of bourgeois civilization (the *Ringstrasse*), and political power (the *Hofburg*).
16. Cf. Dietmar Goltschnigg, "Die Bedeutungsformel 'Mann ohne Eigenschaften,'" *Vom "Törless,"* pp. 325–47. Goltschnigg points out that Ulrich's *Eigenschaften* prove to

qualities are only symptoms of his culture's confusion, and he simply makes these contradictions conscious and explicit. Even his most admirable qualities are functions of what his culture has made him and what it admires. They are not his qualities or properties, not his possessions or property.[17] Instead of possessing these qualities, Ulrich approaches the devalued reality around him so skeptically and relativistically that no position provides leverage from which to define his own identity. This negative definition of the hero is intolerable for the other characters, and Walter insists that this man without qualities is hardly a person at all. His lack of qualities corresponds to Musil's inability to tell a story, since traditional narrative depends on character. Ulrich sees this complete devaluing and self-emptying as the precondition of authentic action. Put positively, his lack of judgment is a lack of prejudice and a complete openness to the future, but he also leaves himself with no firm ground on which to stand. In this sense his undermining of reality is self-ironic from the start. Ulrich is free, left without a story in his pocket.

People become firm, real, secure by acquiescing in the assumptions of the social order in which they are placed. Ulrich's refusal to do this makes him a man without qualities, attributes, properties, character. Like everyone else in the novel, Ulrich is defined by nine qualities: professional, national, state, class, geographical, sexual, conscious, unconscious, and private. What is peculiar about Ulrich is his failure to take these qualities personally. Whether in sports, in love, or in his profession, the qualities seem to belong more to each other than to him. The way in which B always follows A quite apart from his intervention leads him to the inference that experiences have won their independence from people. The center of gravity lies in things rather than people, so that one cannot even be sure one's anger is personal. He concludes that the ego is the point of intersection of quite impersonal functions. The fact that a particular bundle of qualities happens to intersect in him for the moment seems to him an entirely impersonal occasion. He is the exact

---

be *Aller-schaften* and characterizes Ulrich's task as the recovery of the real self from the accumulated social functions of the pseudo-ego. See also Stefan Reinhardt, *Studien zur Antinomie von Intellekt und Gefühl* (Bonn, 1969), p. 194.

17. Dinklage ("Musils Definition," in *Studien*, p. 113) quotes Musil from a *Nachlass* entry (Mappe II/9) of 1939: "'A man with qualities would be one who possesses his qualities not as a necessity of nature, but also morally. Thus who possesses himself morally. Or who has morality.'" Cf. Kierkegaard's distinction between having mood and being in a mood.

opposite of Arnheim, who is overwhelmed by the significance of the fact that time and space intersect in the great Arnheim, or that the sun goes down to his left. Ulrich's identity, in the ordinary sense, hardly belongs to him at all. He is a man without reality, or qualities without a man.

Ulrich notices that what most people take seriously as the self arises over time out of events, accidents, deaths, moods, and the like, little of which has been unequivocally motivated in the first place. By mid-life, the youthful sense of expectancy has spilled into the fixity of a few pleasures, "a world view, a wife, a profession, and a character":

But the strangest thing of all is that most people don't even notice that; they adopt the man who has come to them, whose life has entwined itself with theirs; his experiences seem to them now the expression of their qualities, and his fate is their reward or misfortune.

At thirty-two Ulrich stands at mid-life, between the indefiniteness of youth and the reality of adulthood. He observes that in the course of the previous decade all the rebels and new people of his youth have made their way out of the mist and fog and into rigidity. Watching the arbitrariness of this process, Ulrich concludes that the reality of the personality is not at all what it seems to be. Most people around him seem content to have the world pre-formed for them when they arrive, except for a few personal peculiarities, but Ulrich dislikes the feeling that the life he leads does not concern him much inwardly. Ulrich finds himself set down in a rigidified world where everything happens without sufficient reason. He experiences his world as lived-out, used-up, as "a died-out little breath about which God no longer concerns himself." [18]

Ulrich is opposed to everything that assumes a firm order: to all finished laws and ideals and to the satisfied character. He suggests the possibility of giving up the normal possessiveness toward experience. Each person has roughly the same qualities, the same capacities for experience or goodness. He wonders what is changed about success because he has it, about a hundred marks because they are in his pocket. Ulrich suspects an archaic need to insist that the physical and moral universes revolve in a very concrete way around oneself. People who possess their experience in the ordinary way are not yet alert to the impersonality of a shared process and shared functions. Instead of seeing the connections which lie in things, people insist on taking their successes,

18. *MoE* I, chap. 34.

dinners, discoveries, and vacations in the country quite personally. Ulrich wants to explore the possibility of living objectively and impersonally. He wants to be a man without qualities, no longer living like a fixed person in a fixed world with only a few buttons left to button, but born to variation in a world born to variation, like "a drop of water in a cloud":

> He sensed that this order was not so firm as it pretended to be; no thing, no self, no form, no principle was certain. Everything is caught up in invisible but never-resting metamorphosis; in the unfirm lies more of the future than the firm, and the present is nothing but a hypothesis which one has not yet gotten beyond.

Ulrich sees the possessive relation to one's qualities, experiences, and ego as a function of the rigidification of the world, of principles, and of the given social order.[19]

Ulrich does, however, take his tenth quality seriously: "The passive fantasy of spaces left unfilled . . . an empty, invisible space, in which reality stands like a little toy-brick town abandoned by the imagination."[20] For him, the soul is a hole of which only the sides (the other nine qualities) are real. What he values is the hole, the possibility, the imagination, the spirit, the fire. Put positively, Ulrich's lack of qualities is the potentiality of the self, refusing to be rigidified into specific qualities which are not motivated as his own. As a man of possibility, Ulrich hangs onto the fire, the conscious utopianism, sustaining the indefinite energy of the child against the random accretions of age. The man of possibility invents reality, thinks in the subjunctive, and always bears in mind that no matter how something is done, "it could probably also be otherwise." In his first schoolboy essay on patriotism, he wrote that "probably even God preferred to think of his world in the *conjunctivus potentialis* . . . , for God makes the world and thinks it might just as well have been otherwise." The God of possibility invokes the subjunctive, the dominant voice of Musil's novel.[21]

The man of possibility values everything that dissolves the firmness of reality, releasing in it the sense of possibility. The ordinary man of reality values science for its ability to confirm and sustain his view of what is: the man of possibility uses science to melt down reality in order to

19. *MoE* I, chaps. 66, 62.
20. *MoE* I, chap. 8.
21. *MoE* I, chap. 5. The subjunctive is one of Musil's principal weapons for the dissolution of reality and the creation of a world which is more than imitative realism. See Albrecht Schöne, "Zum Gebrauch des Konjunktivs bei Robert Musil," *Euphorion* 55 (1961):196–220.

liberate possibility. The sense of possibility arises from the shattering of
the two *idées fixes* of the ordinary sense of reality: the physical, literal
model of the self and the world (uncontaminated by modern science),
and the social identity of the self fixed in bourgeois society. This represents a challenge to the two dominant forms of determinism and reductionism of nineteenth-century positivism: the biological and the social.
(These realistic values are, of course, deeply embedded in the tradition
as well.)[22]

A man of possibility is not an idealist who suffers from a weak sense
of reality. His constructive will does "not shrink from reality, but treats
it, on the contrary, as a mission and an invention." He is the empiricist
in the realm of the spirit, the "underwater swimmer in an ocean of reality," always risking the danger that he may never come up for air. He
needs to understand reality because it is reality that awakens possibility.
It is less a matter of evading reality than of creating a tension with it.
This is not otherworldliness, but a positive, active indifference to his
own qualities, a refusal to be possessed by a pre-established logic of desire to which he brings nothing. A man of possibility is someone to
whom what is real is no more important than what is thought or imagined. This type of the creative person is in search of a possible experience or a possible truth. In his refusal to grant solidity its solidity, his
approach to life sometimes makes the admirable appear false and the
forbidden permitted or at least indifferent. Instead of thinking of reality
as something finished and perfected, the man of possibility creates new
possibilities and gives them their meaning. The man of reality expects
something from experience which has already been defined, and he is
happy to settle for the old meanings.[23]

As a scientist-mathematician Ulrich represents the bold confidence of
a new way of thinking about feelings and morality, or at least the fragments of such a way of thinking and feeling. His scientific spirit treats
life as a great experimental laboratory where he is investigating the best
way to be a human being. The precision and energy of mathematical
thought enhance his awareness of the impersonality of knowledge and
the world. The thrill of scientific discovery is keyed to something imper-

22. Erich Heintel, "Der Mann ohne Eigenschaften und die Tradition," *Wissenschaft und Weltbild* 13 (1960):179–94.
23. *MoE* I, chap. 4. Cf. Musil, *Prosa*, p. 704: "*Anders*: Act not so that your action would be a rule for all, but rather so that it would be valuable. Whereby 'value' comes out of the sphere of the *other condition*, is that indefinable 'lively' moment."

sonal, to "the affinity and interconnectedness of the things themselves which bump together in the head." Like his prototype, *Monsieur le vivesecteur,* Ulrich wants to apply the ruthless objectivity and disciplines of scientific thought to human relationships, feelings, and values. He sets out from the side of science to inquire into how the devil can find his way back to God, and how truth can again become the sister of virtue. He needs a way of thinking that can bridge the gap between the side of him which is powerful and wants to have impact on the world and that other self which can never quite come to expression. This other self is "small, tender, dark, and soft like a Medusa floating in water, as soon as he read a book that seized him, or was brushed by the breath of the great homeless love, whose being-in-the-world he had never been able to comprehend."

A man who wants the truth becomes a scholar; a man who wants to give free rein to his subjectivity becomes, perhaps, a writer; but what should a man do who wants something which lies between the two?

Ulrich decides on essayism as the intermediate mode suitable to his search for a moral way of thinking which learns from the experience of science. As an essayist, Ulrich falls between science and art, between his father's firm logic and Walter's softness.[24]

In the absence of philosophical totality and narrative coherence, essayism provides the thread of continuity for Ulrich and the novel, as the form of spirit appropriate to the dissolution of bourgeois culture. Ulrich prefers essayism to the philosopher's impulse to give knowledge and feelings a military order which no longer makes sense in an age of democracy and pluralism. These systematic philosophers (like Stumm) belong to an age of despots, and not to the contradictory ideological situation of modernity. Instead of a systematic presentation of all the rules and principles regarding good and evil, Ulrich develops a form of ethical thought that is not meant to be reduced according to the model of academic philosophy. What is essential in the essay is the inner movement, and that is precisely what is lost in the exegesis. It is like taking a jellyfish out of the water to admire it, so that everything admirable about the jellyfish is gone. An essay is the inner form which crystallizes in a decisive thought, and the essayist is the master of the floating life within. Ulrich's moments of essayistic insight and focused consciousness

24. *MoE* I, chaps. 28, 40, 62.

punctuate the narrative throughout. They inquire into problems of love and knowledge in a search for a new combination of "the exact and the indefinite, of precision and passion."[25]

Essayism is a life-form as well as a mode of thinking. Ulrich's essayism is a preparation for meaningful experience, the active passivity of the prisoner waiting for an opportunity to break out. It is a conscious human essayism, which constantly takes everything back and starts over. For an essayist like Ulrich, the most intense and meaningful life-experiences are those that fall between law and subjectivity, the genuinely ambiguous situations which make us sweat with uncertainty. Ulrich wants to do something with his whole soul, which means that he could just as well do it or not do it. He respects no compulsion or aversion, but only a complete freedom. Ulrich does not suffer from the Hamlet-syndrome of inhibited capacity to decide or act, nor is he like Dostoevsky's Underground Man, who finds freedom in arbitrariness and pathology. He is convinced that only a man without identity or pathology can be free; only such a person could sustain the knowledge that his society offered him only inauthentic actions and whims. Ulrich is searching for a form of meaningful participation in social reality, but he wants action that fulfills both intellectual and emotional criteria of authenticity. His essayistic mode is a response to the fragmentary character of modern culture, of the "weakness of the whole in relation to its parts. With passion and will there is nothing to be done against it. Hardly will you be completely in the middle of something, and you see yourself already spilled over the edge: that is the experience today in all experiences."[26] Ulrich yearns to be caught up in experience like a boxer in the ring, to find experience which is somehow final and valid.

Positivism, relativism, and decadence have left Ulrich's generation without religion, morality, or unifying culture. Thus, Ulrich has no idea how to furnish his house, no guiding idea or principle of order. But he sees precisely in this an opportunity for disinterested thought and creativity. The debris had inadvertently cleared itself away; one could see this as an empty room or as a new opportunity. Many of Ulrich's contemporaries are inclined to blame science for the missing whole of the culture and the self, but Ulrich sees science as a model of a more modest

25. *MoE* I, chap. 62. Although Musil defended intellect and made mathematics a model for ethical thought, he was also an aggressive critic of the kind of academic reason which wants to make the essayistic mode or any form of life-teaching into a life-science.
26. *MoE* II, chap. 25.

style of thought that sticks to the facts and partial solutions. It suggests
the possibility of living hypothetically, finding the courage to make each
step a risk, without certainty or knowledge. This means taking responsibility for one's own life, and feeling the breath of the irrevocable over
each step—or, as Ulrich puts it, it is like living in a book or a fable. This
draws him not to firm commitments, but to whatever is inwardly enhancing. He feels himself capable of every virtue and every perversity,
and conventional morality seems to him merely an outmoded remainder
of a form which the ethical energy-system had taken on in ancient
times. While this view reflects a certain insecurity, Ulrich believes that it
corresponds to the inadequacy of the conventional assurances.

Observing the empirical basis and modesty of the scientific method,
Ulrich wonders if it might not be better to live for three treatises instead
of one long book. In geology, the discovery that stones speak would be
disposed of in a single scientific paper, while every day there is another
book on human nature and morality. This suggests the utopia of exact
living:

> It means roughly the same as keeping silent when one has nothing to say; doing
> only what is necessary when one has nothing particular in mind; and what is
> most important, remaining without feelings when one does not have the inde-
> scribable feeling of spreading one's arms and being raised on a wave of creativi-
> ty! One will notice that thereby the greater part of our psychic life would have to
> cease, but that would perhaps not be such a bad thing.[27]

Ulrich imagines that there may be at most three occasions in a life which
call for real passion, individuality, or morality. Otherwise, life lives itself
without assistance from the individual. Ulrich suspects that it might be
better if for a time people made less use of morality, reserving it for the
special cases when it is required and treating the rest of life as routinely
as the conventions of handwriting. He refuses to exalt as morality what
is only a set of practical arrangements for organizing life and getting
through the day. This exact way of living would, instead, live objectively the connections which lie in things and in impersonal qualities
and functions.

The exact temperament of the utopia of the three treatises is characterized by a cold-bloodedness which is also required in science, in professions, and in sports. The normal passions are replaced by a primal

---

27. *MoE* I, chap. 61. Musil's notion of a utopia was modeled on the humble vision of
the scientific method: it is "an experiment in which the possible variation of an element
and its effects are observed" (ibid.)

fire, which is something like remaining in constant creative activity. This would be too much to ask were it not that this attitude was already common in the early twentieth century. Musil referred here not only to scientists, but to technicians, businessmen, organizers, and athletes, though of course only on days when they were at their professions. He wonders why this frame of mind could not be carried over into life: to live like a scientist or like a boxer in the ring. In sporting events and laboratories, the most impersonal gathering of energy seems to lead to the greatest sense of fulfillment. Similarly, only the intensity of exact living is likely to awaken moments of real discovery in life.

In chapter 7 Musil portrays his ironic hero for the first time in active relation to social reality. Ulrich is beaten unconscious in the street by three muggers, and many critics have discovered in this scene the Achilles heel of the man of possibility: his inability to act decisively. In a split second's hesitation Ulrich wastes the chance to use his carefully cultivated physical skills. Although Ulrich's preference for thoughtful inaction is well-known, Musil is in fact establishing not Ulrich's lamed capacity to decide, but most of the main themes of the novel. The presence of three assailants expresses the impotence of the individual in relation to the greater weight of circumstances. This senseless crime is also, of course, a graphic demonstration of the blindness of desire and the chaos of individual actions which neutralize each other. It is, equally, a reminder of "a certain atmospheric hostility, of which the air is full in our age." Despite the aspirations of culture, a block away from a policeman the state of nature resumes again. It is not only the scale and chaos of modern life that thwart the effectiveness of individual action; it is also the ambivalence of human life which makes progress on the whole so difficult, since an old form of stupidity seems always to be replaced by a new one. Hostility and love seem to be constants, no more separated from each other than "the bright wings of a silent bird." The individual seems unable to diminish or expand these constants by his reforming zeal, thanks to the dualistic nature of a humanity which makes "Bibles and weapons, tuberculosis and medicine. . . . It is the well-known matter of contradictions, the inconsequence and incompleteness of life. One smiles at it or sighs at it. But now Ulrich was simply not that way. He hated this mixture of resignation and monkey-love." Ulrich is not mesmerized by his own indolence or complacently resigned to passive meaninglessness. He explicitly hates all this halfwayness. This experience reminds him of how little difference the individual makes in the sum of good and evil; the arrival of Bonadea recalls the proximity in human affairs of hostility and love; and the arbitrariness of both these incidents reminds Ulrich that what happens in life is roughly the opposite of what a trained mind is accustomed to expect.[28]

But this experience is also a model of release from normal reality, a moment that breaks in to shatter the utopia of the status quo. It is an experience of total participation which is ordinarily quite rare in bourgeois life. Ulrich describes this interruption of normal reality as a spontaneous expression of speed and energy in which rational will, intention, and consciousness play no role. His encounter with the muggers is a moment of magic, a decision of the body which simply happens and which permits conscious reflection only afterward. It is at the furthest possible remove from decisions about furnishing one's house; it has nothing to do with deliberation and decision. Ulrich explains to Bonadea that boxing and other sports have brought this experience into a kind of system which amounts to a modern theology. For a moment, the body and soul become a harmonious whole: "This experience of the almost complete removal or penetration of the conscious personality is fundamentally related to the lost experiences which were well-known to the mystics of all religions." Ulrich's discussion of the body stimulates Bonadea in a way that recalls the similarity between sexuality and gooseflesh in a culture where the "bodily drives have really come to be in fashion." Bonadea becomes not only Ulrich's new mistress but also a symbol for such transforming experiences and their relations with shifts of perspective and weakened conditions: "Even love belongs to the religious and dangerous experiences, because it lifts people out of the arms of reason and removes them into a truly groundless condition of soaring." This incident typifies the novel's pattern of breaking out of reality and then returning to discover what reality really is.[29]

While the first part of the novel concentrates on introducing the man of possibility, the second part leads Ulrich into the complexities of social reality and a nearly inexhaustible cast of characters. Ulrich's problems simply mirror the problems of his culture as a whole, and his pecu-

28. *MoE* I, chap. 7. This chapter also highlights the fact that Ulrich is a bit bored by everyday goodness and inclines "in morality more to the service of the general staff than to the daily heroism of doing good."

29. Ibid. Peter Berger points out that normal reality, or what Musil calls the utopia of the status quo, requires a "perspectival abridgement" of consciousness. See Berger's valuable essay, "The Problem of Multiple Realities: Alfred Schutz and Robert Musil," in *Phenomenology and Social Reality*, ed. Maurice Natanson (The Hague, 1970), pp. 213–33.

liarity as a man without qualities is to be aware of this. Critics often emphasize Ulrich's isolation but say less about his awareness of interdependence with other human beings. The title of part two, "Seinesgleichen geschieht," is translated by Kaiser and Wilkins as "The Like of It Now Happens." This emphasizes the arbitrary and inessential quality of human action in society and history—at least in a pluralistic culture without a center. But it may also be read as a pun: "The Like of Ulrich Now Happens." The other characters are variations of Ulrich and his problems. Whether in the Parallel Action or the Moosbrugger plot or the adventure with Agathe, Ulrich is portrayed as consciously interconnected with his age, culture, and society. This also means that when Musil wrote about Walter, Clarisse, Meingast, Hans, Moosbrugger, Diotima, Arnheim, Stumm, Hagauer, Lindner, Agathe—he was also writing about Ulrich . . . and himself. The yield of Musil's inquiry into science and the self is that "personal happiness (or balance, contentment, or however one wants to describe the most automatic, most inward goal of the person) is only as enclosed in itself as a stone in a wall or a drop in a stream, through which the energies and tensions of the whole pass."[30] This interconnectedness of human forms and energies is the positive content of the dissolution of the ego. It also defines the convergence of scientific objectivity with Musil's ironic voice.

Musil's irony focuses not on persons and their moral failings, but on the social forms and moralities in which individuals are taken up. His "new irony" rests on the assumption "that all the qualities which have come to expression in humanity rest rather close to one another in the spirit of each person, if he has any spirit at all":[31]

----

30. *MoE* I, chap. 109.

31. *TE,* pp. 269, 117. The debate in the critical literature over irony and satire has been polarized ideologically along the same lines as the attempts to finish writing the novel for Musil. Even for specialists (see Robert Elliott, "The Definition of Satire," *Yearbook of Comparative and General Literature* 11 [1962]:19–23) satire is a concept with blurred edges; and it is not the historian's task to adjudicate metaphysical essences for the literary guild. Musil himself made no strict technical distinction between irony and satire. His objectivity was inevitably satiric, since it brought out the limitations of points of view that represented themselves as complete. Musil does correct and criticize, and he is not merely resigned and world-weary, but certainly his ironic posture of impersonality and ignorance differs from the traditional conception of the satirist as the representative of fixed moral ideals. Part of the Musil literature has attempted to accommodate this moral style to a more modern definition of satire. Among the more important works on this extensively discussed subject are: Arntzen, *Satirischer Stil*; Cristoph Hönig, *Die Dialektik von Ironie und Utopie* (diss., Berlin, 1970); and Jürgen Brummack, "Zu Begriff und Theorie der Satire," *DVJS* 45 (1971):275–377.

Irony is: to portray a clerical in such a way that a Bolshevik is captured in the same description. Portray an imbecile so that the author suddenly feels: I am that in part myself. This kind of irony—the constructive irony—is relatively unknown in Germany today. It is the connection of things from which they come forth naked. One takes irony for mockery or ridicule.[32]

Without actively mocking, Musil's irony allows objectivity to be what it is and lets judgment arise out of the structure of the situation. At the same time, Musil was convinced that satire ought not to be a partisan device: "One must think through and master what one loves as well, so that it seems satirical."[33] Irony undermines the realities that make his characters feel important and justified, but it is also self-ironic; the narrator and his hero are also implicated in this structural irony. As spirit dissolves the rigid forms of European culture, there is no privileged place to stand. Musil's irony is critical but without righteousness, urbane but loving. It communicates his ambivalence, of being of two minds about something; it seeks in a single gesture to accept and yet give away, to negate and yet love. The decisive quality of Musil's mature poetic voice is the ironic blend of hostility and empathy, objectivity and love, which he displays in the first volume of *The Man without Qualities.*[34]

2. THE SEARCH FOR ORDER

What a person does and feels himself is insignificant by com-

parison with everything which he must assume that others

will do and feel for him in an orderly way. No human being

---

32. *MoE, Nachlass*, p. 1603.

33. *TE*, p. 260. Musil certainly meant to keep his distance from his culture's conception of the satirist. No Austrian of Musil's generation could say the word *satire* without thinking of Karl Kraus, but Musil did not like the self-righteousness and simple-mindedness of this model: "Kraus is the savior-figure; because Kraus is there and scolds, everything is all right again. The objectively bad conscience. Naturally this effect is not good. Kraus's opposition to the war is morally just as sterile as enthusiasm for it" (*TE*, pp. 271–72).

34. See ibid., p. 500. In the 1920s Musil concluded that his early books had been too serious, that he was too inductive to achieve a satisfying pathos: "One could say, philosophical humor. For the world is not ripe for seriousness. At that time I decided for irony. The almost purely positive work on the second volume and also the preparation for the aphorisms have, to be sure, not let me forget that, but it has robbed me of its effectiveness." Musil saw the moral peril of his ironic style in an objectivity so wise as to offend through *Besserwisserei*. Here he felt himself protected by the questionableness of knowledge and virtue. He distinguished between Socratic irony, which means "seeming to be ignorant," and modern irony, which means "really being ignorant" (*TE*, p. 558).

lives only his own balance, but, rather, each depends on the
layers which surround him.[35]

An escaped metaphor of order: that was what Moosbrugger
was for him![36]

The characters in *The Man without Qualities* are searching for order
in the chaos of a culture which has broken down into competing partial
ideologies. These people feel the incoherence of knowledge, ideology,
society, and the self. They express a situation in which culture failed in
its mysterious task of giving order to the soul. Musil points out that
only "an extremely artificial condition of consciousness" permits a
human being "in the midst of the almost infinite unknownness of the
world to place his hand with dignity between the second and third
buttons of his jacket." Ordinarily, people are saved from thinking of
this by convention, self-deception, and common sense, but there are
historical periods when cultural forms fail to bind the firm order that
human beings seem to require for "the artificial contentedness of the
soul." Kakania is a paradigm of European culture at such a time, "the
first country in the contemporary slice of development from which God
withdrew his credit." The cultivated Austrians of this period felt as if
the debt were getting higher all the time, though not because of anything demonstrable. Something imaginary was felt to be missing, and
this nothing became as disturbing as not being able to sleep. This
nothing is the main subject of conversation in part two.[37]

The huge cast of characters allows Musil to explore the variety and
interdependence of attempts to achieve ideological reassurance. Musil
portrays the multiplicity of human responses to this situation, the manifold relations between truth and feeling, the shadings and layerings of
types as they blend into one another. Most of the ideologies are directed
against science and intellect. The willingness of these people to sacrifice
intellect for the sake of feelings leads toward an end to words, toward
the release of senseless action. The reassuring totality which science
cannot provide is discovered in the emotional union of war. The failure
of traditional ideas and institutions to give security and stability to the
feelings of people in modern civilization drives their feelings to a panic

35. *MoE* I, chap. 109.
36. *MoE* I, chap. 122.
37. *MoE* I, chap. 109.

of order. The attempts of Ulrich (and of Musil) are directed toward a kind of spiritual therapy, both intellectual and emotional, to overcome the rigidity of bourgeois culture.[38]

Whether in politics or romantic love, these characters exhibit the collapse of a unified tradition which could inform meaningful action. The ideological discussions are superficially concerned with politics and truth, but beneath these grand formulations, Musil uncovers the vacuity of emotional life and the strange system of compensation between private and public, person and ideology. The Parallel Action deals with a range of political issues which lead to war, but these are not the main themes of the novel. Musil is interested not in real events but in the emotional need for great events. Similarly, the ideological debates revolve around civilization and soul, order and chaos, reason and feeling, but the real issue for Musil's characters is the acoustic of emptiness which haunts their personal lives. The novel seeks to clear away the pathos common to both politics and bourgeois private life by resisting false attempts at ideological order. General Stumm is the satiric vehicle of this search for order. His visits to the library and the insane asylum caricature the absence of firm order in knowledge and in the emotional life. His attempt to find an ordering idea in the inner sanctum of the card catalog drives the search for order to absurdity; his role recalls that the general can provide for the feelings what the philosopher cannot provide for knowledge—order.

The focus of the novel gradually moves away from the collapse of a unified tradition to explore the emerging forms of modern culture. This points not only in the direction of war and fascism, but also toward the new cultural forms which arose before the war and became more prominent in the 1920s. Here Musil finds not decay but energy and impatience without ideological focus: impressionism and expressionism, dynamism, lyricism, technicism, accelerism, biomechanics, and film. This new culture, in its passion for technology, sensation, the body, and concepts such as "the race-horse of genius," seems to express the mistrust of the age "against the whole higher sphere."[39] This means the dethroning of the ideocracy, of Diotima's bourgeois culture, and of the traditional elites. A new culture was emerging in which sports, fashion,

---

38. Musil was aware that this situation required a social and institutional analysis as well, but he believed that his background and talents equipped him better to deal with ideology and feelings. The complex interconnections of belief and desire which he explored are, in any case, too nuanced and varied for the abstractions of social science.

39. *MoE* I, chap. 13.

health, sexuality, and technology had more allegorical power than the thoughts of philosophers. In opposition to the nineteenth century's emphasis on reason, concept, conviction, and character, the world was now being built up from the outside in. The center of change now lay at the periphery, so that the profounder reality was the length of women's skirts, not the writing-desk of the philosopher. A new collectivism was emerging that made the old individualism look ridiculous.

Even the Parallel Action attempts to come to terms with mass political culture. But Leinsdorf and the traditional elites do not understand that the populace is full of people who hide within their normal selves, little, secret sectarians, whose injured, unrealized fantasies fix on a multitude of saving solutions for the world. Instead of the single patriotic voice Leinsdorf expects to rise from the people, Ulrich finds a chaos of partial truths and sectarian ideologies. These demands range from "Away from Rome" to "Forward to Vegetarianism." "Forward to" and "back to" solutions alike attempt to reduce complexity to reassuring simplicity, and all assume that some final solution is possible. The most common salvation-motif is the elimination of the single evil: Jews, Roman Catholicism, socialism, capitalism, big landowners, intellectualism, or salt-shakers in restaurants. The universality in this culture is the pattern of contradiction: individualism vs. collectivism, militarism vs. pacifism, elitism vs. democracy, capitalism vs. socialism. All stand side by side in the same age in equal certainty of their saving power. These ideologies are solutions to emotional needs rather than practical problems; together they reflect the chaos of modern culture. The disorder of civilian thought makes Stumm itch, and he discovers that he cannot live without a higher order in his head.

The real answer to the search of the Parallel Action for a saving idea is Moosbrugger. A journeyman carpenter, often unemployed, Moosbrugger is a victim of both the old status hierarchy and industrialization. A social outsider and pariah of the lower orders, Moosbrugger points back to Christ and forward to Hitler. With a little education he might have become an anarchist; instead, he is only a sex-murderer—though he denies this description, since he does not even like women. Ignored from Turkey to Stuttgart, Moosbrugger finds his principal means of human contact in violence, since his society's conventions give more authentic access to hostility than to love. His brutal stabbing of a prostitute leads to a lengthy trial and inquiry into his legal responsibility or insanity. The psychiatrists and lawyers can bear Moosbrugger's presence in the courtroom only because of the magic of their specialized words, which makes Moosbrugger suspect that they should have their tongues cut out. The trial fascinates the civilized people of Vienna. Like a sporting event or a war, Moosbrugger binds all these people together through the newspapers, touching them more directly than their neighbors do. He expresses the yearning for the unconscious and the primitive in civilized people, who, if they could dream collectively, would dream Moosbrugger.

As both symbol and sensation, Moosbrugger brings to consciousness the revolt of the bourgeoisie against itself. As a pathological intensification of the human need to break with the given social order, he summarizes what the other characters feel (and dream) and their inability to give real expression to these feelings. He expresses the need for action and the end of words—the lack of an integral truth to inform this integral action. He is pure immediacy; his unconscious meets the world without mediation or negotiation. Moosbrugger abolishes reality through violence, and normal reality finally has no choice but to abolish him. As the pathological variation on the possibility of release from normal consciousness, Moosbrugger is a loose thread: tug on it, and the whole social fabric comes unraveled. His presence keeps recalling the catastrophe that awaits the elites who can no longer give sense or direction to their experience.

The Moosbrugger case formulates the polarity of science and soul that is the focus of the ideological complaints of Ulrich's friends. The opposition between Moosbrugger and the psychiatrists is the characteristic polarity of modern consciousness: between whole experience and broken-up, abstracted, specialized knowledge. The old-fashioned philosopher's way of bridging this gap between feeling and knowledge is logic, but this primitive thought-form no longer corresponds to the complexity of modern knowledge and social experience. The legal mind of Ulrich's father represents this primitive logic, which requires that a person be either responsible or insane, despite the empirical gradations in reality. Psychiatry, on the other hand, still knows so little that it easily forgets itself when it listens to legalistic notions of logical abstraction. The psychiatrists "declare to be really sick only those people whom they cannot heal, which is a modest exaggeration, for they cannot heal the others, either."[40] The slow, empirical tasks of science seem inadequate next to the logical forms required for decisive action.

Moosbrugger, on the other hand, is a world. His pathological capac-

40. *MoE* I, chap. 60.

ity for metaphorical thought allows him to dream himself into the world, to become the table or chair he had wanted to destroy a moment earlier. As a "whole personality," he is what Walter and Clarisse, Arnheim and Diotima are looking for. Ulrich believes that whole personality is no more possible than the pre-scientific unity of knowledge. Yet he does not agree with the psychiatrists that all such cases of heightened intensity are pathological, representing something unpleasant and undesirable. He wants to combine Moosbrugger's feelings with the fragmentary, partial knowledge of modern science in a way that does not require hysterical action.

Ulrich does not take a moral attitude toward Moosbrugger: he is neither satisfied by this murderer's condemnation nor determined to protest it. Just as Ulrich's father wants him to advocate conservative legal theory, Clarisse and Bonadea urge Ulrich to intervene on Moosbrugger's behalf. For Ulrich, social meanings are too tangled for the firm, rational theories of his father or Schwung, but neither can he accept the senseless gestures of rebellion and liberation advocated by Clarisse. Although Ulrich cannot execute his father's legacy of imposing practical rationality on the chaos of the world, he rejects the romanticism of the grotesque and the impulse to react pathologically to a pathological society. Moosbrugger is a paradigm of inner intensity and transformed consciousness, but his insanity is unfree and without shaping idea. A man without qualities is capable of all illnesses; a pathological person is capable of only one. Similarly, a pathological society lurches between violent moods, while a pluralistic society tolerates all moods at once. Ulrich believes that the need for a firm, rational order does not correspond to the complexity and uncertainty of knowledge on which action must rest. On the other hand, he is convinced of the impossibility of the whole person or the final solution for which the feelings yearn.

Moosbrugger is described as Ulrich's client or friend, and Ulrich feels that in some way this giant touches him more closely than the life he is leading. Moosbrugger reminds him of the sisterly relationship which Ulrich feels for the soft language of soul which he had given up long ago for the hard commands of mathematics.[41] Ulrich still recalls these is-

41. Even Musil's sober protagonist is implicated in this compromising word. One definition of *soul* in *The Man without Qualities* is that the essential is never what one does or sees or hears. "It lies just beyond as a horizon or a hemisphere." Whatever one is caught up in and does is only half of the sphere. This appears as the uncertainty about everything one does as a youth and in the astonishment about what one has become in old age. *Soul* has to do with the need to think of oneself as good when nothing justifies that, or with the feeling that the world is not as it should be. Some people think of God as the missing piece, and love seems to have a special role in awakening this dormant half.

lands between his practical activities, islands which hint that there might be a whole continent of firm land reaching beyond them. Moosbrugger reminds him of a second home where one feels innocent. Ulrich often discusses the Moosbrugger case with Bonadea, whose nymphomania embodies one form of the transformation of consciousness which recalls the rapid changes of normal people into fools:

But it occurred to him that this transformation of consciousness in love was only a special case of something far more general; for also an evening at the theater, a concert, a worship service, all expressions of the inner life are today such quickly-dissolved-again islands of a second condition of consciousness which are inserted from time to time in the ordinary.[42]

These connections remind Ulrich of the "forgotten, supremely important story with the major's wife." He can hardly recall the face of this woman with whom he had tried to make use of the concept of love provided by his society, but his passion for her had led him into a lovesickness which was "not a yearning for possession, but a tender self-unveiling of the world."[43] Moosbrugger, Bonadea, and the affair with the major's wife suggest another relation to the world which is the recurring preoccupation of Book I. This condition of being is what the other characters are looking for. Ulrich's problem is to decide how to give continuity to these islands of transformed consciousness and bring them into relation with normal reality.

Ulrich refuses to accept the polarity between intellect and feeling as it is ordinarily formulated in his culture. He finds that modern thought oscillates between exaggerated formulations of rationality, freedom, and control over human destiny and exaggerated evasions of intellect, knowledge, and responsibility. Most of his friends assume that feelings are superior to intellect and in conflict with it. These neo-romantic theorists reject science, knowledge, technology, and urban life in favor of early nineteenth-century values such as horses, sunsets, houses, families, and nature walks. These anti-intellectual ideologies argue variously for soul, intuition, simplicity, the whole personality, deep feelings, sex, romantic love, the old Austria, nationalism, community, anti-Semitism, heroic action, music, the great man, and political irrationalism. Science appears to these characters as evil, fragmenting, narrowly professional, and destructive to the soul. Soul is associated with lack of knowledge, nature, women, youth, aristocrats, and criminal insanity. These expressions of pessimism about science and modernity do nothing to change

42. *MoE* I, chap. 29.
43. *MoE* I, chap. 32.

knowledge or the conditions of modern life, but they do provide the feelings with an escape from lucidity, knowledge, and responsibility.

Ulrich serves as the advocate of intellect and impersonality and attempts to dissolve the emotional attachment to dead metaphors and dysfunctional solutions. He rejects these neo-romantic attacks on science and intellect as evasions of the present which fail to see that there is no way around the extension and specialization of knowledge: "'There is no longer a whole person confronting a whole world, but a human something floating in the universal stream of culture.'" Ulrich sees science as an impermissible passion that will not quit. He sees mankind standing at the beginning of a project it does not yet understand, and he is convinced that it makes no sense to sing like a child in the dark to keep one's courage up. He refuses to blame the problems of soul on the specialization and depersonalization of knowledge. He notes that in science, where the person is ignored, there is always a new and adequate person available, while in the realms of culture, which are dominated by genius and great personalities, all the great people seem to belong to the past. Ulrich wonders if a bit more objectivity in matters of culture and soul might not be a good thing.[44]

Modeling himself on the hard spiritual courage of Nietzsche, Ulrich rejects these laments over the loss of a better time. In opposition to the irrationalist impulse to freeze into an immediate state of despair and ignorance or to escape into action and sensations, Ulrich recalls how much we still do not know and how open the future is. In this context, Ulrich becomes the advocate of evil. He is identified with masculine images of evil smiling in its beard, with Tuzzi's dry skin, Leinsdorf's muddling-through, and Fischel's Jewish money, progress, and paternity. Book I becomes the book of evil and truth, the squinting eye sighting down the barrel. The man of possibility is a truthsayer who actually believes that the truth liberates, but the others cannot stand it. Against the sublime values of neo-romanticism, Ulrich advocates the view that in climbing a staircase the firmly planted foot is always lower. When his culture says high, he says low; when it says moral, he says immoral; when it says love, he says statistics. Since the dominant elites stress the virtue of the good, ironic objectivity becomes the satiric mode of revealing that the good is not only good. This ignoble voice of irony prefers the low and vulgar values of Tuzzi and Fischel to the sublime romanti-

44. *MoE* I, chap. 54.

cism of Diotima, Walter, Arnheim, and Dr. Strastil. This reflects not cynicism but cleanliness in relation to the verbal dishonesty of his culture's apotheosis of soul.

Beneath the ideological rhetoric lies the emptiness of personal life. Musil's portrayals of Walter and Clarisse, the Fischels, Hans and Gerda, and Diotima and Tuzzi indicate that the forms of bourgeois culture were not responding well to the emotional experience of modernity. In a variety of personality types and generations, Musil shows the failure of the bourgeois house, family, and "egoism by twos" to cope with the fragmentation of feeling which people actually experience in the modern world. The rigidity of institutions and fixation on irrelevant ideas and metaphors keep these people from bringing their feelings into relation with the reality of modern life. These characters live out the roles of bourgeois culture without a sense of participation in their own experience. In the absence of intimacy and meaningful human relations, political and cultural ideologies exercise a compensatory function for failed private lives. This pattern highlights the needs for security, order, and self-justification, as well as the dependence of the individual for his inner balance on the culture as a whole.[45]

The unhappy marriage between Diotima and Tuzzi suggests the difficulty of bringing soul into relation with reality and civilization. Diotima is the culmination of the Austrian tradition of the salon and high culture—the chaste, beautiful woman, surrounded by mandarins, capitalists, and poets. Her spiritual virginity leads her into a dishonesty of language which never comes to terms with reality and specifics. Precisely this irrelevance to reality confirms the ideality of her thought and models the irrelevance of romantic culture to the situation of the twentieth century. Diotima feels that Austria offers the solution to the prob-

45. Musil's exploration of the disintegration of liberal culture led him toward a phenomenology of the feelings and private life. Bourgeois family life seemed to Musil not to enhance the individual in a way that led to a full life. Instead, it generated a collective egotism which marked no real progress beyond the possessive, self-interested style of individualism. The family was an extension of this individualism with an eye to morality, sexuality, and the practical requirements of property organization. It led not so much to a "we" as to a new "I" which was more serviceable in bourgeois society. Thus, Ulrich sees the conventions of the house and the family as anachronisms no longer related to the actual flow of feelings in modernity. Luxury hotels and tennis tournaments seem to him closer to the hearts of modern young people than warm, secure, permanent homes. The declining importance of kinship and family seem to him to point toward a homeless life to come. Meanwhile, however, the feelings of the individual are left adrift and without a firm criterion by which to judge and value. Ulrich believes that only intellectual and emotional flexibility, patient spiritual courage, and a refusal to act out of panic or inauthentic grounds can begin to cope with the stresses of this situation.

lems of an age of sterile, logical civilization (by which she means Tuzzi)
and the true counterbalance to technological Germany (which seems to
have something to do with the way Arnheim makes her soul float over
her head like a balloon). Tuzzi, who has no idea how it is that one has
soul, is eager to encourage his wife's cultural activities, which, he is confident, make no difference to the state or his marriage. Meanwhile, Diotima (like Walter) explains her unhappiness in terms of an age of materialism, atheism, socialism, positivism, and civilization. Diotima and
Tuzzi represent the polar roles of female and male in bourgeois culture,
as well as the gulf between sublime ideals and practical functions in the
early twentieth century. While Diotima believes in the force of great
ideas, Tuzzi works with the lowest common denominator. When Tuzzi
points out that without bureaucracy there would be hardly a trace of
Christianity left in the world, Ulrich replies that spirit alone is mostly
talk, and that without something more reliable history would never
arise at all. Ulrich concludes that the human being is both enthusiasm
and evil, that both high and low methods are required: "that spirit and
goodness would not be capable of enduring without the assistance of
the evil and material, and you answer me roughly that the more spirit at
hand, the more caution required."[46] This is the practical man's warning
to the age of soul that Diotima embodies.

Arnheim is both a great industrial entrepreneur and a Great Writer, a
Pope of capitalism who can bring Maeterlinck and Bergson to bear on
the price of coal and the politics of the cartels. When he is not busy with
princes and bankers, this ideal union of economics and soul markets the
spirit and assures his age that it is there and important. He agrees with
Diotima that understanding and knowledge have lamed the soul, that
women are more admirable than men because they know nothing and
are thus still whole. He is convinced that the mechanization of the age
can be overcome only by heart, will, and intuition, while the understanding has nothing more to offer. At the same time, Arnheim sees
money as the crown of a moral and rational existence. The world is si-
lently convinced that wealth (like suntan) is a quality of character, and
Arnheim is persuaded that this unpleasant burden (which he inherited
from his father) derives its meaning from him and not the other way
around. As the great Jewish industrialist from Prussia, Arnheim embodies the ambivalence of a culture which both worships and deplores

46. *MoE* I, chap. 91.

money and its vulgar relatives. The moral quality of money is that it is dependable, while "the higher intentions are unreliable, contradictory, and fleeting like the wind."[47] Arnheim's vanity concentrates on male virtues, but he is not quite in charge of the fairytale side of himself, which yearns, like a little boy, for hugs and kisses.

Arnheim's experience tells him that ideals and morality are the best materials with which to fill up the hole called soul. Thanks to bourgeois morality, law, and duty (about which Arnheim and Ulrich's father agree), only logical questions of exegesis remain as to which rule an act falls under. The soul in this tradition comes to look like a battlefield after the battle, where one watches intently for dangerous signs of life. The ideal is to turn as quickly as possible from soul to morality. A person troubled by doubt turns immediately to the persecution of unbelievers. If disturbed by love, he makes a marriage out of it. Enthusiasm always leads him to conclude the impossibility of living *in* the fire; and he goes over instead to living *for* the fire, through law, duty, or some variety of higher but unattainable order. As a man of reality, Arnheim prefers to give up living in the fire in order to live on behalf of the good. His predicament with respect to Diotima could be best described as "the despondency of the moralist who suddenly and unexpectedly encounters heaven on earth."[48] Arnheim and Diotima suffer feelings which have very little in common with happiness, feelings which threaten all the fixity and security of their worlds. Arnheim is shocked by this opportunity to live *in* the fire rather than *for* it; it would be unbearable to give up great tasks and being the great Arnheim. Rather than suffer these idiotic feelings (like wanting to be shot out of a cannon into outer space), Arnheim turns to other tasks in Kakania: oil fields and his budding friendship with Stumm.

Musil was convinced that in his generation the interests of power and domination were particularly eager to use culture as an instrument (or ornament) of their own ends. Under the circumstances, the task of spirit was to keep its distance like a chaste woman. Ulrich and Arnheim represent a split between spirit and power so fundamental that no authentic connections can be made between them. Diotima praises Arnheim's sense of reality and compromise, while Ulrich seems merely negative, always praising the worst (Tuzzi or science) out of sheer quarrelsomeness. Arnheim connects with the present, while Ulrich acts as though

47. *MoE* I, chap. 106.
48. *MoE* I, chap. 50.

the world will begin only tomorrow. Arnheim is as sublime and personal on behalf of reality and power as Diotima is on behalf of idealism
and soul. He finds Ulrich's resistance to reality and practical achievement in the name of the spirit something physically immoral, like sleep-
ing on the ground next to a comfortable bed. Ulrich threatens Arnheim
with his unpredictable nature and his theories of precision and soul, but
Arnheim does not make Walter's mistake of seeing Ulrich as a soulless
man of intellect. Arnheim finds himself superior in every way; yet,
Ulrich has something unused and free that reminds Arnheim of the mystery of the whole. While everyone else has dissolved soul into understanding, morality, or great ideas, Ulrich has something left over, "still-
unused soul." Ulrich's objectivity seems to require no ownership of
the object, like "someone possessed who does not want to be a pos-
sessor."[49]

The tender, but not quite overtly sexual, relationship between Diotima
and her cousin foreshadows the Agathe-Ulrich adventure. Diotima feels
a tension between her body and her soul, while Ulrich feels one between
his body and his spirit. They play a game of Diotima-Socrates, of beauty
vs. irony, of love vs. statistical curves of birthrate. Diotima is offended
by Ulrich's vulgar ideology of materialism and civilization, and she
wonders how someone who does not look at all Jewish can hold these
cynical ideas. Diotima's combination of beauty and soul makes Ulrich
mistrust soul and feel a revulsion against bourgeois culture. Her slightly
too fat body seems the embodiment of all idealism; Ulrich wants something leaner. This drives him back to the passionate first morality of
childhood, which was without purpose or direction in the world. Although Ulrich vastly prefers Tuzzi to Arnheim, he contends that it is Diotima's duty to run off with the great man from Germany if she loves
him. Diotima says she is immeasurably in love, but Ulrich explains that
this is much more difficult to achieve than most people assume. He argues that it would almost require pedantry to get it right and not make a
mistake. It would require two egos who knew "'how questionable it is
to be an ego today'" and the discipline to be entirely objective and precise: "'That is the way I imagine it, if it must be entirely love and not
merely an ordinary activity,'" if two people are to be "'so interlocked
with each other that one is the cause of the other. . . . For only if human
beings were entirely objective—and that is, to be sure, almost the same

49. *MoE* I, chap. 112.

thing as impersonal—then would they also be entirely love.'" In this case the elements would unite with an almost inhuman tenderness, but Ulrich concludes that being immeasurably in love might be something which Diotima "'would perhaps not like at all!'" In these conversations, Diotima feels about her cousin as she would about a naked person in whose presence everything is permitted.[50]

Through his conversations with Diotima and his relations with Bonadea, Gerda, and Clarisse, Ulrich begins to focus his critique of sexuality in bourgeois culture. He decides that the appeal of bourgeois love lies primarily in the discovery of one's capacity to drive another human being insane. Although he has the face and the body that his culture requires for these experiences, he finds himself steadily less inclined toward this form of love. He senses that all his relations with women have been somehow wrong. Thanks to convention, sexuality goes smoothly from the first attraction, when there is goodwill on both sides: "But nothing any longer flowed from the source; the sheer liking of two people for each other, this simplest and deepest of human feelings, which is the natural origin of all others, simply no longer even arises in this psychic inversion of relations."[51] Ulrich begins to feel that the possibility of recovering simple, human liking and a more personal relation to his life would require giving up the old erotic. Romantic love is only the most stereotypical of the roles made available to the human being in bourgeois culture. It is symptomatic of the assumption that it is necessary to live out the given system of reality—to act out the roles of love and murder and success because they are there. The question of authentic participation in one's experience means nothing next to the bad theater of what happens to whom, when, and where.

Instead of emphasizing what is real and personal in experience, Ulrich wants to live in general, as though thought impersonally, as though his life were painted or sung. He wants to abolish reality and live the history of ideas, but Walter insists that this would be mere literature. Ulrich replies that if one understands under that concept all the arts, life-teachings, religions, and the like, then "'our existence ought to consist of nothing but literature!'" To Walter, this means marketing packaged vegetables as fresh, while Ulrich thinks of it as cooking only with salt. Yet it is Walter who wants the arts to flourish, while Ulrich insists that "'every complete life would be the end of art.'" Walter is upset by

50. *MoE* I, chap. 101.
51. *MoE* I, chap. 68.

the thought that in a fulfilled life beauty would become superfluous, while Ulrich thinks that "'one ought to live more or less as one reads.'" Ulrich wants to overcome the romantic separation between art and life represented by Walter, Diotima, and Dr. Strastil. He wants to find his way beyond the senseless alternation between force and love and the feeling that his life does not concern him very much inwardly.[52]

In the last ten chapters of Book I, Ulrich finds himself undergoing a change in the direction of "tenderness, dream, relatedness, or God knows what." Diotima's reference to the holy path as "'an always available other form of reality'" seems (like the speeches of Hans and Bonadea) to be stealing Ulrich's lines. Standing in front of the library, Ulrich invites Diotima into an experiment in love: "'Let us try to love each other as though you and I were the figures of a poet, who met each other on the pages of a book.'" He wants to let go of the grey reality of compromise for a life without vacations: "'What a life, that one must intermittently perforate it with vacations!'" This perforation of life with vacations, this rhythmic alternation of force and love, is Arnheim's ideal, but Ulrich wants "'feelings without vacation,'" what people avoid for fear of drowning: "'Every feeling other than the limitless is worthless.'" Diotima is shocked at the thought of abolishing reality, and she turns Ulrich down. Ulrich cannot reach this goddess of love because she is one of those people with solid ground under her feet, who is satisfied with herself and takes her own reality quite literally and personally.[53]

Ulrich is convinced that until the relations in modern culture between intellect and feeling, between the practical and the unreal, between force and love, are fundamentally sorted out, all the strenuous ideological efforts of his time will come to nothing but disaster. Leinsdorf, Stumm, Diotima, Arnheim, Walter, Clarisse, Meingast, and Hans all express the same panic—from empty words to the pessimism of the act—but Ulrich challenges the assumption that doing something dramatic will help. At a plenary meeting of the Parallel Action near the end of Book I, Ulrich suggests that they proceed as if the Last Judgment were to fall in 1918. Since something has to be done with the part of human nature that had once been cared for by the church, Ulrich suggests a General Secretariat of Precision and Soul. The others are ready for authority, order, and action, and Count Leinsdorf announces the answer: "*Etwas muss*

52. *MoE* I, chap. 84.   53. *MoE* I, chap. 114.

geschehen." [54] This expresses the capitulation of the elites, the renunciation of intellect for senseless action. Leinsdorf wants to salvage the conservative state, perhaps with a blend of socialism and anti-Semitism, but
he realizes the need for beautiful words in modern politics. At the opposite pole of German political culture in Kakania, Hans Sepp wants to
break free from rationality, capitalism, and the bourgeois-Jewish order.
The charismatic philosopher Meingast offers the bridge of ecstatic, musical politics without ideological content.

This universal passion for liberating action takes the form of the rejection of bourgeois liberal values, whether from above, below, or
within. Musil portrays an ideological situation in which the failure to
deal with life in the modern world leads toward will, action, and heroism simply to gratify the feelings. This need for saving action is the
other side of decadence, the last spasm of a culture in crisis. The music
that had been a narcotic evasion for elites without purpose (Walter and
Clarisse) now becomes an image of emotional solidarity without intellectual or functional content. The politics of Kakania portrays the dan-
gers of bringing this musicality directly into life without rationally eval-
uating whether action will help. As Musil points out, there are many
things we do not know, but it is difficult to think about them while you
are singing your national anthem. Politics in Kakania is even more vacuous than Ulrich's social relationships, and Ulrich can find no meaningful relation to it.

Ulrich is torn between the pull of solidarity and the refusal to achieve
it through senseless action. He feels both the inadequacy of his isolation
and the hopelessness of trying to redeem his age. The climax of Book I is
the confrontation between the conservative elite and the German middle class (from Walter to Hans). During this demonstration Ulrich is
physically associated with Count Leinsdorf, as opposed to Walter in the
streets below; and he is reminded of his own extreme solitude as an
intellectual, cut off from the common experience of his society. This
dramatic political action against Count Leinsdorf leads Ulrich not to a
commitment to social action but to the realization of the bankruptcy
of the life he has been leading: "'I cannot go along with this life any
longer, and I cannot hold myself back from it!'" [55] For the first time in
his life, Ulrich is inwardly ready for a decision, but none of the people
around him can help. The aristocracy has given up and the army is

54. *MoE* I, chap. 115.   55. *MoE* I, chap. 120.

ready for action. The middle class is divided between bureaucratic routine and empty rhetoric.

Ulrich concludes that the condition of moral standstill in which he finds himself arises from his inability to unite the two tracks of force and love, activity and rest. He decides that for his life to have meaning, he must bring back together the two basic spheres of humanity: force and love, science and art, evil and good, the unambiguous and the metaphorical. The preliminary critical task requires "that out of all human relations the false soul sitting in it must be completely distanced first," and Book I is largely devoted to this task. Ulrich is ready now for a more constructive attempt, but "alone he was not in a position to bring back together again what had fallen apart." [56]

Ulrich's real options for action are symbolized by Arnheim and Moosbrugger. When Ulrich draws back from Arnheim's paternalistic arm around his shoulder, he makes a consequential rejection of reality, status, power, and the opportunity for impact under the conditions of modern industrial civilization. When Ulrich hesitates to accept Arnheim's offer of power, the great man from Germany challenges Ulrich with the opposite temptation: would he release Moosbrugger if he had it in his power? Ulrich replies that he would not, even though he knows he could argue "'that in a falsely arranged world I ought not at all to act as it seems right to me.'" In response to Arnheim's lament that the modern world has lost track of the demonic and the divine, Ulrich imagines "'that the devil has built up the European world and given God permission to do what he can!'" Ulrich's decisions against domination and rebellion symbolize the rejection of the view that the word is nothing until it is made act. Musil is arguing that the act is nothing until it is made word. At the same time, his notion of a life by experiment means "the will in a certain sense to accept unlimited responsibility." Given the inauthenticity of senseless action in his culture, Ulrich makes the case for spirit and for investigating the presuppositions of action.[57]

The last two chapters of Book I ("The Way Home" and "The Conversion") lead Ulrich to heightened experiences of the other condition. Walking the streets "as though he were only a ghost lost in his way through the gallery of life," Ulrich thinks for the first time of his dead mother and her claims on his future. Amidst all the contradictions of his life, "something arises unconsciously" in which he "feels himself to be

56. *MoE* I, chaps. 116, 120, 118.
57. *MoE* I, chap. 121.

master in his own house." He realizes that the law he is yearning for in his life is "nothing other than that of narrative order!" This would be living a page at a time instead of standing in front of the library with a book under his arm like Arnheim. It would mean cooking only with salt. In the last few chapters of Book I, Ulrich turns away from Arnheim, Moosbrugger, the prostitute, and Clarisse; he frees himself of male virtues, solutions, and temptations in favor of living in a girl's dormitory, remembering his mother, and treating all women like sisters. In the last chapter Ulrich grows steadily more sober as Clarisse's hysteria mounts. Clarisse and Moosbrugger stand at the opposite pole from Arnheim and Diotima, but all are now shaping Ulrich's will in the same direction. When Clarisse leaves, Ulrich is ready to respond to the telegram from his father, posthumously reporting his father's own death— the death of reality, of bourgeois culture, and of the male ideal. Ulrich is ready to abolish reality.[58]

3. THE CONDITION OF LOVE

Today the poet is at the end of his energies. He has written many things, but not the book of love.[59]

This book is religious under the assumptions of the irreligious.[60]

Part three of *The Man without Qualities* is primarily an exploration of the other condition and an attempt to think about morality and the world out of the condition of love. The adventure of Ulrich and Agathe symbolizes the reconciliation of intellect and feeling, male and female, science and art—not the rejection of intellect in favor of intuition, irrationalism, or sexuality. Together Ulrich and Agathe find themselves happy without reflection, but this is no ordinary love-story. It is the context for an experiment and an inquiry into the foundations of genuine enthusiasm and the sources of meaningful experience. While Ulrich and Agathe recover the condition of love and a mystical relation to the world, they also begin a collaboration in the understanding of the feelings and morality. Their conversations—which constitute the main

58. *MoE* I, chaps. 122–23.
59. *TE*, p. 265 (early 1920s).
60. *MoE*, *Nachlass*, p. 1604.

thread of Book II—explore the other condition, mysticism, love, sexuality, the morality of performance, faith, evil, history, and the tension
between the creative person and the norm, but these insights remain
contextual. The point is not a general theory, but a lived process of
thinking and feeling.[61]

The attempt by Ulrich and Agathe to found the realm of the spirit
requires of them the capacities of the fool, the saint, the criminal, and
the adventurer. The Pierrot costumes they are wearing when they meet
announce the "ludic" mode. They are also prepared to throw everything into the fire, to give up every connection with the lives they have
led. This relationship has criminal dimensions as well: the possibility of
incest and Agathe's willingness to murder her husband, forge her father's will, or commit suicide. They enter into a relationship of intimacy
and trust which is otherwise entirely presuppositionless and open to
risk:

> A journey on the margin of the possible, which led past the dangers of the
> impossible and unnatural, even of the repulsive, and perhaps not always past: a
> "borderline case," as Ulrich later recalled it, of limited and peculiar validity,
> recalling the freedom with which mathematics sometimes employs the absurd in
> order to reach the truth. He and Agathe found themselves on such a way, which
> has a good deal to do with the business of those seized by God, but they went
> this way without being pious, without believing in God or the soul, yes, not even
> in a beyond and a once-again. They came upon it as people of this world and
> they went this way as such; and precisely that was what was so notable.

In the context of this relationship of trust, Ulrich and Agathe are searching for self-acceptance, love, and the presuppositions of meaningful
action. These are, of course, the issues that underlie the devastated
emotional lives of the other characters in the novel. Ulrich and Agathe
take up these concerns, but without denigrating intellect or falling into
the fetishism of personality.[62]

Agathe is the vehicle for the religious and mystical themes of the

---

61. After 1933 Musil erred in the direction of a theoretical treatise on psychology, but
he realized his own mistake: "Only in love are these somewhat overdone questions and
theories and experiences possible and justified, and in their continuity they also constitute
the history of this love" (*MoE, Nachlass*, p. 1588).

62. *MoE* II, chap. 12. Musil's summary from the Holy Conversations shows a striking
similarity to *Young Törless*: the distancing of the perspective and the allusion to the
square root of minus one. Cf. Berger, "The Problem," p. 326: "It is not without interest to
recall here that, at their very first meeting in the novel, they appear dressed in 'Pierrot
costumes.' There is a 'ludic' or 'clownish' dimension to their entire 'experiment.'" Nonetheless, Book II departs in tone from Book I: this adventure is treated with more seriousness.

novel; she also provides Ulrich with a counterbalance in an androgynous exploration of the dualities of male and female, force and love. She is ready for the adventure in love and objectivity that Diotima fears, and she is an ally in a project that Ulrich cannot work out alone. Agathe is described as Ulrich's self-love, as that completion of the self which had always been missing from his life, but she is a real person in her own right, and she is embarked on her own spiritual quest, which is somewhat different from Ulrich's. Agathe is neither conventionally feminine nor liberated, but more nearly hermaphrodite. She has a childlike capacity for trust, but Ulrich is struck by her hardness and lack of sentimentality. Her severe illness in adolescence has given her a certain distance from experience and a quality of spirituality about which she makes no pretensions. By introducing this intelligent, sensitive, modern woman into the story, Musil allows Ulrich to explore the lost half of his self and to take up religious questions as his own.

Musil's portrayal of Agathe emphasizes the value of the woman as ally, the lost half, separated out of Western history—in Agathe's case, by a convent school, marriage, and indolence. Protected from reality, left to be an object without purpose or achievement, Agathe is open to her primitive side and has a claim to be the most illogical of women. Her only activity has been passively to resist the process of socialization, whether in family, convent, or marriage. She "despised women's liberation just as much as she mistrusted the feminine need for marriage, which lets the man provide the nest." Her experience of romantic love was shattered by the gruesome death of her first husband, and she has rigidified since then at the side of Hagauer. Despite the unhappiness of her second marriage, "she had demonstrated little talent for infidelity," and she found it difficult to take seriously the cultic seduction patterns of the European male. Her relations with Hagauer have always been good, and she has no specific quarrel with this good, enlightened man and model liberal pedagog, but she is contemptuous of the normalcy of a bourgeois life which is "like piled-up things, which have ordered themselves into no higher demand."[63]

For Ulrich, Agathe provides the only possibility of union available to him in his culture, his specific path to the recovery of the suppressed half of his self. She is love in a way that means no special person, representing the claim "on tenderness and selflessness" to which he has paid so

63. *MoE* II, chaps. 9, 21, 29.

little attention. Her role floats "between sister and wife, stranger and girlfriend, and yet [is] identical with none of them." Under the impact of his sister's presence, Ulrich finds that "for the first time in his life he love[s] his everyday life entirely without thought." As someone who has never been in sympathy with life, Ulrich values this relationship for being "'in agreement with someone before the fact, before one understands'"; this lends a "'fairytale beautiful senselessness, as when water in springtime runs from all sides to the valley!'" His first attempt at loving his neighbor opens Ulrich to pleasure in the flow of life. He finds that as soon as he gives up any self-serving egotism toward Agathe, "'she draws the qualities out of me like a pile of magnets to a ship's nail!'" With Agathe he finds "an island of meaning" in which it is hard to say whether his state of feeling comes from the physical world or from a heightened inner participation. "Agathe" is, of course, the feminine form of the Greek word for *the good*, and the island of meaning to which she and Ulrich journey is a magical awakening of the world in the other condition.[64]

The Ulrich-Agathe story is an attempt to overcome the extreme polarity in Western culture between male and female. Ulrich realizes the age-old dream of a twin in the opposite sex, a younger sister whom he had loved as a child and rarely seen since adolescence. They are siblings, yet uninhibited by years of living together. Ulrich compares them to the *Symposium*'s myth of the original unity of humanity which had been torn apart by the gods into male and female; for millenia human beings have frantically sought the other half. The Siamese Twins realize this dream, but, like the myth of Isis and Osiris, this story is also an image of the possibility of union in the personality. The male-female polarity is portrayed as a symbol for the fragmentation of the self and the devaluation of experience and personal relationships. Ulrich's deeper connection with Moosbrugger is that he has always experienced "the inclination to women as a violently inverted dislike for people."[65] For Ulrich, the revaluation of his relationships with women is the key to the reconstruction of his inner life so that he can be happy without pretense.

Ulrich and Agathe are both dissatisfied with European romantic love. Ulrich finds "that the ideal demand to love thy neighbor is followed

64. *MoE* II, chaps. 11, 28, 46. The metaphor of the island suggests that Musil transposed the journey to an island in the Adriatic into metaphor. Cf. chap. 45: Ulrich predicts that Agathe will "'sleep as restlessly in this night as before the departure on a great journey.'"

65. *MoE* II, chap. 25.

among real people in two parts, of which the first is that one cannot endure his fellow human beings, while the second is made good by bringing oneself into sexual relations with half of it." In his dissatisfaction with his culture's limitation of love to sexual love, Ulrich looks to his relation with Agathe as a model of seraphic love, "the sisterly love of an age which had no place for brotherly love." Each of them rejects the prefabricated sexual role, while leaving the other entirely free in this respect. Agathe thinks men are right to exploit women for sharing their lives like dogs; and Ulrich would wish to be a woman, except that women love men. Ulrich wants to give up the male style of the predator toward women. Lying in bed with Bonadea, he explains the arrival of Agathe and his decision not to continue his affair with Bonadea: "'My life is constructed like a machine which ceaselessly devalues life! I want for once to be different!'" He adds: "'I have undertaken for a long time to love no woman in any way other than if she were my sister.'" When Agathe joins him in Vienna, Ulrich finds himself in a feminine environment, as though a girl's dormitory had grown up overnight around him. Acquiescing in this softness, Ulrich moves away from his years of accomplished performance of the male role as soldier, seducer, and scientist.[66]

When Book I begins, the mother is dead and the sister is absent; this leads to the male book, of the son measuring up to the father. Book II, the female book, begins with the death of the father and bourgeois culture and leads to the discovery of the sister, who leaves her husband and forges her father's will. Agathe empowers Ulrich's other side. His decision to treat all women like sisters would mean the end of the old erotic, of objects, and of generations. It would mean the end of the bourgeois house, the end of Oedipus, property, and ego. Here the daughter takes the heroic role against the male order to which she has submitted for so long. Her importance in Book II—along with Diotima, Bonadea, Dr. Strastil, and Clarisse—reflects the new importance of the feminine in modern culture. But Musil's goal is not the victory of Agathe, the good, the feminine. He wants at last to bring the polar concepts of good and evil, female and male into right relation with each other. The male, evil, active type moves in the direction of inactivity and rest. Together Ulrich and Agathe explore not a new world but a new relationship to reality.

---

66. *MoE* II, chaps. 22–23. Ulrich looks forward to an age of "simple sexual comradeship" when boys and girls will stand in amazement before the "'old pile of broken drives which used to constitute man and woman!'"

For Musil and Ulrich, the male-female polarity expresses a still more fundamental dualism in nature between force and love. The sexual duality and the duality of his own personality suggest to Ulrich the possibility that "an ancient double form of human experience lies behind it," as in the dualities of concave-convex, being inside and seeing from the outside. Ulrich wants to recover the lost relation to experience that he stumbled across in the affair of the major's wife, that "'being-in-the-middle, a condition of the undisturbed insideness of life.'" He wants to limit practical rationality and the morality of performance in a way that enhances his relation to the world. He wants to live *in* something rather than *for* something. He wants to recover value, feelings, dream without distorting reality, diminishing the intellect, or giving up on the achieved illumination of the spirit. This is the significance of his adventure with Agathe. He is interested in neither the gooseflesh of sexuality nor the emotional upheaval of romantic love, but, rather, in "'the real inward experience of love: it simply does not necessarily have anything to do with the other two parts at all. One can love God, one can love the world; yes, perhaps one can love only either God or the world.'" Ulrich's task is to do for the feelings what science has done for knowledge of the physical world, and he wants to risk the values of truth, freedom, and objectivity with the feelings. When he recommends the attitude of the exact scientist in the realm of the feelings, Arnheim warns that this would mean "'a mounting relationship to God.'" Although Ulrich points out that the inquiry into the feelings need not go far, he wonders if this would be "'the most terrible thing.'"[67]

In their heightened love relation, Ulrich and Agathe become sensitive to the second way of relating to the world, which Musil called "the other condition." The lovers feel no need for possession by or of each other; they simply enter into this newly discovered world together. Walking in the countryside or sitting in the garden, they experience a spiritual union. In this dissolution of the borderline between ego and non-ego, their conversations express the inner movement required to maintain the balance. The siblings experience a sense of participation in the world, a supra-heightening, and a mild splitting of consciousness. This holiday experience, beyond the tyranny of churches and moralists, provides the sense of insideness that has been missing from their lives.

67. *MoE* II, chaps. 3, 25, 28, 38.

Out of this condition of love, Ulrich and Agathe discuss not only their own lives but more general questions such as morality, mysticism, and history. In the Holy Conversations (Chapter 11 and 12) and in the garden chapters of the *Nachlass* (45–47, 51–55) this experience achieves its most heightened expression. In these portrayals of the kingdom of love, of the realm of God on earth, Musil achieved his most intense literary expression of the idea of the other condition, an idea that had become steadily more central to this thought since the early 1920s. These dyadic experiences touch on several different levels of thought and feeling, and they take on their significance in relation to the characters and issues of the novel as a whole.

Musil used the expression "the other condition" only in passing in the Holy Conversations, but his sketch in the *Nachlass* gives some insight into the central place of this concept in his thought. Although Musil did not provide a systematic explanation of this model, it offers a rare glimpse into the structure and interconnections of his thought.

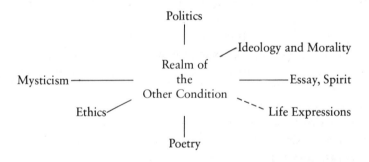

This is a late crystallization of a relation to the world which had accompanied him most of his life. It made sense of life-forms in relation to "the soul and the other condition at the center." It is not only a model of the world but a map of the relations within *The Man without Qualities*. On the same page, Musil describes politics or activism as "a middle realm between mysticism and spirit" and defines morality as "only a search for more intelligent forms of living." It should be noted that mysticism is not identical with the other condition, but (like politics, ideology, morality, essay, spirit, ethics, and the novel itself) one form of its expression. In ordinary life-expressions, many of which are portrayed in *The Man without Qualities*, Musil apparently saw a less intense and direct connection with the source of value. These are, presumably, forms which have rigidified into reality and lost connection with the primal fire and conscious utopianism.[68]

For Musil, morality is central to the explication of the other condition, since it is morality which gives form to the feelings. Most of the novel is devoted to the portrayal of the available moralities and ideologies, and Agathe reports to the other characters that her brother talks of nothing but morality. In these conversations, Musil uses *morality* to mean both conventional morality and morality in the sense in which he had previously used the word *ethics.* Conventional morality not only has difficulty keeping up with the practical requirements of life, but it tends to lose track of the other condition. Ulrich describes this kind of morality as "'the crystallizing-out of an inner movement which is utterly different from it!'" Ordinary moral precepts have value as attempts to regulate a society of wild animals: "Another meaning shimmers behind them. A fire which ought to melt us." However dried-up moralities and ideologies may become, "'some sort of drop of this mysterious wonder-water is left over and nonetheless burns a hole in all our ideals.'" Through these various images of movement, light, fire, water (spring, ocean, flow), Musil gives metaphorical expression to a condition of being that he believes to be more fundamental than moralities, religions, or ideologies. Ulrich's relationship with Agathe is a search for the experience of "'that love which does not flow like a brook to its goal, but rather constitutes a condition like the ocean!'"[69]

The recurring motif of the Ulrich-Agathe conversations is that rules and principles smother the life out of being good. Conventional morality seems to proceed on the assumption that the good has no appeal; its best hope, then, is to bind evil. Agathe's friend Lindner and her husband Hagauer represent the main options of conventional morality: Christianity and the secular good man. Lindner is the man who read Nietzsche and then became a pastor. He regulates every minute of his week in an attempt to bind evil with unshakeable principles and routine. Hagauer, who defines his morality through the profession rather than the church, is also a good man. But Ulrich believes that people like this are distasteful in their preoccupation with good principles and good works: "'They make a condition into a demand, a state of grace into a norm, a way of being into a goal!'" Conventional morality regulates the feelings to permit only those feelings that are necessary for its preferred

68. Quoted from the *Nachlass* in Kaiser and Wilkins, *Robert Musil,* pp. 298–99.
69. *MoE* II, chaps. 11, 12, 15.

activities. This procedure makes even new virtues unappealing, simply the scraps left over from a feast which has been vaguely preserved in the memory of morality. Under this repressive system of morality "'the power for good, which in some way or other is probably present in us, immediately eats through the walls when it is enclosed in a firm form, and immediately flies through the hole to evil!'"[70]

Ulrich is convinced that the feelings do not tolerate being bound. Immorality wins its appeal as a release from boredom and lack of passion and through its power as criticism. Ulrich describes Agathe (who leaves her husband and forges her father's will) as a person "'who is bad in a good way,'" as opposed to Hagauer, "'who is good in a bad way.'" The bad-good people like Hagauer have never seen the good fly and sing, so they ask their fellowmen to get excited about stuffed birds in lifeless trees. The good-bad people are then inclined to react that moral vitality is still to be found only in bad acts, which have not yet been used up as the good ones have. In Ulrich's generation, most people were either sterile moralists or passionate immoralists. There were very few bad-bad people, and the good-good was a task as remote as star mist. As an advocate of the good which flies and sings, Ulrich had always defended bad deeds against the bad-good people, but the tension in his relationship to Agathe arises from the resistance to the simple inversion of values in reaction to the bad-good. He feels "'a yearning for the good in the way someone who had unnecessarily driven himself into foreign lands might imagine going back home sometime—and return immediately in order to taste the water from the well of his village.'"[71]

Ulrich begins to develop a positive understanding of morality as "'the coordination of every momentary condition of our life to a permanent condition!'" He is convinced that happiness is possible only through a firm morality and a profound conviction, but the chaos of cultural styles and individual moods does not allow him to focus on a single guiding idea to give his life sense. He concludes that it is the ideas which grow old, while the essence of morality is that "the important feelings always remain the same" and the individual must somehow act in harmony with them: "'Feelings must either serve or belong to a not-yet described condition which reaches into infinity, which is great like a shoreless ocean.'" He discovers that he abhors evil, that his love for good is his central impulse rather than his love for truth (since science knows that

70. *MoE* II, chaps. 11, 12.
71. *MoE* II, chap. 18.

truth comes only at the end of days) or beauty (since art contradicts life). This discovery does not make him turn his back on intellect, for he is still confronted with the task of bringing good and evil into right relation with each other. Ulrich believes that good and evil are a whole which cannot be separated out in any of us, that in every plus there is a minus. He even expresses a belief in something like original sin or the fall: "At some time there must have been a transformation in the attitude of people which reached to their very basis, as when a lover becomes sober: he sees then, to be sure, the whole truth, but something greater is torn, and the truth is everywhere a part. . . . But Ulrich did not believe in such stories as they were inherited from the tradition, but rather as he had discovered them for himself." These transitions from the other condition to sobriety define the crucial structure of Ulrich's perception of reality; they correspond to good and evil when he uses these terms in a positive sense. Ulrich is persuaded that "'it is far more difficult to be good than has been believed, and that a similarly endless collaboration would be required, as is the case everywhere in research.'" His conversations with Agathe constitute a first step toward the union of precision and soul, toward applying intellect and passion to these questions with the kind of discipline and collaboration which have been so fruitful in science.[72]

For Ulrich, morality is "neither obeying commandments nor wisdom of thoughts, but rather the unending whole of the possibilities for living." Against the old injunction to hold yourself stiff, he offers the new criterion for experience of "'whether its presence makes me rise or sink,'" whether he is "'awakened to life or not.'" This new morality comes into focus as the morality of the next step: "'Never is that which one does decisive, but always only what one does after that.'" Conventional morality judges the past, as self-justification or as regret, while Ulrich's morality asks only about the next step. This path beyond righteousness and regret requires a tolerance for incompleteness and openness to the future: "'Such a person would have to live without end and decision, yes, precisely without reality. And, nonetheless, it is so that it always depends only on the next step.'" Only a man without qualities could bear this lack of fixed character and identity, this lack of a fixed and final form for morality and the world. Ulrich believes that nothing is finished, that nothing stands in balance, that there is no firm

72. *MoE* II, chap. 22.

point. The other side of this principle of openness is that the "'demand that one act out of one's full reality is then a quite unreal desire.'" Then the release from a fixed reality and morality is also the possibility of regaining connection with the deeper sources of motivation. Even this morality of the next step is expressed not as a general theory but as Ulrich's own process of thought and feeling on his walk with Agathe.[73]

Ulrich and Agathe explore the interconnections between religion and mystical experience. Ulrich is "a religious person, who simply happened to believe in nothing at the moment: his deepest commitment to science never succeeded in making him forget that the beauty and goodness of human beings comes from what they believe and not from what they know." He believes that faith must not be an hour old, but he does not want a faith which stands in opposition to knowledge, "that deprived desire to know which one ordinarily understands by it." Lindner uses Christianity as a way of saving human beings from freedom, unhappiness, and modern science. Much like Arnheim and Walter, Lindner wants to blame science for not meeting all our needs, while Ulrich refuses to set himself in opposition to science as though he were a nomad in the desert three thousand years earlier. Instead of working against better knowledge, it is given to Ulrich, "in the 'presentiment after the best knowledge,' to know a special condition and region of travel for enterprising spirits."[74]

Agathe has no clear ideas in these matters, and she sometimes finds it difficult to discuss them with Ulrich. In questions of religion, as in their personal relationship, she is simply in the experience, plunged into the world or Ulrich's life like an ocean; Ulrich is struck by "'how wild her being is in comparison with mine.'" Agathe is described when they meet as not believing in God, and she has learned to mistrust pious talk from her years in the convent school, yet she experiences a presence which is physical: "She had begun in the last weeks somehow or other to believe in God again, but without thinking of him." Her conversations with Ulrich lead her to a new conviction which is "close to an inner metamorphosis and complete conversion." She is prepared to believe in God, but "Ulrich said that was not necessary; it could at most be harmful to make a pretense to more than one could experience. And it was his business to decide something of that sort. But then he had to lead in order not to lose her. He was the threshold between two lives.

73. *MoE* II, chaps. 12, 10, 22, 38.
74. *MoE* II, chap. 18, and *Nachlass*, chap. 46.

... She loved him as shamelessly as one loves life." This need for clarification about God is one aspect of conflict in her relationship with Ulrich that leads her into the friendship with Lindner. To her dismay,
Lindner talks only of morality, duty, marriage, and selflessness, while
saying nothing of God. Lindner misunderstands himself and Agathe,
but for all his ridiculous qualities, he saves Agathe from suicide at a
time when Ulrich's theorizing makes him oblivious to Agathe's feelings.
Nonetheless, Agathe needs Ulrich in order to go further.[75]

Throughout the second book Ulrich educates himself in the ways of
the holy life to discover if it is possible to drive on this path with a truck.
Reading the mystical books of the world religions, Ulrich finds

> "the same construction of inner movement, which turns away from the ordinary
> but remains unified in itself. They differ from each other solely in terms of their
> relation to the teaching structure of theological wisdom from which they derive.
> Thus, we may assume a specific second and unusual condition of great impor-
> tance, of which the human being is capable and which is more fundamental than
> the religions."

Ulrich's assumptions are purely empirical and worldly and do not require that a person be a saint to experience something of this—perhaps
when sitting on a fallen tree in the mountains: "'One loses oneself and
comes all of a sudden to oneself: you have already spoken of it yourself!'" The normal human pattern is to take vacations from one condition of being into the other. "'Mysticism, on the other hand, would
be bound up with the intention of a permanent vacation.'" What interests Ulrich about the mystics is a response to life which is somewhere
"between an infinite tenderness and an infinite solitude." He wants to
explore these experiences without going beyond the phenomena to the
pretense of being chosen by God. Modeling himself on the successes of
science, Ulrich thinks "not so much Godlessly as much more God-free,
which means, in the manner of science, to leave every possible turning
to God to the feelings." Rather than seeking the supernatural, Ulrich
wants to transform "the supernatural content infinitely slowly into
something mundane." Rather than lamenting science and modern civilization, Ulrich is inclined to suspect that someday human beings will
"'become in part very intelligent and in the other part mystics. Perhaps
it happens that our morality today has already split into these two elements. I could say: into mathematics and mysticism. Into practical ame-

75. *MoE* II, chap. 31, and *Nachlass*, chaps. 43, 46.

lioration and unknown adventure.'" If the bulk of moral life could be
recognized finally as a merely practical task of organizing social life, it
might be possible to reawaken the inner life.[76]

Ulrich reads about mysticism, but a great deal of the mystical experience seems to flow through Agathe, who is less clear about how to give
it intellectual form. Agathe finds herself believing for a moment that
"she had touched a higher truth or reality or at least found herself at
the edge of existence, where a little door led out of the garden of the
worldly into the supernatural." Ulrich points out how hard it would be
to believe in the kingdom of love; and Musil notes that neither of them
believed this experience was the immortal part. It was simply a second
condition. Their experiences, which draw freely on Buber's mystical
texts, are described as "only a half-comprehensible reality; no reality
for the whole world or truth for the whole world, but, rather, simply a
secret one for lovers."[77]

In the garden chapters of the *Nachlass* (1933–1942), *Gottesleiden-
schaft*, love, and conversation flow together. Ulrich wonders if every
great love or passion contains something mystical. When Agathe asks
what this mystical participation is if it is not real, they conclude that
"there are two kinds of mundane reality." Ulrich finds that the speaking
animal's "lovingness is essentially bound up with his talkativeness,"
since love "is the most talkative of all feelings and consists in large part
entirely of talkativeness." He does not mean by this that love is tied to
opinions, but rather that words are made magic by love. In fact, he
wants to emphasize the "mysterious, beautiful causelessness of love."
Love appears in these conversations as a "supra-sensuous tenderness,"
as a feeling "between being and non-being" a "progressive approxima-
tion and the approaching fulfillment," for which talkativeness, like still
water, seeks a balance.[78]

The conversations are not a model of withdrawn, indifferent mysticism. Not only are they grounded in the sociability of the siblings and
their love relation, but they flow into the meaning of loving one's neigh-

76. *MoE* II, chap. 12, and *Nachlass*, chap. 42. Musil occasionally gives short definitions of mysticism: "Mysticism: One can only advise every reader: lie down in the woods
on a beautiful or even a windy day; then you will know everything yourself. It ought not
to be assumed that I never lay down in the woods." *MoE, Nachlass*, p. 1603.
77. *MoE* II, *Nachlass*, chaps. 51–52.
78. Ibid. For Musil, love is something which is brought to the object; it is the opposite
of desire and stands outside the chaos of arbitrary feelings. At the same time, the variation
and individuality of love seem to refer in some way to the object. Love for a girl is different from love for a boy, love of chocolate eclairs is different from love of God.

bor and the tasks of history. Even in their closeness to one another, Ulrich and Agathe feel a connection with other human beings, as though
"they had become sensitive through their expectancy and asceticism to
all the undreamed inclinations of the world." The love-story of Ulrich
and Agathe is not an anarchy of feelings but an attempt to see the world
out of the condition of love. It does not pose a choice between a moralistic-scientific final straightening out of reality and a resigned, contemptuous, superior retreat from reality. It is, rather, a shattering of a world
caught up in rigidity and a self-emptying beyond any need for self-justification. In an unpublished variation on the difficulties of loving, Musil
connected the implications of the man without qualities, the mystical
dissolution of the ego, and his early formulations of the possibility of
loving:

Being egocentric means feeling as though one bore in the middle of one's person
the midpoint of the world. Being allocentric means not having any midpoint at
all. Participating in the world without remainder and holding nothing back for
oneself. In the highest degree, simply ceasing to be.[79]

The conversations of Ulrich and Agathe often turn toward understanding their social world and history. They find themselves in an age
which is "beginning to devalue the individual human being without
being able to make good the loss through a new achievement of community." The world seemed to be on the way to an ant-state, in which
the human has the whole of humanity in himself, while the human part
has come to seem purest illusion. The decline of bourgeois individualism, heroism, and the family had so far produced a world dominated by
the "typical, mechanical, statistical, ordered," but not yet shaped by a
new collective value. Ulrich wonders "if it were God himself who devalued the world? Would it not thereby gain sense and desire once
again? And would he not have to devalue it first, if he were to come even
the smallest step closer? And would it not then be the only real adventure just to see even the first shadow of it?"[80]

Ulrich is not equipped with firm ideological certainties in his understanding of history. He believes that world history arises without authors, without center, out of accidental, peripheral causes. The law of
world history is muddling through, and the path of history is more like
a cloud's than a billiard ball's. The scientific functions are rational and

79. MoE II, *Nachlass*, chaps. 47, 59.
80. MoE II, *Nachlass*, chap. 46.

constant, while the events themselves are always without sufficient reason. When Agathe charges Ulrich with romantic pessimism, he points out that the traditional insistence that the world correspond to preformed concepts of the good and the beautiful has had very uneven success. He prefers to acknowledge that in history "the higher and special values are far fewer than the mediocre ones . . . in fact, they almost never appear" and remain "at best or at worst marginal values." But this means simply that history is not the pleasure-garden of the genius but the arena of the average person; and nothing is sillier than "to reproach an average for its averageness!" Ulrich argues that in order to avoid the extremes of genius and catastrophe in history, it is necessary to settle for mediocrity and statistics, to renounce sublime expectations for "the pre-established disharmony." History then would fall, not under a spiritually ordered law of truth, but under the law of the logically probable: "'If human history were to have a task at all, and it were this, then it could not be better than it is, and achieved in the strange fashion thereby a goal, that it has none.'" The task of history is not the genius but the probable person. Rather than demanding rational purpose from history, Ulrich prefers to allow the chaos of individual wills gradually to raise the level of the average in a random and statistical way. This yields the "'profoundly necessary project'" of "'furthering the average.'"[81]

The literature on Ulrich and Agathe has frequently emphasized the decadent, elitist, and antisocial aspects of this relationship—much as Ulrich has often been seen as cynical, pessimistic, or incapable of decisive action. Ulrich himself points out that his relationship with Agathe "had been mixed from the very beginning with a great measure of the asocial." The Ulrich-Agathe adventure emerged in Musil's mind in close connection with the theme of crime. The possibilities of murder, suicide, and incest, as well as the actuality of Agathe's violation of the laws of property, all establish a distance from the given social order. Agathe feels the need for a crime to define her distance from society, and even Ulrich is tempted by the notion that a crime might give his life ballast and a steadier ride. Ulrich actually satirizes their relationship, pointing out that they are both a little suspicious in their toying with incest taboos, and he carries off a nice satire of himself and his critics when he notes "'that the desire to possess another person so entirely that a third

---

81. *MoE* II, *Nachlass*, chap. 47.

cannot approach at all is a sign of personal solitude in human society which even socialists seldom deny. If you want to look at it that way, we are nothing but a bourgeois extravagance. See, how marvelous!'"[82]

The most hostile formulation of this bourgeois extravagance might see the mystical adventure of siblings as a holiday for decadents. In relation to the specific historical situation of Austria 1914, Ulrich and Agathe express an elitist refusal to expend their energies in wrongly formulated ideological quarrels and hysterical action. But there were two time frames at work in Musil's own mind. The literal narrative of Book II keeps piling up ever closer to August 1914 without quite arriving; but the symbolic weight of 1914–1942 mounts steadily as the focus shifts away from decadence to the task of salvaging something of value. Even as decadent elitists, Ulrich and Agathe represent the right of human beings to see the world from the horizontal now and then, and a positive move beyond the old erotic and hysteria to intimacy. Yet the irresponsibility in which they live is no merely personal occasion; it is a conscious working-out of the real historical situation of their class, generation, and culture. Some critics assume that this relationship must end in incest as an analog to the outbreak of war—or, at the very least, that their relationship is objectively incestuous and in rebellion against society. But this is only to say that Ulrich, for all his sanity and clarity, remains even in his isolation a function of his society and its problems. This is not an argument for or against him, but an axiom of his reality. Given the inadequacy of his social order, his honesty does not permit him an artificial position of righteousness, as though he were a stone untouched by the wall in which he is set. But Ulrich also has dim suspicions that contemporary decadence and irresponsibility might be the first stage of a new responsibility, and the particularity of these two lives is constantly enlivened by the universality of their insights. Certainly, incest is not the central issue it is often made into, and to see their adventure as merely elitist or escapist is to reduce it beyond recognition.[83]

The Ulrich of Book II no longer feels the need for psychotic experi-

---

82. *MoE* II, chaps. 22, 25. Musil read Scipio Sighele's study of crimes by lovers, often against spouses (*Le Crime à deux* [Paris, 1910]), but Musil seems gradually to have lost interest in such demonstrative conflicts. Ulrich understands Agathe's impulse to kill Hagauer, but he is sure the act would turn out to be something other than what she had in mind.

83. Incest, in the sense of physical union, is a question which distracts from Musil's main concerns. It is the obvious narrative device for returning this adventure to reality, but it is not the main issue between Ulrich and Agathe: "The trance belongs to the magical effect of the real world. Thus it is logical that Agathe and Ulrich would not want coitus.

ences: i.e., the experiences of panic, flight, suicide, or criminality to be found in Musil's earlier heroes such as Törless, Johannes, Achilles, and Anders. The society from which Ulrich distances himself is the society of psychotic experiences and irrational action: the musical politics of Moosbrugger, Walter, Clarisse, and Meingast, and the *etwas muss geschehen* of Leinsdorf, Arnheim, Diotima, and Stumm. Ulrich seems steadily less inclined either to incest or to the liberation of Moosbrugger. Even the need to break with society and paternal roles becomes more complex and the simple inversion of bourgeois values becomes less attractive. On a pathological level, Book II leads toward action and hysteria (1914 or 1933), but Ulrich is outgrowing his generation's fascination with evil: "'This contemporary preference for the morally gruesome is naturally a weakness. . . . I myself originally thought that one had to say no to everything; everyone thought so who is today between twenty-five and forty-five.'" Ulrich and Agathe are both tired of the bourgeois morality which their father and Hagauer represent. When Ulrich resists Agathe's impulse to murder her husband, Agathe protests: "'But you said, after all, that the virtues of society are burdens for the saint!'" Ulrich agrees, but he reminds her that he did not say "'that the burdens of society are virtues for the saint!'"[84]

Ulrich admits to Agathe that the individual cannot influence whether a future good age comes or not. But he is convinced that if the people who understand the situation fail to act correctly, "'then it will certainly not come and the decline is not to be halted!'" Thus, near the end of Volume II, Ulrich speaks to 1933 with the metaphors of 1914: "'I do my duty, do you understand? Perhaps like a soldier.'" Despite his critique of bourgeois morality, Ulrich refuses any formula that denies solidarity, and he therefore prefers inactivity to an unmotivated crime:

"In the moment when you remove yourself from harmony with the others, you will never in all eternity know again what good and evil are. If you want to be good, you must be convinced that the world is good. And the two of us are not. We live in an age when morality is either in dissolution or in convulsions. But for the sake of a world which could still come, one must hold oneself pure!"

But the contemplative quality of the *other* condition is something other than the trance; it is, moreover, a surrogate for a total way of being. It is a European attempt without the loss of consciousness and so forth. Thus it could probably—with the a priori imprecision of the achievable degree—come to seem possible and desirable as an attempt" (*TE*, p. 435). At the same time, Musil did want to explore the mystical implications of eroticism and spiritual union.

84. *MoE* II, chaps. 30, 28.

Despite the ambivalence of their moral world, Ulrich explores the good with Agathe as a kind of interim project on behalf of a faith in the continuity of the human project beyond the catastrophes of Musil's own generation.[85]

The complexity and richness of Musil's novel have often not been taken seriously by his critics. This massive portrayal of human interaction is frequently reduced to a single position (for or against sex or society), so that a single concept of the good is applied to one of the most subtle and complex works of literature ever written. Musil's difficulty in finding a way to bring Ulrich and Agathe back into social reality is clear enough. But Philip Beard's study of the other condition in *The Man without Qualities* offers a valuable challenge to the critics' impulse to reduce Musil's literary achievement (or failure) to a single, rigid concept of mysticism which cancels out the complexity and variation that he obviously valued:

And regardless of how the love between the siblings would finally have ended, if Musil had been able to write it to the end: it posits the indispensable conditions—existential conditions, if you will—conducive to the valuable continuation of life in a human society which otherwise gave only grounds for despair.[86]

The Man without Qualities is not an attempt to take an abstract position for or against practical involvement in society. In Vienna 1914 Ulrich can find no general idea that would give sense to such involvement, but this conventional distinction has already been annihilated as an anachronism. Objectively, scientifically, the individual is involved, interconnected with the biological, cultural, and technological flow of his society. Functionally, the effective mode for the man of spirit is less spectacular than that of the politician, but Ulrich is consciously involved, accepting responsibility for everything. His isolation and the corruption of cultural forms are the givens from which he sets out, and his response is chosen in relation to the historical predicament of his culture. He suspends the compulsive power of social roles and identities, rather than joining the pathological activity of people who can find no sense for all this action: "'In truth, we ought not to be requiring actions from each other, but, rather, first of all creating their presuppositions: that is my feeling.'" The utopia of precision and soul and the love-story with Agathe are images for embarking on this task. The life

85. *MoE* II, chaps. 30, 29.
86. Philip Harper Beard, "Der 'andere Zustand' im Mann ohne Eigenschaften und in der Musil-Kritik" (Ph.D. diss., Stanford, 1971), pp. 130, 427, and *passim.*

Ulrich and Agathe live together completes them emotionally, but it is also an alliance of male and female to explore the possibility of a more loving and meaningful way of thinking and being in the world. Ulrich wants a life without vacations, but this is hardly the same as saying that they will never return to social reality. The repeated implication is that there might be a way to have a permanent vacation *in* reality; one which is neither tied to the conventions of normalcy nor cut off from the good. The novel implies that romantic love may not be the way to achieve this, because it is exclusive and devalues everything else. The next step for Musil would have been to portray the other condition *in* lived reality, in all its complexity and evil. In a sense, this was the task of Book I, but that meant portraying a social order bound for destruction. This suggests that the real puzzles and adventures of the human spirit may not lie in repeating the emotional conventions of 1800. But Musil's values and ethical method have value beyond the social order he portrayed.[87]

Musil assumed that human beings are both good and evil, and he rejected the tendency in the Western tradition to alternate between exaggerations of human goodness and exaggerations of human depravity. In a note from the 1930s, Musil wrote: "On the whole, the novel must invent the 'good-bad' and portray it, since the world needs it more than the utopian 'good-good.'" His defense against the charge that he portrayed only bad people in his novel was that all the "good people were for the war. The bad against it!" The goal of his novel was neither to lead Ulrich from evil to good, nor to show that the good is an illusion. His goal was to bring good and evil, virtue and truth, feeling and intellect back into relation with each other. Thus, Musil asked to be read twice: in part, and in whole. His novel is more like a sustained poem than a conventional story; its ending, if it had one, would not be a resolution but a clarification of the beginning. But the novel is also not a philosophical treatise; the thoughts are not there on their own account but as "partial elements of a form. And if this book succeeds, it will be a Gestalt." Musil's delicate balance of intellect and imagination penetrates the realm of feeling and seeks to found the realm of the spirit. Rather than stating his philosophical position directly, Musil proceeded contextually, as though speculating with someone else's money. Setting out from the assumption that the world was not made to conform to his concepts, he sought the relations within the flow. He was a poet rather

87. *MoE* II, chap. 10.

than a philosopher, because he did not know what he meant until after he had said it.[88]

Musil's task was simply to climb into the structure of his culture as it expressed itself in lived situations and think it out—portray it, show it. Defending himself against the reproach that his examples were old-fashioned, Musil replied that the problems of his age were old-fashioned. Its metaphors were a hundred years old, taken from romanticism instead of modern experience. The novel portrays the difficulty of bringing into relation soul and civilization, romanticism and technological society, female and male stereotypes, youth and age, nature and the streets of the city. Musil believed that modern experience had meant a gain in reality and a loss in the dream. Put in scientific terms, this means that "'the percentile of participation of the human being in his experiences and actions is very small today.'" The remainder of magic, which is still stored up in analogy, dream, childhood, myth, poetry, and love, is ordinarily demolished in the individual's life to make way for success, family, character, profession or some other form of rigidification. Against the reification of the dream into a handful of dead conventions, Musil wanted to recover the feeling that everyday life is written in capital letters. This meant doing for the city what Wordsworth did for the country, and liberating modern, urban man from someone else's metaphors. Thus, despite the setting in 1914, Musil fantasized the structure of modernity far beyond anything that actually happened. The other condition offered insight into the ethical resources of humanity and room for the feelings to burn brightly, but it also left the intellect free to criticize outmoded forms, to create new solutions, and to invent the inner person. Musil was convinced that the problems of the day arose not from the arrival of intellect but from its insufficient realization. He wanted to liberate the spirit from the rigid conventions of ego, role, and reality without destroying the world or sacrificing the achieved illumination of the spirit.

88. *MoE, Nachlass,* pp. 1591, 1602.

CHAPTER SIX

Geist und Politik: 1933-1942

You must believe in the future of National Socialism or in
the decline of Germany. In any case, then, in the end of
the tradition in which I know myself to be embedded. How
can one still work under these circumstances?[1]

Spirit and the Jew have statelessness in common; that they
never in the world have their country.[2]

The decline of liberal politics in the 1930s destroyed the conditions under which European intellectuals had thrived for two centuries. Hitler's victory completed the break with traditional liberal society which had begun with the First World War, and the transformation of Germany after 1933 was defined in opposition to liberal intellectuals and Jews. As an intellectual and the husband of a Jew, as a poet whose audience was almost entirely liberal and Jewish, Musil found the last decade of his life determined by the politics of the fascist era. Stripped of the illusion that spirit has a history of its own, Musil turned his thought to politics and to the problems of culture in an age of transition to mass social forms. Even as he retreated from the attempt of politics to legislate for the spirit, Musil was convinced of the interdependence of *Geist* and *Politik.* Even in self-exile from German culture, he was conscious of his elective affinity with Germany: "I am a German flea. I have an inner relationship to German blood. I am a flea in the ear."[3]

The last chapter of Musil's life was an epilog. This decade has a posthumous quality about it, and the last four years in Switzerland completed his self-vision that he had given up everything to become

1. *TE,* p. 412.   2. Ibid., p. 405.   3. Ibid., p. 395.

"the least-known man of our time."[4] In addition to his uncertainty about how to continue the novel, his situation was not conducive to creative work. For nine years he contended with political instability, financial insecurity, poor health, and anonymity. Discussions of this period have, understandably, concentrated on Musil's attempts to finish the Ulrich-Agathe story and on the biographical details of his life in Austria and Switzerland. This dual focus gives back an image of isolation, resignation, and apolitical mysticism. What is missing from this picture of the late Musil is the tension between spirit and politics—his relationship as *Dichter* to an era of violence and collectivism. Musil was never a political activist in the conventional sense, but his essays, diaries, and public addresses reveal a continuous and thoughtful preoccupation with politics after 1933. Moreover, these reflections need to be seen not in relation to an abstract conception of mysticism or politics but in terms of the historical situation of a defeated intellectual elite. Musil's fate between 1933 and 1942 was largely determined by the politics of the fascist era, but this was not a merely personal occasion. It was the last chapter in the crisis of the bourgeois liberal intellectuals of the generation of 1905 in Central Europe.

THE EXILE

Musil's self-exile from Germany between 1933 and 1942 echoes the familiar pattern of emigré intellectuals. Whenever Hitler arrived, Musil left: in the summer of 1933, he moved from Berlin to Vienna; in the summer of 1938 he moved to Switzerland. But the motivation and tone of his exile were idiosyncratic: he was neither Jewish nor politically active. In both 1933 and 1938 he thought of himself as moving voluntarily, and even in Zurich and Geneva he considered himself to be merely the temporary guest of the Swiss people. Ignazio Silone, who met Musil in Zurich, recalled him as an oddity among the emigrés. Asked by Silone why he had bothered to leave Vienna at all, Musil replied: "'Nearly all of my readers and critics were Jewish. In the last few years they have all left one after another. Should I have stayed behind alone, and what for?'"[5] Musil's self-irony need not stand too literally—a writer with a Jewish wife and a Jewish audience could

4. Karl Otten, "Eindrücke," in *LWW*, p. 359.
5. Silone, "Begegnung mit Musil," in *Studien*, p. 350. Efraim Frisch had introduced them. Musil told Silone that Frisch had been the only one who had understood him: "'But actually even he did not understand me. . . . Unfortunately, I do not understand myself.'"

hardly expect a bright future in the Third Reich—but Musil understood his motivation more simply: to protect his autonomy as a poet and a thinker against the determination of the German state to regulate culture. This also defined his isolation against all the ideological attempts of the fascist era to make spirit the instrument of politics.

Musil's years in Vienna between 1933 and 1938 offered a life which at least resembled normalcy, and it might at first seem strange to think of them as exile. But it was the political situation in Germany which had forced his move. Moreover, he no longer had the financial support of Rowohlt or of Kurt Glaser's Musil-Gesellschaft. His friends and his readers were in flight, and his prospects of ever finishing or publishing his novel were dim. His return to Vienna simply reminded him of his anonymity in Austrian culture. As in 1910, 1914, and 1920, it was necessity rather than preference that kept him from Berlin. Nonetheless, he and Martha were able to return to the familiarity of their apartment in the Rasumofskygasse. In 1934 Bruno Fürst organized another Musil-Gesellschaft to support the completion of the novel, and between 1935 and 1937 Musil gave several public lectures in Vienna, Zurich, Basel, and Paris. Returned to his library and his work-routine, Musil did manage to continue with the novel, and he actually made plans with the Bermann-Fischer Verlag to publish a third volume.[6] When it became clear that this would not soon appear, Otto Pächt arranged the publication of some of Musil's essays and stories in Zurich. The title of this collection, *Nachlass zu Lebzeiten* (1936), captured the posthumous mood of these Vienna years.

The negative mood of these years was marked in every respect. Musil's health was very poor, thanks to constant cigarette-smoking and overwork. Plagued by high blood-pressure in the early 1930s, he suffered a heart attack in 1936. He resumed his smoking and his daily calisthenics, but the vitality required for his creativity seems to have been undermined. He was depressed much of the time, and Martha worried constantly about money. Convinced of the importance of his work, Musil found himself consigned to an old age of obscurity, beg-

6. By 1938 Musil was working on the galleys. The *Anschluss* interrupted publication, but Musil had reservations about these chapters, in any case, and continued to revise them in Switzerland. After Musil's death, his wife published a third volume out of the materials Musil had taken with him to Geneva. Bausinger's meticulous study concludes that Musil had decided firmly on only fourteen chapters of continuation between 1933 and 1942. Certainly, the six hundred pages of *Nachlass* in the Frisé edition can be treated only as a representative sample of Musil's thoughts and attempts over a twenty-year period.

ging charity in hard times. His fate as a posthumous writer was now
apparent to him, and it sometimes seemed pointless to go on at all.
Moreover, the threat of *Anschluss* was never far away. In 1934 he wrote
that Austria would be National Socialist already if it were not for Dollfuss and Cardinal Innitzer. In 1936 Martha's daughter, Annina Rosenthal, moved with her husband to Philadelphia. By then Austria was
protected only by the British bulldog, who turned his face in 1938.
Following the *Anschluss*, the publisher Eugen Claasen visited Musil
from Hamburg; he urged Musil to remain in Vienna and offered him a
contract and financial security. Musil declined and arranged a vacation
to Italy in August.

Musil arrived in Zurich from Italy in September, 1938, and remained
in Switzerland until his death in April, 1942. He emphasized that he
had moved to Switzerland on his own, and that he was not a refugee.
But for the Swiss authorities he was just another foreigner without a
home or a regular income, and he was even less known in Switzerland
than in Vienna. The move to Switzerland broke up the continuity of his
work and left him more anxious about the conditions of his existence.
Simply to remain in Switzerland required the grace of a bureaucracy
inundated by refugees. He and Martha changed apartments several
times in these four years, and financial insecurity continued to be the
norm, but they were allowed to stay in Switzerland, and the aid
of friends and refugee organizations allowed them to live in modest
comfort.

The highlight of the Swiss years was Musil's friendship with Robert
Lejeune. Lejeune was the pastor of the Neumünster in Zurich, and a
scholar with interests in art and theology. They met through the sculp-
tor Fritz Wotruba while the Musils were staying at the Pension "For-
tuna" in Zurich. Lejeune not only helped the Musils financially but
introduced them to other refugee intellectuals. Despite his shyness and
reserve, Musil was consistently the center of the gatherings Lejeune held
in his home. Lejeune deeply admired Musil as a person, and he later
recalled that Musil's extraordinary intelligence was more spiritual than
intellectual. Even after Musil moved to Geneva in 1939, he corresponded regularly with Lejeune and occasionally visited him in Zurich.
In a letter to friends in the United States, Musil referred to himself as an
"anomalous son" of Protestantism to whom Lejeune had recalled his
Christianity.[7] It was through his conversations and correspondence

7. *Prosa*, p. 799.

with Lejeune that Musil began to write what he called a *Lay Theology*.

In light of his friendship with Lejeune and the supportive situation in Zurich, it seems strange that Musil decided to move to Geneva in 1939. Lejeune warned him that he would not feel at home in French culture, but Musil thought he could live more comfortably there and was apparently looking for an exit to the West. Musil was never entirely convinced that he wanted to leave Switzerland, but he was flattered to learn that the PEN Club in London (including Thomas Mann, Hermann Broch, Arnold Zweig, and Robert Neumann) was trying to arrange for him to emigrate. Throughout 1941 Musil corresponded with his friends in the United States—the Rosenthals, the Churches, and Ervin Hexner—to explore the possibility of a stipend from the Rockefeller Foundation. Despite the efforts of Albert Einstein and Ernst Cassirer, Musil's lack of a special field of scholarship worked against him. By the end of 1941 he was inclined to risk the transit to the United States if a stipend without conditions could be arranged, but these negotiations came to nothing.

The last years in Geneva have an atmosphere of unreality. As Lejeune had feared, Musil felt isolated in French culture, but he continued to lead his orderly and aesthetic private existence, to talk with Martha in the garden, and to write to his friends. He worked on a variety of projects, including the aphorisms, the lay theology, and a biography of Martha. He thought of writing an intellectual autobiography (*Das eigene Leben*), as an example of life in his time, for even in the anonymity of exile he was convinced of his identity in one respect: "In any case, a writer of this epoch." He remained quietly secure in the importance of his work, certain that it would be posthumously recognized. While obscurity was hard to bear, he reminded himself that acclaim would almost have invalidated his work. But his situation was not ideal for productivity. His novel went slowly, and he imagined that he had perhaps twenty more years to complete it and the other projects. He fought stagnation as best he could. On April 15, 1942, thirty-one years after his marriage to Martha, Musil died of a stroke. He was sixty-one. His novel and a number of other projects remained unfinished. His library and most of his papers were destroyed in Vienna at the end of the war, but the diaries, aphorisms, and public addresses of these last nine years contain valuable reflections on his relationship to the politics of the fascist era.[8]

8. *TE*, p. 473. Martha Musil died on August 24, 1949, three years before the Frisé edition of *Der Mann ohne Eigenschaften* appeared.

NATIONAL SOCIALISM AS SYMPTOM

As in August 1914, so in 1933 Musil was in Berlin to witness the
dawn of the new era. He was struck by the passivity and cowardice of
the German people as the Nazis moved swiftly against the KPD and all
the liberal freedoms. Election day in March was like an artificial rerun
of August 1914, a holiday atmosphere without real seriousness or upheaval:

> In the beautiful *Kaiserwetter* the streets are full of people. "Life goes on."
> Although daily hundreds are killed, imprisoned, beaten, etc. That is not levity,
> but the inability of a herd to compare; it is slowly pushed back, while those in
> the front are killed. . . . National Socialism is right when it despises the unled
> masses.[9]

A nation, evenly divided between stormy conquerers and quiet cowards,
waited to be disposed of. If Hindenburg, the army, and the bureaucracy
did not resist, Musil suspected that the other half of Germany would
soon acknowledge Hitler as well. The promise of this catastrophe was
that it might clear away the old morality and rigidity of German culture
and leave no choice but to open toward the future. In any case, Musil
was convinced that this was not simply another conventional, conservative reaction, but a fundamental break with the past which allowed no possibility of a return.

The dramatic collapse of liberal politics and individual rights in 1933
was the beginning of a decade of reflection on the significance of National Socialism for German political culture and the modern mass-
state. The most careful and complete of Musil's analyses of National
Socialism, "Bedenken eines Langsamen," was originally intended for
publication in the *Neue Rundschau* in 1933. But these "scruples of a
slowpoke" who had trouble keeping up with world history remained
unpublished, as did his other explicit reflections on National Socialism.
Musil argued that the fundamental ideological content of National Socialism was anti-Semitism, the condemnation of the Jew as a symbol for
all the suspect values of the old system: humanity, internationalism,
freedom, and objectivity. But if the Jew was corrupt, so was the main-
stream of the German intellectual tradition; in this revolution against
Jews and intellectuals Musil identified a deeper emotional incapacity to

9. Ibid., p. 359.

tolerate pluralism. The events of 1933 in Germany signaled a new total-
ism that was well on its way toward dominating Europe.[10]

Musil rejected the charge that German culture had become too Jewish
(*verjudet*). He calculated that, in his own generation, "we Aryans were
richly represented" in the best and the worst. If the fault lay in the decadence of the tradition, then surely the Aryans were responsible: from
Goethe and Novalis, to Dickens and Baudelaire, to Nietzsche and Dostoevsky. The last resort was to blame the Jews for the "industrialization
of the spirit": the standardized, uncritical trendiness of newspapers, ra-
dio, and film. But Musil argued that the sins of the provincial and party
newspapers far outweighed those of the free-thinking press, and among
those who had sought to mitigate this corrupt situation, Musil had in
his experience found quite a few Jews. National Socialism had called on
the individual's higher sense of responsibility to the nation as an antidote to the corruption of modern culture, but focusing this process of
spiritual purification on the Jew amounted to "mistrust of real spiritual
achievement." In punishing the Jew, National Socialism was forced to
reject what was finest in the German spirit and tradition.[11]

Musil was critical of the dogmatic liberalism of the late nineteenth
century and the Weimar establishment, but his place in the spiritual tradition rejected by Nazism was clear enough. He denied National Socialism's claim to represent a revolutionary tradition of opposition to the
black-coated moguls of the liberal era. Musil considered himself a member of the opposition, even if *Geist* had also been the ideology of the
liberal establishment. And he argued that the spiritual precursors of National Socialism, such as Chamberlain and Langbehn, were not revolutionaries but conservatives, vastly overvalued by the Wilhelmine period
whose values they expressed. Musil saw National Socialism as a politically successful version of an old-fashioned style of thinking which had
been common in Germany for at least two generations. This earnest,
dogmatic, sectarian literature was pasted together out of racial theory
and religious reaction against free-thinking and the emancipation of
the Jews. Musil's characterization of the paranoid literature that had
shaped Hitler's mind as a young man in Vienna could hardly have been
more precise, but Musil could not quite bring himself to make explicit
the distinction between an elite intellectual tradition that had found a

10. Musil, "Bedenken" (1933), in *TE*, pp. 864–77.
11. Ibid.

home (however alienated) in the institutions of the old regime, and a vulgar, lower-middle-class tradition that had never found its resentments properly satisfied. In any case, Musil thought it was a mistake to take too seriously the roots of National Socialism in ideas. The key was emotional rather than intellectual.

Musil argued that in order to understand the extraordinary success of National Socialism one must distinguish "the power of the affects from the ideas in which they are dressed." Anti-Semitism was, to be sure, the central idea, but any attempt to give intellectual coherence to the cluster of prejudices that surrounded it missed the point. The selection and compilation of these ideas were accomplished by the feelings: "And the method which purifies and unites these elements is roughly such that one could just as well use it to found a world view on the inferiority of women or the beauty of the stars." The appeal of National Socialism arose not from a system of thought but from a particular situation and an attempt to deal with feelings of humiliation and panic. The drive toward power and unity was directed against the experience of national impotence since the war. These feelings were unleashed against the ideas associated with the post-war order: "Democracy, internationalism, progress, etc., in other words, the European cultural inheritance as it attempted (insufficiently) to realize itself in the German Republic." Musil would have preferred to direct this resentment against the insufficient realization of these values, "but the psychological truth is that its object is the conceptions themselves." This rejection of everything which made possible Musil's function as a German intellectual was nicely coupled with National Socialism's quite German instinct for bourgeois life. The German revolt against bourgeois culture had salvaged the emotional rigidity of bourgeois society and expelled its intellect.[12]

The dramatic role of emotions in this scenario corresponded to Hitler's genius for aesthetic politics. Here Musil found the apotheosis of one of his favorite ideas: twentieth-century politics as the arena of the failed artist. To the earlier incarnations of Princip, Clemenceau, and D'Annunzio were now added Mussolini, Goebbels, Vansittart, the lesser Nazi leaders, but, above all, Hitler himself. Hitler's capacity to arouse "the will without purpose" stood in radical opposition to Social Democracy's failure to recognize this side of politics. Musil pointed out that the poet had always been dangerous in politics because of the

12. Ibid.

human need to love someone and "to eat feelings with a big spoon," but now the vast capacities of modern media were ready to manipulate the emotions that art sought to educate. Musil considered the Germans particularly vulnerable to such manipulation, because they had "frightfully little sense of reality" in their celebrations, entertainments, or politics. Hitler was musical, like Moosbrugger, Wagner, and the average German, lifting the emotions beyond the merely practical and mundane. Enchanting a people who liked to "be ruled by fools," Hitler was the form in which modern political culture came to Germany with the utmost of technical sophistication. This capacity to coordinate the feelings of the masses with a single leader seemed to Musil to open up a wonderland of manipulation: his wish is their desire. Art on a grand scale.[13]

Musil saw the *Anschluss* in 1938 as a dramatic victory of the *völkisch* values of "the irrational, religion, the community" over the more skeptical values of liberalism. He believed that Hitler's political situation had been on the verge of collapse, and that Chamberlain's policies had saved him with a series of moral and political victories. The capitulation of Daladier and Chamberlain at Munich suggested that the "cowardice of the pluto-democracy" might be "inherent." Musil had no admiration for Chamberlain's morality of peace, since the business of the diplomat was not high ideals but actually achieving peace. Musil did not consider failures of calculation and nerve synonymous with morality, and he was convinced that the "man with the umbrella" would "soon count as a false holy man." Looking back on the collapse of bourgeois liberalism in the 1930s, Musil recalled his reactions:

Recollection from the time of Dollfuss or Schuschnigg: the era of the bourgeoisie goes under inwardly. Later impression at the time of the GPU-trials: perhaps it is the achievement of National Socialism to spare the Germans such a ruinous path to the forms of social life. Third impression: the astonishing achievement of Russia; the military and industrial strength, the cohesiveness.[14]

Musil characterized the 1930s as post-political, focusing on the mass organization of human beings and giving meaning to the life of the ordinary person. He saw National Socialism as an attempt to overcome the decline of discipline in the democratic system. Thus, the militarization of a whole nation was a value in itself and an instinctive movement of defense under difficult historical circumstances. Failure to deal with the

13. *TE*, pp. 511, 358, 360, 373.
14. Ibid., pp. 404, 485, 531, 520.

conditions of life in modern civilization had led Germany in 1914
"from the inability to imagine that there could be anything else for us
besides peace to the permanent condition that one lives for war." This
mobilization of the nation also responded to the human need to belong.
Just as in the Soviet Union, the system of "unspiritual political re-education" satisfied the need to believe in something. Musil suggested a
maxim of political modernization for National Socialism: "Act so that
it would also be valid for Bolshevism. As transitional forms. Post-
political." [15]

Musil believed that the liberal ideology of the West ignored the
deeper problems of organizing large modern polities. Even assuming the
defeat of Germany, the basic problems of mass societies would remain.
The empires of "America (USA with dependents), the British Empire,
Russia, China" would have to "be ruled according to the large number." This would require the homogenization of local traditions and individual variations into a single state-system. It also meant evolving a
system of contentment that answered the needs of the average person.
The success of National Socialism had resulted in part from its discovery of the poverty of individual goals and virtues in the structure of
modernity, yet it was not entirely undemocratic, since its worship of race
and the reproductive drives was a kind of *reductio ad absurdum* of the
average. Whatever the ideology or system, Musil was convinced that the
key to West European politics was the mentality of the lower middle
class. The contentment of this average person required not only freedom
from envy in the ordinary things of life, but also a "certain emotional
equilibrium under the guidance of some idea or other, like any other
person." Hitler's gift had been to address the needs of this ordinary person, whose organization and contentment was the main business of
modern politics. [16]

Musil saw the state's new task of indoctrinating the European *Klein-
bürger* as a transformation of values. The state was no longer there to
serve; instead, everything was there for the state. Musil was convinced
that new forms had to be found which met the needs of mass society
while protecting the interests of the individual and culture: "As a begin-
ner I despised *the masses*; later I held that to be an error of youth; and
now I am probably correcting it back again a little." Musil felt trapped
between revolutionary fascism and communism and the inadequacy of

15. Ibid., pp. 360, 566, 374.
16. Ibid., pp. 529, 424.

conservatism. He wanted an evolutionary mode that avoided the complementary pathologies of rebellion and stagnation. The content of the revolutionary mode seemed to him the same, whether in its fascist or communist form: "I do not like this form of expression, the being in revolution of mankind and its typical spiritual consequences. But neither do I like the stationary, the conservative." While the age of the masses tried out its forms, Musil tried to make sense of what was indispensable to culture and spirit.[17]

CULTURE AND POLITICS

Musil did not consider himself politically gifted, but he believed his responsibility as a *Dichter* in the fascist era was to clarify and preserve the values of the culture. In Vienna, Paris, Basel, and Zurich, he spoke on the predicament of spirit in an age of political crisis and ideological oversimplification. Although his detailed political analyses remained unpublished, his public critiques of the subordination of culture to politics displayed an unconventional autonomy in the politicized atmosphere of the late 1930s. His audiences in Vienna were astonished at his candor under the political circumstances of 1936–1937, and his audience of left-wing intellectuals in Paris hissed him for noticing the similarities between fascism and communism. Musil did not keep to a political line. His main interest was the independence of spirit, not the defense of a specific political ideology. He pointed to the threat to culture from intensified collectivism, whether fascist or Bolshevik, but he also refused to assume that parliamentary democracy was the only solution to modern politics. His analyses were often shocking, because he did not love democracy uncritically enough to find fascism bad *a priori*. *A posteriori* he had no doubts about which of them had to be defeated; but he was aggressively opposed to the failures and limitations of what passed for liberalism in his generation: "I do not fight against fascism, but in democracy for her future, thus also against democracy." His convictions about objectivity led him to criticize what he loved as well as what he hated.[18]

Speaking in Paris in 1935, Musil argued that culture was not national or bourgeois or liberal or revolutionary, but something more general

17. Ibid., p. 415.
18. Ibid., p. 496. Musil was puzzled to see how the strangest people sought his judgment in political matters, as though a higher essence were hidden behind him which knew all the answers. Nonetheless, he was convinced that the poet could not afford to be indifferent to politics—and this one evidently was not.

280]	Geist und Politik: 1933-1942

and autonomous. He condemned the apparently harmless tendency of the nineteenth century to perceive poets as expressions of national culture. Even antagonism between culture and politics seemed to him preferable to modern collectivism's tendency to need culture the way knights once needed women, as a final ornament of their achievements. Parliamentary democracy had at least offered freedom to culture, as well as to what harmed it, but he denied that the health of culture was bound to a single political form. On the other hand, Musil rejected the conception of culture as a single, fixed value passed on from hand to hand. Culture was hard to define; it was susceptible to distortion and recovered in unpredictable ways—despite the interests of nations, classes, and ideologies. However the community might choose to support culture, the burden rested with the individual: "For those of us who create, culture is something inherited, something experienced, not at all in every respect sympathetic, that is more nearly a will, which lives in us and over us, than a definable conception." [19]

Musil refused to suspend the values of culture in the interests of immediate political conflict. Trapped between fascism and the Popular Front, he warned the intellectuals of the 1930s against the temptation to identify themselves "without remainder with a momentary condition of their national culture." He reminded his audience of Nietzsche's maxim that the "victory of a moral ideal is achieved through the same immoral means as any victory: force, deceit, slander, unrighteousness." Musil was not arguing that all political forms were equally beneficial to culture or that culture could be walled off into a higher realm. Political forms could be expected to vary historically, and culture could not be defined precisely. But Musil believed that culture always had a stake in certain values. He was convinced that no great culture could rest on opposition to the truth, whether the motivation was irrationalism or the quest for political righteousness. The life of culture seemed invariably to depend on a cluster of values which included "freedom, openness, courage, resistance to corruption, responsibility, and criticism—this more against what attracts us than against what repels us." [20]

There is an obvious affinity between these values and the historical attempts of the liberal-democratic tradition in the West, but the task of intellect was to save this tradition from self-righteousness. The pieties of liberalism inspired Musil's skepticism: "The anti-fascist *Geistesfront*

19. Musil, "Vortrag in Paris," in *TE*, pp. 899–902.
20. Ibid. Musil was convinced that "the good is not so different from evil as it thinks" (*TE*, p. 500).

presumes that the true, the good, and the beautiful exist. Only the Catholic church is entitled to that. Therefore, the outrageous thinness of dogmatic liberalism." Like Nietzsche, Musil found something ridiculous and dishonest in liberalism's smug assumption of metaphysical righteousness and moral absolutism. While liberalism talked as if it had a final package of the truth, the free spirit was left with only the regulative values of freedom, openness, and criticism. Parliamentary democracy was not an absolute value: it had not seemed to help Germany and a host of other European countries in the 1920s. It gained its staying power in the West through other values: patriotic nationalism in France, and in England a strong conservative counterbalance and imperial mission: "You have to be able to see that, even if democracy seems to you more deserving of life." Musil's commitment to the creative freedom of the individual was unequivocal, but he saw the problem in a Central European frame. His generation had experienced the loss of this freedom as they had known it before 1914 in the authoritarian-liberal institutions of Austria and Germany. He could compare a tradition of enlightened absolutism which nourished culture and freedom to the failures of parliamentary democracy in France and England to respond creatively to the social and economic problems of the 1930s. For Musil, the danger lay not in the evolution of new political, social, or economic forms but in the threat to inward freedom since 1914.[21]

Musil had no objection to collectivism on principle, since "the human being is by nature as much collective as individual." Moreover, collectivism "is not to be called undemocratic in any of its forms; it is sooner a new form of democracy or at least has the striving for it alongside its other strivings." In war, in politics, and in economics, the moral power of the individual seemed now to be weak in relation to its environment, but collectivism itself was not new. Scientific thought, with its indifference to the particular and personal, had always been supremely collective. The German humanist tradition of Lessing, Kant, and Schiller had been dominated by a vision of the interdependence of humanity as infinite totality, as evolving moral and social being. But this requirement of an infinite process for the moral fulfillment of mankind had been brought abruptly into the present by a collectivism "which is not exactly a passionate admirer of humanity." Twentieth-century collectivism was original in the power and multiplicity of its forms and in "a certain one-sidedness of its arguments." The dramatic political changes

21. *TE*, pp. 506, 513.

since 1914 were obviously responses to the new requirements of social life, but Musil denied that there was any sublime metaphysical necessity hidden in the political forms and constellations of 1936. On the contrary, he inclined toward the view that the current situation would be overcome, not on the basis of any historical metaphysic, but "as an analytical conclusion from the assumption that everything is not yet and not so soon over." To the despairing liberal intellectuals of the 1930s Musil offered the inelegant maxim of the old Austria that "we are erring forward!"[22]

In an address to Austrian writers in 1936, "Der Dichter und diese Zeit," Musil argued that the distortion of the tasks of culture could not be blamed entirely on the emergence of modern technology, popular culture, and mass politics. He knew only too well that the tradition had been normalized to the point of sterility by bourgeois culture, and he located the decline of culture in the bourgeois trivialization of art in the nineteenth century, before democracy, fascism, and communism. Nineteenth-century bourgeois art had been lured away from the classical ideal of *Bildung* to the ideal of entertainment, renouncing the task of educating mankind in order to accommodate "the smallest human power of comprehension." The most obvious symptom of this had been the demand that characters be good or at least that the good hero be victorious. Hitler, like most middle-class Germans, loved this kind of kitsch. The bourgeois audience had insisted that the thoughts and feelings of ordinary people be reproduced as faithfully as the uniforms of the princes. This literal realism had gone so far by the twentieth century that people "do not want to believe any more at all in an unpolitical feeling and thinking."[23]

Musil opposed the reduction of the inner as well as the collective life to the categories of politics. But he also insisted that politics had a stake in preserving this unpolitical thinking and feeling "as a reservoir for itself." Art expressed a will to abstraction from life that disturbed the normal response to experience, of which politics was only a part:

All our higher feelings have probably arisen from the opposition from time to time to the simple and the instinctual, from the hindrance of immediate gratification.

22. Musil, "Der Dichter und diese Zeit," in *TE*, pp. 903–917. Musil presented this address both to the "Schutzverband deutscher Schriftsteller" in Vienna and to the PEN Club in Basel.
23. Ibid.

I would like to assert that whoever cannot look at even the nastiest, but also the most spiritual, caricature of his self with enjoyment has not yet understood that entirely!

Both German literature and its audience had lost track of the freedom and discipline which this irritating, critical, and self-critical vision of the spirit required. By the 1930s this corruption of culture had reached a low point, but Musil placed his hopes in the significance of the individual as a spiritual force, and his individualism stood firmly within the totality of culture which it nourished and reawakened.[24]

Musil's notion of spirituality depended equally on qualities of intellect and feeling. He believed that the crucial qualities of thinking were qualities of the feelings as well: "Narrowness, breadth, flexibility, simplicity, and fidelity." Thought and feeling could not be autonomous, since they expressed themselves through the same person, even if the relations between them remained imprecise. The dependence of literature and politics on the perplexing innerconnections between thought and feeling made these aspects of life peculiarly vulnerable to stupidity, and Musil's last public analysis on the political culture of his day was an ironic commentary on the meaning of this word. He considered "Über die Dummheit" (1937) one of his most important works, but the indirection, ambivalence, and painstaking care of this analysis of everyday language defy summary. In spirit this essay echoes Erasmus and Nietzsche. In method it is closer to Wittgenstein in its patient unpackaging of the overlapping usages and implications of this simple German word. An essay which at first seems idiosyncratic to the point of outrage (or stupidity) gradually emerges as a commentary on German culture and the fascist era.[25]

The burden of Musil's argument was that contemporary psychology had made the definition of stupidity more difficult than in the past. In the nineteenth century it had been easy to think of stupidity as a lack of understanding; now it was apparent that stupidity was a function of both the understanding and the feelings. Musil set himself against a definition of intelligence concerned only with mental capacity and also against the characteristically German prejudice that profound, genuine

24. Ibid.
25. Musil, "Über die Dummheit," in *TE*, pp. 918–38. Musil presented this essay in two addresses to the Österreichische Werkbund in March, 1937. Twenty-three years later Fritz Wotruba recalled it as the last lecture of significance he heard in Vienna. He also noted that seventy-five percent of the audience had been Jewish ("Erinnerung an Musil," in *LWW*, p. 400).

feelings do not require intellect. He was not concerned with "the dear, bright stupidity," that plain stupidity which is often an artist. He identified a second form of stupidity, more dangerous than ordinary weakmindedness, a deviation which is served by innate and unharmed intelligence. Musil wanted to do battle with this higher stupidity, the intelligent stupidity that is a function of the feelings as well.

Musil believed that this pretentious stupidity, this renunciation of the intellect for the wrong reasons, was the real disease of German education and culture. Musil belonged to the most literate, academically eduucated culture in Europe; certainly, a lack of intelligence, in the ordinary sense of capacity for mental labors, could not explain its passion for stupidity. German culture had produced the world's most distinguished cults of university learning and romantic feeling, but each had been compartmentalized in its appropriate sphere of sterility and rigidity. The conventions of science and literary culture had encouraged a false polarity between disciplined rationality and sentimental soul. The cultivation of higher stupidity in German literature and politics amounted to a renunciation of reason for the sake of the affects. Musil wanted to replace this rigid polarization of intellect and feeling with a utopian concept of meaning: "The significant [*Das Bedeutende*] unites the truth . . . with qualities of feeling which have our trust, to something new, to an insight, but also to a resolve, to a refreshed sense of commitment." This essayistic mode of spirit shaped both intellect and feeling, rather than succumbing to the renunciation and panic of higher stupidity.[26]

Musil conceded that "occasionally we are all stupid," that "we must sometimes act blindly or half-blindly or the world would stand still," but the contemporary crisis of ignorance and uncertainty in the moral realm seemed to him not so very different from the long-standing predicament of the natural sciences. In an apparently desperate situation, the scientific analogy offered a promising guide to ethical method:

For because our knowledge and capacity are incomplete, we must fundamentally judge prematurely in all sciences. But we make an effort and learn to hold these mistakes within known limits, and at every opportunity to improve them, whereby correctness comes into our actions again.

Science could not provide an infallible, fixed moral system, but it did suggest a useful rule-of-thumb in ethical matters: "Act as well as you

26. Musil, "Über die Dummheit," pp. 933–37. Cf. Musil's note from March of 1934: "Given the contemporary condition of culture, it would be more reasonable if one sent the future natural scientists into the gymnasium and educated the future humanists in the Realschule" (*TE*, p. 366).

can and as badly as you must, and in that remain conscious of the margin of error of your action!" This "exact, proud-humble way of judging and acting" seemed to point toward "a promising way of giving form to life." The universality of Kant's maxim was no longer possible for the generation of 1905, but nihilism, irrationalism, and dogmatism were not the only remaining options. Instead, Musil invoked a moral rule that captured the empiricism of modern science, the ethical intensity of a generation without a systematic ideology, and the aesthetic passion of a man who believed it possible to live one's life like a work of art.[27]

Germany's search for a binding concept of politics appeared to Musil as a symptom of a cultural failure to cope with intellectual uncertainty and affective disequilibrium. Even before Hitler, the German intellectual had shown the way for the average person by renouncing freedom for certainty and submission to the sacred leader. This emotional scenario of authority and dependence seemed to Musil a pervasive disease of his culture, and this need for emotional security was intellectually corrupting as well, since the task of the savior was to carry the Truth in his pocket. Musil identified this worship of the intellectual dictator in the followers of George, Kraus, Freud, Adler, Jung, Klages, and Heidegger. These personality cults displayed a need for complete and final explanations that led to intellectual rigidity and sectarianism. With a few dozen concepts, the members of these sects could explain the world. Watching this failure of autonomy in intellectuals as well as average people, Musil was reminded of the impossibility of an entirely inductive way of thinking. But the too hasty capitulation to partial truths had corrupted the cultural and political life of his generation.[28]

For Musil, the European crisis was the crisis of the liberal tradition, of reason, freedom, and the educated bourgeoisie who had been the bearers of these values since the eighteenth century. He located the origins of the crisis not in the fascist era, but at least as early as the middle of the nineteenth century, and the danger to the tradition lay "less in the success of its enemies than in that of its friends." Since 1880 the crisis of confidence in these values had been too fundamental to permit a return to the unchanged conceptions of the Enlightenment. Musil belonged to a generation whose point of departure had been the collapse of these

---

27. Musil, "Über die Dummheit," p. 938.
28. *TE,* pp. 398, 494, 565. Musil frankly compared the syndrome of the intellectual dictator [*die geistige Diktatorenverehrung*] to the attitudes of the German people to Hitler. Even Thomas Mann wrote "for the people who are there: I write for the people who are not yet there!" (*TE,* p. 386).

286]   Geist und Politik: 1933-1942

bourgeois values. The old guidelines had lost their power to inspire confidence, leaving only formless energy without the fixed parameters of
traditional ideology. The political response to this situation after 1914
had amounted to a panic, one that threatened the European's capacity
for freedom and reasonable judgment over his affairs. The human being
had collapsed under the ideals of the eighteenth and nineteenth century.
In poetry and politics the great leader had satisfied the need for love,
illusion, and security. In the midst of this panic and senseless destruction, Musil believed that the task of spirit was to preserve the broken
fragments of the Western tradition: "Our task, and the sense of the task
which is set for the spirit—and that is the so seldom understood, pain-
ful-hopeful task of such a generation—will, rather, be to complete the
always necessary, yes, even desired transition to the new with a mini-
mum of losses."[29]

THE MYSTIC IN THE GARDEN

Musil's circumstances in Geneva from 1939 to 1942 reflect an image
of the homelessness of spirit in the generation of 1905. With no real
connection in the world, Musil was left to a life of nearly pure contemplation. This was, of course, the logical intensification of a life devoted to exploring inwardness and the presuppositions of meaningful
action, but it was also an extreme, corresponding to the years of Hitler's
unchallenged supremacy in Europe. Musil's reality (or unreality) was
the garden in Geneva, and Ulrich and Agathe in the garden echo the
world of Robert and Martha. But the portrayal of Musil as a withdrawn, asocial mystic ignores his continuing interests in world politics
and distorts the quality of his mysticism. Musil's mysticism was love
and not indifference; not irrationalism, but sobriety and objectivity.
Even in the intense inwardness of these years, Musil continued to reflect
on politics "for the sake of a world which could still come."
    In a note dated 1936, Musil asked himself: "How can someone who
is preoccupied with the sister problem be interested in politics?"[30] And
yet one has not understood Musil until one can imagine just such a person. Both his public addresses and his diaries make clear that Musil
thought a great deal about politics after 1933.[31] At the same time, Kai-

29. Musil, "Über die Dummheit," p. 932.
    30. MoE, Nachlass, p. 1345.
    31. Corino is right to challenge Silone's widely accepted judgment that in exile Musil
had no interest in politics and that its real complexity eluded him: Karl Corino, "Reflexionen im Vakuum. Musils Schweizer Exil," in Die deutsche Exilliteratur 1933–1945
(Stuttgart, 1973), p. 254.

ser and Wilkins have accomplished a valuable service in emphasizing the importance of mysticism and the other condition for Musil's last years.[32] But they equate Musil's mysticism and his late thought with indifference to reality, particularly the reality of world politics, and they allow a single, unelaborated reference to Lao-tse to have decisive importance for Musil's thought. The image of indifference toward politics, society, science, and evil that emerges from Kaiser and Wilkins obscures Musil's love for science and his thoughtful interest in politics. Even in Swiss exile, Musil continued his commentary on the political events of the day in his diaries and aphorisms. Aside from commenting on developments in the war, Musil was interested in the new roles of Russia, China, and the United States in world politics.

In a fragment written in January, 1942, Musil made explicit his continuing concern with politics, and he explored the impact of the fascist era on his conception of *The Man without Qualities*. He still hoped to finish his novel, but he wanted to do so in a way that would allow him to write about both mysticism and the world political situation since 1933. One solution would have been to allow Ulrich to comment on his narrator: "The Ulrich of today as an old man, who is living through the Second World War and on the basis of these experiences writes an epilog to his story and my book." It was in this same fragment that Musil pointed to the importance of mysticism for his argument: "Important: the discussion (*Auseinandersetzung*) with Lao-tse, which makes Ulrich, but also my task, comprehensible." But it would be a mistake to read this one sentence as a summary of a complex and elusive thinker. Musil did not indicate what Ulrich would have to say about Lao-tse, and a reference to Sufism followed in parentheses. In the same context, Musil referred to his aphorisms (*Aus einem Rapial*) as "the liquidation of Volume I," but this was principally a reference to the changed historical situation. Musil was neither indifferent to politics nor trapped in Vienna 1914, but thinking out the meaning of 1942.[33]

What is clear about his last years in Geneva is Musil's complementary interests in mysticism and politics. Like many other writers of his generation (Scholem, Jung, Scheler), Musil was alert to the value of Oriental traditions of mysticism, but even in the mystical epiphanies of *The Man without Qualities* Musil remained very much a European. He was bound to the German language, and (like Schopenhauer, Mach, Nietz-

32. Kaiser and Wilkins, *Robert Musil*, p. 297.
33. *MoE, Nachlass,* p. 1609.

sche, or Wittgenstein) he offered a variant of Western thought. His intellectual journey had led him beyond the tyranny of moralists, psychologists, ideologies, and churches, and the literary portrayals of the
Nachlass should certainly not be read as fixed statements of ideology or
religion. But Musil's approach to mysticism and politics was not compatible with all religious traditions, and its elective affinity with Christianity was very great. His reflections on Christianity and prayer provided a form for connecting his mystical retreat with the politics of the
fascist era, and his decision to write a *Lay Theology* was the most novel
dimension of his thought during the Swiss exile. Although fragmentary
and inconclusive, the notes for this work offer some insight into the connection between mysticism and politics, between contemplative retreat
and loving the world.

Although the mysticism of *The Man without Qualities* might be described as a creative continuation of Western religiosity, Musil wrote
very little before the 1940s about his own attitude toward Christianity.
He had learned to dislike the spiritual imperialism of Austrian Catholicism in his youth. Protestantism had always seemed less offensive, but
on the whole he found that Christianity contained "too many untimely
characteristics and elements. A false relationship to knowledge. Inadequate breadth of spiritual heroism. Too rigid moral law."[34] Although
his reflections on prayer and faith moved his language closer to the
Christian tradition, Musil wrote as an outsider; and his notes to Lejeune are perhaps too detached, ambivalent, irreverent, and unsystematic to be called a theology at all. It is unlikely that Musil ever studied the
Bible seriously, and he had always been critical of theologians. Certainly he did not belong to the theologian's universe of discourse, but he
shared with Buber, Tillich, and Barth the intellectual and political scenario of the generation.

In a sense, Musil had written all his life as a God-free theologian and
critic of Christianity, but there does seem to have been a change in his
attitude, or at least in his way of expressing it, during the Swiss exile.
His conversations with Lejeune apparently encouraged him to give
more careful and sympathetic consideration to Christianity. His own
suffering made him less spiritually elitist and more sympathetic to the
simple Catholic type who was helpful without pretension. He found

---

34. *TE*, p. 424. Comparing his novel to conventional religious attitudes, Musil wrote:
"'There is no rest for the spirit except in the Absolute, no rest for the feelings except in
eternity, no rest for the soul except in God!' That this book is just as opposed to such
answers as to materialism" (*MoE, Nachlass*, p. 1602).

that he now enjoyed Lagerlöf's *Wonder of the Anti-Christ*, even though a few years earlier he had been unable to finish it. Moreover, he envisioned the dialogs between Ulrich and Agathe as a continuation of Tolstoy's thought in *Resurrection*. These feelings must be seen against the broader historical backdrop of an intense sense of human impotence and evil in the early 1940s, but Musil had no patience with a faith which was anti-intellectual or escapist—whether in a Social Democrat or a Christian. Faith as credulity or an impoverished form of knowledge had no appeal for him. His opening to faith does not sound like escapism and resignation stimulated by old age, exile, and the brutality of the fascist era. It seems to have been much more an attempt to reconcile faith in God with a political view of the world.[35]

Musil's notes toward a lay theology leave the impression that he thought he was on the track of something important but had not quite decided what to do with it. As always, he could not come to an articulated system, but the opening to faith seems to have been real enough: "Nothing logical-theoretical came to me, but, rather, an almost spiritual awakening to faith. What then?" At the same time, he had strong doubts about religion. He took seriously the Freudian analysis of man's relationship to God in terms of infantile relations and emotional inertia. Musil also considered the possibility of a drive of submissiveness and self-abasement, or the possibility that God refers to the human incapacity to proceed from childlike faith to knowledge. Yet he did not find such reductions conclusive: "But is so firmly articulated a feeling thinkable without experience or merely on the basis of childhood experience? Or is it precisely a special feeling and of a unique sort? Does not the maintenance of a childlike relationship (the theologians speak of *Gotteskindschaft*, being a child of God) itself require an explanation?" But Musil had nothing decisive to say on this subject: "All my life I have felt nothing against such humility and diffidence or deemed it necessary: Where then would the idea of so superior a being (and the naturalness of the submission) have come from?" His friend Allesch said that for Musil God was only a concept, but Musil's exploratory sentences offer nothing so firm and unambiguous as a concept. His own feelings on this subject seem to have been too ambivalent for firm judgments: "I have no flashes of religious genius: an evasion which means: I do not believe. If you were convinced, the insights would come."[36]

35. *TE*, pp. 414, 412, 379. See also Musil's related letters to Lejeune and his reference to a "painful inner crisis" (*Prosa*, pp. 749, 823, 832).

36. *TE*, pp. 548, 542, 482, 543.

Musil defined faith positively, not as the absence of knowledge or an act of dependence, but as an act of creativity. In place of his older, more intellectual language of presentiment (*Ahnen*), Musil began to think of faith more affectively in terms of surrender (*Hingabe*). Faith amounted to loving God: "Immanence: To live 'in' the will of God. To love him, then, means to dwell, grow, change, and have being in his commands. But does one know these through tradition, reason, or intuition?"[37] This conception of faith was ontological rather than cosmological, and it was continuous with Musil's values of being "in" rather than "for." But the tension between morality and the other condition appears in new form: even granting the hypothesis of the presence of God, the content of God's will did not seem manifest. Musil's notes to Lejeune are largely an inquiry into prayer as a means of mediating tradition, reason, and intuition. This also meant an attempt to balance the inner and the collective life. Musil was skeptical about the notion of divine intervention in human affairs, but he seems to have taken seriously the notion that prayer might be important to a full understanding of evil, freedom, and human action in the world. He kept his distance from conventionally Christian language, and he expressed little confidence in the efficacy of prayer. He left his requests in the outermost vestibule of the outermost courtyard of the unknown highest essence, somewhere on the margin of the subjunctive.

Musil's reflections on prayer centered on the politics of the 1940s. He explored the conventional solutions to the problem of evil and envisioned the attempts of the faithful to moralize with God about politics. It seemed clear to Musil that God was badly compromised in this matter, since the role of the historical criminal seemed to assure long life and good health. This implied either the Manichean view that the devil takes care of his own or the Panglossian rebuff that "in the best of all possible worlds the good extirpate evil themselves. It is wearisome for God to have all mankind dependent on him." Counseling God in these matters must mean either reminding him of his commands or having enormous confidence in one's judgment. This also required some confidence about which were the real (so to speak, decisive) decisions and about the desirability of being a chosen people. (Musil noted that the only case on record had been rather unenviable.) It seemed to him that the prayer of the pious anticipates not as a cause but as "a humble form

37. Ibid., p. 548.

of prophecy." His request is already fulfilled, since "he asks only what is in God's will and anything else is simply not possible for him."[38]

Musil's view of prayer and politics assumed a lawful process which prayer could not be expected to abrogate: outcomes are determined by long-term preparations and not by dramatic interventions. Thus, for example, Czechoslovakia, Poland, and France could not be saved at the last minute from the implications of two decades. On the other hand, the intellectual failings which accompanied the moral failings of the Nazis would save the rest of mankind. The conception of God which emerges in these notes on prayer allows for both transcendence and human collaboration; it leaves human beings with full responsibility for their own fate, without implying that outcomes (or their desirability) can be foreseen. Thinking about prayer and politics led Musil to the view that "God's will reveals itself step by step."[39]

All conventional solutions to the problem of evil seemed to Musil to express the human need to venerate and absolutize morality. In this sense the *Lay Theology* was the last stage in Musil's lifelong struggle with morality: "To be sure, what passes for morality will always seem to be God's will. But that notion must have arisen entirely against God's will or altogether without his help." Even in the Manichean atmosphere of the 1940s, Musil fought against righteousness and insisted on the interdependence of good and evil. He was convinced that the good needs evil, and that even "the devil has something of God in him. So speaks the angel who has left the house. Between God and the devil there is not the crass opposition (of the Orient) between light and darkness as principles; the devil is part of God's world-order." It was precisely this primitive style of moral dualism that had empowered Hitler's sectarian triumph. Musil feared that the triumph of the Grand Alliance would ensure a revival of Manicheanism in the interests of expelling Satan from God's house. He did not disparage the good: "Morality is there so that we are not any worse. Or so that we can more easily excuse the things we do wrong." But even before the victory of the righteous was assured, Musil was already thinking ahead to the rigidity and moralism of the post-war era: "I write in the garden chapters against righteousness. After the experiences of the present, it will presumably become a fundamental value again, assuming Hitler is not victorious."[40]

38. Ibid., pp. 551, 548–49.
39. Ibid., p. 550.
40. Ibid., pp. 550, 377, 412, 481.

However moral or mystical Musil became, he was never social or pious or extroverted enough for the conventional Christian model. He set himself against every form of spiritual imperialism and righteousness, whether religious or moral:

God gives partial solutions, i.e., creative people; they contradict each other. The world constitutes out of them again and again a relative whole which corresponds to no solution. I am poured into this form of the world like molten ore. Therefore, I am never entirely that which I do and think: an attempted form in an attempted form of totality. One must not listen to the bad masters who have erected one of God's lives according to his plan as though for eternity. Rather, one must trust humbly and defiantly in oneself. Act without reflection; for a man never gets further than when he does not know where he is going.[41]

The God of possibility could not offer a final table of values, and a creative morality could not dispose of freedom. For Musil, morality was the point where the innocence of the creature ends, "where the actions implanted in an entire animal species begin to permit and reveal personal deviations: thus, actually with the first hints of freedom, responsibility, and intelligence."[42]

Musil's reflections on prayer led him back to the tension between the creative person and the needs of the average. He was only too conscious of the tension in German culture between Nietzsche and Hitler. He believed that his culture had produced the greatest moralist of the nineteenth century and the greatest moral aberration of the twentieth. Watching the spectacle of Germany's perverted moral energy, Musil could not help wondering if the world required two moralities, a morality for the genius and a morality for the average person. Perhaps, after watching the impact of Nietzsche Musil wondered if it might not be better to be ironic and not say everything that was on his mind. To rush the average person too quickly from Biedermeier culture to Nietzsche might be to invite Hitler, not because Musil wanted elitism or because Nietzsche wanted Hitler, but because the historical reaction of human beings led to this inference. Musil perceived the First World War and the fascist era as a revolt against civilization, as a failure and breakdown of culture, but he did not share the view of the political irrationalists

41. Musil, *Nachlass*, loose sheet: D 76. Cf. the personal side of this theology during the Geneva years: "If God wants to create and develop the spiritual through human beings, if it depends in any way on the individual intellectual contribution, suicide is then a deadly sin—a refusal of service to the creating God" (*TE*, pp. 552–53).

42. *TE*, p. 559.

and "iron-eaters" who believed that Europe had suffered from too much culture: "In truth, we had too little culture."[43]

At Musil's center was that unpolitical thinking and feeling which he called *Geist.* Spirit was often in conflict with politics, but it was not indifferent. Even the most extreme unreality of the conversations between Ulrich and Agathe led Musil to fundamental insights into the structure of political culture in his generation. Just before his death he noted: "After Hitler, the bankruptcy of the male idea; a matriarchy will follow. America."[44] In his generation, politics had acted out one-sidedly a critique of bourgeois culture which spirit had begun. Watching the suicide of Germany and Europe, Musil was convinced that the possibility of a creative future was linked to the recovery and reconstruction of tradition against the conformity which had overwhelmed it. He believed that spirit was always in process and transformation. It had no fixed forms, but it depended on the brake of tradition and it never changed simply for the sake of change. Musil believed it was his responsibility to preserve intact whatever he could that was of value in the Western tradition, and (as in 1900) he wondered if a time without meaning might not clear the ground of accumulated dead meanings and allow the possibility for truth to be discovered again. The catastrophe of Germany and bourgeois culture might also be a new beginning. After the explosion of the European art museum, perhaps new fragments of meaning would be discovered in the rubble. A period of uncertainty and self-doubt might actually be desirable for culture; at any rate, it was the task of Musil's generation of intellectuals to make the best of it.

43. Ibid., p. 580.   44. Ibid., p. 558.

Epilog

usil's significance as a representative writer lies in his thinking through the breakdown of liberal ideology from the inside. He explored the assumptions, limits, and collapse of liberal values in the generation of 1905. Although he expressed many of the traditional liberal values of the Austrian mandarinate, he felt himself in opposition to bourgeois culture. He stood for spirit against the stabilized hopelessness of bourgeois society, but without deciding for its political opponents. He was Austrian and a poet, but he did not think of himself as an Austrian poet within Austrian literature, and he felt himself "prevented from becoming a poet in Austria."[1] On the other hand, in his lifetime he never found the place he sought in German literature. Musil did not define literature or culture in terms of states. For him there was simply European culture and, within that, the German language. As a *Denker* he thought in terms of the common predicament of European culture in his generation. As a *Dichter* he wrote as a German who felt a responsibility to his people. It was not the fate of Austria which concerned him, but the dual catastrophe of European culture and the German nation.

Musil is important less for his individual artistic works than for the shape and utopian direction of his whole corpus, for his essayistic in-

1. *TE*, p. 447.

sights, and for his characteristic way of perceiving the world. He saw his value in the flow and forming power of his evolution as a whole, and he sometimes feared that he would be ranked far below Goethe and Mann because he had produced so few works. But he reminded himself: "Whoever has so many insights and sees into the future is not unfruitful! . . . What a mistake to see the fruitfulness of a poet in the quantity of his achievement!" In his disdain for worldly success, he had always written with an eye to future generations: "I am not for the present, not of it; I do not work, even in the least objectionable sense, for its needs." He lived for the utopia of literature, believing that "timeless cultural achievements are not the expressions of their age, but, rather, that in which their covetousness has not sufficed, the content of their oblivion and confusion." Even here, Musil saved the last irony for himself: "I am still entirely naively convinced that the *Dichter* is the task of mankind, and besides that I would like to be a great *Dichter*. How nicely I hide my self-love!"[2]

Musil's love for science and intellect set him apart from conventional poets. Learning from Nietzsche, Mach, Dilthey, and the world of experimental science, Musil brought the precision and impersonality of science to bear on the realm of culture. His work displays a steadily maturing capacity for cultural and human objectivity—and an unusual gift for balancing apparently conflicting faculties. From *Young Törless* to *The Man without Qualities*, Musil sought to unite the ethical and the aesthetic, and his work explored the perplexing boundaries between the cognitive and the affective. His essayism and his vision of the ethical process argued for the flexible, undogmatic growth of both intellect and feeling. As he put it in *The Man without Qualities*, the essayist falls between mysticism and knowledge, between love and *amor intellectualis*. His passion for both science and art seemed to him to reflect a tension in the structure of human experience between force and love, between love and knowledge.[3] This vision consistently placed Musil between philosophy and literature, making the claims of a philosopher with the for-

2. Ibid., pp. 485, 492, 562–63, 448. Cf. ibid., p. 460: "My concept of literature, my standing in for it as a whole, is probably the counterbalance to my aggression against individual poets. . . . I thus make for myself a utopian concept of literature."
3. Musil noted that the simple exchange "I love you!" is capable of bringing the world into order: "For the soul, for contentment, for self-consciousness, and for the 'enclosedness' of the world as well as human beings, it is not a matter of knowledge." On the other hand, Musil knew that after a while the human being was always eager again to be offered the apple of knowledge. After a time, "even the 'I love you' becomes intolerable. So then knowledge begins again" (*TE*, p. 575).

mulations of a poet, or the claims of a *Dichter* with the formulations of
a philosopher. Spirit was his highest value, but this was something different from the Reason of the philosophers: it was closer to Socrates'
life-wisdom than to the academic philosophy of the university.

Musil's mode of feeling and his openness to the unconscious were
part of the twentieth-century dethroning of reason in favor of the affects. Thanks to Freud, the psyche was now psychologically, as well as
morally and logically, furnished; but the dualistic model and the moralistic domination of consciousness remained. Musil valued the appropri-
ation of the unconscious for the world of science and medicine, and he
was surely no irrationalist or rebel against civilization, but he was concerned that the discovery of the unconscious might lead to a sterile reduction which simply imposed the narrow claims of bourgeois consciousness. As a scientist, Musil saw Freud's work as a stage in the
evolution of modern psychology. As a poet, Musil was closer to Nietzsche, Jung, and Gestalt psychology in his attitude toward the unconscious, illusion, and fantasy. For Musil, morality was imagination, and
he wanted to re-empower the unconscious rather than pacify it. Whatever pathological or neurotic explanations one might give for fantasy,
Musil believed it was time to reclaim the imagination as "the fundamental quality of the poet."[4]

The characteristic quality of Musil's thought was its resistance to
highly formed theory or ideology. His Machian dislike for rigid concepts, his openness to unconscious energies, and his refusal to assume a
firm point made him too unsystematic for a philosopher. His modes of
spirit, essayism, and Gestalt all modified the old systematic vision of
truth, and his irony amounted to the knowledge "that the poet should
not (and cannot) press to the point of philosophical system." His sense
of process and ironic ignorance made him too fruitful in insights for the
conventional philosopher, and the primacy of insight over system gave
even Musil the impression of being "a man who does not agree with
himself." On the other hand, his search for meaning in the forming
power of language made him look like a philosopher, at least to the poets. Since his first exposure to Maeterlinck's symbolism, Musil's passion
for clarity had always been a threat to the obscurity of symbolism: "Always to express oneself correctly is like Midas's gold. It makes valuable
but unenjoyable what it comprehends." Musil often wondered if he

4. Ibid., pp. 583, 586, 363.

were perhaps "too intelligent for a real poet." He was conscious that his attempt to keep intellect in relation to feeling was a threat to his culture's desire for security in literature, for unequivocal feelings and an unchallenged ideological superstructure. His intellect undermined the prejudices of his literary reader, just as his openness to the unconscious irritated the philosopher's need for systematic form.[5]

Musil's thought can best be understood within the context of the essayistic writers of the generation of 1905 in Central Europe. These generational affinities are unmistakable in a host of fields: in the novel, with Kafka, Mann, Broch, Döblin, Rilke, and Hesse; in literary criticism, with Lukács, Benjamin, Kassner, and Kahler; in philosophy, with Wittgenstein, Scheler, and Bloch; in theology, with Buber and Tillich; in psychology, with Jung and Köhler. Like all of these writers, Musil was coming to terms with the absence of a coherent philosophy, with the crisis of bourgeois culture, with the impact of science and Nietzsche, with the experiences of World War I and the fascist era. He stood closest to the conventions of the novel, but he did not define himself within an ideological tradition. Instead, he understood himself within the European cultural situation, defined in the late nineteenth century by the crisis of liberal values and the tension between science and art.

Musil was an authentically great *Dichter*, who in his finest moments achieved that shattering power of language to which only a poet can find access. But as the genius of intermediate modes and states, as the pure type of the phenomenon between metaphysics and the novel, Musil was a *Denker* as well. His novels and novellas belong to intellectual history. His art was not simply the acting out of autonomous and more general ideas, but an original expression of intellect and cultural objectivity. As a thinker, his essayism and mysticism find echoes in Benjamin, Scheler, Broch, Wittgenstein, Tillich, and Jung, but he left behind no finished system, philosophy, or psychology. He was that irritating inconvenience of the thinking human being, the Socrates in process without a doctrine. But that is only to say that he was an essayist, a lost member of a lost generation of liberal intellectuals. Thinking through the crisis of European culture, Musil was, as he hoped to be, representative of his generation, but also—like Nietzsche—"only a fool, only a poet."[6]

5. Ibid., pp. 455, 471, 389, 448.
6. *Prosa*, p. 810.

Bibliography

This bibliography includes works cited in the text, as well as selected primary and secondary works most useful in preparing this study. I have excluded much of the more obvious background literature, such as novels and major works in philosophy and social thought. For more exhaustive bibliographies of the Musil literature, see Jürgen C. Thöming, *Robert-Musil-Bibliographie*, Berlin, 1968; Marie-Louise Roth, *Robert Musil: Ethik und Aesthetik*, Munich, 1972, pp. 210–229; *Robert Musil: Leben, Werk, Bedeutung: Ausstellungskatalog*, ed. Karl Dinklage, Vereinigung Robert-Musil-Archiv, Klagenfurt, 1973; Robert L. Roseberry, *Robert Musil: Ein Forschungsbericht*, Frankfort, 1974; Karl Heinz Danner, "Robert-Musil-Schrifftum 1970-1975," *Modern Austrian Literature* 9 (1976): 210–239. For reviews of the Musil literature, see Roseberry; Ulrich Karthaus, "Musil-Forschung und Musil-Deutung: Ein Literaturbericht," *Deutsche Vierteljahrschrift* 19, 3 (September 1965): 441–483; and Dietmar Goltschnigg, "Kritische Anmerkungen zur Musil-Forschung," *Österreich in Geschichte und Literatur* 16 (1972): 150–162.

I. MUSIL'S WORKS

A. *Unpublished Sources*

All of Musil's major works have been published, but there is a *Nachlass* of more than 10,000 pages. The most important part of this bears on the evolution of *The Man without Qualities* during the 1920s and 1930s, but it also includes Musil's *Tagebücher* (much of which only recently appeared in print), as well as a variety of drafts, conceptions, newspaper clippings, and reading notes. Although many of Musil's personal papers were destroyed in Vienna at the end of the Second World War, the *Nachlass* gives a substantial picture of Musil's patterns of work and thought. I worked with copies of the *Nachlass* in the Vereinigung Robert-Musil-Archiv in Klagenfurt, Austria, where Dr. Karl Dinklage has gathered other materials concerning Musil's life. The original *Nachlass* is in the Nationalbibliothek in Vienna, and copies are available at the Musil-Arbeitsstelle in Saarbrücken.

B. *Major Fiction*

Die Verwirrungen des Zöglings Törless. Roman. Vienna, 1906.
"Das verzauberte Haus," *Hyperion* 3, 6 (1908): 105–116.
Vereinigungen. Novellen. Munich, 1911.
Die Schwärmer. Schauspiel. Dresden, 1921.
Vinzenz und die Freundin bedeutender Männer (Posse). Berlin, 1923.
"Isis und Osiris," *Die neue Rundschau* (May 1923).
Drei Frauen. Novellen. Berlin, 1924.
"Die Amsel," *Die neue Rundschau* (January 1928).
Der Mann ohne Eigenschaften. Roman. Vol. I. Berlin, 1930.
Der Mann ohne Eigenschaften. Roman. Vol. II. Berlin, 1933.
Nachlass zu Lebzeiten. Zurich, 1936.
Der Mann ohne Eigenschaften. Roman. Vol. III, edited from the *Nachlass* by Martha Musil. Lausanne, 1943.

C. *Major Non-Fiction*

Beitrag zur Beurteilung der Lehren Machs. Ph.D. Diss. Berlin, 1908.
"Das Unanständige und Kranke in der Kunst," *Pan* (March 1911).
"Erinnerung an eine Mode" [Anon.], *Der lose Vogel* (1913).
"Penthesileade" [Anon.], *Der lose Vogel* (1913).
"Das Geistliche, der Modernismus und die Metaphysik" [Anon.], *Der lose Vogel* (1913).
"Moralische Fruchtbarkeit" [Anon.], *Der lose Vogel* (1913).
"Über Robert Musils Bücher" [Anon.], *Der lose Vogel* (1913).
"Politik in Österreich" [Anon.], *Der lose Vogel* (1913).
"Der mathematische Mensch" [Anon.], *Der lose Vogel* (1913).
"Die Wallfahrt nach innen," *Die neue Rundschau* (April 1913).
"Essaybücher," *Die neue Rundschau* (September 1913).
"Analyse und Synthese," *Revolution: Zweiwochenschrift* (October 15, 1913).
"Politisches Bekenntnis eines jungen Mannes: Ein Fragment," *Die weissen Blätter* (November 1913).
"Anmerkung zu einer Metaphysik," *Die neue Rundschau* (April 1914).
"Europaertum, Krieg, Deutschtum," *Die neue Rundschau* (September 1914).
"Skizze der Erkenntnis des Dichters," *Summa* (1918).
"Buridans Österreicher," *Der Friede* (February 1919).
"Der Anschluss an Deutschland," *Die neue Rundschau* (March 1919).
"Geist und Erfahrung. Anmerkungen für Leser, welche dem Untergang des Abendlandes entronnen sind," *Der neue Merkur* (March 1921).

"Die Nation als Ideal und als Wirklichkeit," *Die neue Rundschau* (December 1921).

Das hilflose Europa. Munich, 1922.

"Psychotechnik und ihre Anwendungsmöglichkeit im Bundesheer," *Militärwissenschaftliche und technische Mitteilungen* (1922).

"Stilgeneration und Generationsstil," *Berliner Börsen-Courier* (June 4, 1922).

"Symptomen-Theater I," *Der neue Merkur* (June 1922).

"Symptomen-Theater II," *Der neue Merkur* (December 1922).

Der Deutsche Mensch als Symptom. Published posthumously from the *Nachlass*.

"Der 'Untergang' des Theaters," *Der neue Merkur* (July 1924).

"Ansätze zu neuer Aesthetik. Bemerkungen über eine Dramaturgie des Filmes," *Der neue Merkur* (March 1925).

"Bücher und Literatur," *Die literarische Welt* (October 1926).

"Rede zur Rilke-Feier," Berlin (January 16, 1927).

"Literat und Literatur," *Die neue Rundschau* (September 1931).

"Vortrag in Paris." Paris, 1935.

"Der Dichter und diese Zeit." Vienna, 1936.

"Über die Dummheit." Vienna, 1937.

Aus einem Rapial. Published posthumously in *TE*.

D. *Standard Editions*

1. GERMAN

Gesammelte Werke in Einzelausgaben. Ed. Adolf Frisé, Rowohlt, Hamburg.
   I. *Der Mann ohne Eigenschaften.* Roman. (1st ed., 1952). 4th edition, 1968. (*MoE*)
   II. *Tagebücher, Aphorismen, Essays und Reden.* 1955. (*TE*)
   III. *Prosa, Dramen, späte Briefe.* 1957. (*Prosa*)

Theater: Kritisches und Theoretisches. Intro. and ed. Marie-Louise Roth. Hamburg. 1965.

Der deutsche Mensch als Symptom. From the *Nachlass*. Ed. Karl Corino and Elisabeth Albertsen. Hamburg, 1967.

Briefe nach Prag. Barbara Köpplová and Kurt Krolop. Hamburg, 1971.

Tagebücher with *Anmerkung, Anhang, Register.* 2 vols. Ed. Adolf Frisé. Hamburg, 1976. (Wherever possible, I have changed my *Nachlass* references to this new edition, but I have kept the references to *TE*.)

Gesammelte Werke. Ed. Adolf Frisé. Hamburg, 1978. (This edition appeared after my manuscript was complete.)
   I. *Der Mann ohne Eigenschaften.* Roman.
   II. *Prosa und Stücke, Kleine Prosa, Aphorismen, Autobiographisches, Essays und Reden, Kritik.*

2. ENGLISH

The Man without Qualities. Trans. Eithne Wilkins and Ernst Kaiser. 3 vols., London, 1953/1954/1960.

Young Törless. Trans. Eithne Wilkins and Ernst Kaiser. New York, 1964.
Five Women. Trans. Eithne Wilkins and Ernst Kaiser. Preface by Frank Kermode. New York, 1966.

II. OTHER PRIMARY SOURCES

Andrian, Leopold. *Das Fest der Jugend.* Berlin, 1919.
Bauer, Otto. *The Austrian Revolution.* Trans. H. J. Stenning (abridged). London, 1925.
Benjamin, Walter. *Schriften.* 2 vols. Introduction by Theodor Adorno. Frankfort, 1955.
———. *Illuminations.* Trans. Harry Zohn. New York, 1969.
Bergson, Henri. *An Introduction to Metaphysics.* Trans. T. E. Hulme. New York, 1912.
Blei, Franz. *Zeitgenössische Bildnisse.* Amsterdam, 1940. *Schriften in Auswahl.* Munich, 1960.
Broch, Hermann. "Hofmannsthal und seine Zeit" in *Dichten und Erkennen: Essays I.* Zurich, 1955.
Buber, Martin. *Ekstatische Konfessionen.* Leipzig, 1921.
Curtius, Ernst Robert. *Der Syndicalismus der Geistesarbeiter in Frankreich.* Bonn, 1921.
Foerster, Fr. W. *The Art of Living: Sources and Illustrations for Moral Lessons.* Trans. Ethel Peck. London, 1910.
———. *Christentum und Paedagogik.* Munich, 1920.
Haas, Willy. *Die Literarische Welt: Erinnerungen.* Munich, 1958.
Hartmann, Eduard von. *Das religiöse Bewusstsein.* 3rd edition, Bad Sachsa, 1906.
———. *Philosophie des Unbewussten.* 3 vols. 12th edition. Leipzig, 1923.
Hegel, Georg Wilhelm Friedrich. *Vorlesung über die Aesthetik.* Stuttgart, 1928.
Hofmannsthal, Hugo von. *Die prosaischen Schriften Gesammelt.* Vol. I. Berlin, 1907.
Huch, Ricarda. *Die Blütezeit der Romantik.* Leipzig, 1901.
Huysmans, J. K. *Against the Grain.* Introduction by Havelock Ellis. New York, 1930.
Kant, Immanuel. *The Critique of Judgment.* Trans. James C. Meredith. London, 1964.
Kassner, Rudolf. "Der Dichter und der Platoniker" in *Sämtliche Werke.* Vol. 1. Stuttgart, 1969.
Kerschensteiner, Georg. *Staatsbürgerliche Erziehung der deutschen Jugend.* 4th edition, Erfurt, 1909.
———. *Die Seele des Erziehers und das Problem der Lehrerbildung.* Berlin, 1921.
Key, Ellen. "Die Entfaltung der Seele durch Lebenskunst." *Die neue Rundschau* (June 1905):641–86.
Kierkegaard, Soren. *The Concept of Irony: With Constant Reference to Socrates.* Trans. with introduction by Lee M. Capel. New York, 1965.
Klages, Ludwig. *Der Geist als Widersacher der Seele.* Bonn, 1969.

————. *Vom kosmogonischen Eros.* Jena, 1941.
Köhler, Wolfgang. *Die physischen Gestalten in Ruhe und im stationären Zustand.* Erlangen, 1924.
————. *Gestalt Psychology: An Introduction to New Concepts in Modern Psychology.* New York, 1947.
Kraus, Karl. *Literatur und Lüge.* Munich, 1958.
Kretschmer, Ernst. *Physique und Character.* Trans. W. J. H. Sprott. London, 1945.
————. *Medizinische Psychologie.* 13th edition, Stuttgart, 1971.
Landauer, Gustav. *Der werdende Mensch: Aufsätze uber Leben und Schriftum.* Potsdam, 1921.
Lenin, V. I. *Materialism and Empirio-Criticism: Critical Notes Concerning a Reactionary Philosophy.* Trans. David Kvito. New York, 1927.
Lévy-Bruhl, Lucien. *How Natives Think.* Trans. Lilian A. Clare. New York, 1966.
————. *Primitive Mentality.* Trans. Lilian A. Clare. Boston, 1966.
Logos: Internationale Zeitschrift für Philosophie der Kultur 1, 1 (1910).
Lukács, Georg. *Die Seele und die Formen.* Berlin, 1911.
————. *Die Theorie des Romans.* Berlin, 1968.
Mach, Ernst. *The Analysis of Sensations.* Trans. C. M. Williams. New York, 1959.
Maeterlinck, Maurice. *Weisheit und Schicksal.* Trans. Friedrich von Oppeln-Bronikowski. Leipzig, 1904.
————. *On Emerson and Other Essays: Three Transcendental Thinkers.* Trans. Montrose J. Moses. Port Washington, 1967.
Mann, Thomas. *Schriften und Reden zur Literatur, Kunst und Philosophie,* vol. 1. Frankfort, 1968.
Neue freie Presse. Summer, 1914.
Nietzsche, Friedrich. *Beyond Good and Evil: Prelude to a Philosophy of the Future.* Trans. Walter Kaufmann. New York, 1966.
Novalis. *Schriften.* Stuttgart, 1960.
Rathenau, Walter. *Zur Mechanik des Geistes.* Berlin, 1922.
Schoenberner, Franz. *Confessions of a European Intellectual.* New York, 1946.
Scholem, Gershom. "Walter Benjamin," *Leo Baeck Memorial Lecture* 8 (New York, 1965).
Schopenhauer, Arthur. *Essays: From the Parega and Paralipomena.* Trans. T. Bailey Saunders. London, 1951.
Strich, Walter. "Der Fluch des objektiven Geistes," *Der neue Merkur* 3, 7 (1920):494–504.
Tiroler Soldaten-Zeitung (June 2, 1915–April 15, 1917).
Tucholsky, Kurt. *Gesammelte Werke,* vol. 3. Ed. Mary Gerold-Tucholsky. Hamburg, 1960.
Weininger, Otto. *Geschlecht und Charakter: Eine prinzipielle Untersuchung.* 8th edition. Vienna, 1906 (orig. pub. 1903).
Wilhelm, Richard, and C. G. Jung. *Das Geheimnis der goldenen Blüte: Ein Chinesisches Lebensbuch.* Munich, 1929.

Wittgenstein, Ludwig. *Tractatus Logico-Philosophicus*. London, 1960.
Das Ziel: Jahrbücher für geistige Politik 3, 1 (Leipzig, 1919).

III. LITERATURE ON MUSIL

A. *Books and Dissertations*

Albertsen, Elisabeth. *Ratio und "Mystik" im Werk Robert Musils*. Munich, 1968.
Allemann, Beda. *Ironie und Dichtung*. Pfullingen, 1956.
Appignanesi, Lisa. *Femininity and the Creative Imagination: A Study of Henry James, Robert Musil, and Marcel Proust*. New York, 1973.
Arntzen, Helmut. *Satirischer Stil. Zur Satire Robert Musils im "Mann ohne Eigenschaften."* Bonn, 1960 (2nd revised edition, 1970).
Aue, Maximillian. "Novalis und Musil: Eine Untersuchung der romantischen Elemente im Werk Robert Musils." Ph.D. diss. Stanford, 1973.
Bachmann, Dieter. *Essay und Essayismus: Benjamin, Broch, Kassner, H. Mann, Musil, Rychner*. Stuttgart, 1969.
Bauer, Sibylle and Ingrid Drevermann. *Studien zu Robert Musil*. Cologne, 1966.
Baumann, Gerhart. *Robert Musil: Zur Erkenntnis der Dichtung*. Bern, 1965.
——. *Vereinigungen. Versuche zu neuerer Dichtung*. Munich, 1972.
Bausinger, Wilhelm. *Studien zu einer historisch-kritischen Ausgabe von Robert Musils Roman "Der Mann ohne Eigenschaften."* Hamburg, 1964.
Beard, Philip Harper. "Der 'andere Zustand' im *Mann ohne Eigenschaften* und in der Musil-Kritik." Ph.D. diss. Stanford, 1971.
Berghahn, Wilfried. *Robert Musil in Selbstzeugnissen und Bilddokumenten*. Hamburg, 1963.
Birrell, Gordon Eastridge. "The Problem of Ethical Responsibility in Robert Musil's 'Die Schwärmer.'" M.A. diss. Stanford, 1965.
Böhme, Hartmut. *Anomie und Entfremdung: Literatursoziologische Untersuchungen zu den Essays Robert Musils und seinen Roman "Der Mann ohne Eigenschaften."* Kronberg Ts., 1974.
Büren, Erhard von. *Zur Bedeutung der Psychologie in Werk Robert Musils*. Zurich, 1970.
Cantoni, Remo. *Robert Musil e la crisi dell'uomo Europeo*. Milan, 1972.
Corino, Karl. *Robert Musil-Thomas Mann: Ein Dialog*. Pfullingen, 1971.
——. *Robert Musils "Vereinigungen": Studien zu einer historisch-kritischen Ausgabe*. Munich, 1974.
Flanagan, Thomas Eugene. "Robert Musil and the Second Reality." Ph.D. diss. Duke, 1970.
Freij, Lars W. *"Türlosigkeit." Robert Musils Törless in Mikroanalyse mit Ausblicken auf andere Texte des Dichters*. Stockholm, 1972.
Goltschnigg, Dietmar. *Mystische Tradition im Roman Robert Musils*. Heidelberg, 1974.
Graf, Günter. *Studien zur Funktion des ersten Kapitels von Robert Musils Roman "Der Mann ohne Eigenschaften": Ein Beitrag zur Unwahrhaftigkeits-Typik der Gestalten*. Göppingen, 1969.

Gumtau, Helmut. *Robert Musil.* Berlin, 1967.

Hagmann, Franz. *Aspekte der Wirlichkeit im Werke Robert Musils.* Bern, 1969.

Hanke-Tjaden, Irma. "'Der freie Geist und die Politik.' Zum Problem des Politischen bei Robert Musil." Ph.D. diss. Freiburg/Brg., 1962.

Herwig, Dagmar. *Der Mensch in der Entfremdung.* Munich, 1972.

Heydebrand, Renate von. *Die Reflexionen Ulrichs in Robert Musils Roman "Der Mann ohne Eigenschaften."* Münster, 1966.

Hönig, Christoph. "Die Dialektik von Ironie und Utopie." Ph.D. diss. Berlin, 1970.

Honold, Helga. "Die Funktion des Paradoxen bei Robert Musil. Dargestellt am 'Mann ohne Eigenschaften.'" Ph.D. diss. Tübingen, 1963.

Hüppauf, Bernd-Rüdiger. *Von sozialer Utopie zur Mystik. Zu Robert Musils "Der Mann ohne Eigenschaften."* Munich, 1971.

Jässl, Gerolf. "Mathematik und Mystik in Robert Musils Roman 'Der Mann ohne Eigenschaften.'" Ph.D diss. Munich, 1964.

Kaiser, Ernst, and Eithne Wilkins. *Robert Musil: Eine Einführung in das Werk.* Stuttgart, 1962.

Kalow, Gert. *Zwischen Christentum und Ideologie; die Chance des Geistes im Glaubenskrieg der Gegenwart.* Heidelberg, 1956.

Karthaus, Ulrich. *Der andere Zustand: Zeitstrukturen im Werke Robert Musils.* Berlin, 1965.

Krüger, Hans-Peter. *Dichtung und Erkenntnis: Eine Studie zum Sprachstil in Robert Musils Roman "Der Mann ohne Eigenschaften."* Tokyo, 1961.

Kühn, Dieter. *Analogie und Variation: Zur Analyse von Robert Musils Roman "Der Mann ohne Eigenschaften."* Bonn, 1965.

Kühne, Jörg. *Das Gleichnis: Studien zur inneren Form von Robert Musils Roman "Der Mann ohne Eigenschaften."* Tübingen, 1968.

Laermann, Klaus. *Eigenschaftslosigkeit: Reflexionen zu Musils Roman "Der Mann ohne Eigenschaften."* Stuttgart, 1970.

Lepinis, Asta. "Der Kritiker Robert Musil." Ph.D. diss. Yale, 1970.

Literatur und Kritik 66/67 (July–August, 1972). Articles on Musil by Edgar Buchleitner, Karl Corino, Paul Hatvani, Eberhard Hilscher, Egon Nagonowski, Wolfgang Freese, and C. A. M. Noble.

Luft, David S. "Robert Musil: An Intellectual Biography, 1880–1924." Ph.D. diss. Harvard, 1972.

Merrill, Charles Seeley. "A Calculus of the Mind: Robert Musil's Anti-Epic Narrative 'Die Vollendung der Liebe.'" Ph.D. diss. Texas, 1972.

Müller, Gerd. *Dichtung und Wissenschaft.* Uppsala, 1971.

Müller, Götz. *Ideologiekritik und Metasprache in Robert Musils Roman "Der Mann ohne Eigenschaften."* Munich, 1972.

Nusser, Peter. *Musils Romantheorie.* The Hague, 1967.

Peters, Frederick G. *Robert Musil: Master of the Hovering Life.* New York, 1978.

Pike, Burton. *Robert Musil: An Introduction to His Work.* Ithaca, N.Y., 1961.

Rasch, Wolfdietrich. *Über Robert Musils Roman "Der Mann ohne Eigenschaften."* Göttingen, 1967.

Reinhardt, Stephan. *Studien zur Antinomie von Intellekt und Gefühl in Musils Roman "Der Mann ohne Eigenschaften."* Bonn, 1969.

Reniers-Servranckx, Annie. *Robert Musil: Konstanz und Entwicklung von Themen, Motiven und Strukturen in den Dichtungen.* Bonn, 1972.

Rieder, Heinz. *Österreichische Moderne.* Bonn, 1968.

Rieger, Elisabeth. "Musil in Frankreich: Ein Beitrag zur Rezeptionsgeschichte seiner Werke (1922–1970)." Ph.D. diss. Vienna, 1972.

Rieth, Renate. *Robert Musils frühe Prosa: Versuch einer stilistischen Interpretation.* Tübingen, 1963.

Robert Musil: Leben, Werk, Wirkung. Ed. Karl Dinklage. Hamburg, 1960. Includes articles on Musil by Marie-Louise Roth, Wilhelm Grenzmann, Johannes Loebenstein, Johannes von Allesch, Ervin P. Hexner, Hajo Bernett, Eithne Wilkins and Ernst Kaiser, Joseph Strelka, Armin Kesser, Dinklage, Oskar Maurus Fontana, Josef Luitpold Stein, Franz Theodor Csokor, Karl Otten, Wolfdietrich Rasch, Bruno Fürst, Martin Flinker, Otto Pächt, Valerie Petter-Zeis, Fritz Wotruba, Carl J. Burckhardt, Robert Lejeune, Adolf Frisé, Philippe Joccottet, and letters and articles by Musil.

Robert Musil: Studien zu seinem Werk. Ed. Karl Dinklage, Elisabeth Albertsen, and Karl Corino. Hamburg, 1970. Includes articles by Dinklage, Albertsen, Annie Reniers, Gerhart Baumann, Walter H. Sokel, Marie-Louise Roth, Johannes Hösle, Wolfgang Freese, Fritz Martini, Wolfgang Rothe, Ulrich Schelling, Henri Avron, Jürgen C. Thöming, Corino, Adolf Frisé, Ludwig Kunz, Karl Baedeker, Walter Grossmann, Ignazio Silone, Robert Lejeune, and Dietrich Uffhausen.

Roth, Marie-Louise. *Robert Musil: Ethik und Aesthetik. Zum Theoretischen Werk des Dichters.* Munich, 1972.

Schaffnit, Hans Wolfgang. *Mimesis als Problem. Studien zu einem ästhetischen Begriff der Dichtung aus Anlass Robert Musils.* Berlin, 1971.

Schelling, Ulrich. *Identität und Wirklichkeit bei Robert Musil.* Zurich, 1968.

Schneider, Günther. *Untersuchungen zum dramatischen Werk Robert Musils.* Frankfort, 1973.

Schramm, Ulf. *Fiktion und Reflexion: Überlegungen zu Musil und Beckett.* Frankfort, 1967.

Seeger, Lothar Georg. *Die Demaskierung der Lebenslüge: Eine Untersuchung zur Krise der Gesellschaft in Robert Musils "Der Mann ohne Eigenschaften."* Bern, 1969.

Sera, Manfred. *Utopie und Parodie bei Musil, Broch und Thomas Mann.* Bonn, 1969.

Strelka, Joseph. *Kafka, Musil, Broch und die Entwicklung des modernen Romans.* Vienna, 1959.

Text-Kritik 21/22: Robert Musil. Ed. Heinz Ludwig Arnold. Aachen, 1968. Includes articles by Elisabeth Albertsen, Helmut Arntzen, Wolf Überling, Karl Corino, Jörg Jesch, Stephan Reinhardt, Wolfdietrich Rasch, Eithne Wilkins, Aloisio Rendi, and Jürgen C. Thöming.

Trommler, Frank. *Österreich im Roman: Eine Untersuchung zur dargestellten*

Wirklichkeit bei Joseph Roth, Robert Musil und Heimito von Doderer.
Munich, 1965.
Vom "Törless" zum "Mann ohne Eigenschaften." Ed. Uwe Baur and Dietmar
Goltschnigg. Munich, 1973. Includes articles by Baur, Karl Corino, Golt-
schnigg, Erich Heintel, Christoph Hönig, and Egon Nagonowski.

B. *Articles*

Aler, Jan. "Als Zögling zwischen Maeterlinck und Mach" in *Probleme des
Erzählens in der Weltliteratur,* ed. Fritz Martini. Stuttgart, 1971.
Appignanesi, Lisa. "Femininity and Robert Musil's 'Die Vollendung der Liebe,' "
Monatshefte 65, 1 (1973):14–26.
Bachmann, Ingeborg. "Ins tausendjahrige Reich," *Akzente* 1 (1954):50–53.
Bausinger, Wilhelm. "Musils mystische Wandlung?" *Frankfurter Allgemeine
Zeitung,* September 15, 1962, p. 11.
———. "Robert Musil und die Ablehnung des Expressionismus," *Studi Ger-
manici* 3 (1965):383–89.
Berger, Peter. "The Problem of Multiple Realities: Alfred Schutz and Robert
Musil" in *Phenomenology and Social Reality,* ed. Maurice Natanson. The
Hague, 1970.
Boehlich, Walter. "Untergang und Erlösung." *Akzente* 1 (1954):35–50.
Boeninger, Helmut. "The Rediscovery of Robert Musil," *Modern Language
Forum* 37 (1952):109–119.
Bolton, Neil. "Robert Musil and Phenomenological Psychology," *Journal of the
British Society for Phenomenology* 6, 1 (January 1975):42–89.
Braun, Wilhelm. "Musil's Siamese Twins," *Germanic Review* 33 (1958):41–52.
———. "Moosbrugger Dances," *Germanic Review* 35 (1960):214–30.
Brosthaus, Heribert. "Zur Struktur und Entwicklung des 'anderen Zustands' im
Robert Musils Roman 'Der Mann ohne Eigenschaften.' " *DVJS* 39, 3 (Sep-
tember 1955):388–440.
Brummack, Jurgen. "Zu Begriff und Theorie der Satire," *DVJS* 45 (May
1971):Sonderheft, 275–377.
Cohn, Dorrit. "Psycho-Analogies: A Means for Rendering Consciousness in Fic-
tion" in *Probleme des Erzählens in der Weltliteratur,* ed. Fritz Martini.
Stuttgart, 1971.
Corino, Karl. "Reflexionen im Vakuum. Musils Schweizer Exil" in *Die
Deutsche Exilliteratur 1933–1945,* ed. Manfred Durzak. Stuttgart, 1973.
Fischer, Ernst. "Das Werk Robert Musils: Versuch einer Würdigung," *Sinn und
Form* 9, 2 (1957):851–901.
Frisé, Adolf. "Fragen nach Robert Musil," *Frankfurter Allgemeine Zeitung,*
November 21, 1959.
———. "Angriff auf eine Edition," *Frankfurter Allgemeine Zeitung,* September
3, 1962, p. 16.
Geulen, Hans. "Robert Musils 'Die Versuchung der stillen Veronika,' " *Wirken-
des Wort* 15 (1965):173–87.

Goldgar, Harry. "The Square Root of Minus One: Freud and Robert Musil's 'Törless,'" *Comparative Literature* 17 (1965):117–32.

Hatfield, Henry. "An Unsentimental Education," in *Crisis and Continuity in Modern German Literature: Ten Essays.* Ithaca, 1969.

Heintel, Erich. "Der Mann ohne Eigenschaften und die Tradition," *Wissenschaft und Weltbild* 13 (1960):179–94.

Kaiser, Ernst. *See* Wilkins, Eithne, and Ernst Kaiser.

Kermode, Frank. "A Short View of Musil," *Encounter* 15 (December 1960): 64–75.

Mattenklott, Gerd. "Der 'subjektive Faktor' in Musils Törless; Mit einer Vorbemerkung über die Historizität der sinnlichen Wahrnehmung" in *Neue Hefte für Philosophie,* 4, ed. Rüdiger Bubner, et al. Göttingen, 1972.

Mayer, Hans. "Robert Musil: A Remembrance of Things Past" in *Steppenwolf and Everyman.* Trans. with introduction by Jack D. Zipes. New York, 1971.

Meyerhoff, Hans. "The Writer as Intellectual: 'The Man without Qualities' by Robert Musil," *Partisan Review* 21 (1954):98–108.

Michel, Karl Markus. "Die Utopie der Sprache. Zu Robert Musils Roman 'Der Mann ohne Eigenschaften,'" *Akzente* 1 (1954):23–35.

Minder, Robert. "Kadettenhaus, Gruppendynamik und Stilwandel von Wildenbruch bis Rilke und Musil" in *Kultur und Literatur in Deutschland und Frankreich.* Frankfort, 1962.

Rasch, Wolfdietrich. "Zur Entstehung von Robert Musils Roman 'Der Mann ohne Eigenschaften,'" *DVJS* 39, 3 (September 1965):350–87.

Roth, Marie-Louise. "Musiliana," *Akzente* 12 (1965):649–65.

Rougemont, Denis de. "Nouvelles métamorphoses de Tristan" in *Comme toi-même: Essais sur des mythes de l'amour.* Paris, 1961.

Schöne, Albrecht. "Zum Gebrauch des Konjunktivs bei Robert Musil," *Euphorion* 55 (1961):196–220.

Schröder, Jürgen. "Am Grenzwert der Sprache," *Euphorion* 60 (1966):311–34.

Seidler, Ingo. "Das Nietzschebild Robert Musils." *DVJS* 39, 3 (September 1965):329–49.

Sokel, Walter H. "Robert Musils Narrenspiegel." *Neue Deutsche Hefte* 71 (1960–61):199–214.

Stern, Guy. "Musil über seine Essays: Ein Bericht über eine unveröffentlichte Korrespondenz," *Germanic Review* 49 (1974):60–82.

Titche, Leon L. "Isis und Osiris." *Kentucky Foreign Language Quarterly* 13 (1966):165–69.

Wilkins, Eithne, "Musil's 'Affair of the Major's Wife' with an Unpublished Text." *Modern Language Review* 63, 1 (January 1968):74–93.

Wilkins, Eithne, and Ernst Kaiser. "In Sachen Robert Musils," *Frankfurter Allgemeine Zeitung*, September 14, 1962, p. 63.

―――. "Monstrum in Animo," *DVJS* 37, 1 (1963):78–119.

Zak, Eduard, "Gegen den Strom," *Neue Deutsche Literatur* 4, 10 (October 1956):118–36.

C. *Reviews by Contemporaries*

[Anon.]. "An Austrian Novel." *TLS* (November 19, 1931):914.

[Anon.]. "Empire in Time and Space," *TLS* (October 28, 1949):689–90.

Balázs, Béla. *Oesterreichische Rundschau* 19, 4 (1923):344–49.

Bertaux, F. "Der Mann ohne Eigenschaften," *Nouvelle revue française* (1930): 615–20.

Blass, Ernst. "Robert Musil zum 50. Geburtstag," *Prager Presse*, November 6, 1930.

Blei, Franz. "Robert Musil" in *Zeitgenössische Bildnisse*. Amsterdam, 1940.

Diebold, Bernhard, "Totentanz. Von Proust und Joyce zu Musil," *Neue Schweizer Rundschau* N.F. (1944–45). 157–63, 210–19.

Döblin, Alfred. "Über Robert Musil" in *Aufsätze zur Literatur*. (Olten und Freiburg im B., 1963) (from *Berliner Tageblatt*, February 3, 1924).

Fontana, Oskar Maurus. "Robert Musil und sein Werk," *Prager Presse*, May 21, 1922.

———. "Was arbeiten Sie? Gespräch mit Robert Musil," *Die Literarische Welt* (April 30, 1926).

———. "Robert Musil. Zum 50. Geburtstag," *Prager Presse* (November 5, 1930).

Frisch, Efraim. "Der Mann ohne Eigenschaften," *Frankfurter Zeitung*, December 20, 1930.

———. "Robert Musil," *Frankfurter Zeitung*, October 18, 1931.

Frisé, Adolf. "Der Mann ohne Eigenschaften," *Der Gral* 27 (1932–33):697–99.

———. "Die vergessenen Dichter," *Die Zeit* 3, 42 (1948):4.

Jacob, Paul. "Robert Musil," *Revue d'Allemagne* 6 (1932):503–517.

Kayser, Rudolf. "Die Schwärmer," *Die neue Rundschau* 33 (1922):918–19.

Kerr, Alfred. "Robert Musil," *Der Tag* (December 1, 1906).

Kesser, Armin. "Robert Musil," *Neue Züricher Zeitung* (April 18, 1953).

Müller, Robert. "Der erotischeste Schriftsteller," *Prager Presse*, July 15, 1924.

Schaffner, Jacob. "Verwirrungen des Zöglings Törless" (and) "Vereinigungen," *Die neue Rundschau* 22, 2 (1911):1769–71.

Spunda, Franz. "Der Mann ohne Eigenschaften," *Die neue Literatur* (February 1931):87–88.

Wolfenstein, Alfred. "Robert Musil: 'Vereinigungen,'" *Die neue Kunst* 1 (1913–14):217–19.

IV. GENERAL WORKS

Adorno, Theodor W. *Noten zur Literatur I*. Frankfort, 1969.

Bauer, Roger. *La Realité royaume de Dieu: Études sur l'originalité du théâtre viennois dans la première moitié du XIXᵉ siècle*. Paris, 1965.

———. *Der Idealismus und seine Gegner in Österreich*. Heidelberg, 1966.

Baumgarten, Eduard. *Das Vorbild Emersons im Werk und Leben Nietzsches*. Heidelberg, 1957.

Berendsohn, Walter A. *Die humanistische Front: Einführung in die deutsche Emigranten-Literatur*. Zurich, 1946.

Berger, Peter. *The Precarious Vision*. New York, 1961.

Bernard, Paul P. *Jesuits and Jacobins: Enlightened Despotism in Austria*. Urbana, Ill., 1971.

Blackmore, John T. *Ernst Mach: His Work, Life and Influence*. Berkeley, 1972.

Boring, Edwin G. *A History of Experimental Psychology*. New York, 1929.

Bramsted, Ernest Kohn. *Aristocracy and the Middle Classes*. Chicago, 1964.

Carter, A. E. *The Idea of Decadence in French Literature, 1830–1900*. Toronto, 1958.

Cassirer, Ernst. *Substance and Function and Einstein's Theory of Relativity*. Trans. W. C. Swabey and M. C. Swabey. New York, 1953.

David, Claude. *Zwischen Romantik und Symbolismus, 1820–1885*. Gütersloh, 1966.

Deák, István. *Weimar Germany's Left-Wing Intellectuals: A Political History of the "Weltbühne" and Its Circle*. Berkeley, 1968.

Demetz, Peter. *René Rilkes Prager Jahre*. Düsseldorf, 1953.

Durzak, Manfred. *Hermann Broch: Der Dichter und seine Zeit*. Stuttgart, 1967.

Eder, Karl. *Der Liberalismus in Altösterreich: Geisteshaltung, Politik und Kultur*. Vienna, 1955.

Elliott, Robert. "The Definition of Satire," *Yearbook of Comparative and General Literature* 11 (1962):19–23.

———. *The Power of Satire*. Princeton, 1966.

Erikson, Erik H. *Identity: Youth and Crisis*. New York, 1968.

Ernst Mach: Physicist and Philosopher. Ed. Robert S. Cohen and Raymond J. Seeger. New York, 1970.

Fischer, Ernst. *Von Grillparzer zu Kafka: Sechs Essays*. Vienna, 1962.

Franz, Georg. *Liberalismus: Die deutschliberale Bewegung in der Habsburgischen Monarchie*. Munich, 1955.

Friedell, Egon. *A Cultural History of the Modern Age*, vol. 3. Trans. Charles Francis Atkinson. New York, 1933.

Frye, Northrop. *Anatomy of Criticism: Four Essays*. Princeton, 1967.

Gay, Peter. *Weimar Culture*. New York, 1968.

Goldmann, Lucien. *The Human Sciences and Philosophy*. Trans. Hayden White and Robert Anchor. London, 1969.

Hantsch, Hugo von. *Die Geschichte Österreichs*, vol. 2. Graz, 1951.

Hatfield, Henry. *Modern German Literature*. Bloomington, Ind., 1966.

Heer, Friedrich. *Land im Strom der Zeit: Österreich gestern, heute, morgen*. Vienna, 1958.

Heller, Erich. *The Disinherited Mind*. New York, 1957.

———. *The Artist's Journey into the Interior*. New York, 1965.

Heller, K. D. *Ernst Mach: Wegbereiter der modernen Physik*. New York, 1964.

Hiebert, Erwin N. "Mach's Philosophical Use of the History of Science" in *Historical and Philosophical Perspectives of Science*. Ed. Roger H. Stuewer. Minneapolis, 1970.

Hughes, H. Stuart. *Consciousness and Society: The Reorientation of European Social Thought 1890–1930*. New York, 1958.

Janik, Allan, and Stephen Toulmin. *Wittgenstein's Vienna*. New York, 1973.

Jens, Walter. *Statt einer Literaturgeschichte*. Pfullingen, 1962.

Johnston, William M. *The Austrian Mind: An Intellectual and Social History*. Berkeley, 1972.

Kahler, Erich. "Der Prosa des Expressionismus" in *Der deutsche Expressionismus: Formen und Gestalten*. Ed. Hans Steffen. Göttingen, 1965.

Kann, Robert A. *The Multinational Empire: Nationalism and National Reform in the Habsburg Monarchy 1848–1918*, 2 vols. New York, 1950.

———. *A Study in Austrian Intellectual History: From Late Baroque to Romanticism*. New York, 1960.

Klemperer, Klemens von. *Ignaz Seipel: Christian Statesman in a Time of Crisis*. Princeton, 1972.

Lehmann, A. G. *The Symbolist Aesthetic in France, 1885–1895*. Oxford, 1968.

Leser, Norbert. "Austro-Marxism: A Reappraisal" in *The Left-Wing Intellectuals between the Wars 1919–1939*. Ed. Walter Laqueur and George L. Mosse. New York, 1966.

Lichtheim, George. *Marxism: An Historical and Critical Study*. New York, 1961.

Lukács, Georg. *Deutsche Literatur im Zeitalter des Imperialismus*. Berlin, 1950.

———. *Deutsche Literatur in Zwei Jahrhunderten*. Berlin, 1964.

———. *Studies in European Realism*. Trans. Edith Bone. London, 1964.

Magris, Claudio. *Der habsburgische Mythos*. Salzburg, 1966.

Malcom, Norman. *Ludwig Wittgenstein: A Memoir*. London, 1958.

Mannheim, Karl. *Ideology and Utopia: An Introduction to the Sociology of Knowledge*. Trans. Louis Wirth and Edward Shils. New York, n.d.

Martini, Fritz. *Deutsche Literatur im bürgerlichen Realismus 1848–1898*. Stuttgart, 1962.

Masur, Gerhard. *Prophets of Yesterday: Studies in European Culture, 1890–1914*. New York, 1961.

———. *Imperial Berlin*. New York, 1970.

McGrath, William J. *Dionysian Art and Populist Politics in Austria*. New Haven, 1974.

Merleau-Ponty, Maurice. *Sense and Nonsense*. Trans. H. Dreyfus and P. Dreyfus. Evanston, 1964.

———. *Themes from the Lectures at the College de France 1952–1960*. Trans. John O'Neill. Evanston, 1970.

Mitzman, Arthur. *The Iron Cage: An Historical Interpretation*. New York, 1971.

Poor, Harold. *Kurt Tucholsky and the Ordeal of Germany*. New York, 1968.

Pross, Harry. *Literatur und Politik: Geschichte und Programme der politischen Zeitschriften im deutschen Sprachgebiet seit 1870*. Olten und Freiburg im B., 1963.

Rieff, Philip. *The Triumph of the Therapeutic*. New York, 1966.

Ringer, Fritz. *The Decline of the German Mandarins: The German Academic Community, 1890–1933*. Cambridge, Mass., 1969.

Rohner, Ludwig. *Der deutsche Essay*. Berlin, 1966.

———. *Deutsche Essays*, vols. 1–4, Berlin, 1968.

Schlawe, Fritz. *Literarische Zeitschriften,* 2 vols. Stuttgart, 1961–1962.

Schorske, Carl E. "Politics and the Psyche in *fin de siècle* Vienna: Schnitzler and Hofmannsthal," *AHR* 66, 4 (July 1961):930–46.

———. "The Transformation of the Garden: Ideal and Society in Austrian Literature," *AHR* 72, 4 (July 1967):1283–1320.

———. "Politics in a New Key," *Journal of Modern History* 39, 4 (December 1967):343–86.

Sokel, Walter H. *The Writer in Extremis: Expressionism in Twentieth Century German Literature.* Stanford, 1954.

Steed, Henry Wickham. *The Hapsburg Monarchy.* London, 1913.

Stern, Fritz. *The Politics of Cultural Despair: A Study in the Rise of Germanic Ideology.* New York, 1965.

Stern, Guy. *War, Weimar, and Literature: The Story of the "Neue Merkur" 1914–1925.* University Park, Pa., 1971.

Strelka, Joseph. *Brücke zu vielen Ufern: Wesen und Eigenart der österreichischen Literatur.* Vienna, 1966.

Szondi, Peter. *Theorie des modernen Dramas.* Frankfort, 1966.

Valjavec, Fritz. *Der Josephinismus: Zur geistigen Entwicklung Österreichs im achtzehnten und neunzehnten Jahrhundert.* Munich, 1945.

Watson, Robert I. *The Great Psychologists.* New York, 1968.

White, Hayden. *Metahistory: The Historical Imagination in Nineteenth-Century Europe.* Baltimore, 1973.

Williams. C. E. *The Broken Eagle: The Politics of Austrian Literature from Empire to Anschluss.* London, 1974.

Winter, Eduard. *Romantismus, Restauration und Früh-liberalismus im österreichischen Vormärz.* Vienna, 1968.

———. *Revolution, Neoabsolutismus und Liberalismus in der Donaumonarchie.* Vienna, 1969.

———. *Barock, Absolutismus und Aufklärung.* Vienna, 1971.

Index

Achilles, 161, 203, 204–206, 265
Adler, Alfred, 285
Aeins, 183, 184
Aestheticism, 12–13, 23, 38–41, 201;
  of Allesch, 68–69; critique of, by
  Musil, 45–46, 47–48; and music, 45
Aesthetics, and *ratioïd*/non-*ratioïd*, 164–
  165
Agathe, 75, 174, 176, 183, 204, 205–
  206, 213, 216, 232; as decadent elitist,
  263, 264; as lost half of self, 251–
  252, 253; relation to Ulrich, 249–
  268; religious-mystical themes ex-
  plored through, 250–251, 259–262;
  as Ulrich's self-love, 251–252
Aktion, Die, 103
Alexander, Henriette, 74
Allesch, Johannes von (1882–1967), 64,
  68, 80, 102–103, 138, 139, 184,
  210, 212; as symbol of experimental
  research, 68
Alpha, 176, 183
Altenberg, Peter, 12, 36, 37, 69, 106n,
  139, 141
Altruism, 105, 106, 107
"Amsel, Die," 125, 179, 180, 183–184
Anarchisten, Die, 102
Anders, 161, 203, 206, 210, 265
Androgyny, 182, 251. *See also* Gender
  identity
"Ansätze zu neuer Aesthetik," 188–198,
  200n

Anschluss, 271n, 272, 277; advocated
  by Musil after World War I, 127, 130–
  131, 139
Anselm, 171, 172–173, 174, 176
Antichrist, Der, 204
Anti-Semitism, 143, 239, 247; as basis
  of National Socialism, 274–275, 276
Archivar, 203
Aristocracy, 5, 6, 10; of display and pleasure, 11–12; Musil's wartime critique of, 124
Arnheim, 207, 215, 232, 238, 241, 242–
  244, 246, 254; egoism of, 223–224;
  Rathenau as model for, 116; split between spirit and power in, 243–244;
  and Ulrich's options for action, 248,
  249
Arnold, Matthew, 19
Art, 2; essayism as mediator for, 101;
  ethical role of, 89, 97–98; and exploration of non-*ratioïd*, 156; and organization of experience, 199–201;
  perversity in, 104–105; as portrayal of
  individuality, 88–98; in thought of
  generation of 1905, 14
Austria: class forces stalemated in, 136–
  137; classical culture of, 7–8; from
  Empire to Republic, 132–133; generation of 1905 in, 15–18; mandarinate
  in, 6–9; modernism in, 37–38; politics of, 119, 120–121; portrayal of, in
  Man without Qualities, 214–215;

relation of Musil to, 4–5, 138–139; service in government by Musil, 136–137
Azwei, 183

Bach, Julius Carl von, 49
Bahr, Hermann, 12, 110, 111, 138
Balázs, Béla, 158–159, 160, 175–176, 209
Barber, Albertine, 28
Barth, Karl, 16
Basini, 54, 55, 56, 58, 59
Baudelaire, Charles, 36
Bausinger, Wilhelm, 168n
Beard, Philip, 266
Beineberg, 54, 55, 56, 61
Benjamin, Walter, 16, 18, 19–20, 22n, 183, 198, 201, 202, 297
Benn, Gottfried, 16
Berger, Peter, 177–178, 250n
Bergson, Henri, 14, 18–19, 81
Berlin, 2, 23, 141; academic environment in, 78–81; move of Musil to (in 1931), 212; neo-romanticism in, 69–70; philosophical study in, by Musil, 50–51, 52, 64–77; relation of Musil to, 101, 102–103, 139–140
Berliner Tageblatt, 102
Berta, 26
Besitz und Bildung, 8, 9, 10–11
Biedermeier values, 4, 7
Bildung, 6, 7, 8–9, 170
Biological reduction, 191, 193–194
Blass, Ernst, 211–212
Blei, Franz, 64, 69, 77, 102, 103, 104, 109, 110, 127, 139, 141
Bloch, Ernst, 16, 19, 298
Bohemia-Moravia, 6
Bolshevism, 132, 134, 136, 137, 204, 278, 279
Bolton, Neil, 219n, 221n
Bolzano, Bernard, 8, 79
Bonadea, 215, 231, 238, 239, 245, 253
Boredom, 120–121
Bourgeois culture: moralism of, 104–108; theater as symptom of, 170; and women's role, 108–109
Bourgeois family, 241n
Bourgeois morality, 104–108, 161–178
Bozena, 55, 58
Brandes, Georg, 69
Brentano, Franz, 79, 80
Brest-Litovsk, Treaty of, 131, 132
Brno, 23, 24, 28, 33, 34–35, 38, 50

Broch, Hermann, 4, 4–5n, 9n, 13, 15, 16, 18, 22n, 39, 79, 198, 273, 297
Buber, Martin, 16, 187, 188, 261, 297
Büchner, Georg, 168
Bureaucracy, 127, 136

Capitalism, 10, 155; and bureaucracy, 136; and liberal culture, 8–9; Musil on, 119–120; rooted in the normal condition, 189; and World War I, 128–129
Carlyle, Thomas, 36, 72
Cassirer, Ernst, 273
Cassirer, Paul, 69, 103
Catholicism, 7, 29, 51, 288; in Der Teufel. See also Christianity; Church
Causality, 83–88
Central Europe: crisis of liberal culture in, 16; postwar revolution in, 132
Charcot, Jean, 58n, 80
Christianity, 1, 135, 143, 190; breakdown of, 99; late interest of Musil in, 288–293; morality of, criticized by Musil, 105–106
Church, 6–7; and state power, 114; theological reduction of the other condition by, 190, 194–195, 197–198
Civil courage, 129, 130
Civilization, modern, 61; formlessness of, 149–157; German revolt against, 129–130; science as a basis of, 112–114; World War I as revolt against, 121–138
Claasen, Eugen, 272
Clarisse, 67–68, 183, 193, 215, 221n, 232, 238, 245, 246, 249, 253
Claudine, 94–95
Clemenceau, Georges, 132
Clothing, 108–109, 152
Cohn, Martin, 74–75
Collectivism, 279, 280, 281–282
Communism, 120. See also Bolshevism
Condition of love, the, 189, 191, 192, 195–196; in The Man without Qualities, 249–268; and mystical contemplation, 197; and sexual desire, 196–197. See also Other condition, the
Corino, Karl, 33, 49, 54n, 96, 210
Cosmopolitanism: of generation of 1905, 15–16; and peace settlement, 131
Coudenhove-Kalergi, Richard, 131n
Creative person, 160–178, 250, 292; and Dichter, 165–166; in Die Schwärmer, 171–176; house as sym-

bol of, 171; in *Vinzenz*, 176–177
Crime: as theme in Ulrich-Agathe story, 263–265
Csokor, Franz, 141
Culture, 1–3; distortion of, in bourgeois art, 282; formlessness of modern, 149–157; as international, 279–280; postwar critique by Musil of, 138–157; relation of, to politics, 279–286; search for order in, 233–249
Czechoslovakia, 132

D'Annunzio, Gabriele, 38
Darwin, Charles, 188
Death: Musil's wartime awareness of, 124, 125
Decadence, 12–13, 14, 15, 23, 38, 41, 42, 68–69; defense of, by Musil, 104–105; and music, 45; and Ulrich-Agathe story, 263, 264
Demeter, 95
Democracy, obstacles to, 118–119. *See also* Parliamentary democracy
Denker, Musil as, 295, 298
Determinism, historical, 151, 152–153
Deutsch, Julius, 140
Deutsche Mensch als Symptom, Der, 145–157
Dichter, 103, 104, 138; intellect of, applied to individuality, 165; lack of recognition of, 209; Musil as, 2, 158–213, 279, 295–296, 297; role of, 165–168, 169–170
Dietz, Herma, 33, 48–49, 51, 65, 66–67, 68, 73, 74, 181. *See also* Tonka
Dilthey, Wilhelm, 14, 164–165, 168, 296
Diotima, 72, 207, 215, 232, 235, 238, 251, 253; as culmination of Austrian high culture, 241–242, 243, 246; relation to Ulrich, 244–245, 246
Döblin, Alfred, 16, 18, 141, 186, 187, 297
Donath, Alice, 33, 36, 42, 66, 67–68, 91
Donath, Eduard, 127
Donath, Gustav (1878–1965), 28, 33, 34, 36, 42, 45, 48, 66–68
Dostoevsky, Feodor, 36, 168, 228
Drama, 170–171. *See also* Theater
Dream-life, 17; and neo-romanticism, 69–70
Drei Frauen, 159, 179, 180–183
Duty: in morality, 105–106, 107, 108; and war, 122, 123

Eckhardt, Meister, 96
Ecstasy, modes of, 193
Ego: Cartesian, 70; and Gestalt psychology, 185–186; modes of dissolution of, 193; mystical, 70, 88, 90, 94–95; and the normal condition, 192; and the other condition, 192–193
"Ego-fugal," 105, 106
Egoism, 105, 107; by twos, 241–242
"Ego-petal," 105, 106
Einstein, Albert, 84, 88, 273
Eisner, Kurt, 133
Emerson, Ralph Waldo, 29, 36, 59, 72, 101
Emotions: essayism to free, 101; and evolution of society, 193–194; modern mixture of, 194. *See also* Feelings
"Enchanted House, The," 91–92, 93
Engineering, 24–25, 29, 30
Enlightened absolutism, 7, 281
Enlightenment, 6, 7–8
Epic, 202
Erfahrung, 117, 164–165; and task of art, 199
Erikson, Erik, 87–88
Erlebnis, 117, 164–165; novella as vehicle for, 179; the other condition as, 198; and task of art, 199
Eros, 188
Eroticism, 108–109
Essayism, philosophical, 2, 17, 18–22; analysis of ideologies through, 149; and ethics, 20–21, 100–121, 162; form of, 110; of generation of 1905, 18–22, 296–297; and Gestalt psychology, 185; and ideological uncertainty, 110–111; in *The Man without Qualities*, 208, 217; as mediation between science and art, 101–121, 296; and movement from the other condition to the normal condition, 198; and truth, 41; Ulrich's use of, 227–228
Ethical person, 160. *See also* Creative person
Ethics, 23, 40, 81; and artistic perversity, 104–105; and creative person, 162–164; and essayism, 20–21, 100–121, 162; for generation of 1905, 14–15, 17; versus morality, 163–165; in prewar diaries of Musil, 105–107; problematics of, 144–145; source of, in *The Man without Qualities*, 216, 217, 249–268; source of, in the other condition, 190–191, 196–198, 255–

256; Ulrich's style of, 227–228
Everyday life: metaphysics of, 146–148,
  150–151, 153; recovery of meaning
  in, 268
Evil, 189; relation to good, 257–258,
  267, 291
Expressionism, 39, 61–62, 99, 142,
  200–201, 235; Musil's resistance to,
  166–168, 178

Faith, 288–293
Fascism, 14, 17, 130, 157, 279, 280. *See
  also* National Socialism
Fechner, Gustav, 80
Feelings, 2, 17, 21; and essayism, 101;
  excess of, and World War I, 122, 123;
  formlessness of, in bourgeois culture,
  115, 122, 123; given form in morality,
  256–259; Key on, 71–72; language
  of, 219–220, 222; and morality, 105,
  106, 256–259; organization of,
  through ideology, 146–147; reconciliation of, with intellect, 249–250,
  254, 258, 260–261, 267–268, 296,
  297; role in art of, 199–201; and stupidity, 283–285; Ulrich on link to
  intellect of, 239–241, 246–247
Feminism, 108
Film, 169, 235
Fischel, 240–241
Fischer, Samuel, 103, 140, 141
Flâneur, 43, 44
Flaubert, Gustav, 168
Fontana, Oskar Maurus, 53, 141, 206,
  208, 211n
Formalism in art, 199, 200–201
Formlessness of modern culture, 149–
  157
France, 132, 133
Francis of Assisi, Saint, 72
Franz Joseph, 11, 24, 126, 206
Freud, Sigmund, 12, 13, 14, 31, 40, 57,
  58–59, 81, 108, 109, 184–185, 186,
  188, 285, 296
Frisch, Efraim, 157n, 211
Function, 84–85, 86
Fürst, Bruno, 271

Geist. See Spirit
Gender identity: Austrian, 23; and blend
  of emotions in the other condition,
  194, 195; and bourgeois culture, 108–
  109; in *Drei Frauen*, 181–182;
  Musil on, 45–49; Musil's own, 27–
  28, 32–34; polarization of, 242; rec-

onciliation of polarities of, in Ulrich-
  Agathe story, 249, 250–251, 252,
  254, 267, 268
Generation of 1905, 13–18, 286, 295;
  and philosophical essayism, 18–22,
  296–297
Gentz, Friedrich von, 30
George, Stefan, 141, 285
Gerda, 245
Germany: culture of, as symptom, 129–
  130, 138–157; Musil's identification
  with, 132; and National Socialism,
  274–279; politics of, 119, 120–121;
  revolt against civilization in, 129–130
German Youth Movement, 51
Gestalt psychology, 68, 80, 84, 297;
  Musil on, 185–187
Gide, André, 57
Glaser, Kurt, 271
God: in "Die Amsel," 183; late reflec-
  tions of Musil on, 289–293; neo-
  romantic search for, 115–118; of pos-
  sibility, 225; presence of, and the
  other condition, 197–198; stages of
  belief in, 153n
Goethe, J.W., 7, 72, 138, 218; Musil on
  interpretations of, 156–157
Goldgar, Harry, 58
Gomperz, Heinrich, 164n
Grauauges, 65
Graz, 35
Grieche, Der, 204
Grigia, 125, 181, 182
Grillparzer, Franz, 4, 8
Gütersloh, Albert Paris, 16, 127, 141

Habsburg Monarchy, 120; and crisis of
  liberal culture, 9–10; liberal elite in,
  9–13; and mandarinate, 5–9
Hagauer, 164, 232, 251, 256–257
Hamsun, Knut, 69
Harden, Maximilian, 118
Hartmann, Eduard von, 43n, 59
Haute bourgeoisie, 8–9, 10–13
Hebbel, Friedrich, 168
Hegel, Georg, 8, 151
Heidegger, Martin, 16, 82, 285
Heisenberg, Werner, 86
Helmholtz, Hermann von, 78–79, 80
Herbart, J.F., 80
Hesse, Hermann, 16, 18, 297
Hilflose Europa, Das, 145–157
Hiller, Kurt, 141
Historicism, 151–152, 154
History: for generation of 1905, 17;

Musil's view of, 151–153; Ulrich's
  view of, 262–263
Hitler, Adolph, 129, 130, 137n, 152,
  213, 236, 291, 292; aesthetic politics
  of, 276–277
Hofmannsthal, Hugo von, 12, 13, 15,
  16, 36, 37, 69, 138, 139
Holy life, 260–261
Homo, 181, 183
Homosexuality, 53, 54, 56–57, 58, 61
House: as symbol of self, 171, 222,
  228
Huch, Ricarda, 71
Hughes, H. Stuart, 13–14
Humor: of Musil, 124, 177–178, 233n;
  as vision, 177–178, 250n
Hungary, 6, 133
Husserl, Edmund, 18–19, 81

Ibsen, Henrik, 36, 69
Idealism, 3, 145
Ideology: breakdown of, 99–100; as
  context for story, 202–203; Musil's
  postwar critique of, 142–157; portrayal of, in The Man without
  Qualities, 234–249; professionalism
  as substitute for, 148; relation to the
  other condition, 255, 256; variant
  meanings of, 146
Impressionism, 39, 167–168, 235
Incest, 182, 250, 263, 264–265n
Individuality, 1, 39, 282–283; essay as
  vehicle for, 101; and Gestalt, 185–
  186; intellect applied to, 165; and
  World War I, 128–129
Intellect, 2, 13, 21, 70, 72; commitment
  of Musil to, 98, 296, 296–297; and
  essayism, 101, 110–111; ideologies
  opposed to, 234; mediating role of,
  168; modern German rejection of,
  155–157; and ratioïd/non-ratioïd,
  165n; reconciliation of, with feelings,
  239–241, 246–247, 249–250, 254,
  258, 260–261, 267–268; role in art
  of, 199–201; and stupidity, 283–285;
  Ulrich's commitment to, 215, 219–
  221, 239–241, 246–247; in Young
  Törless, 60–61
Intuition, 157, 165n
Irony, 3, 18, 20, 21, 232–233
Irrationalism, 17, 38, 99, 115, 200; criticized by Ulrich, 239–240; as response to facticity, 155–157
"Isis und Osiris," 182, 183
Italy, 123–125

Jacob, Paul, 211
James, William, 72, 80, 111
Janet, Pierre, 58n, 80
Jaspers, Karl, 16
Johannes, 95, 171–172, 174, 265
Josef, 164, 172, 174
Joseph II, 6
Josephinism, 7, 8–9
Jung, Carl, 16, 184, 186, 285, 287, 296,
  297

Kafka, Franz, 16, 18, 22n, 79, 145,
  168n, 297
Kahler, Erich, 15, 16, 62, 297
Kaiser, Ernst, 96, 203, 210, 286–287
Kakania, 9, 243; as paradigm of modern
  culture, 214–215, 221–222, 234;
  politics in, 246–249; and prewar Aus-
  tria, 120
Kant, Immanuel, 8, 38, 61, 115; aes-
  thetics of, 39–41, 164; opposition to,
  in Austrian philosophy, 79–80
Kassner, Rudolf, 16, 21, 297
Katacombe, 203
Kermode, Frank, 180
Kerr, Alfred, 53–54, 64, 66, 69, 102,
  103, 104
Ketten, Herr von, 181, 183
Key, Ellen, 69, 71–72
Kitsch, 13, 282
Klages, Ludwig, 67, 81, 184, 187–188,
  285
Koffka, Kurt, 80
Köhler, Wolfgang, 80, 185, 297
Krähe, Der, 203, 204
Kraus, Karl, 13, 15, 16, 31–32, 118,
  138, 139, 233n, 285
Kretschmer, Ernst, 186

Lady from Portugal, The, 181, 182, 183
Lagerlöf, 289
Landauer, Gustav, 133
Language, 44–45; dualizing conventions
  of, 191; as medium, 17
Lao-tse, 287
Lask, Emil, 16
Lawrence, D.H., 57
Lay Theology, 272–273, 288–293
League of Nations, 127, 130, 132
Leibniz, Gottfried, 8, 79, 97, 138
Leinsdorf, 215, 236, 240, 246, 247,
  265
Lejeune, Robert, 272–273, 288, 290
Lenin, V.I., 127–128, 129
Lessing, Gotthold, 7, 72

Lévy-Bruhl, Lucien, 186–187
Liberalism, 136–137, 190; Austrian, 8–13; breakdown of, 99, 294–297; crisis of, 1–3, 9–13, 20–22, 32; and essayism, 20–22; as mandarin ideology, 6–7, 8, 10, 134–136; pieties of, 280–281; predicament of, 8–9, 10–13; and sexual polarities, 32
Lichtenberg, Georg Christoph, 60
Lindner, 232, 256, 259, 260
Linz, 123
Lloyd George, David, 132
Logic, 44–45
Loos, Adolf, 15
Lose Vogel, Der, 102, 103, 108, 109–110
Lotze, Rudolf Hermann, 80
Love, 73, 107, 296; experience of, 117–118; versus force, 254; Key on, 71; Klages on, 188; married versus neighborly, 109; mystical and instinctual in, 125; and the other condition, 195–196; role of ideology in, 147; in Vereinigungen, 91–98. See also Condition of love
Lukács, Georg, 16, 18, 19, 20, 21, 109, 132, 139, 142, 198, 201, 202, 297
Lukács, Hugo, 209–210

"Machen Wir" ("MW"), 129–130
Mach, Ernst, 2, 14, 60, 97, 111, 145–146, 167, 185, 188, 296; Musil's study of, 47–48, 64, 78, 81–88
Maeterlinck, Maurice, 38, 59, 69, 296
Mallarmé, Stéphane, 36, 38
Mandarinate, Austrian, 5–9, 295; Alfred Musil as member of, 24–25; and capitalist bourgeoisie, 8, 9; morality of, 164; objectivity of, 79; polarities between thought and feeling within, 166–167; Robert Musil as representative of, 5–9, 24–35, 134–136, Ulrich as representative of, 220–221; in postwar period, 134–135
Mann, Heinrich, 16
Mann, Thomas, 16, 18, 20, 39, 54, 123, 141, 164, 202, 208, 211, 273, 285n, 297
Mannheim, Karl, 16, 134–135, 136
Man without Qualities, The, 1, 2, 3, 4, 21, 35–36, 45, 93, 97, 100, 153, 158, 159, 171, 187, 196, 197, 198, 214–268, 287, 295; Achilles period in evolution of, 203, 204–206; Anders period in evolution of, 203, 206–208, 210; architectural symbolism in, 222n;

complex richness of, 266–268; conception of hero in, 203–213; controlling and rebelling groups in, 215–216; essayistic mode in, 22, 208, 217; evolution of, in 1920s, 203–213; forms of new culture portrayed in, 235–236; Holy Conversations in, 255; intellect and feeling reconciled in, 249–268; irony in, 208, 215, 216, 232–233; the other condition in, 248–249, 254–268; Parallel Action in, 206–207, 208, 215, 216, 232, 235, 236, 246; polar structure of, 216–217; publication of, and critical reception to, volume I, 210–212; science and the self in, 217–233; search for order in, 233–249; unfinished, 212–213; war as frame of, 203, 204–205, 234
Maria, 171, 172, 173, 174
Maria Theresa, 6, 7, 222
Marriage: in Die Schwärmer, 171, 172, 174–175; in The Man without Qualities, 241–242; and normalization of the other condition, 109, 195–196; rigidity of, 241–242
Marx, Karl, 146, 152
Marxism, 1, 99
Materialism, 3, 38
Mathematics: and civilization, 112; Ulrich's use of, 219, 220, 226–227, 228n, 238; in Young Törless, 56, 59
Mauthner, Fritz, 18–19
Meinecke, F., 123
Meingast, 67, 216, 232, 246, 247
Merleau-Ponty, Maurice, 17–18
Metaphor, 76, 88–98, 219
Metaphysics, 17–18, 111–112; and essayism, 18–22; novel as vehicle for, 18–19, 20, 198–213
Militarism, 129–130
Military tradition: Musil's incorporation of, 29, 30–31
Minkowski, Hermann, 84, 88
Modernism, cultural, 9, 15, 35–38, 114–115, 199–200
Monsieur le vivesecteur, 227
Moosbrugger, 186, 193, 205, 215–216, 232; as answer to disarray of culture, 236–238; as pathological, 238; as pure immediacy, 237–238; Ulrich's attitude to, 238–240, 248, 249
Morality: and art, 104–105; bourgeois, 105–109; conventional, 256–257, 258; versus ethics, 163–165; as

form for feelings, 256–259; idea of character in, 151–152; in *Lay Theology*, 290, 291, 292; of the next step, 258–259; in prewar Musil diaries, 105–107; relation to the other condition, 255, 256–259, 260–261; science applied to, 163–165; Ulrich's view of, 229; and verbal polarities, 106–107

Müller, Robert, 141

Music, 45–46, 247, 277

Musil, Alfred (1846–1924), 24–25, 26, 29, 49, 50–51, 52, 76, 102n; death of, 159–160, 183

Musil, Elsa, 26, 27–28

Musil, Hermine Bergauer (1853–1924), 24, 25–26, 29, 33–34, 48, 49, 51–52, 102n; death of, 159–160, 183; portrayal in "Die Amsel," 183–184

Musil, Martha (née Heimann; Marcovaldi) (1874–1949), 63, 64, 69, 73–75, 77, 91, 124–125, 181, 209, 210, 271, 272, 273, 286

Musil, Matthias, 24, 27

Musil, Robert (1880–1942): archival work, 100, 101–102; artistic moratorium from 1905 to 1918, 66–67; artistic vocation and self-identity, 65–67, 76, 77, 87–88; as Austrian mandarin, 5–9, 24–35, 134–136; birth of, 23; childhood of, 23, 27–29; as conservative anarchist, 119; engineering education and work, 23, 30–32, 49–50; exile in Switzerland, 271, 272–273; family atmosphere as child, 26, 27, 28, 29; as homeless modern man, 141–142, 286–293; illnesses of, 102, 271–272; invents color-wheel, 50, 68; literary apprenticeship of, 35–52; military training of, 29–31, 34; military service in World War I, 123–124; as philosophy student in Berlin, 23, 49, 50, 52, 63–88; relation to parents, 24–26, 27, 28, 29, 33–34, 50–52, 75; sees psychiatrist, 209–210; in service of Austrian state, 100, 136–137, 140; theater criticism and art, 169–177; in Vienna, 208–210, 212–213, 271–272; as wartime editor, 125–127; and Weimar culture, 141–142

Mysticism, 3, 21, 286–293, 298; in "Die Amsel," 183–184; experience of, and religion, 259–262; Musil on role of, 70–72; neo-romantic, 116–118; and

politics, 286–293; relation to the other condition, 197–198, 255, 259–262; and revolt against rigidity, 161–162; and science, 101; wartime awareness of, by Musil, 124–125

Mythology, 182, 187–188

Nachlass zu Lebzeiten, 271

Nationalism, 10; appeal of, to Musil, 122–123; Musil's analysis of appeal of, 142–145; and World War I, 129

National Socialism, 274–279

Naturalism, 38–39, 168

Neo-romanticism: in Berlin, 69–70; spirituality of, 115–118; Ulrich's repudiation of, 239–241

Neue Freie Presse, 138, 139

Neue Rundschau, 69, 140; Musil's essays in, 102, 103, 104, 122, 127

Neumann, Robert, 273

Nietzsche, Friedrich, 14, 20, 29, 36, 38, 45, 48, 59, 60, 72, 97, 106, 107, 152, 168, 240, 280, 281, 292, 295, 297; influence on Musil, 40–41, 101

Non-*ratioïd*, 39, 87, 156, 158; intellect applied to, 165n; and the other condition, 179; as realm of art and ethics, 163–165

Normal condition, the, 188–189, 190, 192–193, 194, 197–198; distinguishing marks of, 191–192; reduction of the other condition to, 193–197; relation of the other condition to, 190–191

Normal person, the, 165, 195, 293; exposure of, to the other condition, 195–196

Noske, Gustav, 133

Novalis (Friedrich von Hardenberg), 97

Novel, 169; attitude to, in *Young Törless*, 60; and generation of 1905, 18; as mediation, 159; modern crisis of, 201–202; and portrayal of objectivity/subjectivity dilemma, 201–202; task of, 198–213; as vehicle for metaphysics, 18–19, 20, 198–213

Novella, 179, 183–184

Objectivity: and bourgeois culture, 161–163; limits of, 156; in *The Man without Qualities*, 218, 219; Musil's commitment to, 43–44, 166–168, 184–188; in portrayal of mystical experience, 184; Ulrich's use of, 215, 225, 226–227, 232, 240–241, 244, 254

Other condition, the, 92; biological dimension of, 191, 193–194; described, 189–198; as different relation to real world, 189, 190, 192, 196–197; in *Drei Frauen*, 180–183; ego in, 192–193; as *Erlebnis*, 198; in *The Man without Qualities*, 248–249, 254–268; relation to normal condition, 190–191, 230, 231, 238–239, 266–268; scientific account of, 191; and symbolism, 159, 178–198; theological reduction of, 194–195, 197–198; two modes of, 193; Ulrich's experience of, 238–239, 248–249, 254–268
Other person, the, 163. *See also* Creative person
Otten, Karl, 127, 141

Pächt, Otto, 271
"Paderewski-Phantasie," 45
Pan, 102, 104
Panama, 124, 203
Parliamentary democracy, 279, 280–281
Pasquil, Das, 77
Paulsen, Friedrich, 170
Pavlov, Ivan, 80
Peace psychosis, 128–129, 143
Perfecting of a Love, 90, 91, 93–95
Perversity in art, 104–105
Pfemfert, Franz, 103
Phenomenology, 70–73, 81
Philosophy: and art, 65–66; and essayism, 18–22; Musil's view of, 64, 65–66; relation to science, 78–88, 97. *See also* Metaphysics
Physics, 83–85, 218
Planck, Max, 84
Plotinus, 68, 71
Poincaré, Jules, 84
Polgar, Alfred, 141
Politics, 1–3; aestheticization of, 70, 276–277; in Central Europe, 118–121; cultural basis of problems in, 142–157, 279–286; and essayism, 101; intellectuals in, 142; mediation in, 136–137; Musil's interest in, 137–138, 279–286; and mysticism, 286–293; quest for certainty in, 285; relation to the other condition, 255; romanticism in, 70, 133–135; rooted in the normal condition, 189; in tension with spirit, 269–270, 274–293
Positivism, 3, 10, 14, 103, 226; Austrian,

79; in Berlin, 78–79; rejected by Musil, 38; revolt against, 155
Pötzl, Otto (1877–1962), 102n
Pragmatism, 154–157; as mark of the normal condition, 191–192
Prayer, 288, 290–291, 292
Prince H., 56
Professional as ideal type, 148
Professions, 171, 172, 175; as substitute for ideology, 148; Ulrich on, 219; and utopia of exact living, 229–230
Prostitution, 30, 32
Protestantism, 29, 288
Psychiatry, 236, 237–238
Psychoanalysis, 184–185
Psychology, academic, 78–81; limits and goals of, 89–90; themes of, in Musil's stories in 1920s, 184–188; use of, by Musil in government service, 140n. *See also* Gestalt psychology

R., Karla, 28
Ranke, Leopold von, 151
Rasch, Wolfdietrich, 212
Rathenau, Walther, 116–118, 205, 207
Ratioïd, 39, 85–86, 154–155; intellect applied to, 165n; as realm of science and morality, 162, 163–165; Stader as explorer of, 173–74
Rationalism, revolt against, 142, 153–157
Realism, Musil's turn from, 88–98
Reason, 1, 10, 14, 38, 111–112; and "Valerie-experience," 47–48
Regine, 171, 172, 173, 174
Reiter, Heinrich (1856–1940), 25–26, 28, 29, 34, 51
Reiting, 54, 55, 61
Religion, 28–29, 111–112, 114–115; and mystical experience, 256–262. *See also* Christianity; Church
Revolution, 99, 132, 151, 190, 278–279
Rilke, Rainer Maria, 2, 15, 16, 26n, 54, 139, 168, 179–180, 297
Romanticism, 3; Austrian, 7–8; ideal of love in, 252–253; Musil on, 38, 70–72; phenomenological reduction of, 159 (*see also* Other condition); in politics, 70, 133–135
Rousseau, J.J., 72
Rowohlt, Ernst, 209, 210, 212, 271
Ringer, Fritz, 5–6
Ruskin, John, 72
Russian Revolution: of 1905, 109; of 1917, 126

Saar, Ferdinand von, 4
Sadism, 53, 54–55, 61
Salon, bourgeois, 32, 35
Satire, 232n, 233. *See also* Humor; Irony
Scheler, Max, 16, 81, 123, 287, 297
Schelling, Friedrich, 70
Schiele, Egon, 31
Schiller, Johann, 39, 164
Schlegel, Friedrich, 7, 20, 138, 218–219
Schleiermacher, Friedrich, 72
Schnitzler, Arthur, 12, 31, 37, 69, 211
Scholem, Gershom, 19–20, 287
Schopenhauer, Arthur, 38, 39, 45, 54, 59
Schorske, Carl E., 13, 23
Schutzengel, Der, 92
Schwärmer, Die, 102, 159, 160–161, 164, 170, 176
Science, 2, 10, 13, 14, 23, 111–112, 166–167; and bourgeois culture, 161, 162–163; as civilization-building, 112–113; commitment of Musil to, 2–3, 72, 111–112, 295–296; essayism as mediation for, 101; ideologies opposed to, 234; Mach on, 82–85; in *The Man without Qualities,* 217–233; and morality, 163–165; Musil on, 83–88; and mysticism, 101; and *ratioïd,* 163–165; relation to philosophy, 78–88, 97; rooted in the normal condition, 189; Ulrich's commitment to, 219–221, 222, 226–227, 228–229, 232, 240, 254; and utopia of exact living, 229–230
Sepp, Hans, 216, 232, 246, 247
Sexuality, 15, 17, 249, 250; in Austrian culture, 31–33; and bourgeois culture, 108–109; in *Drei Frauen,* 181–183; as drive, 191, 193–194; in family of Musil, 26, 27, 28; as focus of cultural criticism, 31–32; interest of Musil in, 27–28, 31–32, 45–49; and the other condition, 181–183, 191, 193–195, 196; in *Vereinigungen,* 90–98; in *Young Törless,* 54, 55–59
Sexual union, 195–197
Sighele, Scipio, 264n
Silone, Ignazio, 270
Simmel, Georg, 18–19, 81
Skepticism, 110–111, 153–154
Social democracy, 104, 119
Socialism, 119, 190, 191, 195; attraction of Musil to, 37; and bureaucracy, 136; Musil's analysis of, 133–134, 135–136, 137, 143

Sorel, G., 129, 152
Soul (*Seele*), xii–xiii, 70, 225; and bourgeois morality, 243; of creative person, 161; and essayism, 101; experience of, 117–118; Key on, 71–72; in *The Man without Qualities,* 238–239, 243; Musil on, 70, 71, 72–73; in *Vereinigungen,* 96–98
Soviet Union, 278
Spengler, Oswald, 16, 141, 149n, 151, 152
Spion, 203, 204–206
Spirit (*Geist*), xii–xiii, 7; at center of Musil's vision, 293, 297; in tension with politics, 269–270, 274–293
Spirituality: bourgeois, 161–162; intellect and feeling in, 283; neo-romantic, 115–118; search for, 59–62
Spiritual union, 195–197
Sports, 230, 231, 235, 237
Spunda, Franz, 210–211
Stader, 172, 173–174, 176
Stalin, Joseph, 129
Stallburg, 215
State: culture not attribute of, 139; functional view of, 136, 138, 143–144, 145; growth in power of, 114–115; and organized society, 120, 143–145; and nationalist ideology, 143–144
Steyr, 27–28
Stifter, Adalbert, 4, 8
Story, breakdown of, 183–184, 201–202
Strastil, Doctor, 241, 246, 253
Strich, Walter, 161–162
Stumm, General, 215, 227, 232, 235, 246
Stumpf, Carl, 50, 64, 68, 76, 80–81
Stupidity, 283–285
Stuttgart, 23, 49, 52
Subjectivity, 2, 192–193
Südpol, 102
Switzerland, 271, 272–273
Symbolism, 17, 23, 38, 159; in aesthetic of Musil, 38–40; in "Die Amsel," 183–184; French, 38–39; and Gestalt psychology, 185–187; and mythology, 187–188; and the other condition, 178–198

Temptation of Quiet Veronica, The, 90, 91–92, 95, 182
Teufel, Der, 203, 204
Theater, 169–170

Thomas, 161, 171, 172–176, 178
Thoreau, H.D., 72
Tillich, Paul, 16, 297
Titche, Leon, 182
Tolstoy, Leo, 36, 289
Tonka, 48–49, 67, 181, 182–183
Törless, 54–57, 265
Trakl, Georg, 16
Truth, 2; in essayism, 41; in *The Man without Qualities*, 234, 235
Tuzzi, 215, 240–242, 243
Tryka, Frau, 35, 52, 55
Tyrol, South, 123, 124–125

Ulrich, 65, 68, 153, 161, 173, 174, 176, 193, 203, 213, 215, 242, 287; active relation to society of, 230–233; as advocate of evil, 240–241; as aesthete, 221; attitude to Moosbrugger, 238–240, 248, 249; on bourgeois sexuality, 245; commitment to science, 219–221, 222, 226–227, 228–229, 232, 240, 254; connected to social reality, 264–265, 266–268; as decadent elitist, 263–264; essayistic style of, 227–228; firm order opposed by, 224–225; history for, 262–263; lack of qualities of, 222–226, 228, 231–232; as mandarin, 220–221; as man of possibility, 224–226, 229, 230–231, 240–241; on morality, 256–259; mugging of, 230–231; other characters in novel as variations of, 232; the other condition experienced by, 248–268; and overcoming of separation of art and life, 245–247; on politics, 246–249; prototypes of, in Musil diaries, 42; relation with Agathe, 249–268; relation with Diotima, 244–245, 246; relation to women, 216, 239, 244–245, 249–268; similarity of, to Musil, 221n; and split between spirit and power, 243–244, 248; transition to, 203, 210; as vehicle for study of motivated life, 216–217, 219–231
Unconscious, 10, 13, 14, 17, 44–45; Musil's openness to, 297, 298; and neo-romanticism, 69–70; in *Young Törless*, 59
Undset, S., 164
Utopia of exact living, 229–230
Utopia of status quo, 231

Vaihinger, Hans, 84, 111
Valerie, 46–47

"Valerie-experience," 58, 63
Variationskreisel (color-wheel), 50, 68
Vereinigungen, 64, 68, 76, 88–98, 125, 159, 180, 181; and essaysim, 101; soul in, 71
Veronica, 95–96
Versailles, Treaty of, 99, 127–132, 137n
Verstehen, 165
Vienna, 1, 2, 23, 64; archival work of Musil in, 100, 101–102; modernism in, 15; Musil's life there, 140–142, 213; theater in, 169
Vienna Circle, 79, 80, 87, 141
Vinzenz, 65, 159, 161, 164, 171, 176–177, 178, 182
Vitalism, 17, 115
Völkisch ideology, 143, 277
von Saar, Ferdinand, 4

Wagner, Richard, 36, 45
Walter, 45, 67–68, 215, 221, 223, 232, 238, 241, 245–246, 247
War, 99–100; appeal of, to formless modern man, 149–151; communal solidarity in, 122–124; as frame for *The Man without Qualities*, 203, 204–205, 234
War psychosis, 143, 151
Weber, Max, 13, 14, 18–19, 29, 32, 51, 82, 145, 146, 148, 148–149n, 188
Weimar culture: Musil's relation to, 141–142
Weininger, Otto, 13, 15, 16, 32, 59
Werfel, Franz, 16, 127
Wertheimer, Max, 80, 84
Whitman, Walt, 72
Wilde, Oscar, 36, 69, 168
Wildgans, Anton, 168n
Wilhelm II, 206
Wilkins, Eithne, 96, 203, 210, 287
Williams, C.E., 137n
Wilson, Woodrow, 127–128, 132
Wittgenstein, Ludwig, 15, 16, 19, 22n, 79, 87, 139, 283, 297
Women: in *Drei Frauen*, 181–183; Musil on, 26, 28, 31–34, 45–49, 108–109; and the other condition, 181–183; Ulrich's relation to, 216, 239, 244–245, 249–268; in *Vereinigungen*, 90–98
World War I, 99–100; as revolt against civilization, 121–138, 292–293
Wotruba, Fritz, 272, 283n
Wundt, Wilhelm, 80

Young Törless, 23–24, 29, 52–62,
    65–66, 88; as autobiography, 57–58;
    discovery of unconscious in, 59; di-
    vided self in, 55–56, 61–62; domina-
    tion and revolt in, 61–62; power of
    thought in, 59–61; soul in, 71
Young Vienna, 12–13

Zak, Eduard, 214
Zweig, Arnold, 16, 273
Zweig, Stefan, 16, 139

Designer:	Al Burkhardt
Compositor:	G&S Typesetters, Inc.
Printer:	Thomson-Shore
Binder:	Thomson-Shore
Text:	Sabon
Display:	Typositor Garamond
Cloth:	Holliston Roxite B #53549, Linen finish
Paper:	50 lb. P & S Offset, B-32